Ulysses S. Grant, 1861–1864

To Sandy,

Best Regards,

William Farina

Ulysses S. Grant, 1861–1864

His Rise from Obscurity to Military Greatness

WILLIAM FARINA

McFarland & Company, Inc., Publishers
Jefferson, North Carolina, and London

LIBRARY OF CONGRESS CATALOGUING-IN-PUBLICATION DATA

Farina, William, 1955–
     Ulysses S. Grant, 1861–1864 : his rise from obscurity to military
greatness / William Farina.
         p.   cm.
     Includes bibliographical references and index.

     ISBN-13: 978-0-7864-2977-6
     softcover : 50# alkaline paper ∞

     1. Grant, Ulysses S. (Ulysses Simpson), 1822–1885.
2. Grant, Ulysses S. (Ulysses Simpson), 1822–1885—Military
leadership.   3. Generals—United States—Biography.   4. United
States—History—Civil War, 1861–1865—Campaigns.   I. Title.
E672.F235   2007
973.7'3092—dc22   2007012452
[B]

British Library cataloguing data are available

On the cover: *General Grant on the Battlefield,* ©2006 Pictures Now

Manufactured in the United States of America

McFarland & Company, Inc., Publishers
  Box 611, Jefferson, North Carolina 28640
  www.mcfarlandpub.com

To

William Eugene Cox (b. 1926)
U.S. Fourth Marine Division (Iwo Jima)
(and who shares our Confederate heritage)

and

Louis Philip Farina (b. 1923)*
U.S. Seventh Army (Battle of the Bulge)

and to all those who served.

*Bronze Star / Purple Heart / Citation for Gallantry in Action

Acknowledgments

Thanks to Edward A. Cox for showing me where American history and family history come together. Thanks to Philip and Kathleen Farina for letting me bounce off ideas, as well as allowing me to use the books of Kathleen's father, the late William Georgius, who was likewise fascinated by the American Civil War. Thanks to Jerome Bloom for helping me to navigate through some difficult waters. Thanks to Lineages, Inc., for their professional genealogical research. Thanks to Professor Philip Kolbe of the University of Memphis, for reading portions of my draft manuscript and offering encouragement. Thanks once again to my better half, Marion Buckley, for being supportive and making countless good suggestions.

Special thanks to Dr. John Y. Simon of the Ulysses S. Grant Association at Southern Illinois University. Professor Simon, in addition to being generous with his time, has devoted his life to incredible and monumental projects such as editing Grant's complete papers and Julia Grant's memoirs. This book would not have been possible without his invaluable work.

Last but not least, thanks again to the staff at the Newberry Library and Harold Washington Library Center in Chicago. You make it possible.

Table of Contents

Introduction

The noble son on sinewy feet advancing,
I saw, out of the land of prairies, land of Ohio's waters and of Indiana,
To the rescue the stalwart giant hurry his plenteous offspring,
Drest in blue, bearing their trusty rifles on their shoulders.
                                                            —Walt Whitman[1]

The biography of Ulysses S. Grant, unlike that of Abraham Lincoln, defies mythologizing. Had it not been for the first three years of the American Civil War, Grant likely would have been forgotten to history; thus his is a case study in greatness thrust upon an individual, to borrow Shakespeare's phrase.[2] Although individual rise from obscurity to fame was a frequent occurrence in 19th-century America, Grant was unusual even for his times, and was recognized as such by contemporaries. In less than 36 months, he went from being a lowly, unwanted veteran to general-in-chief of the most powerful army on earth, and a shoo-in for next president of the United States. Beginning as a down-and-out assistant store clerk in Galena, Illinois, Grant metamorphosed into Lieutenant-General of the U.S. armed forces, a rank last held by George Washington. Such rapid and dramatic promotion appears unprecedented in the annals of history—American or otherwise. The poet Walt Whitman, who observed Grant's transformation, did not exaggerate when he asserted, "In all Homer and Shakespeare there is no fortune or personality really more picturesque or rapidly changing, more full of heroism, pathos, contrast."[3] British military historian J.F.C. Fuller added, "Such a romance as his staggers the Arabian Nights."[4]

Grant may be rightfully viewed as one of the most successful and admirable military leaders that this country has ever produced, not only for his victories but the manner in which he achieved them, yet he is also perhaps the most misunderstood. His many critics (Northern and Southern alike) argue that Grant succeeded merely because of his army's superior, overwhelming numbers and industrial support, an insensitive willingness to sacrifice life, ridiculously good luck, and the ineptitude of his opponents. Robert E. Lee was, of course, an exception to the last item, and these same critics are fond

1

of pointing out how Lee proved himself a superior tactician to Grant during the Virginia Overland campaign of 1864–1865, despite the fact that Grant eventually forced Lee to surrender at Appomattox. While it is true that Grant had many factors working in his favor, an unparalleled career trajectory suggests that much more was at work, if for no other reason than that many, many other Union officers had similar advantages but failed to achieve a fraction of Grant's success. In addition to luck, one must still ultimately ask what made Grant different from his colleagues.

Another reason Grant, in spite of his achievements, has been denied a deified place among the pantheon of American legends such as Washington and Lincoln is that his personal imperfections were so glaringly conspicuous. Many would-be admirers have been put off by his spectacular failures as a businessman, his shortcomings as a politician, his surprisingly dispassionate attitude towards slavery, his anti–Semitic outbursts, and his alleged alcoholism. Even his talents as a military commander and memoirist have been called into question, despite a ubiquitous track record in both areas. A more enlightened view is that Grant's many faults underscore the profundity of his greatness. It also points the way to a better historical understanding of other American heroes, who were perhaps not as flawless as they are often made out to be by mythmakers posing as educators.

This study posits that the primary additional factors contributing to Grant's sudden success and prominence were his unique personal qualities and background, plus near-complete chaos caused by the war itself, which allowed many unknowns on both sides—Grant among them—to quickly rise to the top. Among other factors frequently cited by his critics, the ones which impress us the most are his amazingly good fortune (which Grant repeatedly cited in his own writings), as well as the weakness of his early opponents. This latter item, of course, can easily be viewed as a corollary to good luck. Regardless, the reader will hopefully appreciate that it is possible to admire Ulysses S. Grant while at the same time criticizing his occasional misbehavior. Conversely, Grant's contemporaries whom we do not admire, such as Jefferson Davis and John McClernand, were nevertheless occasionally capable of doing good things during the course of their careers. These individuals, however, are not the subject of this study.

For complete coverage of Grant's fascinating pre–Civil War life, from his birth in 1822 at Point Pleasant, Ohio, to his late-1860 relocation to Galena, Illinois, I refer readers to Grant's own *Personal Memoirs* and to several excellent biographies, beginning with the underrated and fascinating work of Lloyd Lewis. Perhaps the most striking yet overlooked aspect of Grant's early background, however, was that he, like seemingly countless outstanding Civil War personalities, originally hailed from the Ohio River Valley and environs. Not the least of these other major figures included Abraham Lincoln and Jefferson Davis, who were born not far apart from each other in Kentucky. While the war produced a galaxy of legendary soldiers and statesmen from around the country, the region surrounding Grant's native soil had far more than its fair share. Once again, the specific reasons for this concentration of talent are beyond the immediate scope of this study, although it does tie into one of our major themes: namely, that the American Civil War was first won and lost in the West before it was in the East. This view, incidentally, is nothing new. It was mostly shared by those who lived through the conflict and, after a curious period of eclipse, has been making a steady comeback among professional historians (if not in the public imagination) over the last 70 years or so.

Grant as the Reluctant Warrior

Unlike many successful generals of the war, such as, say, Philip Sheridan, who discovered his true self in the army, Grant was pushed rather than drawn towards a military career. An unlikely series of events involving his strong-willed father Jesse and two Ohio politicians resulted in the young Grant being admitted to the West Point Military Academy in 1839. Almost with a tone of regret, Grant near the end of his life maintained in his memoirs, "A military life had no charms for me,"[5] and that his stern father forced him to attend the academy; hence, he had "to face the music."[6] After graduating with indifferent grades, Lieutenant Grant found himself hurled into the Mexican War of 1843, where he earned a distinguished combat record despite his personal belief that the war itself was "one of the most unjust ever waged by a stronger against a weaker nation."[7] Indeed, Grant as a young officer defied all of the typical military stereotypes. He had a unique aversion to swearing,[8] considered himself a failure as a sportsman,[9] and mocked the practice of dueling,[10] which was very *en vogue* at the time. Physically, he was short and slight of build, while his personality was quiet and shy. The young Lieutenant Grant displayed artistic talent and enjoyed the contemplative life of the mind. Moreover, he deeply loved his wife Julia and their children, and preferred their company above all others. Grant's only outward soldierly quality was that he was a superb, even miraculous equestrian, and was acknowledged as such by his military colleagues. Promoted to captain, Grant was next stationed for tedious garrison duty along the Pacific coast, separated from his family (who remained in Missouri), and barely able to support them on his army paycheck.

Grant's notorious string of pre–Civil War failures began with his resignation from the army in 1854, reputedly forced upon him for being drunk while on duty at Fort Vancouver, Washington. Though he was immediately reunited with his wife and children near St. Louis, the next six years brought multiple professional failures that seemed to consign Ulysses S. Grant to a life of obscurity, if not wrenching poverty. After bottoming out in 1860, he desperately accepted a solicited offer from his father to help mind the family leather goods store in Galena, Illinois, since his younger brother Simpson (who had successfully run the business), was rapidly failing from consumption. Though providing the Grant family with a sufficient income, working in Galena was also an admission of failure, since Grant hated the leather business. His return to the family fold under such circumstances also did little to ease a thorny relationship with his father. Part of the reason for this was Jesse Grant's strong disapproval of his son's slave-owning in-laws, the Dents, plus Jesse's criticism of Julia herself. This was no doubt much harder for Grant to endure than any criticism of his own hapless business acumen.

A Second Chance

Then came the war, and Grant's luck changed, to say the least. In his memoirs, Grant catalogues with absolute candor the many times he could have been killed, captured, demoted, or cashiered. His very re-commissioning at the outbreak of hostilities was surrounded by fortuitous circumstances. A favorite theme among military historians, especially the ancient Greeks such as Plutarch and Thucydides, was the way in which virtuous and even brilliant commanders were often betrayed by bad luck, or (conversely) how unworthy leaders were sometimes smiled upon by good fortune. In truth, Grant during his first 39 years enjoyed many windfalls, despite his dismal experiences in the world of commerce. For example, he relates that, unlike the tragic case of his younger brother, his own sickliness was cured and life probably saved by the outbreak of the Mexican War, which forced him to relocate into healthier environs.[11] During the Mexican War, Grant literally dodged the bullet several times. For example, during one battle he loaned his horse to a fellow officer who was then instantly killed.[12] Grant's admittance to West Point, which proved absolutely essential to his later advancement, had been facilitated by Democratic Congressman (and later Army Major) Thomas Hamer of Ohio. Grant noted that Hamer ("one of the ablest men Ohio ever produced"[13]) likely would have been president of the United States (rather than Grant himself, it is suggested) had it not been for his premature death.[14] Even Grant's reluctant move to Galena, made so grudgingly at the time, placed him within the sphere of Congressman Elihu Washburne and attorney John Rawlins. These men would play indispensable roles in Grant's resurrected military career. Good luck not only applied to Grant's military life, but to external circumstances as well. To repeat, the American Civil War was a cataclysmic event in which conventional wisdom for success no longer applied, allowing unprivileged men like Grant to advance both during and after the event.

Personal Qualities

Part of the reason Grant's extraordinary talents were (and still are) underappreciated is that most were of a type concealed from casual view. Foremost among these hidden traits was a quick and perceptive mind. While many commentators balk at applying the term "genius" to Grant as they would unhesitatingly to numerous other Civil War generals, it is a threshold and fundamental error to discount his intellectual capacity. Essayist Gore Vidal put it best when he wrote, "More to the point, it is simply not possible to read Grant's memoirs without realizing that the author is a man of first-rate intelligence."[15] Examples of this "first-rate intelligence" are countless, but my own favorite is the manner in which a discerning Grant recalled how slavery, in addition to being the cause of the war, was justified by its many antebellum apologists as a divinely approved institution.[16] Thus Grant shrewdly suggested that religion can be used to justify any atrocity. As for Grant's personal opinions, he played a leading role in the abolition of slavery—the defining event of his epoch—yet never considered himself an abolitionist. To his critics, such contradictions are incompatible with characterizations of "genius" in the conventional sense of the word. Nevertheless, by the time Grant was through with his opponents on the battlefield who were supposedly more sophisticated than he, a plausible case could be argued that he was in fact brilliant, at least in the instinctive sense of the word.

Education

A more satisfactory explanation, or at least a partial one, for Grant's unique qualities involves his education. All-too-frequent attempts to present him as not being well-educated for his time and place are unpersuasive, and come across more as pandering to our own modern ignorance and comparative lack of education. Grant was placed in a good position at birth to take advantage of resources not widely available to his contemporaries. Though his father Jesse lacked formal schooling, and often quarreled with his eldest son, Grant nevertheless praised his father's attitude:

> ... his thirst for education was intense. He learned rapidly, and was a constant reader up to the day of his death—in his eightieth year. Books were scarce ... but he read every book he could borrow.... The habit continued through life. Even after reading the daily papers—which he never neglected—he could give all the important information they contained. He made himself an excellent English scholar, and before he was twenty years of age was a constant contributor to Western newspapers....[17]

The elder Grant, according to Ulysses, was eventually "Mindful of his own lack of facilities for acquiring an education," and therefore "his greatest desire in maturer years was for the education of his children."[18]

Grant's admittance to West Point gave him additional career opportunities not readily available to his Midwestern contemporaries. While his formal grades were mediocre, we learn in Grant's memoirs that this was partly due to his love of reading fiction (both classic and pulp), while he praised the library at West Point, where he spent much time engaged in non-academic study.[19] One of his few accomplishments at the academy was to be elected president of the cadet literary society,[20] and throughout his life he exhibited an enthusiasm for theater and drama, including the works of Shakespeare. His memoirs quote Shakespeare with phrases such as "it was Greek to me" (*Julius Caesar*)[21] and "ocular proof" (*Othello*),[22] plus he later acted in amateur army productions, once auditioning for an unlikely Shakespearean role (see Chapter 36). After graduation from West Point, his first ambition was to be a mathematics professor, but this humble desire was thwarted by the outbreak of the Mexican War.[23] Perhaps the most tangible products of Grant's formal education (and mental aptitude) were his superb written communication skills, which later proved a great benefit both for himself during the war and for his posthumous legacy. Interestingly, the two military commanders whom he admired most—Zachary Taylor and Winfield Scott—are praised in his memoirs specifically for their own outstanding skills at writing clear and concise orders.[24]

The Western Federal Armies

Grant's definitive biographer, Jean Edward Smith, appropriately reminds us, "At the root of Grant's success was his army."[25] And what an army it was, the likes of which will probably never be seen again. This analysis accepts the view that the American Civil War was first won and lost in battles fought by western soldiers. Grant shared the opinion that the typical western Federal soldier was, if nothing else, a breed apart from his eastern counterpart.[26] In deference to those who fought on the eastern front (and not to belittle their memory), I, along with others, merely maintain that the fate of everyone was eventually determined by the war fought in the West. By the spring of 1863, the Army of Northern Virginia appeared indomitable after repelling yet another attempted, all-out Federal invasion at Chancellorsville. At nearly the same moment Chancellorsville was being fought, however, the turning point of the entire conflict was being decided at a place called Champion Hill near Vicksburg, Mississippi. One year later, Robert E. Lee and his Confederates would find themselves confronted by Grant in Virginia. This was after they had been bloodied at Gettysburg the previous summer—a battle that likely would never have been fought if not for Champion Hill. By the spring of 1865, the Confederates found themselves behind fortifications outside of suburban Richmond, while the relentless Federal western army (now under Sherman) was simultaneously knocking at their back door in North Carolina. No matter how much blood and treasure were expended by each side, the stalemate in the East was not effectively broken until Grant, Sherman, Sheridan, and the western Federal armies came into the picture. Those who fought and fell from Bull Run through Appomattox eventually found themselves on the winning and losing sides, respectively, depending on outside events occurring in the West.

In addition to having under his charge one of the most intimidating armies to ever take the field, Grant's informal and unorthodox command style was perfectly fitted for his mostly volunteer troops. As a junior officer, Grant recalled that there tended to be an overlap between commanders who studied to annoy their subordinates and those who were absent from duty during a crisis.[27] His approach was not to be lax in discipline, but rather to be hard on junior officers while going easy on the men under their authority. I am at a loss to name a single instance in which Grant criticized his infantry, even at Shiloh, where thousands ran away in terror; his criticism of officers, on the other hand, was continuous and consistent. Grant also is often depicted as a man who accomplished his goals by being single-minded and uncompromising; this, too, is an oversimplification. It would be more accurate to say he often approached his tasks experimentally and scattershot by trying everything, sometimes simultaneously, to see what would work, then exploiting whatever did. His greatest campaigns (the most spectacular examples being Vicksburg and Chattanooga) all reflect this trait, and it is remarkable how many of his contemporaries seemed unwilling or unable to do anything remotely similar.

Empathy with the South

Like Lincoln, Grant had strong personal and family ties to the South. Beginning with the Confederate sympathies of his boyhood home in southern Ohio, extending through his days at West Point and during the Mexican War, Grant befriended many of his future antagonists such as James Longstreet and Simon Bolivar Buckner. Certainly, his marriage to Julia Dent, a woman with a Southern antebellum upbringing who continued to legally own slaves after January 1, 1863,[28] put Grant at odds not only with abolitionists, but with his own father as well. Accordingly, Grant's personal attitude towards slavery was disconcertingly under-zealous: he seems to have been quite at ease among its most fervent defenders. Like most Southerners at the time, Grant had political sympathies with the Democratic Party and was never a great advocate for the Republicans, even after entering the White House. Moreover, after defeating Confederates in the field, Grant often protected them. For example, former Confederate Colonel John S. Mosby later eulogized Grant by writing, "I felt that I had lost my best friend."[29] Mosby explained that he was not alone in this sentiment: "In common with most Southern soldiers, I had a very kindly feeling towards General Grant, not only on account of his magnanimous conduct at Appomattox, but also for his treatment of me at the close of hostilities."[30]

A Disclosure

If a tone of harshness towards Confederate leaders occasionally colors these writings, it is possibly because most (if not all) of the author's maternal ancestors fought for the Confederacy. Although most of these ancestors were from the state of Georgia, a surprisingly large number of them rushed east to fight at Bull Run and then later under Robert E. Lee during all of his major campaigns, with the exception of Appomattox. This was because, as things came to an end, most were allowed to rejoin their western brethren in North Carolina for surrender to Sherman, rather than to Grant. Many no doubt were not about to stack their weapons in front of the Army of the Potomac, whom they continued to regard with defiance, if not contempt. Their choice to fight in the East reflected family roots in Virginia and the Carolinas, along with a perception that the eastern theater was, as Sam Watkins ironically put it, "the big show."

In conducting formal genealogical research for the first time, the author was surprised to learn how much of family oral tradition held up under scrutiny. I had previously assumed that many of these traditions were overblown, as indeed a few turned out to be. Most, however, were harrowingly confirmed. For example, my great-great-grandfather, Burl Washington Nail, along with three brothers,[31] served under Lee with the 27th Georgia Infantry for the duration of the conflict, and all emerged alive but with wounds of various severity. Burl's first cousin, Corporal Joseph Henry Nail, served in the West with the 56th Georgia Infantry and managed to survive being engaged in some of the deadliest fighting there. The Cox brothers of Wilkes County, Georgia, which included my great-grandfather, Private Frederick A. Cox, were all members of the 37th Georgia Infantry and not so fortunate. Frederick and his brother, Private John T. Cox, both survived but were severely wounded, while their 14-year-old younger brother, Private William Richardson Cox, died during Sherman's spring campaign of 1864. Their father (my great-great-grandfather), Private Thomas J. Cox, had not long before been permanently disabled while fighting at Sharpsburg/Antietam in 1862 with the 13th Georgia Infantry. Before the war, Thomas J. Cox and his family appear to have been fairly prosperous farmers. Thomas had in fact married into the distinguished Anthony family of Wilkes County. Then in short order, his wife, Mary T. Anthony, died in 1859, Thomas was disabled in 1862, and his youngest son was dead by 1864. The two wounded sons and other surviving family members then migrated out of Wilkes County during Reconstruction. In fact, it appears that my maternal family branches all were affected by the war in a bad way. For these misfortunes, I blame Confederate leadership far more than I blame Ulysses S. Grant. Then again, perhaps some of them were willingly misled.

Most of my Confederate ancestors were non-slave-owning farmers and privates in the army. The biggest exception appears to have been Major James Rembert Anthony of Wilkes County, kinsman to my great-great-grandmother, Mary T. Anthony, who fought under Lee and whose aunt married the famous Robert Toombs, Georgia Senator, Confederate General, and outspoken critic of Jefferson Davis. Another was the Dozier family of Columbia County. Georgia, a branch of the celebrated clan by the same name originally from Virginia and who were extensive owners of land and humanity. Most, however, were modest farmers like another one of my great-great-grandfathers, 18-year-old Private James Jesse Prickett, who served in the 1st Georgia Cavalry, while James' brothers, Privates John W. Prickett and George P. Prickett, were members of the 34th and 53rd Georgia Infantry Regiments, respectively. George did not survive the war. As a member of the 53rd Georgia Infantry, he probably knew my great-great-grandfather, Private Allen Rape, and Allen's sons, Private James M. Rape and Private Milton A. Rape, also members of the 53rd. Only James survived. These were the brothers of the author's great-great-grandmother, Martha Hannah Rape, who after the war married the aforementioned Private Burl Washington Nail. All of the survivors were no doubt drawn together by a shared heritage and the recent memory of fallen friends and loved ones.

Source Material

Many excellent full biographies of Grant have been written, and it is not the purpose of this study to present another. For readers who seek a broader overview, the splendid and revisionist account given by Professor Jean Edward Smith in *Grant* (2001) is highly recommended. Here we are mainly concerned with the three years that saw Grant's extraordinary rise, from April of 1861 to March of 1864. Particularly interesting to us are events taking place between the battles—the politicking, rumors, blustering, backbiting, intrigue, psychological warfare, etc., but above all, the incredible twists of fate that punctuated these events. My quotations from Grant's voluminous writings have corrected his occasional phonetic spelling but not his inimitable grammar, which often accomplishes what strictly proper grammar cannot. Moreover, no detailed attempt has been made to retell the stories of famous battles, because the author cannot do it half as well as the late Shelby Foote or the late Bruce Catton, whose classic works are required reading for this topic. Others who have ably tackled the subject of Grant's early Civil War career include Arthur Conger, Kenneth Williams, and Michael Ballard. Hopefully, this study will add something meaningful to their many worthy observations.

I have made an effort to present Grant's story as seen through the eyes of his adversaries, as well as his admirers. Contemporary impressions of events, such as those by Tennessee Private Sam Watkins and Southern socialite Mary Chesnut are occasionally cited, as are modern historians from the South whose work I admire, such as James Lee McDonough and Thomas Connelly. It was continually surprising, however (at least to me), to learn that Grant's harshest critics tended to be his Northern contemporaries: Grant's worst enemies were not Confederate combatants, but rather his own Federal colleagues. I further observe that modern historians, though most agree on Grant's greatness, tend to diverge considerably when discussing the reasons for this greatness. Grant, with typical humility, suggested it was simply because his side had won: "I commanded the whole of the mighty host engaged on the victorious side."[32]

Not long ago I attended a lecture and book-signing event in Chicago featuring the eminent, Pulitzer Prize–winning historian James McPherson of Princeton University. For my money, Professor McPherson has written the best all-around book on the American Civil War, *Battle Cry of Freedom*. After an erudite presentation followed by some generic Q&A, a woman with the appearance of a suburban housewife raised her hand and asked Professor McPherson which side he thought won the war (this was right after the 2004 election). For a split second, irritation flickered across the honored speaker's expression, then he patiently and comprehensively explained to the audience that the North had indeed won. Nevertheless, the question continues to resonate. With only a few days left to live, Grant concluded his own memoirs by predicting future harmony between Federals and Confederates, and that harmony has come to pass in many ways. Slavery was abolished and the Union restored, but States' Rights have made a strong resurgence, both in popular government and judicial interpretation. What the future holds no one can tell, but we hope and pray that if the United States ever experiences a similar crisis, there will still be ordinary American citizens possessing a small portion of U.S. Grant's character, courage, and skill.

CHAPTER 1

April 1861: Galena, Illinois

It seems that man's destiny in this world is quite as much a mystery as it is likely to be in the next. I never thought of acquiring rank in the profession I was educated for; yet it came with two grades higher prefixed to the rank of General officer for me.

—Grant writing to his last visitor[1]

Many tourists who visit Galena, Illinois, fail to appreciate that the splendid U.S. Grant Home on the east side of town was not given to its namesake by city fathers until after the war, and was occupied by Grant and his family only intermittently before their permanent move to New York in 1881.[2] At the time of the war's outbreak in April 1861, the Grant family lived in a much more modest house at 121 High Street, which is still to this day a private residence. Grant's wife Julia remembered this earlier home with affection as "a nice little brick house of seven rooms, which was nestled up on the hill on the west side the town in the best neighborhood and with a lovely view," adding, "We were most pleasantly situated."[3] Compared to earlier Grant abodes such as Hardscrabble Farm in Sappington, Missouri, the High Street setting would have truly been idyllic.

The only disadvantage to a Galena High Street address is the location, literally high upon a bluff overlooking the Galena River Valley. To get to Main Street and the Grant family store from High Street, one had to walk down (and later up) no fewer than three city blocks of steep outdoor stairs. This would have been Grant's commute in April of 1861—whatever his personal shortcomings may have been, lack of physical stamina was not one of them. Conversely, Grant's daily ladder-like descent to work would have put his home life conveniently above and removed from, yet geographically close to, the shop, a concept typically foreign to the modern American workforce, though not so during the mid–19th century.

The counter behind the Grant leather goods store at 145 Main Street[4] was the future Lieutenant-General's place of employment when Confederate batteries fired upon Fort Sumter in Charleston Harbor on April 12, 1861. His annual salary at the time was $600[5]—a merely adequate amount that was nevertheless more than he was used to earning, especially since resigning from the army in 1854. Although Grant and his family were in effect now living off the largess of his father and younger brothers, it would be going too far to portray him as being under the thumb of his siblings (one of whom, Simpson, would be dead within the year from consumption).[6] Nor was there any ill will towards Grant from other numerous store employees.[7] On the other hand, no one is known to have expressed envy. Grant was, in the words of historian James McPherson, "A man of no reputation and little promise,"[8] or as Shelby Foote more succinctly put it, "a confirmed failure."[9] It was from these lowly beginnings that Ulysses S. Grant began his rocket-like career trajectory in the world during the spring of 1861.

Whether Grant achieved military success in spite of his personal faults or because of them may be an open question; however, there can be little doubt as to his having a number of conspicuous traits perceived as being less than enviable. Foremost among these negatives was an unimpressive physical bearing in an age that seemed to demand the opposite from its military leaders. Shelby Foote's rendering of Grant's "seedy appearance" is hard to forget:

> ... he was five feet eight inches tall and weighed 135 pounds; one eye was set a trifle lower than the other, giving his face a somewhat out-of-balance look; he walked with a round-shouldered slouch, pitching forward on his toes, and paid as scant attention to the grooming of his beard as he did to the cut and condition of his clothes....[10]

James McPherson simply described Grant as "slouchy and unsoldier-like in appearance."[11] Grant's wife Julia, though much better dressed, was well-matched in terms of physical unimpressiveness. Essayist Gore Vidal cruelly described Julia as a "goose of a wife" and said that "If photographs are to be trusted ... [she] was short and dumpy, with quite astonishingly crossed-eyes." Vidal characterized husband and wife together as "two odd little creatures."[12]

Grant's near hobo-like demeanor no doubt contributed to his ineptitude in business matters, or perhaps it was vice-versa. One of his most admiring biographers, Brooks Simpson, judged that "Grant proved adequate at best at the general store."[13] Others, however, have tended to share the opinion of Grant's fellow Galenan, the merchant John E. Smith, who flatly maintained that the future President was "a very poor businessman."[14] In his own memoirs, Grant dispassionately noted that he was "nominally only a clerk" in Galena but "In reality my position was different."[15] In reality, he was a family employee trying to fill in for a terminally ill brother and could dress and act on the job pretty much any way he pleased, while the remaining healthy brother, Orvil, ran the shop.

There was, however, surely one major exception to this license. By almost universal agreement among those who knew Grant in Galena, he fastidiously avoided drinking, even when offered.[16] Given that Grant's resignation from the army had been clouded in ugly rumors and that his subsequent civilian life in the world of commerce had been a total flop, this reported abstinence comes as no surprise. In short, Grant had a reputation for drinking that seemed to only increase proportionately with his later public visibility. It is likely that in Galena he was aided decisively in his effort to stay on the wagon by the proximity of his wife, and perhaps as well by his early acquaintance with attorney John Rawlins, who would later play the unofficial role of Grant's conscience and personal disciplinarian during his resurrected military career.

Although Grant had his weaknesses, no one can accuse of him of not having been a dutiful husband and father. It may be no exaggeration to say that devotion to family kept him from completely descending into drink, debt, and despair. One of the most

Later portrait of Julia Grant in the White House. Julia was usually photographed in profile to hide her crossed eyes (courtesy Library of Congress Prints and Photo Division).

endearing stories about his early Galena days is related by biographer Lloyd Lewis. After a hard day of work, Grant climbed the long flight of stairs back to his house only to be met on the porch by his three-year-old son Jesse, who challenged his father with, "Mister, do you want to fight?"—to which Grant replied, "I'm a man of peace, but I'll not be hectored by a person of your size."[17] The two would then wrestle on the spot until the father capitulated. Cynics may argue that Grant's conspicuous family values were a by-product of his New England Puritan ancestry (as related in his own memoirs), rather than any sincere peace-loving personal tendencies; nevertheless, and whatever the source, his family-man-on-the-wagon image no doubt later served him well as a commander of Midwestern volunteers. Beyond his drinking problems and financial difficulties, Grant from all accounts was good to his wife and children, and this trait probably counted for something in the eyes of those who served under him. It certainly stood in marked contrast to a number of other Civil War leaders, particularly on the Union side.

While in Galena, Grant attended the Methodist church conveniently located on Bench Street, midway along his stair route between work and home. Grant apparently patronized this church because he shared the pastor's political views. In fact, Grant in his memoirs joked with some bitterness that in the southern Ohio of his youth "hostility to ... the liberation of slaves, was far more essential [for church membership] than a belief in the authenticity or credibility of the Bible."[18] Grant was not, however, a Methodist "church member," according to the pastor,[19] although his parents affiliated with this denomination as well. More certain is that Grant, though he admitted to praying in private, disliked all religious ostentation, as opposed to the current fashion of religious worship in America.

Far less obscure than Grant's religion were his political beliefs: he was more or less a Democrat. This was in spite of a father with Whig sympathies and serving under Whig generals during the Mexican War. By his own admission, Grant would have voted for Stephen Douglas for president rather than Abraham Lincoln in 1860 had he been eligible (he was not, due to less than one year of residency in Galena), just as he had voted for Democrat James Buchanan in 1856.[20] In addition, Grant's mother was a lifelong Democrat who despised the Republicans and refused to later visit her son in the White House, possibly because she viewed him as a political turncoat. Moreover, Grant (like Lincoln) had married into a slaveholding family—the Dents of Missouri—and had many family relations with strong Southern sympathies. Above all, Grant was a pragmatist who seemed to gravitate towards the moderate elements of both political parties. Grant knew Southerners well and before Fort Sumter had cautioned his Galena neighbors, "The South will fight"[21]— although even he did not realize at the time how hard they would fight. Thus one of the great icons of the Republican Party had in 1861 no great liking for the party itself, for abolitionists, or (in the beginning at least) for Abraham Lincoln.

Grant's minority political status in Galena as a Douglas Democrat gave him another military career advantage, although it did not seem that way at the time. Galena's own political rainmaker in April 1861 was the venerable Republican Congressman Elihu B. Washburne, a strong Lincoln man, opponent of slavery, and the embodiment of everything that the South feared and loathed in Yankee politicians. Thanks to the recent election of Lincoln as President, Washburne now found himself in a position of unusual strength for making recommendations on military appointments to Illinois Republican Governor Richard Yates, although he and Yates had previously butted heads over other issues.[22] One sentiment the two men did share was a recognized, urgent need to bring into their fold Illinois Democrats such as Grant and his friend John Rawlins. Both Washburne and Yates foresaw that a successful Northern war effort had to be bipartisan, and Grant became an early beneficiary of this foresight.

In addition to having a mother with strong Democratic sympathies— though not so his father, who was a Whig—Grant's wife Julia, to repeat, came from a Missouri slaveholding family that had both Democratic and Southern leanings. Julia's own personal views, as recorded in her memoirs, seem to have been as pro–Southern as it was possible to be without necessarily being pro–Secessionist. In her own words:

> I was very much disturbed in my political sentiments, feeling that the states had a right to go out of the Union if they wished to, and yet thought it the duty of the national government to prevent a dismemberment of the Union, even if coercion should be necessary. Ulys was much amused at my enthusiasm and said I was a little inconsistent when I talked of states' rights, but I was all right on the duties of the national government.[23]

Julia's inconsistent views aside, there can be no doubt that Grant's home and family life encouraged his comparatively centrist attitudes on states' rights. Nor were his opinions mere acquiescence; in addition to growing up in southern Ohio, where erstwhile friends were at each other's throats over politics, Grant's father Jesse apparently disapproved of his daughter-in-law's slave-owning family and political outlook in general. The Dents and the Grants, like many other clans, were at odds amongst themselves over the great questions of the day, and one could not simply go along with another's politics without offending someone else nearby who disagreed. Individual views such as Grant's, by necessity, had to hold their own in the face of constant challenge.

Even more than centrist politics and conspicuous family values, Grant enjoyed the advantage and distinction of being the only Mexican War veteran in Galena,[24] plus he was a former officer and an educated West Pointer. Once put to the task, Grant would display organizational skills and a flair for written communication, as well as physical courage. In hindsight, this ideal combination of personal qualities and background put him in a rather uniquely advantageous place at the outset of the war, although these could have easily been offset by his various faults and lack of connections; nor did these give him any special advantage over hundreds of other commissioned officers once hostilities began. In fact, Galena produced a total of nine generals during the American Civil War (though none so illustrious as Grant).[25] This is further indication, however, that he was in exactly the right place and the right time to begin his successful use of the superior resources offered by a Federal war machine. As eminent Grant scholar John Y. Simon has written, "Grant was fortunate in living in Galena when the Civil War began. He had slight chance for a regiment, even less for a general command, without the intervention of an effective politician."[26]

Thus whatever dubious reputation the faded ex-soldier had in Galena as a poor businessman, shabby dresser, or recovering alcoholic, he was still looked up to by his fellow townsmen as a veteran,[27] especially since he was the only one amongst them. What was not realized by his neighbors until after the war began was that—in spite of his failings in the private sector—he was also a competent soldier, notably at army paperwork. Reading in between the lines of those who described those early days, one wonders if Grant was the only person in Galena, perhaps in the entire state of Illinois at that time, who had any clue as to how this paperwork should be completed. This hidden talent would serve as an additional springboard for his quick promotion from civilian and disgraced former Captain to Brigadier General within a few short months.

Grant biographer Jean Edward Smith wrote, "Had peace prevailed he would have lived out his days as a slightly rumpled shopkeeper in the upper Mississippi valley, indistinguishable from his friends and neighbors."[28] In the early morning hours of April 12, 1861, an event occurred that would completely change the course of Grant's life, as well as American history: forces authorized by the Confederate government of South Carolina bombarded the Federal garrison at Fort Sumter. Two days later, on April 14, the Federals surrendered. On April 15, the same day Lincoln issued his first call for volunteers, news reached Galena, whose citizens, like most others throughout the Northern states, were virtually united in outrage. According to one source, Grant that very same day realized that his career as a soldier had been instantly reactivated:

> I thought I had done with soldiering. I never expected to be in military life again. But I was educated by the Government; and if my knowledge and experience can be of any service, I think I ought to offer them.[29]

This comment, expressed in Grant's usual terse fashion, reflected his own surprise at returning to the military, as well as his own self-appraisal of being "educated" and having a strong sense of obligation towards "the Government" that had provided him with this invaluable commodity.

On April 16, Galena held its first town meeting dealing with the national crisis, consisting mainly of patriotic speeches, the keynote of which was delivered by John Rawlins, who eloquently spoke of the need for unification between Democrats and Republicans while preserving the Union.[30] Two days later, on April 18, a second meeting was held for the purpose of organizing volunteers. To the amazement of an embarrassed and reluctant Grant, he was nominated to preside from the floor by Washburne's right-hand man John E. Smith (the same who criticized Grant's business acumen)—Grant being the only bona fide veteran in town.[31] The momentousness and unlikelihood of this nomination, coming as it did from such unexpected quarters, may well be compared to the surprise nomination of Plutarch's Timoleon as leader of the Corinthian expedition to Syracuse during the fourth century B.C.[32] In his memoirs, Grant conflated the two meetings of April 16 and 18, and according to him, Congressman Washburne expressed "surprise that Galena could not furnish a presiding officer for such an occasion without taking a stranger."[33] In reality, though Grant apparently never got to the bottom of the source, it may well have been that Washburne was behind the nomination all along, recognizing in his lowly fellow townsman a perfect combination (for political purposes) of war veteran, family man, and Democrat. Grant concluded his account of this incident with, "I never went into our leather store after that meeting, to put up a package or do other business."[34]

At the second Galena meeting, Grant declined to be elected an officer by the volunteers, no doubt hoping to receive a direct appointment at a later date. He did pledge, however, to offer his assistance in any capacity needed. Soon afterwards, Grant wrote a letter to his slave-owning father-in-law in Missouri, declaring to Colonel Dent that "all party distinctions should be lost"[35] now that the war had begun in earnest. Thus, not only was Grant himself, as a Democrat with Southern ties, committing himself to the Northern cause, he was urging family and friends with similar anti–Republican sympathies to do likewise. After helping to organize and drill the companies, Grant and the Galena volunteers left by train for Springfield on April 25.[36] One of my favorite stories about Grant—the most successful general of the war—is that, according to eyewitnesses, as the volunteers marched to the train station with great fanfare and sharply outfitted in new uniforms, Grant unimpressively brought up the rear in anticlimactic style, dressed in shoddy clothes and holding a carpet bag.[37] The whole scene represented a microcosm of Grant's public image at the beginning of the war. Both North and South judged military leadership in terms of appearances, but many would eventually learn that appearances could be deceiving.

Grant arrived in Springfield, via a roundabout route through Decatur, Illinois, on April 26.[38] At Camp Yates in Springfield he encountered the mustering officer, Captain John Pope, a fellow Illinoisan and future Federal army commander.[39] Pope pompously offered to pull some strings for Grant, but the latter, according to his own account, "declined to receive endorsement for permission to fight for my country."[40] The following day, April 27, was Grant's 39th birthday, of which it could be safely said that few great men have spent their 39th birthdays in more obscurity.

That weekend, Grant was introduced to Governor Yates by Congressman Washburne, who was less than impressed by what he saw and did not immediately offer Grant a job. Soon afterwards, though, when word got out that the disappointed ex–Captain was returning to Galena on the evening of the 28th, Yates buttonholed Grant at the hotel front door and asked him to come back to his office the next morning. Grant's account of these events is somewhat at odds with other witnesses in that he denied (or at least claimed not to recall) having been introduced to or spoken with Yates before that fateful evening at the Chenery Hotel. It may have been that Washburne had earlier neglected to properly introduce Grant to Yates, or that the preoccupied Yates initially paid no attention to him, or that Grant made such a poor initial impression that words were not exchanged. More certain is that, in later years (and consistent with his lifelong disdain for seeking political favors), Grant was reluctant to credit Washburne or any other politician for his career advancement—despite the fact that he clearly received help from Washburne, Yates, Lincoln, and others. Perhaps Grant found their manner less offensive than, say, the blatant and unapologetic patronage offers of John Pope, or perhaps Grant correctly judged that Pope was someone he did not want to hitch his wagon to.[41] In any event, Grant wrote to his sister on April 29, recalling how he had been personally detained by the governor the night before.[42] As Jean Edward Smith observed, Grant's disinclination to accept political support almost kept him out of the war, but "at the last minute, [his] luck changed."[43]

As it turned out, Yates hardly offered Grant what he was hoping for, which would have been an officer's commission. Instead, he received a dingy cubicle of a room plus two dollars a day salary as a sort of unofficial consultant and paper-pusher. Grant accepted the offer without complaint, although later in an unguarded moment he confided to fellow Galenan Augustus Chetlain that he felt useless.[44] In a more humorous vein, he wrote to his wife Julia that his new occupation was "principally smoking and occasionally giving advice...."[45] Nevertheless, Grant's valuable facility for paperwork now came into play, and in his memoirs noted, "The army forms were familiar to me and I could direct how they should be made out."[46] His contribution was soon recognized by Yates in an official letter (dated April 29) to the Speaker of the State House, transmitting an inventory of arms at the Illinois State Armory conducted by "Capt. U.S. Grant."[47] Apparently, rumors of Grant's past drinking problems also surfaced while he was in Springfield, possibly spread by his old army acquaintance John Pope. He invariably made a poor appearance to casual observers, at least one of whom described Grant as "a dead-beat military man—a decayed officer from the regular army." John Pope, however, was about to inadvertently come to the rescue of the same man he may have attempted to earlier marginalize with gossip.[48]

CHAPTER 2

May 1861:
Springfield, Illinois

Our armies were composed of men who were able to read, men who knew what they were fighting for, and could not be induced to serve as soldiers, except in an emergency when the safety of the nation was involved, and so necessarily must have been more than equal to men who fought merely because they were brave and because they were thoroughly drilled and inured to hardship.... [They were] as good soldiers as ever trod the earth; better than any European soldiers, because they not only worked like a machine but the machine thought. European armies know very little what they are fighting for and care even less.

—Grant[1]

On May 3, Captain John Pope was enraged to learn that he had been passed over for promotion to Brigadier General in favor of Benjamin Prentice,[2] and the next day indignantly stormed out of Springfield. Camp Yates was now without a mustering officer. Governor Yates simultaneously learned that there was insufficient railroad transportation to move troops from Springfield to the Missouri border. With a nudge from State Auditor Jesse Dubois, Yates then turned to his lowly office consultant, ex–Captain Grant, for an opinion. Grant told an astonished Yates that it would be good practice to make the troops march the 100-odd miles to Missouri, should that become necessary. The governor was so impressed that, on the same day that Pope left town, he named Grant as Pope's successor at Camp Yates. It is possible that Grant was the only person in the world who both wanted and could do the job. He also received a pay raise from $2.00 to $4.20 per day.[3]

Historian James McPherson wrote that Grant's appointment by Yates was, in effect, "scraping the barrel,"[4] since qualified military professionals were in short supply during the chaotic early months of the war, particularly in Northwestern states such as Illinois. It can certainly be argued that, one way or another, Grant would have eventually found his way into service. On the other hand, the manner in which he did find it proved to be the ideal initial step, positioning him eight months later to lead the first great Federal campaign of the war. One is also struck by what a near-miss his provisional, temporary appointment was—quite understandable given his tarnished reputation, slovenly appearance, and lack of political connections. On at least one occasion he prepared to return to the family storefront in Galena (before fate intervened), and one wonders what would have happened to Grant if John Pope had not been such an impatient hothead. Thanks to this unexpected opportunity, Grant would demonstrate over the next month his impressive organizational talents.

Grant spent the next several weeks performing his new duties with a quiet zeal, traveling throughout the state and organizing troops. His letters from this period reflect a common misconception regarding the impending conflict. To his father he wrote, "My own opinion is that this War will be of but short duration,"[5] and to his wife, "My own opinion is there will be much less bloodshed than is generally anticipated."[6] On the other hand, Grant was probably concerned at this time, like many other volunteers, that the war would be over before he could make a significant personal contribution. With more foresight, to his father he expressed contempt for Confederate General Gideon Pillow, who reportedly commanded a nearby force. Grant mocked the *"valiant* Pillow," reminisced serving under him in Mexico, and implied that Pillow was a coward and a fool. Grant specifically alluded to Pillow's notorious mistake during the Mexican War of having dug a moat on the wrong side of a wall, then discounted rumors of an attack on Cairo, Illinois, noting that there the ditch had been dug on the correct side.[7] Grant's remarkable killer instinct towards a potential adversary foreshadowed and anticipated his confrontation and defeat of Pillow nine months later at Fort Donelson.

During early May, Grant reported to Belleview in southwestern Illinois, but upon learning that the volunteers had not arrived yet, he made a side trip to nearby St. Louis, at that time the volatile epicenter of civil unrest in the region. Part of his motive in crossing the Mississippi, no doubt, was a hope that the Federal officers in charge there (Colonel Francis Blair and Captain Nathaniel Lyon) needed experienced help. Grant received no offers but he did meet Blair, who would later serve under him at Vicksburg. Before going into the city, Grant also paid his respects to his in-laws at Wish-ton-Wish, Missouri (Julia's old home), but was distressed to learn that his father-in-law Colonel Dent was essentially Confederate in his sympathies. Writing to Julia, Grant noted that her father was "opposed to having the army sustain it [the Union]" and was "...really what I would call a secessionist." Somewhat jarringly, he joked to Julia about his slave-owning in-laws eventually being left to the mercy of their "darkeys."[8]

Later that same day, on May 10, Grant entered St. Louis and witnessed the memorable and forcible suppression of the Secessionist movement in that city. He observed the Confederate flag that was flying on Pine Street (near

Fifth) being ordered down by Federal soldiers in "tones of authority." In Grant's opinion, the "timely services" of Blair saved St. Louis from falling into enemy hands. Immediately afterwards, he found opportunity on a streetcar at nearby Pine and Fourth to completely deflate the harangue of a Southern sympathizer by pointing out to him that no "rebels" had been hanged yet, though many deserved to be. Grant humorously referred to his own minis-cule contribution to the war effort in St. Louis as "More Yankee oppression"[9] and would always reserve special contempt for agitators whom he felt were responsible for starting the war but were nowhere to be found once the shoot-ing began.

In Grant's memoirs, it is hard to miss an air of personal satisfaction regarding events in St. Louis. In short, he saw highly disciplined troops— mostly German immigrants, tagged "the damned Dutch" by locals—led by a redheaded Irishman (Lyon) and commanded by a stone-cold abolitionist (Blair) go in and restore order.[10] Elated, the civilian-clothed Grant then proceeded to put in his own two cents' worth against a Confederate sympathizer whom he labeled a streetcar "dude."[11] Grant's outlook was likely colored by numer-ous unhappy memories associated with St. Louis during his stay there between 1857 and 1859, evoking memories of what Jean Edward Smith characterized as his "unfitness for commercial life." It was there that Grant, after first fail-ing at farming in Missouri, then failed in real estate and ended up peddling firewood to survive and pawning his watch to buy Christmas presents.[12] This was after having fruitlessly walked the streets in search of employment. It was also in St. Louis that Grant unsuccessfully ran for county engineer and was laid off as a customs house clerk—in favor of a fellow Democrat. In the wake of these multiple setbacks, Grant commiserated with another ex-soldier civil-ian who came to grief in St. Louis, William Tecumseh Sherman, with whom he would three years later forge one of the most successful partnerships in military history. Near despair, Grant told a friend at the time, "I can't make a go of it here."[13]

In spite of these hardships, Grant during this same period elected on March 29, 1859, to emancipate William Jones, the one and only slave that he ever owned.[14] Grant, however, as noted by almost all of his biographers, was no abolitionist. In fact, he had expressed loathing for the abolitionist move-ment and (like Sherman) was known to have occasionally used the "N" word.[15] I would venture to guess that Grant was inspired to make this move (surely against the wishes of his slave-owning Missouri in-laws) by his complete dis-gust with the immoral and unforgiving world of St. Louis commerce. In these personal contradictions, Grant was very much a man of his time and place. In May of 1861, he seems to have been impressed by watching two dedicated Federal officers (Blair and Lyon) with a small but disciplined body of troops overawe a large metropolitan area into submission. After retreating to Casey-ville, Illinois, Grant—by now depressed in spirits—once again confided in fellow Galenan and gubernatorial assistant Augustus Chetlain, telling him, "I don't think I'm conceited ... but I feel confident I could command a regiment well; at least I would like to try it."[16] Grant's discouragement may have been triggered by a brief reunion with the volunteer troops from Galena, now part of the 12th Illinois Regiment stationed in Caseyville.[17]

Grant mustered the famed Eighth District Regiment the following day on May 11 at Belleview. Belleview was the home of Illinois Senator Lyman Trumbull, who would soon afterwards be among those who endorsed Grant's fast-track promotion to Brigadier General. The Eighth District Regiment would eventually see some of the heaviest fighting of the war, from Donelson to Shiloh to Corinth to Vicksburg. Its colonel, Decatur lawyer Richard Oglesby, would soon become one of Grant's key point men, and after the war was elected governor of Illinois. Thus in the space of a week, between May 8 and May 15, Grant had traversed the state from Springfield to Mattoon to Belleview, across the state line to St. Louis, then back to Belleview, Caseyville, and Mattoon. This pace surely had to have been taxing, especially given that Grant was separated from the emotional prop provided by his wife and children.

On May 15, Grant arrived back at Mattoon, Illinois, to muster in the Seventh District Regiment (later known as the 21st Illinois) that would later be instrumental in helping Grant obtain his first officer's commission.[18] Mattoon was also the home town of State Auditor Jesse Dubois, who had been among the first to bring Grant to Governor Yates' attention in Springfield.[19] In his letters, Grant himself disparagingly and incorrectly described Mattoon as part of "Egypt"[20] or southern Illinois, with the town of Cairo (to this day, pronounced "*Kay*-roe" by locals) at the southern tip of the state. Later in his memoirs, Grant stated in an almost defensive tone, "My Regiment was composed in large part of young men of as good social position as any in their section of the State...," with the disclaimer, "There were also men in it who could be led astray."[21] Although Grant specifies the sons of doctors, lawyers, ministers, etc., one cannot escape the image of farmers and backwoodsmen, at least in comparison to these volunteers' eastern counterparts. The Seventh District Regiment did in fact have a rowdy reputation. Nicknamed "Governor Yates' Hellions,"[22] they were, in the beginning, mainly noted for carousing, vandalism, and outright insubordination. This is very reminiscent of Mark Twain's infamous and semi-fictional "Marion [County] Rangers" who were purportedly active at this same time not far away across the Missouri border.[23]

"Egyptian" southern Illinois, which would supply the heart of Grant's legendary Federal army, had reputedly received its nickname from missionaries many years before the war. This agricultural region eventually became the economic breadbasket of the Midwest, and the great confluence of the Mississippi River and its tributaries suggested the biblical Nile River to many settlers, which of course most had never seen. In addition to Cairo, other town names in the region, such as Thebes and Boaz (not to mention regional centers such as Memphis, Tennessee), picked up on this association. The inhabitants of Egyptian Illinois were generally looked down upon by both Northern city-dwellers and genteel Southern planters as being unsophisticated and uncouth.

Initially, the Seventh Regiment elected (in a closely contested vote) as its colonel one Simon Goode, city clerk of Decatur, Illinois, an election that Grant himself apparently supervised and certified as mustering officer.[24] Unfortunately for the regiment (but fortunately for Grant), Colonel Goode turned out to be not so good. Although of impressive physical appearance, flashy apparel, and bombastic oratory, Goode's only military credentials, such as they were, were that he had been a "veteran" of William Walker's boneheaded filibustering excursions into Central America during the 1850s. In brief, Goode's hallmark was drunken incompetence (accusations that would later be flung at Grant), often joining in with the misbehavior of his troops.[25] He soon earned the disrespect of those serving under him, who decided that they did not want to be led into combat by the man whom they had elected. By way of contrast, and as a compliment to their recently departed mustering officer, the volunteers of the Seventh decided to name their base "Camp Grant."[26]

Lieutenant Joseph Vance recalled the Seventh's initial impression of their future commander: "He was a bit stooped at the time, and wore a cheap suit of clothes and a soft black hat." This sort of comment, incidentally, was the kind that irritated Julia Grant in later years, who wrote, "I have been both indignant and grieved over the statement of pretended personal acquaintances of Captain Grant at this time to the effect that he was dejected, low-spirited, badly dressed, and even slovenly."[27] But Lieutenant Vance added that Grant was "the first officer to come to us clothed with authority from the State" and that "we also saw that he knew his business, for everything he did was done without hesitation.... Anyone who looked beyond that [his appearance] recognized that he was a professional soldier."[28] This singular, remarkable passage sums up the story of how a group of young Midwestern volunteers from the 19th century learned through hard experience to distinguish between incompetence and competence—between appearances and reality. It was a crucial lesson that many soldiers and civilians would never learn, and still never learn.

From Mattoon, Grant plunged deeper into the "Egypt"[29] of Southern Illinois, where he mustered in the Ninth District Regiment (later the 18th Illinois Regiment) on May 20. Even by then, his own opinion of volunteers from this part of the state was beginning to improve. From Anna, Illinois, he wrote to his wife:

> It is the prevailing opinion abroad that the people of this section of the State are ignorant, disloyal, intemperate and generally heathenish. The fact is the Regt. formed here is the equal, if not the superior, of any of the Regiments raised in the State, for all the virtues of which they are charged with being deficient.[30]

This was not necessarily a slur against the rest of the state. Grant was beginning to develop a fondness for the regiments that he had mustered, and mutual respect was growing. The handily elected Irish colonel of the Ninth Regiment, Michael Lawler, later wrote to request the continued assistance of "Capt. U.S. Grant" for drilling the troops.[31] Lawler represented a growing number of regimental officers who would later serve with great fervor under Grant, in Lawler's case most notably during the Vicksburg campaign.

This unusual relationship between Grant and his troops marked the genesis of the formidable western Federal armies that would eventually win the war for the North. It really began in obscure places like Belleview, Mattoon, and Anna during the month of May in 1861, and ended at Appomattox, Virginia in 1865. Even though these particular regiments would be defeated in individual engagements,[32] they would never be beaten in a campaign. As many a military historian has noted, the American Civil War was first won and lost in the West, and the winning can be more or less traced to Grant's footsteps from the very beginning of his resurrected career in Galena. For the moment, however, Grant had to collect his first desperately needed paycheck issued by the state around May 22.[33] Before this, he and his family had been living off borrowed money from his brother Orvil, as well as the charity and good will of others.[34]

Over the course of a mere 10 days, Grant had mustered into service three regiments that would later help to form the nucleus of the indomitable western Federal armies. After completing his duties as mustering officer and obtaining a week of leave on May 22, Grant visited his family in Galena and on May 24 wrote a humble, if somewhat pathetic letter to Adjunct-General Lorenzo Thomas[35] in Washington, D.C. (whom he had previously known), requesting a colonelcy appointment in the regular army.[36] Grant laconically noted in his memoirs, "The letter failed to elicit an answer from the Adjunct-General of the Army," adding that years after the war the letter was found mysteriously stashed away in "some out-of-the-way place." Almost apologetically, Grant explained the only reason he had asked for the rank of colonel was that he had observed other inexperienced colonels in action and felt he could do no worse.[37] It appeared that Grant's checkered reputation in the regular army still dogged him and would continue to do so. To his father, however, he wrote, "During the six days I have been at home I have felt all the time as if a duty was being neglected that was paramount to any other duty I ever owed."[38]

Returning to Springfield at the end of the month, Grant moped around the Chenery Hotel, where Governor Yates had personally detained him from returning home the previous month. The antsy and frustrated ex-captain responded to a journalist who asked him what he was doing with, "Nothing— waiting."[39] Despite a remarkable series of events over the last six weeks, Grant still did not have the officer's commission that he coveted. These events, or rather twists of fate, included his nomination to preside at the meeting of volunteers in Galena, his last-minute detainment by the governor in Springfield, and the unexpected opportunity to replace John Pope as mustering officer of Camp Yates. Long afterwards, in his memoirs, Grant maintained that it was improper for anyone to solicit a commission with too much eagerness,[40] and he appears to have been good on his word. To borrow the phrase of historian James McPherson, Grant at the end of May 1861 found himself in Springfield, like Dickens' Micawber, waiting for something to turn up.

CHAPTER 3

June 1861: Colonel Grant

It is men who wait to be selected, and not those who seek, from whom we may always expect the most efficient service.

—Grant[1]

With the death of Illinois Senator Stephen A. Douglas on June 3, 1861, passed the political idol of the Grant family and most Northern pro–Union Democrats. Julia Grant recalled the draped portrait of "our late leader" in their Galena home and Grant himself noted briefly meeting Douglas in Springfield shortly before his death.[2] After the war (in 1866), Grant would reluctantly travel to Chicago with acting President Andrew Johnson—a man he disliked—for a dedication ceremony of the Douglas tomb, no doubt partly out of his respect for Douglas' memory. Later, there was an absurd legend in the Douglas family that the late Senator had prevented Grant from seeking a Confederate officer's commission[3]; yet, there was a grain of truth in that Grant before the war was a Douglas Democrat with strong Southern family ties (his Missouri in-laws). The important point is that *at the beginning of the war Grant was a political outsider.* This worked to his advantage only insofar as Congressman Washburne and Governor Yates had the foresight to make the war effort bipartisan by including those with reputed Democratic sympathies such as Grant.

On June 1, Grant wrote to his wife from Springfield that he was making plans to travel to the Cincinnati area, ostensibly to visit his parents and ailing brother, who were across the Ohio River in Covington, Kentucky. The main purpose of the visit, however, would be to make a house call on Major-General George McClellan, whose headquarters were in Cincinnati. At this point in time, the frustrated ex–Captain had decided that he wanted nothing more than to be a staffer for the renowned McClellan, whom he had known many years previous while stationed at Fort Vancouver, Washington. Grant and McClellan had also both been cadets at West Point and served together during the Mexican War.[4] In the same letter to Julia, though, Grant mentions a rumor that "...I find that I had been spoken of for the Colonelcy of a Regiment now partly made up." Professor John Y. Simon has suggested that this was possibly a reference to the Seventh District Regiment mustered by Grant a few weeks earlier in Mattoon. In spite of this prospect, Grant opted to approach McClellan for a regular army job, rather than wait around any longer in Springfield for something to happen. Five days later, on June 6, Grant wrote again to Julia, confirming his imminent plans to go to Cincinnati.[5]

By June 10, Grant was writing to Julia from Covington. After expressing rightful concern over his brother Simpson's deteriorating health, he disparages a mutual acquaintance, one Louisa Whistler, daughter of an old army acquaintance in the area, for her Confederate sympathies. In Grant's words: "She [Louisa] has been fed on Government pap all her life, since marriage as well as before, and now she would like to see that Government broken up. Such is human nature." Grant's letter of June 10 also indicated that he intended to visit army headquarters that same day.[6]

At McClellan's office Grant met with petty humiliation familiar to any job-seeker in the modern world. After announcing himself, Grant was told that McClellan was out; then after two days of intermittent sitting and waiting, he grew tired of being invisible and walked out, never to return. It was the greatest non-meeting between Union commanders of the war. Reflecting a pattern of behavior, McClellan later dealt out similar treatment to Lincoln (to whom he owed his job), by having the President sit and wait in the parlor (in company with Secretary of State William Seward, no less), while an indisposed McClellan seems to have hid upstairs.[7] Taken in perspective, as historian James McPherson noted, McClellan "had never known, as Grant had, the despair of defeat or the humiliation of failure. He had never learned the lessons of adversity and humility."[8] Later, McClellan claimed that he had already left town and would have given Grant a job had he been there, but it was good thing, wrote McClellan, since he and most of his staff were eventually cashiered.

McClellan's version of these events seems highly implausible because, for starters, no one said anything to Grant. Moreover, McClellan was reported to have left for Cairo, Illinois, on June 12, two days after Grant in his letters said he was going to McClellan's office in Cincinnati on June 10. The final coda to this farce occurred back in Springfield a few days later on June 15 when McClellan personally inspected the same Seventh District Regiment that Grant had mustered in Mattoon. McClellan publicly expressed satisfaction with the regiment, then still under the command of the incompetent Colonel Goode, despite its suffering from arguably the worst regimental reputation in the state.[9] A more likely explanation for the entire episode than the one given years later by McClellan is that he, like many other army regulars, knew about Grant's tarnished reputation, had previously witnessed his drunkenness at Fort Vancouver, and simply avoided the man. In any event, it is probable, as Jean Edward Smith wrote, that "McClellan's slight hit Grant hard."[10]

By now, Grant—in desperation—was telling anyone who would listen that he had been a good baker (as quartermaster) during the Mexican War and could contribute to the war effort by baking bread.[11] What is remarkable about this period in Grant's life is that, discouraged as he had to have been, quitting did not seem to be part of the equation. When not floating ideas on commissary duties, he seemed to consider seeking an officer's commission in Ohio or Indiana, if he could not find one in Illinois. Although this dogged-ness may have been due to Grant's famous "never turn back"[12] philosophy, the fact remains that his sheer determinedness by itself had not translated into success during the pre-war years. As the ancient historian Plutarch wrote in reference to Julius Caesar, "[T]here is no beginning so mean, which con-tinued application will not make considerable...."[13] Like Caesar, no beginning was apparently too mean or humble for Ulysses S. Grant. In retrospect, Grant's sojourn to Cincinnati in early June 1861 probably represented the absolute low point of his Civil War career, even more so than the numbing disgrace that followed Shiloh or the hailstorm of criticism he endured during the Vicksburg campaign. At this point, he was still just a seedy, non-commissioned civilian whom nobody seemed to want; yet, even as his former colleagues rebuffed him, good—if not miraculous—things were happening back in Spring-field.

In the words of Jean Edward Smith, "Providence now took a hand in Grant's future."[14] Governor Yates was approached and informed by the jun-ior officers of the Seventh District Regiment that the volunteers were no longer willing to serve under their buffoonish colonel-elect, Simon Goode, and would in fact prefer their original mustering officer, U.S. Grant, as their new colo-nel. Under normal circumstances, Yates probably would have reminded these men of their oath and sent them packing; however, the volunteers held a proverbial hammer over the governor's head. It was recently announced that the original three-month enlistment term and been peremptorily converted by the government into three years of service—a bait-and-switch technique not unique to modern times. After conferring with advisers, including State Audi-tor Jesse Dubois from Mattoon, Yates informed the junior officers of the Sev-enth District Regiment that Grant was now appointed their new Colonel. The executive order was issued a few days later and officially dated June 15, 1861.

Yates' slowness and hesitancy to issue perhaps the most momentous com-mission in American military history requires a bit of explanation. Over the previous two months the lowly Grant had firmly established a reputation among Illinois politicians—indeed, drawn attention to himself—as one who absolutely refused to come to them hat-in-hand for favors. This idealistic but impractical attitude provoked reactions of (at best) incredulity and bewilderment among those who had the power to help him, Yates included. For this reason alone, it is therefore not surprising that Grant was initially passed over during the first wave of military appointments handed out in early 1861. Finally, after a few weeks, as the crunch hit to find qualified field officers, Grant got a second chance. Yates was told by an assistant that Grant's hard-to-get attitude stemmed from a desire for a regular army commission, but that he would probably accept a gubernatorial appointment if he could get it without solicitation.[15] Simultaneously, a disgruntled regiment asked for Grant by name. This has to be viewed in retrospect as a highly fortuitous series of events for the North's future commander-in-chief. Professor Simon provided the useful observation that "...USG's appointment can only be explained in terms of the peculiarly demoralized state of the regt.," adding that it "...was generally believed necessary to encourage the men to enlist for three years and received favorable newspaper comment."[16] After appeasing the junior officers of the Seventh Regiment, Yates then telegrammed his offer to Covington, Kentucky, where Grant had been visiting his parents and unceremoniously rejected by George McClellan.[17]

By the time the governor's telegrammed offer reached the home of Jesse Grant, however, his disappointed son had already left to return to Illinois. When the offer of a commission reached Grant in transit, he was laying over in Lafayette, Indiana, staying with an old friend from his St. Louis days, Colonel (later Brigadier General) Joseph Reynolds. In writing to Julia on June 17, Grant noted that he had been with the Reynolds family on the previous Sunday, and proudly announced to her (after expressing more concern over the deteriorating health of his brother Simpson), "You have probably seen that I have been appointed to a Colonelcy?"[18] According to tradition in the Reynolds family there was some hesitancy on Grant's part to accept Yates' offer, probably because he still held out hopes for a regular army appointment, but that Reynolds' brother William talked him into accepting.[19] Grant telegrammed his acceptance to Yates on June 14 and arrived in Springfield the next day to personally take command of the regiment. Before he left Lafayette, however, there was a curious incident reported, completely out of character for Grant and perhaps inspired by his sudden good fortune. He happened to encounter an Ohio colonel who declared that he was not willing to defend the Union if that meant the abolishment of slavery. This qualification of loyalty apparently enraged Grant, and the two Union colonels had to be physically separated by bystanders.[20] On the surface, this outburst was a surprising reaction from the famously imperturbable Grant, certainly no abolitionist himself and whose wife and in-laws owned slaves; on the other hand, having a fellow native Ohioan lecture him on the fine points of military duty may have hit a nerve. Perhaps deep down he realized—from hard experience in the Mexican War— that hedging one's commitments during a time of national crisis, especially for an officer, just would not do.

While Grant had been trying without success to get an interview with McClellan in Cincinnati, Julia later claimed to have had a premonition of his appointment in a dream. Nevertheless, when the commission officially arrived in the mail at Galena, she did not initially notice that it was addressed to "Col. U.S. Grant."[21] Now Grant—unlike his father-in-law "Colonel" Dent—was a real colonel. In a small Indiana town (today the home of Purdue University), the military career of Ulysses S. Grant had instantly gone from being a forlorn hope to leader of a regiment. As Professor Smith summed it up, "Grant, who had been considering baking bread for the army, was now a colonel of Illinois volunteers."[22] In two months, Grant had metamorphosed from underemployed small-town retail clerk to a colonel, higher in rank than he had ever been during his former army days.

Colonel Grant's arrival at Camp Yates in Springfield on June 15 to take charge of the notoriously rowdy Seventh Regiment is case study in how unlikely methods can sometimes produce even more unlikely results. Galenan John E. Smith, always with a keen eye for Grant's limitations, accompanied him on the first day they rode a trolley out to camp. Smith tells us that Grant "...was dressed very clumsily, in citizen's clothes—an old coat, worn out at the elbows, and a badly dinged plug hat."[23] His disrespectful reception by the volunteers was predictable. At one point, there was some shadowboxing behind Grant's back until a deviously playful shove sent one volunteer careening into his newly-appointed commanding officer. The new, untested Colonel responded only with a glare that appears to have unnerved those who witnessed it. Then, instead of punishing everyone in sight, Grant surprised the raw recruits by immediately disbanding a large unit of military police assembled by the previous Colonel for the sole purpose of nabbing anyone who tried to sneak out of camp.[24] The result of this single directive was an immediate improvement in morale, as reported by the press,[25] but before the recruits could extract more favors, Grant—with equal unexpectedness—dashed back to Galena for a couple of days, where he borrowed money from his father's business partner in order to buy a uniform and a horse.[26] He then backtracked to Camp Yates, where he issued his first written order of the war, dated June 18, 1861.[27]

According to an eyewitness, Grant, upon entering his tent—perhaps with the greatest understatement in military history—said that "he guessed he'd take command."[28] Once again with great insight, Professor Smith (himself a former army professional) noted that Grant's first orders seemed tailored for volunteer troops (as opposed to career soldiers) by merely appealing for their "hearty support," while simultaneously demanding the total cooperation of officers.[29] Thus Grant consciously opted to begin with a light touch in correcting lax discipline while squarely placing most of the pressure on his officers rather than the rank and file. It was his first tough decision as a commanding officer and proved to be a good one. One week later, soldiers were writing home of improved morale in the regiment.[30] In regards to this process,

Grant in his memoirs states, "I found it very hard work for a few days...," but that "...the great majority [of volunteers] favored discipline, and by the application of little regular army punishment all were reduced to as good discipline as one could ask."[31] In a letter to Julia dated June 26, Grant wrote that his officers had responded to the challenge and interestingly noted that most were light drinkers ("For the Field officers ... one pint of liquor will do to the end of the war"), and jokingly complained that he could not have a game of cards with several due to their religious disapproval of gambling.[32]

On June 28, the Seventh District Regiment was sworn in for three years of service and rechristened the 21st Illinois Regiment. The following day, Grant wrote to Julia, expressing disgust with his cousin Orly (Orlando Ross), who ostentatiously rode up to Grant and his regiment on a hired livery horse during the swearing-in ceremony, bearing all of Grant's "fine trappings" that he had previously purchased with borrowed money in Galena. Colonel Grant seems to have responded to this intended grandiose gesture by snubbing his cousin in front of the troops. Thus even after receiving his commission, Grant still made it a point to emulate his own former commanding officer, General Zachary Taylor, famous for his aversion to all uniforms, show, and ceremony. This attitude seems to have repeatedly gone down well with the enlisted men, just as Taylor's unpretentious demeanor had indelibly impressed Grant as a young officer during the Mexican War. A few days prior to the swearing-in, Grant was joined in camp by his 11-year-old son Fred, who quickly proceeded to endear himself with the troops as the unofficial mascot of the regiment.[33]

Pep talks do not appear to have been the forte of the tight-lipped Grant, but the impending end-of-the-month re-enlistment ceremonies in Springfield seemed to naturally demand some kind of oratory. It was at this time that the newly-appointed Colonel of the 21st was introduced to two Illinois Democratic congressman-turned-soldiers, both of whom would soon serve under him and, for better and worse (respectively), figure prominently in Grant's early Civil War career. These two men were John Logan and John McClernand, both representing congressional districts from southern Illinois. Grant's memoirs relate that McClernand at the time was well-known in the press for his bellicose pro–Union views, but that Logan had been relatively silent on the issue, at least insofar as Grant was aware at the time. Despite heavy criticism in the press for his comparative reticence, "Logan was not a man to be coerced by threats," as noted by Grant. He did hesitate, however, when Logan and McClernand requested an opportunity to address the volunteers, acquiescing in Logan's case only because McClernand was with Logan at the time and appeared to be kind of a chaperon. After a fervent but predictable speech by McClernand, Grant wrote of what happened next, his surprise still evident over 20 years after the fact:

Logan followed with a speech which he has hardly equaled since for force and eloquence. It breathed loyalty and devotion to the Union which inspired my men to such a point that they would have volunteered to remain in the army as long as an enemy of the country continued to bear arms against it. They [the volunteers] entered the United States service almost to a man.[34]

Grant goes on to praise Logan's abilities in both war and peace, but offers no such accolades for McClernand, with whom he would have a combative relationship over the next two years. He does write, however, of how the southern part of Illinois, like the southern part of many Northern states at the outbreak of the Civil War, was hanging in the balance of loyalty to the Union, with the residents of these districts typically heading in opposite geographic directions for volunteer military service. It was thanks to men like Logan, according to Grant, who tipped the balance in favor of the North. As he put it, "The very men who at first made it necessary to guard the roads in southern Illinois became the defenders of the Union."[35]

As the month of June 1861 came to a close, Grant could pride himself in having acquired his coveted officer's commission and successfully disciplining his adopted home state's most challenging regiment. On a more subtle level, Grant appears to have re-entered the service holding a common prejudice that the residents of "Egyptian" Illinois would not make good Federal soldiers. Within a few weeks after mustering these volunteers and assuming command, he seems to have modified his opinion. Few realized it at the time, but this development spelled doom for the Southern Confederacy.[36] Two western armies were being built out of more or less the same raw materials. Whoever now supplied better leadership and successfully harnessed available resources would eventually win. No battles had been fought yet, despite the secession of the Confederate states and the bombardment of Fort Sumter in April, but this relatively quiet state of affairs was about to change.

CHAPTER 4

July 1861: Florida, Missouri

The last camp which we fell back upon was in a hollow near the village of Florida, where I was born—in Monroe County. Here we were warned, one day, that a Union colonel was sweeping down on us with a whole regiment at his heels.... In time I came to know that the Union colonel whose coming frightened me out of the war and crippled the Southern cause to that extent—General Grant.

—Mark Twain[1]

As most students of the war know, on July 21, 1861, a large Federal army under General Irvin McDowell was completely routed by allied Confederate forces at the first Battle of Bull Run near Manassas, Virginia, approximately 25 miles southwest of Washington, D.C. Few know, however, that at the same moment Bull Run was being fought, Colonel of Volunteers Ulysses S. Grant was quietly stationed with his regiment in an obscure place called Mexico, Missouri, having yet to see any fighting whatsoever. Grant and his regiment, the 21st Illinois, had recently managed to traverse the northeastern part of Missouri in a fruitless search for rebel activity, although at one point they apparently came very close to finding it. Bull Run was of course the first great shock of the war for the North in that it demonstrated the South was all too capable of fielding a powerful army and defending its own soil with tenacity and skill. The Union fiasco at Bull Run also represented the first indication to the Northern public, surprising to many, that the war might be long and bitterly contested. This unexpected revelation would be harrowingly confirmed the following April on the west bank of the Tennessee River near a small Methodist chapel.

Less than three weeks before Bull Run, on July 3, 1861, Colonel U.S. Grant and his regiment had marched out of Springfield, Illinois.[2] Almost two years later to the day, he would be negotiating the surrender of Vicksburg—the eventual turning point of the war—but in July 1861 no one could foresee such a thing, let alone the war lasting that long. For the present, just as Grant had proposed to Governor Yates in early May as a mustering officer, the troops were marching on foot towards the Missouri border, as opposed to sitting and

33

waiting for rail transportation. Their preliminary objective was Quincy, Illinois, on the east bank of the Mississippi River, in order to be well-positioned for lending assistance to vulnerable Federal garrisons threatened in eastern Missouri. While the first big battle was about to be fought in Virginia, Colonel Grant's movements out west during the same period now offer a case study in how a competent officer must sometimes cope with (and try to make the most of) orders that are vacillating, contradictory and vague. This is a fascinating period of the conflict that commentators tend rarely to address, presumably because there was little shooting going on. Back in Galena, Julia Grant noted that since her husband's appointment as Colonel and assignment to operations in Missouri, they had become local celebrities. As she proudly noted in her own memoirs, "Our house was now the center of attention in Galena."[3]

Grant would certainly make many mistakes during the early years of the struggle, and during the summer of 1861, he would have been the first to admit that he still had much to learn. Nevertheless, his first march in July from Springfield to Missouri clearly demonstrated many of the special qualities that would serve him well throughout the war. Writing to Julia on July 7 from the town of Naples on the Illinois River (a Mississippi tributary), he related with pride that his regiment "...was in a terribly disorganized state when I took it but a very great change has taken place." A few days later, he repeated the sentiment in a letter to his father: "I ... flatter myself ... that I have done as much for the improvement and the efficiency of this regiment as was ever done for a command in the same length of time."[4] Grant also informed Julia that their son Fred was continuing in his makeshift role as regimental mascot, even riding Grant's horse during the march while he himself hoofed it with the men. Then in a courtly gesture to Julia, he disclosed that he had received a flower bouquet from an anonymous lady admirer while passing through the town of Jacksonville, Illinois.[5] Grant was obviously concerned about stopping ugly rumors (with which he had experience) that might reach his wife.

In Jacksonville (on July 5) occurred another incident shedding a bit of light on Grant's priorities. A local tried to sell liquor to the troops. Grant reacted by immediately confiscating the jugs and giving the would-be profiteer "one minute to 'hitch up' and make tracks." This the individual promptly did, not even stopping to retrieve his coat.[6] If Grant was not concerned about his own frailties, he certainly had in mind those of his troops, who under their former C.O. had shown a keen propensity for reckless behavior. Although Grant confiscated booze in Illinois, it is certainly true that at the outbreak of hostilities he showed a marked concern for respect of private property wherever he was overseeing military operations. This civilized attitude would of course change as the war was prolonged and Grant's troops plunged deeper into an intractably rebellious South. In the marginally loyal districts of eastern Missouri and northern Kentucky, however, his kid-gloves policy bore early, tangible fruits for which Grant is rarely given credit. He began by forcing his own regiment—who not so long ago had trashed everything in their path between Mattoon and Springfield—to observe this policy in west-central Illinois.

Grant also quickly demonstrated, in marked contrast to many of his colleagues at the time, a deep concern (as well as aptitude) for keeping his regiment well-supplied. Jean Edward Smith noted that "Grant's experience managing the supply trains for Generals Taylor and Scott during the Mexican War was much in evidence."[7] Grant's prioritization for keeping his troops adequately fed, clothed, and armed would later lead to one of the first great epiphanies of Civil War strategy during the initial, abortive phase of the Vicksburg campaign, and later would be taken up with terrifying fury by Sherman in Georgia and the Carolinas. It would also two years later contribute heavily to Grant's breathtaking victory at Missionary Ridge in Chattanooga.

By July 8, Grant's regiment was ordered to halt and await steamboat transportation on the Illinois River that would supposedly ferry them to join the forces under Nathaniel Lyon stationed in St. Louis. The designated steamer, however, grounded on a sandbar before it could arrive, and Grant's men had to cool their heels for a couple of days. The 21st Regiment was then ordered on July 10 to resume its original course to Quincy, this time by railroad with all possible dispatch. Professor Smith remarked that Grant's delay and subsequent rerouting represented a significant intervention of fate,[8] presumably because it is possible (if not likely) that had Grant linked up with Lyon, he would have shared Lyon's tragic fate a month later at the battle of Wilson's Creek. The urgency of the new order was due to updated reports that another Federal regiment stationed at Palmyra, Missouri (south of Quincy near Hannibal), was being surrounded and needed help. The order had been issued by John Pope, now a brigadier general and Grant's immediate superior since the day after Grant marched out of Springfield.[9] Thus once again John Pope appears to have come inadvertently to Grant's aid by ordering him out of harm's way, probably thinking at the time that he was doing just the opposite.

Upon his arrival in Quincy on July 11, Grant sent his son Fred home by riverboat, and prepared for the imminent prospect of combat with Confederate partisans. What happened next has never been better described by anyone other than Grant himself. A veteran of some of the most savage fighting of the Mexican War, Grant confided in his memoirs, "My sensations as we approached what I supposed might be 'a field of battle' were anything but agreeable." He adds, however, that his anxiety was due more to the fact that he was now in command, as opposed to his subordinate rank in the Mexican War, where as a young officer he had admired Zachary Taylor's cool demeanor while leading American forces under fire. Before the 21st Illinois could launch out of Quincy, though, the troops that they thought needed rescuing came straggling into town. There had been no battle, per se, and precise accounts of what exactly had happened were obscure. Grant's own deadpan explanation was "I am inclined to think that both sides got frightened and ran away."[10]

The next assignment for Grant (again, ordered by General Pope) was to round up Confederate guerillas reported to be concentrating under General Thomas Harris in the vicinity of nearby Florida, Missouri, today famous as the birthplace of Mark Twain.[11] In July 1861, however, Twain was an unknown 25-year-old named Samuel Clemens and purportedly a member of the self-styled "Marion [County] Rangers."[12] This motley band of young men from Hannibal, Missouri, aspired to be Confederate heroes and were immortalized in Twain's autobiographical sketch titled "The Private History of a Campaign That Failed," published in 1885—the same year as Grant's own memoirs. It thus appeared that on July 14, as the 21st Illinois moved out from West Quincy, Missouri, that Ulysses S. Grant was headed on a direct collision course against his future *Memoirs* publisher and friend, Mark Twain. Grant wrote to his wife and father on July 13 informing them of his mission against General Harris the next day.[13]

In his memoirs, Grant yet again portrays himself as a highly reluctant warrior. He matter-of-factly states, "I would have given anything then to have been back in Illinois, but I had not the moral courage to halt and consider what to do; I kept right on."[14] This admission was reminiscent of Grant's earlier expressed feelings upon approaching his very first battlefield during the Mexican War: "I felt sorry that I had enlisted."[15] Grant's reference to his own lack of "moral courage" also recalls his observation that "Once [a war was] initiated there were but few public men who would have the courage to oppose it."[16] For the second time in a week, however, the anxieties of Grant and his men were relieved. Upon approaching the Confederate camp, they realized that their would-be opponents had hightailed it in the opposite direction. In one of the most famous quotes from the war, Grant relates his learning experience:

> My heart resumed it place. It occurred to me at once that Harris had been as much afraid of me as I had been of him. This was a view of the question I had never taken before; but it was one I never forgot afterwards. From that event to the close of the war, I never experienced trepidation upon confronting an enemy, though I always felt more or less anxiety. I never forgot that he had as much reason to fear my forces as I had his. The lesson was valuable.[17]

Twain had a slightly different take on the whole affair: "There was more Bull Run material scattered through the early camps of this country than exhibited itself at Bull Run."[18] In one sense, Twain humorously implied that his own conspicuous cowardice at Florida, Missouri, contributed to an additional build-up in Grant's own courage. I see no reason to necessarily disagree with this and probably neither would have Grant. With even greater insight, Twain reflected on the obscurity of the Civil War's most famous hero during the first year of the conflict:

> I came within a few hours of seeing him when he was as unknown as I was myself; at a time when anybody could have said, "Grant?—Ulysses S. Grant? I do not remember the name before." It seems difficult to realize that there was once a time when such a remark could be rationally made; but there *was*, and I was within a few miles of the place and the occasion too, proceeding in the other direction.[19]

To what extent Twain was fabricating his own account of these events is beyond the scope of this study. His remark about "Bull Run material" may have been an unconscious realization that the actual battle of Bull Run was fought a mere four days after his hapless, tragicomic Marion Rangers had skedaddled out of Colonel Grant's path on July 17, 1861.[20]

The aftermath of Grant's "campaign that succeeded" saw the 21st Illinois backtracking through the hamlet of Florida itself where, as Grant related in a letter to Julia two days later, they witnessed a scene quite different from the one encountered earlier in the day. "As we went down houses all appeared to be deserted. People of the town ... left on our approach but finding that we behave respectfully ... returned and before we left nearly every lady and child visited Camp...." He added that these women and children "no doubt felt as much regret at our departure as they did at our arrival."[21] In his memoirs, Grant explained that the town folk of Florida "had evidently been led to believe that the National troops carried death and devastation with them wherever they went."[22] To repeat, the orderly and restrained conduct of troops under Grant's supervision in Missouri at this preliminary stage of the war needs to be distinguished from what would later transpire in Mississippi, Georgia, and the Carolinas.

After the great anticlimax at Florida, the comedy that constituted Grant's excursion and dashing about through northeastern Missouri had one final act to play. Grant was now summoned by General Pope to the town of Mexico, Missouri, apparently to help relieve his ambitious commander of the petty duties involved in running an army, which included baby-sitting two additional volunteer regiments besides his own. Here, the worst thing that Grant had to worry about was a surly and suspicious civilian population; on the other hand, this problem proved somewhat thornier than vainly attempting to come to grips with fleeing partisans. By July 20 (one day before Bull Run), Grant and his regiment had arrived in town,[23] where he noted that proper discipline had not been maintained among the other regiments already stationed there. These troops were more or less in the habit of terrorizing locals as their mood dictated. After publishing strict orders against going where not invited, Grant noted that the abuses stopped at once and as a result he "received the most marked courtesy from the citizens of Mexico as long as I remained there."[24] Although Grant was trying to encourage Union loyalty in the border states during this time, he was also no doubt highly cognizant that his own in-laws lived not far away in the St. Louis area. Had he allowed plundering, he might as well have plundered his own father-in-law. The same principle applied with respect to forced loyalty oaths, molestation of private property, slaves, etc.

Grant spent the quiet remainder of July in Mexico, Missouri, where he decided to use downtime as an opportunity to brush up on tactics. During the day he would use the town common to drill troops, after having spent the previous evening studying a textbook on tactics—his worst subject at West Point—written by none other than Confederate Brigadier General William Hardee of Georgia, who also happened to command a hostile force not far away within the state of Missouri. In point of fact, Grant did not appear to stand much in awe of Hardee, noting that his textbook was "a mere translation of the French with Hardee's name attached" and that Hardee's so-called tactics were, in Grant's opinion, simply an updated, common-sense version of the same tactics used by Winfield Scott, Grant's other commander during the Mexican War. Thus Grant hints that Hardee was not the true author of the textbook (with some justification), similar to the manner in which Grant himself—with far less justification—would later be accused by some of not having actually written his *Memoirs*.[25] After studying a particular lesson, Grant (with barely concealed delight in his recollections) would then proceed the following morning to see how many of these rules he could abbreviate, bend and break during parade drill.[26] Once again, before his troops ever fired a shot in anger, we are given a fleeting glimpse of Grant's military acumen, if not genius. Military maxims of the past, as he would often later remind anyone willing to listen, were frequently meant to be broken, and Grant's success in the field over the course of the war would be largely predicated on this idea.

Also during his stay in Mexico, Missouri, Grant came under the sphere of a new commanding officer. This was the high-profiled and superbly résuméd Major-General John Frémont, who arrived in St. Louis on July 25 after having been appointed by President Lincoln to take overall command of Federal forces in the West. A native Southerner (from South Carolina), Frémont had won a name for himself before the war as a western explorer, Republican California senator, and 1856 presidential candidate.[27] Frémont, along with George McClellan, was one of the should-have-been great commanders during the American Civil War, and instead had at best a checkered career. Both Frémont and McClellan had enviable prewar images that rivaled that of Robert E. Lee in terms of paper qualifications and physical appearance. Frémont's short and stormy tenure as head of the Western Department would, in the long run, be mainly notable for the incredibly good fortune that Grant's career experienced during the same time frame. Frémont would also first commission the Federal river gunboats that would later prove instrumental in Grant's western campaigns.

Even before embarking on his Missouri adventures, Grant seems to have lost all regrets at not being an officer in the regular army. Less than a month after receiving his commission, he was writing to his father from the regiment's launching pad in West Quincy, "You ask if I should not like to go into the regular army. I should not." He had obviously grown proud of his handiwork with the volunteers. Rather than express this directly to his father, though, Grant gives us one of his priceless, surprise explanations: "I want to bring my children up to useful employment, and in the army the chance is poor. There is at least the same objection that you find where slavery exists."[28] The still obscure Union colonel clearly felt that his youthful training in the regular army—originally his father's idea—had ill-prepared him for the world of commerce, a world that his non-military father thrived in.[29] Grant wanted his own children to be more like his father, adding that a slave-state environment (translation: the antebellum Missouri of his Dent in-laws) was unsuitable for the same reason. This profound but sad observation came from Grant during his six-week stint as a Civil War colonel. In less than seven months he would become a household name, but at the end of July 1861 his unlikely career was about to take another great forward leap when it was least expected or looked for.

CHAPTER 5

August 1861:
Brigadier General Grant

... circumstances always did shape my course different from my plans.
—Grant[1]

As Colonel Grant's regimental chaplain read the *Missouri Democrat* for August 1, 1861, he brought to Grant's attention for the first time that he had been nominated for promotion to brigadier general, only six weeks after his hard-earned appointment to a colonelcy.[2] At the time, Federal regiments under Grant's supervision were still quietly stationed in Mexico, Missouri, awaiting further orders while trying not to annoy a surly civilian population that was overwhelmingly Confederate in its sympathies. President Lincoln had submitted his list of nominees to the Senate the previous day (July 31), and these were confirmed a few days later on August 5.[3] Crucial in the appointment was its backdating to May 17, which on the surface seemed to place Grant on equal footing with other Illinois political generals, such as Benjamin Prentice, but in reality allowed him to rank Prentice and others due to his previous military experience. Someone pulled a fast one and I suspect it was Washburne. In any event, Grant, with no warning or expectations, now found himself suddenly placed 35th in the overall chain of command for Union forces.[4] Shelby Foote characterized this promotion as "a political fluke."[5] Viewed in retrospect, however, this dramatic and unlooked-for boost had been developing for some time.

While Grant had used his six weeks as a colonel to the best advantage, the primary reason for his latest promotion can be summed up in one word—Washburne. The Union fiasco at Bull Run in July[6] had established that the war was going to be more than a mere Federal police action, and a true military buildup had now begun with additional troops being called into service, and (necessarily) more officers to manage them. At this early point in the conflict, virtually every Northern congressman was sponsoring his own potential war hero, and the influential Elihu Washburne from Lincoln's adopted

40

home state was no exception. In the words of historian John Y. Simon, "He [Grant] was promoted because he was the likeliest candidate for general from Galena." After Grant had come to Washburne's attention in Galena as a Democrat still loyal to the Union, Washburne took a chance and hustled the Mexican War veteran before Governor Yates as someone who might be able to help. Then, after a painful six-week process of doing work that no one else wanted to do, Grant got his big break when an unruly and near-mutinous regiment persuaded the still-skeptical governor to make him their colonel. Now after another six weeks of amply demonstrating his competence with several regiments, Grant was in a good position to justify Washburne's endorsement for yet another promotion, this time with the full support of his congressional colleagues and the president. Professor Simon again: "Washburne's first effort in Grant's behalf had been a partial success; his next, which shaped the whole of Grant's Civil War career, developed from his influence with the President." In one sense, it proved easier for Grant to become a brigadier than a colonel: the first step to colonelcy was the hardest. In any event, Grant gratefully acknowledged Washburne's patronage at the time,[7] something that he would not do many years later.

Aside from political clout, Grant helped his own cause by being highly efficient. Unlike many of his colleagues, he had a notable tendency to obey orders and not complain. More prosaically, he proved himself to be among the best, if not *the* best disciplinarian of western volunteers in the service. Paradoxically, he was able to achieve this without being a blusterer or a martinet. He had to date personally mustered three regiments and now commanded three more. While having yet to be involved in any fighting, his comical but successful excursions throughout northeastern Missouri—Palmyra, Florida, and Mexico—had effectively achieved desirable results, and this surely had been noted by his superiors. More remarkably, Grant had achieved these results while maintaining the good will of both his troops and the local citizens—an unusual combination, to say the least. Even General John Pope, his commanding officer and one not known for gratuitous praise, by now had favorable words for Grant.[8] This was quite a change if Pope had in fact earlier spread rumors about Grant's drinking; he may have been grateful to Grant for shoring up troop discipline in the town of Mexico.

As Grant prepared to leave Mexico for St. Louis to receive his new commission, he shared his observations on the locals in letters to his father and wife. To his father he gave his views on Southern sympathizers: "The majority in this part of the State are secessionists.... Many too seem to be entirely ignorant of the object of present hostilities." Then he complained about lies in the local press:

> There is never a movement of troops made that the Secession journals through the Country do not give a startling account of their almost annihilation at the hands of the States troops, whilst the facts are there are no engagements. My

Regt. has been reported cut to pieces once that I know of, and I don't know but oftener, whilst a gun has not been fired at us. These reports go uncontradicted here and give confirmation to the conviction already entertained that one Southron is equal to five Northerners. We believe they are deluded and know if they are not we are.

When a frustrated Grant tried to point out these reporting errors to the towns-folk of Missouri, he wrote to his father that "they don't believe a word." On a more positive note, he was pleased with the progress of the regiment under his supervision. "I took it in a very disorganized, demoralized and insubordinate condition and have worked it up to a reputation equal to the best...."[9] Writing to Julia the same day (August 3), Grant confided to her, "I am glad to get away from here." As for the town residents, they were "remarkably polite" but still "seceshers." Lastly, he pronounces judgment and offers Julia a glimpse of the near future:

People here will be glad to get clear of us here notwithstanding their apparent hospitality. They are great fools in this section of the country and will never rest until they bring upon themselves all the horrors of war in its worst form.[10]

Grant had realized, perhaps before most, that reason and logic were not going to persuade Confederates of their errors.

Upon his arrival in St. Louis on August 7,[11] Grant learned that big-city sentiment was not much different than in the hinterlands. Writing to Julia a few days later, he described his unpleasant encounter with her cousin (and his former employer-landlord) Harry Boggs, who greeted him with a browbeat-ing:

He cursed me like a Madman. Told me that I would never be welcome in his house; that the people of Illinois were a poor miserable set of Black Republicans, Abolition paupers that had to invade their state to get something to eat. Good joke that on something to eat. Harry is such a pitiful insignificant fellow that I could not get mad at him and told him so where upon he set the Army of Flanders far in the shade with his profanity.[12]

One needs to recall that Grant nearly starved while working with Boggs during his unhappy years in St. Louis. From St. Louis, Grant was ordered by Frémont to immediately take command in Ironton, Missouri, further south, where a disorganized group of Federal volunteers were being threatened by a gathering Confederate force.

At about this same time Grant wrote to fellow Galenan John Rawlins, offering him a job as aide-de-camp.[13] Two other acquaintances, Clark B. Lagow (then with Grant's regiment) and attorney William S. Hillyer of St. Louis, were also offered staff positions. Photographs taken after their appointments reveal three men who appear to be very uncomfortable in their uniforms, and Grant later more or less admitted that the offers to Lagow and Hillyer were mistakes. The appointment of Rawlins, however, was an instinctive stroke of genius, one of which Grant remained proud of to his dying day. Rawlins seemed the most unlikely of the three—a small-town lawyer with no military background, Democrat, eccentric personality, and consumptive (he would die shortly after the war in 1869)—yet he proved invaluable in the long run both as Grant's personal disciplinarian and as a sort of P.R. man, both of which the new brigadier general needed badly. As Grant put it (tongue in cheek), Rawlins had a talent for saying "no" and not getting the same request again.[14]

Upon his arrival in Ironton on August 8,[15] Grant relieved Colonel Benjamin Gratz Brown, later to become governor of Missouri, who had been attempting to preside over an underfed, under-clothed, under-armed, and undisciplined mob of volunteers. Grant noted that "Brown himself was gladder to see me on that occasion than he ever has been since." Meanwhile, approximately 40 miles to the south in Greenville, Missouri, Confederate General William Hardee, whose tactics textbook Grant had been recently studying, was trying to organize an offensive against a target he probably sensed was easy pickings. Grant believed that a single cavalry detachment could have overrun Ironton before he arrived.[16] After he determined the danger was not imminent (Hardee wanted more troops but could not get them), Grant wrote to headquarters on August 9, discounting the possibility of enemy attack, plus offering the priceless observation that

> It is fortunate too if this is the case for many of the officers seem to have so little command over their men, and military duty seems to be done so loosely, that I feel at present our resistance would be in the inverse ratio of the number of troops to resist with.[17]

Grant's next decision was whether to organize an offensive against Hardee, but with his own regiments rather than the volunteer mob in Ironton. Three hand-picked regiments stayed; Colonel Brown's regiment was sent home and mustered out of the service.[18]

Grant's correspondence during his stay in Ironton expressed keen interest (verging on obsession) in Hardee's movements, although the next major battle of the war was about to be fought in a different sector of Missouri. Hardee's name is mentioned by Grant in letters to various parties dated August 10, 12, 13, and 16 (twice).[19] Once again confiding in family, this time to his sister Mary, Grant on August 12 reiterated his mistaken belief that "the Rebels will be so badly whipped by April next that they cannot make a stand anywhere I don't doubt." His specification of "April next" would come back to haunt him at Shiloh Church. Appearing to sense his mistaken read on the Confederates with an eerie foreboding, Grant then qualified himself: "But they are so dogged that there is no telling when they may be subdued." In exasperation he contrasts the good behavior of Union troops and the bad behavior of Confederate forces toward Southern civilians, both of which seemed to result in more volunteers for the South, noting, "Every change makes them [the civilians] more desperate." Startlingly, he tells Mary, "I should like to be sent to Western Virginia but my lot seems to be cast in this part of the world." Lastly, Grant tells his sister that he still needs a uniform.[20] Thus in August 1861, Grant was still predicting swift victory for the North, thought the East was where the real action was, and was still poorly dressed.

West Virginia was then in the process of becoming a separate state as local Unionists, in tandem with Federal armies under George McClellan and William Rosecrans, managed to out-skirmish, out-maneuver, and outsmart poorly-led, rag-tag Confederate forces between the months of July and October. Not widely known is that this Union success was mostly achieved before the battle of Bull Run was fought, with McClellan demonstrating more of a Napoleonic flair for posturing rather than actual fighting, the latter (such as a it was) being done mostly by Grant's future rival, Rosecrans. Unsuccessful Confederate commanders included the notoriously inept John Floyd, later defeated by Grant at Fort Donelson, and Robert E. Lee, who was unable to salvage a bad situation that he had inherited.[21]

On August 10, 1861, the same day Grant wrote expressing interest in Hardee's forces, the North suffered its second major defeat in two months (and its first in the West), as Union forces led by Nathaniel Lyon and Franz Sigel were routed by Confederates under Benjamin McCulloch and Sterling Price at the battle of Wilson's Creek in southwestern Missouri. Lyon himself was killed and his army suffered 1,300 casualties,[22] while panicked survivors retreated to the central part of state. All of this transpired while Grant was stationed in far-off Ironton, Missouri, and contemplating a move against Hardee. Once again, one can't help but be struck by Grant's good fortune. Three months previous he had been itching to join Lyon's command in St. Louis, and a month prior to Wilson's Creek he had been ordered to do so. Had it not been for a steamboat hitting a sandbar on the Illinois River, Grant may have gone into his first Civil War battle (as a subordinate) at Wilson's Creek, and may well have ended up a casualty, as opposed to facing off against Mark Twain's cowardly Marion Rangers in Florida, Missouri.

Seven days after Wilson's Creek on August 17, Union Brigadier General Benjamin Prentice arrived in Ironton with orders to take command. Rather than argue, Grant immediately boarded a train for St. Louis to personally explain to Frémont why he ranked Prentice.[23] It was a savvy move that produced desirable results on several fronts. For starters, Grant's difficult and premature campaign against Hardee in Greenville was necessarily aborted.[24] Furthermore, in wake of the Federal disaster at Wilson's Creek and the arrival of Prentice in Ironton, Grant found himself ordered by Frémont to restore order in Jefferson City, the state capital of Missouri. Although Frémont was busy wrecking his own career with a rapid series of military and political missteps,[25] his use of Grant during this same period appears brilliant, if possibly somewhat serendipitous, in retrospect. Finally, Grant would soon be able to have a successful and inestimably important showdown with Prentice over priority of rank.

Assigned to Jefferson City by Frémont on August 19,[26] Grant arrived to find near-total chaos. Though his troops were nearly as battered as Federal forces after Wilson's Creek and limping towards Springfield, Sterling Price was nevertheless widely perceived as a victorious commander threatening the state capital, and Union-sympathizer refugees were pouring in. A motley combination of raw Federal volunteers and Home Guard militia were unable to keep order among themselves, let alone the city's population, which was facing starvation with no government support. No one seemed to be in charge, but that changed immediately upon Grant's arrival. Within a week, a semblance of order was restored and the threat of attack from Price's Confederates seemed to recede. The shock of what Grant observed in central Missouri's civil affairs, however, still came through in his memoirs long after the fact, as he noted that "worldly goods were abandoned and appropriated ... for the Union man in Missouri who staid at home during the rebellion, if he was not immediately under the protection of the National troops, was at perpetual war with his neighbors." Part of Grant's immediate reaction to this crisis was to press into service teams of horses belonging to known Confederate sympathizers.[27] This appears to have been his first tentative step towards utilizing the brutal tactics of "total war" that would later become standard operating procedure during the Vicksburg campaign. Even so, Grant's reaction to the panic in Missouri following Wilson's Creek was mild—if not imperturbable—compared to that of others, such as Frémont, who declared martial law and attempted to free Confederate slaves. At this early point in the conflict, Grant's deliberate go-easy policy towards Southern sympathizers, even in time of crisis, stood in complete opposition to the panicky retaliations often resorted to by many of his Union colleagues.

As the situation in Jefferson City began to stabilize, Grant's letter to Captain Speed Butler on August 23 provides a useful glimpse of his strategic outlook and a number of other principles that (for him) would remain constant throughout the war. First, Grant expresses disdain for fortifications, using as an excuse a lack of available engineering expertise. Then, instead of requesting engineers, he stresses the importance of drill and discipline on local troops, who evidently had nowhere to go but up in these categories. After expressing a rightful concern over the security of Lexington, Missouri—which would in fact soon be temporarily captured by the Confederates—Grant admitted that he had "very little disposition" in building forts and did want to achieve a "Pillow notoriety" for incompetence in that area.[28] Many of Grant's personal traits come out here in the space of a few sentences: an instinctive prescience of where the real enemy threat was (Lexington) and a desire to preempt it, a skepticism towards fortifications while fighting a war of invasion, and a focus on tight control of his own forces. Again striking is Grant's written contempt, for the second time in four months, of Gideon Pillow, who would soon become his first adversary in combat.

No sooner had things calmed down in Jefferson City than Grant was relieved by Colonel Jefferson C. Davis the last week of August and ordered to report back to St. Louis, where he would receive "important special instructions" for his next assignment.[29] It is difficult not to conclude that Grant was being used at this point by Frémont as a kind of trouble-shooter, since everything he was ordered to tackle seemed to eventually work out for the better, whether by Grant's skill or incredible luck. On August 28, Grant was ordered by Frémont to take command at Cape Girardeau on the west bank of the Mississippi River in southern Missouri, where he would attempt to lead an expedition against Confederate partisans led by General Jeff Thompson. While this expedition would never take place (for reasons discussed in the next chapter), the true significance of Grant's reporting back to St. Louis was that ambiguities of command seniority with Benjamin Prentice had been resolved in Grant's favor. Frémont then told Grant that he needed a uniform,[30] and wrote to Prentice that previous orders had been issued under the mistaken impression that he ranked Grant.[31] Prentice, however, was not about to abandon the issue. Grant, now as Prentice's superior, could afford to be magnanimous, writing to his father that "Gen. Prentice is not a particular favorite as you suspect nor is there a prejudice against him."[32] The net effect of Frémont's decision was that he had chosen Grant to spearhead the Federal movement down the Mississippi Valley. Jean Edward Smith wrote that the choice of Grant was comparable "to FDR's selection of Eisenhower to lead the Normandy invasion,"[33] although the wisdom was more apparent in retrospect. This was perhaps Frémont's finest moment during the war, and one for which he is rarely given credit.[34]

By the time Grant assumed command at Cape Girardeau on August 30, Union sympathizers both east and west had been deeply discouraged by the decisive Federal defeats at Bull Run and Wilson's Creek. Yet even as Northern prospects seemed to be sinking fast, Grant's career was taking off at a rate that was surely beyond his wildest dreams. Less than five months previous he had been an obscure, middle-aged, Midwestern assistant store clerk. Now, without fighting a single battle, he had become the designated point person for the most strategic sector in the American Civil War, though few probably realized this at the time—possibly not even himself, since he claimed to desire a transfer to West Virginia. Before Grant could come to grips with battlefield enemies, however, he had to first win his ongoing seniority dispute with a fellow officer, Brigadier General Benjamin Prentice.

CHAPTER 6

September 1861: Paducah, Kentucky

Grant's new assignment in Cape Girardeau began badly, or at least it must have seemed that way at the time. As related in his memoirs, a few days after arriving Grant was informed that Union forces under Brigadier General Benjamin Prentice were approaching nearby Jackson, Missouri, from Ironton. Grant, who wanted Prentice to pause in Jackson before embarking on a joint mission in pursuit of Thompson's raiders, began personally to ride out so as to meet Prentice and give him his new orders. By chance, at the same moment Grant began his journey, he noticed an advance column of Federal cavalry arriving in Cape Girardeau one block from where he was setting out. He speedily wheeled about and found himself confronted with Prentice and his escort. Grant then for the first time informed Prentice that Grant had senior command and ordered Prentice, along with his men, to immediately return to Jackson whence they had come.[1] Four months earlier, the promotion of Prentice to brigadier had been the source of John's Pope anger that had so fortuitously benefited Grant. Now it was Prentice's turn to be upset.

Grant in later years always took pains to point out that Prentice was a high caliber of soldier, at least compared to many other political generals. In his memoirs, Grant was even able to empathize: "He [Prentice] had been a brigadier at Cairo, while I was a mustering officer at Springfield without any rank." Grant went on to praise Prentice as "a brave and very earnest soldier. No man in the service was more sincere in his devotion to the cause for which we were battling; none more ready to make sacrifice or risk life in it."[2] Nevertheless, Prentice reacted badly to the whole affair. First, he immediately requested that Grant give him three days to present his case to Frémont, which Grant refused to do. Then Prentice requested that each submit written statements to Frémont, who would arbitrate. This was also refused. Finally, Prentice requested that command be assigned to a senior colonel until Frémont could decide the case.[3] Grant rejected this as well, and with good reason, since Frémont had already decided the case a few days ago when he wrote Prentice to that effect (see Chapter Five), but Prentice had not yet received or had chosen to ignore that letter. Defeated, Prentice immediately tendered his resignation, placed himself under arrest and reported back to St. Louis. After Prentice cooled off, Frémont reassigned him to a different sector. This reassignment now brought to a halt the projected mission against Thompson's raiders, and later caused Prentice to miss the Fort Donelson campaign. It also allowed other less able officers to supercede him, particularly John McClernand. Had he not reacted so poorly, Prentice could have easily ended up second in command to Grant, rather than Sherman and others.[4] As for Grant, he immediately (on September 3) wrote to Prentice saying that he had "no personal feeling" in the matter and was "perfectly willing to see the charges quashed and the whole matter buryed in oblivion" if it was okay with Frémont.[5]

The immediate result of Grant asserting his authority was that he inherited disciplinary problems in Prentice's regiments back in Jackson. The same day that he was writing to bury the hatchet with Prentice, Grant received a letter from a member Prentice's staff[6] complaining that the new officer left in charge, Colonel John Cook, was not up to the task, and that the troops were acting like "freebooters and robbers."[7] Grant wrote to the new colonel the following day, stressing to him the need to control his men.[8] Nothing more was heard of the problem. It appears that Grant's reputation as an insistent but moderate disciplinarian who put pressure on his junior officers (rather than the rank and file) had preceded him.

Another immediate, tangible result of Prentice's withdrawal was that Grant now assumed uncontested command at Cairo. That same day he arrived to find Colonel Richard Oglesby of Decatur, Illinois, in command and being continuously distracted by, as Grant put it, an "office full of people, mostly from the neighboring states of Missouri and Kentucky, making complaints or asking favors." Grant, who was still not yet in uniform (and in his typical manner) took a piece of paper, wrote an order assuming command, and handed it to a flustered Oglesby who "put on an expression of surprise that looked a little as if he would like to have some one identify me." After getting over the initial shock of seeing his commanding officer jostling with other petitioners, however, Oglesby "surrendered the office without question."[9]

On September 4, as Grant wrote to Colonel Cook and assumed command in Cairo, a major event occurred in the western theater, setting the stage for most of what later followed. A Confederate army under General Leonidas Polk, which on September 3 had invaded the self-proclaimed neutral state of Kentucky, proceeded to occupy—with the covert support of the local residents—the town of Columbus, located on the east bank of the Mississippi, approximately 20 miles downriver from Cairo.[10] In addition to provoking the state legislature into authorization of Confederate expulsion, Polk's ill-advised move also provoked Grant into making a response. The question of rank with Prentice had been resolved not a moment too soon. Had Grant submitted to arbitration, a crisis would have broken in the face of a divided Union command. Moreover, had Grant not noticed Prentice arriving in Cape Girardeau, or had Prentice not hurried to get there, the same problem would have likely occurred. Because of the way things did in fact transpire, Grant was able to take decisive control of Federal forces in this sector at a critical juncture. This proved to be fortuitous. As Jean Edward Smith remarked, "Grant was lucky once again."[11]

After informing Frémont of the Confederate occupation in Columbus, Grant alerted him to the enemy's immediate intent to do the same at Paducah, Kentucky, on the south bank of the Ohio River about 45 miles east of Cairo. If accomplished, this would put the Federal garrison at Cairo directly between two formidable pincers. Grant then did what any competent professional would have done. He informed his superior that, unless ordered to do otherwise, he intended to beat the Confederates to the punch. Hearing no immediate response from Frémont, Grant issued a direct dispatch to the Kentucky legislature informing them of his intent,[12] gathered all available manpower at Cairo, put together an improvised flotilla, and set out, arriving at Paducah the morning of September 6. According to Grant in his memoirs, secession flags that had been hoisted in the town were swiftly lowered, and a large Confederate force that was only a few hours' march away, when it heard that Grant had arrived first, turned around and retraced its steps back to Columbus. Then the Federals confiscated all enemy supplies stored in Paducah.[13] As the Federal occupiers moved in, Confederate General Lloyd Tilghman[14] and his staff—who had already arrived in Paducah and whom Grant would encounter again a few months later at Fort Henry—beat a quick retreat south.[15] As for the local populace, Grant noted, "I never saw such consternation depicted on the faces of the people."[16] Grant's rapidity of movement against the perceived threat at Paducah, Kentucky, would become a hallmark of his generalship throughout the war.

After securing his position, Grant then went one better with a move that eventually became another of his outstanding leadership traits: he issued a written proclamation.[17] This was perhaps the boldest move of all. Only one week previous (at the end of August), Frémont had done the same for the entire state of Missouri in the wake of Wilson's Creek and other disasters, but only succeeded in incurring the enmity of both Missourians and his own superiors in Washington, with its presumptuous and alarming heavy-handedness.[18] After being tactfully asked by President Lincoln to withdraw the proclamation and unwisely declining to do so, Frémont was ordered to take it back. This affair marked the beginning of the end of his tenure as western commander in chief. As if to show his superior how it should be done, Grant now issued his own proclamation in Paducah, one of an entirely different cloth and deserving full quotation:

PROCLAMATION, TO THE CITIZENS OF PADUCAH!

I have come among you, not as an enemy, but as your friend and fellow-citizen, not to injure or annoy you, but to respect the rights, and to defend and enforce the rights of all loyal citizens. An enemy, in rebellion against our common Government, has taken possession of, and planted its guns upon the soil of Kentucky and fired upon our flag. Hickman and Columbus are in his hands. He is moving upon your city. I am here to defend you against this enemy and to assert and maintain the authority and sovereignty of your Government and mine. I have nothing to do with opinions. I shall deal only with armed rebellion and its aiders and abettors. You can pursue your usual avocations without fear or hindrance. The strong arm of the Government is here to protect its friends, and to punish only its enemies. Whenever it is manifest that you are able to defend yourselves, to maintain the authority of your Government and protect the rights of all its loyal citizens, I shall withdraw the forces under my command from your city.

U.S. Grant, Brig. Gen. U.S.A., Commanding.
Paducah, Sept. 6, 1861.[19]

Particularly noteworthy is the line, "I have nothing to do with opinions." This is in complete contrast to Frémont's declaration that he intended to summarily shoot Confederate partisans and free their slaves. It is also reminiscent of Julius Caesar's proclamation during the Roman Civil War that, as far as he was concerned, those citizens who were not against him were for him.

As a coda to Grant's crucial and successful occupation of Paducah, Frémont belatedly gave him the green light to do so, but covering himself with the qualification that it should be done only if Grant had sufficient strength.[20] Then Frémont reprimanded Grant for communicating with the state legislature—no doubt because his own wrists were slapped by Washington after the Missouri proclamation.[21] In later years, Grant once again pondered the mysteries of fate: "It proved fortunate that the expedition against Jeff. Thompson had been broken up. Had it not been, the enemy would have seized Paducah and fortified it, to our very great annoyance."[22] In point of fact, had it not been for the spat with Prentice, Grant most likely would have been off on another wild goose chase against partisans in Missouri when a major crisis in the West (in Kentucky) transpired on September 4.

In the immediate aftermath of dramatic events at Paducah, as Grant busied himself by suppressing saloon activity in Cairo,[23] two new military colleagues entered his world, both of whom were to play inestimable, though tragically brief roles in the advancement of Grant's career. One was Commodore Andrew Foote, who assumed command of all naval forces stationed at Cairo on September 7.[24] Perhaps the greatest advantage enjoyed by the North throughout the war was its absolute naval superiority, and Foote was the right man at the right place and time to assert this advantage during Grant's first campaigns. The other was Brigadier General Charles Ferguson Smith, who was assigned to take charge at Paducah. In addition to being his elders, these two men complimented Grant's personality and reputation. Foote was a pulpit-pounding teetotaler, while Smith was famous for his swearing and impressive physical appearance.[25] Smith and Foote also brought a combined 80 years of military experience to their jobs. At first glance, both appear to have been designated watchdogs over Grant, given his recent aggressive movements in Kentucky and checkered personal past. Whatever the intent of these assignments may have been, however, the effect quickly worked to Grant's advantage (as well as to that of the Federal cause), in ways that few could have imagined at the time. About the same time Grant was receiving this double windfall, General Albert Sidney Johnston, considered by many (including Jefferson Davis) to be the premier soldier of his generation, was assuming command of all Confederate forces in the western theater.[26]

Both Smith and Foote commanded the absolute respect of the military hierarchy, and both had the competence to justify it. Less obvious but more important, both enthusiastically shared Grant's aggressive killer instinct towards their adversaries in the field. If the administrative intent of these two appointments was to cool Grant's enthusiasm, the result proved to be just the opposite. Jean Edward Smith referred to Grant's technical rank over C.F. Smith in particular—arranged by Congressman Washburne—as a "quirk of fate," since Smith had been Grant's commandant at West Point many years earlier.[27] Grant himself esteemed Smith as "a most accomplished soldier"[28] and felt great unease at being his superior until reassured by Smith that he had no problem with the arrangement.[29] Now, by good fortune, Grant suddenly found himself rubbing shoulders with some of the most experienced, efficient and aggressive military men remaining loyal to the Union. This was in addition to having under his command some of the most spirited volunteer troops in the Federal army, many of whom Grant had personally mustered and trained that summer. Over the next six months, this gathering whirlwind would be unleashed against an overconfident and mismanaged Confederate army occupying the western states of the South.

On September 11, Grant's new uniform finally arrived, but without a sword belt.[30] The following day, the conqueror of Paducah wrote to his wife, informing her that "I have never enjoyed better health in my life."[31] In addition to good physical health, Grant had other reasons to feel satisfied. In less than six months, he had been promoted to brigadier general and was now poised to lead a powerful Federal force down the Mississippi Valley. He had good colleagues and subordinates who were like-minded, plus a commander (Frémont) who, however great his limitations may have been, seemed to respect Grant for the results achieved thus far, albeit without fighting even a skirmish. It was in the midst of all these positive developments that, on September 13, 1861, Grant's esteemed younger brother Simpson died in St. Paul, Minnesota, after a long struggle against consumption.[32] It had been the poor health of Simpson that provided his elder brother with the opportunity to migrate to

Galena, Illinois, and a steady living—not to mention the friendly congressional district of Elihu Washburne—during the previous year. This came after a prolonged brush with destitution among his in-laws around St. Louis. The last time he had seen Simpson alive was at his parents' home in Covington, Kentucky, when he was vainly knocking on the door of George McClellan for an appointment. Now, scarcely three months later, Grant's main complaint was that his new uniform was incomplete. It is often at moments such as these in life that tragedy seems to strike.

On September 20, the same day that a Federal garrison at Lexington, Missouri (east of Kansas City), surrendered to Confederates,[33] Grant, in a letter to Julia, expressed grief at Simpson's death, expected though it had been for some time.[34] He repeated the sentiment in another letter to Julia written two days later[35] and another one written to his sister Mary on September 25.[36] Touching are Grant's repeated requests to his wife during this period for her to send him his deceased brother's watch as a keepsake.[37] The timing of Simpson Grant's demise, just as his older and habitually misfit brother was poised to make a huge mark in history, is striking, to say the least. It is also suggestive that Simpson's death followed in the immediate wake of Grant's bloodless but brilliant occupation of Paducah. From this point onwards, there would be casualties wherever Grant went, and the first ones under his command would be incurred some six weeks later in a very controversial and ambiguous engagement that was more or less engineered by his own initiative. Amateur psychology strongly suggests that, with the passing of his younger brother, Grant was now ready in the truest sense for the shooting to begin.

Throughout the month of September 1861, Grant's letters and dispatches repeatedly return to the same fixation—a place called Belmont, Missouri. He variously mentions Belmont in his communiqués to Generals Frémont and McClernand, as well as those to Colonels Oglesby and Wallace.[38] The references are brisk, within differing contexts, and almost offhand in tone; yet this tiny point on the map was clearly on Grant's mind. Belmont is not a town or even a village—it is a small boat landing located on the west bank of the Mississippi River, directly across from the same Columbus, Kentucky, that was taken over by the Confederate army on September 4, 1861. Today, Belmont is still a small boat landing surrounded by woods and fields along an alluvial plain and defined by a levee cutting through its center. Except for a small back-road marker, there is no indication (at least, on the Missouri side of the river) that this is where Ulysses S. Grant was destined to fight his first battle during the American Civil War. Across the Mississippi on the bluffs of Columbus is an attractive Kentucky state park (complete with museum) that overlooks the site, but there is no bridge across the river. To walk on the battlefield one must drive many miles through a sparsely populated district of Missouri and then trespass over private property whose owners probably prefer that no one know what happened there in late 1861.

Strategically, however, Belmont was a lure to everyone at the time. While Polk's Confederates fortified and held Columbus, on the opposite bank, Belmont was far less defensible and provided a foothold on the Missouri side of the river.[39] Just as Polk had seized an obvious point of defense at Columbus, Grant and his associates surely dreamed of securing the point opposite Columbus. Conversely, Confederates wanted to control Belmont Landing and win over the state of Missouri, as well as Kentucky. The battle of Belmont lay in the near future; for now, Grant was in Cairo busying himself with the drudgery of running an otherwise idle force. Meanwhile, in Washington, General George McClellan was successfully transforming a defeated and disorganized mob back into a bona fide army, having been appointed to the task after the disaster at Bull Run in July. As for the man who had unsuccessfully tried to interview with McClellan in May, Grant spent the rest of September dealing with fortifications around Cairo, skirmishing and reconnaissance in the surrounding areas, handling prisoners and spies, maintaining discipline among his own men, and above all, making sure that they were properly supplied. This was a very productive time for the Federal forces on all fronts, even though no battles were being fought. While Northern politicians and generals puzzled as to how to defeat Southern armies, Grant had played a central role in securing for them large portions of eastern Missouri and northern Kentucky (not to mention southern Illinois), and had accomplished this without firing a shot. Perhaps most remarkable of all, wherever Grant went, the storm clouds had seemed to move away. This, however, was about to change.

CHAPTER 7

October 1861:
Calm Before the Storm

As any casual glance at a map will show, Cairo, Illinois, is located at the great confluence of the Mississippi and Ohio rivers, with the Tennessee and Cumberland rivers not far away. Today, this region—apart from the imposing natural scenery—is very unassuming and Cairo itself is an economically challenged community by any standard. In 1861, however, these environs, along with northern Virginia, became the flashpoints of the American Civil War, and by the end of the year the former served as the launching pad for the great Federal offensive that eventually won the war for the North. Contrary to frequent perceptions, the Northern strategy of splitting the Confederacy along the Mississippi Valley was not Grant's brainchild. Among others, aging General Winfield Scott had proposed it as part of his "Anaconda Plan" even before Bull Run had been fought. Every military and political leader of intelligence (including John Frémont) recognized it early on, but it was Grant, by his own energies plus a tremendous boost from fate, who was destined to initiate it.

In terms of armed hostilities, October 1861 represented a comparative lull in the western theater. Grant himself wrote that "nothing important occurred"[1] during this period; yet studying Grant's correspondence at this juncture (along with the movements of friends and foes) reveals a wealth of insight into what transpired the following month at the battle of Belmont. The situation in Missouri, from a Federal point of view, was unstable but about to improve considerably, thanks in no small part to Grant's personal efforts. St. Louis and Jefferson City were secure, in spite of resentful local populations. With the exception of the remote area located across the river from Columbus—Belmont and environs—the eastern part of the state along the Mississippi Valley did not seem threatened by anything worse than Jeff Thompson's guerillas. The main problem was in western Missouri, where Sterling Price, victor of Wilson's Creek, was trying against nearly impossible obstacles to mold a permanent army into shape for offensive purposes. It was the Federals under Frémont, however, who succeeded in doing this first, as a

38,000-strong Union force set out to recapture Lexington, Springfield, and other strongholds.[2] This was the situation in early October as Grant's forces in Cairo warily faced off against Confederates at nearby Columbus.

Possession of the neutral state of Kentucky was no less important than Missouri to both sides; unfortunately for the Confederates, the occupation of Columbus proved to be a major political blunder, and was not the last such mistake made during the course of the war. Kentucky was not only a neutral border state (situated north of Mason-Dixon), but held tremendous psychological importance as the birthplace of both Abraham Lincoln and Jefferson Davis. Although the majority of the Bluegrass State was more than sympathetic toward the Confederacy, Kentucky politicians had been backed into a corner by the recent aggressive and unexpected movements against Columbus initiated by General Leonidas Polk, notwithstanding that this move had been made in cooperation with the citizens of Columbus themselves. By way of contrast, Grant's rapid-response seizure of Paducah proved in hindsight to be the right move at the right time, both in the military and political sense.

Grant's dispatches and letters for the month of October are dominated by a keen interest in affairs both at Columbus and Belmont Landing.[3] On October 7, per Grant's orders, Federal gunboats made a reconnaissance downriver to Columbus and exchanged fire with Confederate batteries. Eleven days later on October 18, the performance was repeated.[4] Before and after these demonstrations, Grant had his subordinates keep a close watch on the movements of Jeff Thompson to the west, and attempted unsuccessfully to intercept him. Writing to Julia on October 20, Grant made his intentions plain: "What I want is to advance."[5] Earlier (the previous month) he had written to her, "I would like to have the honor of commanding the Army that makes the advance down the river, but unless I am able to do it soon cannot expect it."[6] Four months prior he had been expressing his willingness to bake bread for the army; by September and October he was repeatedly telling his wife (in effect) that he now wanted to score the first great Northern victory of the war. This goal would take another four months for Grant to achieve, but in another two weeks he would make his first attempt.

Another remarkable aspect of Grant's October correspondence is his near-fixation on Confederate General Gideon Pillow. Writing to Julia on October 1, he lists the notable enemy commanders in his vicinity such as Albert Sidney Johnston and William Hardee, sarcastically adding as an afterthought, "to say nothing of the great Gen. Pillow."[7] The following day (October 2) he again mentions Pillow in a dispatch, this time in connection with Belmont,[8] and later on October 19 repeats rumors that Pillow intended to attack Paducah while Hardee remained at Belmont.[9] Having been in the old army and knowing most of these people, Grant seems to have identified a weak enemy commander in his sector, one that he deemed not worthy of leading a large group of men. Taken in isolation, there is nothing extraordinary in the contempt of one army colleague for another; given, however, that these two men would soon collide at Belmont—then again at Fort Donelson in less than four months—one marvels at Grant's instincts for pouncing on vulnerable enemy points both in terms of fortifications and generalship.

Grant's October letters mention another Confederate commander, but this one without any disparagement—the respected and popular Brigadier General Simon Bolivar Buckner.[10] Buckner, like Grant, was a West-Pointer and Mexican War veteran, and seven years earlier had loaned a destitute Grant money to pay a New York hotel bill. At the outbreak of the Civil War, Buckner commanded the Kentucky State Militia and was expected by many to remain loyal to the Union, being immediately offered a brigadier's commission. Jefferson Davis also offered to make Buckner a brigadier, however, and when Polk's army violated Kentucky neutrality, Buckner and his state militia had to choose sides. Both the commander and most of his men immediately joined the Confederate army, and after saluting his new superiors in Columbus, Buckner was expeditiously garrisoned at Bowling Green in the south-central part of the state.[11] This point formed the center of the new Confederate defensive line that now stretched across southern Kentucky by the beginning of October. On October 13, Western Confederate general-in-chief Albert Sidney Johnston was in Bowling Green to personally confer with Buckner, Hardee, and others on how to win and maintain control of the border states.[12]

By October 1861, Confederate perceptions in the western theater appear to have been flush with victory but considerably overconfident. Though dreaming of conquering Kentucky and Missouri and even crossing the Ohio River, the hard reality was that the Confederacy was more disorganized from winning battles than the North was from losing them. As for Grant, on October 14, he completely rebuffed Polk's written proposal regarding the exchange of prisoners that had accumulated from recent skirmishing in the area.[13] Two days later, on October 16, Albert Sidney Johnston approvingly inspected his forces in Columbus, but correctly judged that these were inadequately supplied for any kind of meaningful offensive against Cairo.[14] Johnston may well have had on his mind the recent unsuccessful attempts in Missouri by Sterling Price to hold onto ground gained, such as Lexington, which fell back into Federal hands the same day that Johnston arrived in Columbus.

Military historian Colonel Arthur Conger, during the early 20th century, made a number of interesting observations concerning this early but fascinating period of the war in the West. For starters, both sides in the conflict recognized that the Cumberland River (flowing from Nashville to the Ohio River near its junction with the Mississippi and Tennessee Rivers) formed a sort of natural seam that split the Kentucky-Tennessee front into two separate regions, east and west. He noted, "Thus by a curious coincidence the making of the Cumberland the dividing line between departments, by the North, was repeated by Johnston in making it the boundary between the territorial divi-

The first known Civi War photograph of Grant as a recently-appointed Brigadier General (with his staff) at Cairo, Illinois, October 1861. The battle of Belmont was less than one month away (courtesy Library of Congress Prints and Photo Division).

sions of his very large department."[15] In spite of this recognition, whether conscious or unconscious, everyone's focus at this point (including Grant's) seems to have been on the Mississippi and Ohio Rivers, rather than the vulnerable Confederate forts still under construction along the Tennessee and Cumberland.

Among Grant's personal qualities that enabled him to achieve the enviable and strategic striking position from Cairo (coveted by many an ambitious Union commander), was a rare ability to read the minds and intentions of his opponents. Writing to one of his captains[16] on October 7, a week before Johnston arrived in Columbus, Grant correctly judged that the Confederate army concentrating at that point was in a defensive, rather than offensive posture. This surmise was made after he had sifted through numerous conflicting reports and disseminated Southern propaganda.[17] Colonel Conger proclaimed this assessment to be "A complete reading of the minds of Johnston and Polk, however he may have gained it. What could promise better for the making of a higher commander?"[18] Conger then added that "after reading the old-time records, we cannot but feel that Grant of the October phase of Cairo is, as compared with the Grant of the month before, a rapidly and steadily maturing and mellowing general."[19] Grant was not simply another blue suit that fortune had tossed into a favorable position. He had helped to earn that position with his own unusually good judgment.

The month of October in Cairo also saw Grant re-establish contact with another old army acquaintance who would play a gigantic future role in the Northern push down the Mississippi Valley—Brigadier General William Tecumseh Sherman. Grant's correspondence from October 16 acknowledged receipt of a telegram from Sherman, dourly warning that a major Confederate offensive directed towards Louisville was imminent.[20] Sherman's Civil War career thus far had shown none of the astonishing rapidity of promotion, or even promise, that his younger colleague's had during the same time frame. Like Grant, Sherman was originally from Ohio, a West Point graduate, and a Mexican War veteran, but here the similarities ended. Commissioned as a colonel at the outbreak of hostilities, Sherman had led a regiment (not without some controversy)[21] at Bull Run. Later he was promoted to brigadier general (much to his surprise and thanks to his Senator brother) when it was realized that a bigger Federal army was going to be needed in order to win. No sooner had Sherman received his new rank than he was assigned to the Department of the Cumberland, headquartered in Louisville under the shell-shocked hero of Fort Sumter, General Robert Anderson.

Again to Sherman's surprise, he found himself appointed (against his will) to the head of the department when Anderson suddenly resigned and retired on October 8. Already battling an acquired reputation for nervous instability, Sherman appears to have been completely overwhelmed by his new, unexpected and unasked-for duties and responsibilities. After correctly assessing the disorganized, demoralized condition of his own men, the determination of his opponents, and the hostility of Louisville civilians, Sherman convinced himself that he was facing massive enemy hordes preparing to attack. In fact, much smaller numbers under Hardee and Buckner were at a great distance, even more disorganized than Sherman's forces.

The future conqueror of Georgia and the Carolinas first sent out an abject plea to Grant for reinforcements, and then more egregiously (on the following day) shared his anxieties in person with visiting Secretary of War Simon Cameron. Not content with this, Sherman did the same with his own immediate superior, George McClellan, soon afterwards. Within days, leaks to the press resulted in headlines declaring Sherman insane, and he was relieved of his command by the first week of November.[22] Sherman had this breakdown almost at the same time that Grant was writing to Julia of advances and dreaming of a Union offensive against Columbus. Rather than belittle

Sherman's panic attack, however, Grant merely passed the word to C.F. Smith in Paducah and Frémont's adjunct in St. Louis, expressing a willingness to cooperate if they deemed it necessary. Remarkably, the very same day (October 16), Grant also wrote to his newly appointed brigade commander (and veteran of Wilson's Creek),[23] Colonel Joseph Plummer, that he had been reliably informed of Jeff Thompson's raiders threatening the southeast corner of Missouri, and immediately dispatched Plummer to deal with the problem.[24] Within five days, Grant's instincts proved correct.

As Grant skillfully managed his crucial command post in Cairo, disaster struck the Federals again, this time in the East. On October 21, 1861, the Union suffered its third crushing defeat in four months, this time at Ball's Bluff in Leesburg, Virginia, near Washington, D.C. An attempt to reclaim a small piece of Virginia soil by the North resulted in hundreds of casualties and the death of its commanding officer, Colonel Edward Baker, who was also a Republican Senator and personal friend of President Lincoln. Moreover, this was the second time in a row—the first time being at Wilson's Creek on August 10—that a Federal commander had met his death in the field. Physical bravery in Northern soldiers and officers was apparently not lacking, but other qualities necessary for victory—skill and/or luck—still seemed elusive.

The very same day (October 21) that Federal forces under Colonel Baker were coming to grief in Virginia, the expedition ordered by Grant under Colonel Plummer[25] scored the Union's first notable armed victory in the West, though this clash was a mere skirmish compared to what would soon follow. Jeff Thompson's irregulars had combined with troops under Colonel Aden Lowe and occupied Fredericktown, Missouri, in preparation for a move against Grant's former headquarters at Ironton. When Thompson learned of Plummer's approach, the Confederates withdrew about a mile outside of Fredericktown and offered battle. In the ensuing skirmish, the Confederates suffered nearly a hundred casualties, including the death of Colonel Lowe, while Plummer's forces reported "very slight"[26] losses amongst themselves. This small victory helped to consolidate recent Federal gains in southeast Missouri, and Grant subsequently issued congratulatory letters to Plummer.[27] This action was fought while Grant was preparing to travel from Cairo to St. Louis and Springfield, Illinois, for the purpose of procuring much-needed supplies.[28] His correspondence from the previous week, including his letter to Julia the day before expressing his determination to hold scattered Union outposts, show that Grant anticipated Thompson's move and acted decisively.[29]

As this success was being achieved in Grant's sector, his superior, General Frémont, continued to lead a plodding campaign through central Missouri amidst rumors of incompetence and corruption. On October 24, President Lincoln made the decision to cashier Frémont, but directed that the order not be delivered until it had been confirmed that Frémont had not won a battle or was not in the middle of fighting one.[30] In retrospect, it appears that Frémont could do little right during his tenure in the West, except elevate his subordinate Grant to a position of responsibility. Frémont's official exit nine days later, however, would prove to have important consequences for Grant in terms of deciding when to fight his first major battle of the war.

As Grant quietly spent October 1861 dealing mainly with supply and administrative problems[31]—for example, taking time to crack down on the sale of liquor in the vicinity of Cairo[32]—few seemed to realize that this period represented the calm before the storm. Grant himself may have realized it, though. Sometime in October he posed for his first Civil War photo portrait, revealing an image quite at odds with the one he later cultivated. Professor John Y. Simon has noted that, among other things, the portrait shows Grant in his new general's uniform holding a sword in his lap (perhaps because he never received a sword belt)[33] and sporting a long beard that would have done John Brown credit. He then sent a copy to his sister Mary after having promised to send one to Julia later.[34] It is known that Julia subsequently complained about his long beard.[35] It appears that the sensible and fashion-conscious Julia Grant told her husband to lose the look, which he then did. In any event, it is certainly possible that in the back of Grant's mind, he knew that personal danger was imminent.

CHAPTER **8**

November 1861:
Belmont, Missouri

He [Lincoln] was afraid that the hot pursuit had been a little like that General Cass was said to have been, in one of our Indian wars, when he was an officer of the army. Cass was pursuing the Indians so closely that the first thing he knew he found himself in their front, and the Indians pursuing him.
                                                                    —Grant[1]

On November 2, 1861, John Frémont was belatedly and officially relieved of his short-lived western command.[2] Immediately prior to this, however, he had ordered Grant (largely due to Grant's own urging) to make a demonstration against Columbus that would aid Frémont's grandiosely conceived but incompetently executed Missouri offensive. Then, as an afterthought, Grant was ordered to try to nab the elusive Jeff Thompson.[3] By November 6, General C.F. Smith, along with Colonels Oglesby, Plummer and Wallace, had all been dispatched in various directions for these purposes.[4] The most notable result of these excursions was Oglesby's total disgust for the locals, later expressed in a letter to Grant: "A more unhappy and deluded people I have never seen—Wherever the column moved, Consternation filled the whole Community, and the fact that—without regard to sex or age, the whole people were not outraged and destroyed, seemed to Stupify them."[5] The real action, however, would be with Grant's movement downriver, while Frémont's permanent successor had yet to be appointed. On November 7, after feinting towards Columbus, Grant—on his own initiative and disobeying orders[6]—attacked Belmont Landing, thus bringing on his very first engagement of the Civil War.

Having assembled a strike force of approximately 3,000 troops supported by two gunboats,[7] Grant had set out the previous night with his flotilla, apparently telling no one—insofar as the record shows—what he intended to do. In fact, the entire operation was based on incorrect information that General Leonidas Polk at Columbus intended to detach troops that would interfere with Frémont and/or pounce on Oglesby, who was busy pursuing a long-gone

Jeff Thompson. In reality, Polk was hunkered down and begging for reinforcements while being aggravated by his vainglorious subordinate Gideon Pillow, plus suffering a major inferiority complex after the appointment of Albert Sidney Johnston as top western Confederate commander. As Shelby Foote wittily put it (with a Shakespearean turn of phrase), the Federal plan was "an Intelligence comedy of errors," although one advantage to the confusion was that "Grant's faulty intelligence ... made the Federal plans impenetrable."[8] Indeed, not until the battle was in full swing did Polk seem to understand what Grant was after.

Grant's motives in making the attack on Belmont have been analyzed and second-guessed by several generations of military historians, many far more capable than this one. A few general observations, however, are worth repeating. For starters, Grant himself, writing near the end of his life, offered a rather candid explanation:

> I had no orders which contemplated an attack by the National troops, nor did I intend anything of the kind when I started out from Cairo; but after we started I saw that the officers and men were elated at the prospect of at last having the opportunity of doing what they had volunteered to do—fight the enemies of their country. I did not see how I could maintain discipline, or retain the confidence of my command, if we should return to Cairo without an effort to do something.[9]

Thus Grant, in his final reflections on the event, began by arguing the necessity of channeling his troops' aggressive fighting spirit. In addition, as pointed out by historian John Y. Simon, another "reason for Grant's boldness at Belmont is that he knew his opponents."[10] For Gideon Pillow in particular he had repeatedly expressed contempt. As for Grant's senior colleagues in command, they, rather than encouraging caution, appear to have been co-instigators. Colonel Lew Wallace[11] thought that Grant had been encouraged to make the unauthorized strike following personal conferences with General C.F. Smith at Paducah.[12] As for Commodore Foote, instead of criticizing Grant afterwards for making the attack, he was upset that Grant had not allowed him to participate in the venture.[13] In effect, the battle of Belmont was an unnecessary diversion that turned into an impromptu raid, looking to exploit advantages that never materialized. Above all, the temporary vacuum created in the Federal command following Frémont's ouster surely affected the timing of Grant's decision.

The day before the battle (November 6), as Grant was launching his expedition, Leonidas Polk submitted his written resignation to Jefferson Davis.[14] Little did he seem to know that the fun was about to begin. When reports arrived on the morning of November 7 that Federal troops were deploying on the west bank and moving towards Belmont, Polk dispatched a similar number of troops to meet them commanded by (appropriately enough) General Gideon Pillow. By late morning, Grant's forces had encountered and completely routed Pillow and his detachment, driving them back beyond their encampment at the landing where survivors hid beneath the river bank.[15] Grant later praised his men and officers for their conduct during the first phase of the battle, most of whom were seeing action for the first time. He wrote that "Veterans could not have behaved better than they did...," but then qualified this with, "...up to the moment of reaching the rebel camp." Instead of taking prisoners or preparing for the inevitable counterattack, the Federals celebrated, made speeches and looted, while their helpless commander struggled in vain to control them. As Grant euphemistically put it, his men "became demoralized by their victory."[16] Had it not been for the carnage, the whole situation would have been comical.

Meanwhile, Polk finally had an epiphany that the Federal objective was Belmont and not Columbus. He then personally led reinforcements as they ferried across the river. This occurred just as the Federals were breaking out in celebration. By the time Grant's troops realized the battle was not over, they had been surrounded. At this point, the Federals recovered their discipline to some extent, mainly due to the imperturbability of Grant, who in the midst of the crisis informed his dismaying officers that "We cut our way in and we can cut our way out." Grant then instantly selected the right men for the job, Irish-American Colonel John Logan and the Chicago Light Battery. Logan, along with Grant's second-in-command Brigadier General John McClernand, were the same two Illinois downstate politicians that had given Grant's Seventh Regiment pep talks less than six months ago. Now Logan was in his element. After the Chicagoans had scattered everything in front of them with a concentrated artillery blast, Logan ordered everyone to follow him and the flag, and proceeded to successfully lead most of the force back to the transport ships while Grant personally brought up the rear.[17] The Federal retreat from most accounts was disorderly, but no more so than the Confederate pursuit. This was still November 1861—a war between amateurs.[18] In fact, according to Grant, the attempted pursuit was one of the costliest phases of the battle for the Confederates, as Union gunboats, after being repulsed by the Columbus batteries, joined in the fray upriver, providing cover for the retreat.[19]

While the battle of Belmont inaugurated a long and distinguished Civil War combat record for Logan, it also marked the beginning of mistrustful relations between Grant and McClernand. Although McClernand displayed fearlessness, having his horse shot out from under him three times and later being praised by Grant in the official record,[20] there were problems with his conduct. For one, it appears that McClernand was one of the worst offenders when troop discipline broke down in the captured Confederate camp. Possibly sensing this was a good time begin a future presidential campaign, McClernand gave speeches rather than noticing the boatloads of enemy infantry headed across the river in his direction.[21] In the eyes of Grant, who believed that officers should bear ultimate responsibility for the behavior of volunteer troops under their command, this was considered a serious offense, and he surely took mental note for future reference. In any event, personal bravery lacking in judgment would become the hallmark of McClernand's abbreviated Civil War career.

As for Grant, he emerged from Belmont with, if nothing else, an unshakable reputation among his men for physical courage and coolness under fire. In fact, he came very close to being killed at least three times, not to mention almost being stranded on shore during the retreat. Historian Bruce Catton accurately surmised, "As far as personal peril goes, this was as bad a spot as Grant got into in all the war."[22] First, during the initial attack, he had his horse shot out from under him.[23] Then, while bringing up the retreat, he backtracked to make sure there were no stragglers and encountered, in a corn field at 50 yards, General Polk in person with his staff, though the generals did not recognize each other (Grant, as usual, wore a private's uniform). Polk reportedly said, "There is a Yankee; you may try your marksmanship on him if you wish." Before anyone could take up the offer, though, Grant deliberately wheeled about and retraced his steps out of sight and range.[24] Returning to the transport ships, Grant was the last one to board, but not before his replacement horse, seemingly on its own initiative, slid down the steep river bank and walked over an extended plank to the waiting ship's deck.[25] As the steamer pulled out, with both sides still exchanging fire, Grant momentarily caught his breath on a sofa in the captain's room, but then decided to see what was going on outside. No sooner had he risen than a musket ball came through the room and struck the head of the sofa.[26] At this point, we must ponder how close Grant came to being killed or captured in his very first Civil War battle at a place that few people have ever heard of.

While guns were thundering and rattling at Belmont, Julia Grant was back in Galena preparing to set out for Cairo after having long been urged by her lonely husband to do so. Before setting out, she took an afternoon nap and had a dream later recorded in her memoirs. In the dream she saw her husband appear as if on horseback, giving her an earnest and reproachful look because "I thought he was displeased with me for not coming sooner." According to Julia, she was later told by Grant that her dream had occurred during the same hour of the afternoon as the perilous retreat from Belmont.[27] Readers may draw their own conclusions from this reported incident.

Belmont was the bloodiest battle in the West since Wilson's Creek, with each side suffering over 600 casualties. John Y. Simon summed up the result as accurately as anyone by writing, "Both sides claimed victory; neither deserved to."[28] He then added the important observation: "Considered in terms of casualties or strategy, the battle of Belmont was inconclusive, but in morale the Union troops won."[29]

To fully appreciate the truth of this, one must distinguish between the immediate, short-term results of the raid and the long-term aftermath, which will be discussed further in the next chapter. As for early November 1861, newspaper reaction in the South was predictably favorable, as recorded in the diary of Mary Chesnut from South Carolina. For November 8 she writes, "Papers say Pillow has a victory—away off somewhere. First he lost, then he was being reinforced. Faraway news—I care not for it."[30] Was this mere lack of interest in the frontier war or mistrust of the Confederate propaganda machine? Either way, it is interesting that Pillow was given credit when in fact he and his forces had been driven pell-mell by Grant from the field.

As for the Northern press, the *Chicago Tribune* began by severely criticizing Grant's actions, but later reversed itself after standing somewhat alone in this opinion.[31] A major factor in this perception and the *Tribune* about-face emanated from Grant's own troops. On the surface, Belmont was like Bull Run and Wilson's Creek, in which an invading Federal force achieved initial success only to be repulsed by a spirited counterattack, but as Shelby Foote added, "certain facts were there for whoever would see them."[32] In the first place, the Confederates thought they had been outnumbered, when in fact— as was subsequently learned—they had enjoyed a 2–1 advantage. Viewed in this new light, Grant's repulsed Midwestern invaders (now known as "Grant's men") took on a much scarier demeanor.[33] This was especially true after coffins and maimed bodies were shipped back home south to Memphis.

As for the Federal troops, despite their losses, Grant later wrote without exaggeration that they arrived back at Cairo with "every man feeling that Belmont was a great victory and that he had contributed his share to it."[34] This was not a surprising attitude given that, before Belmont, Northerners had been smarting from repeated demoralizing defeats. Colonel Arthur Conger made a convincing case for how the Federal soldiers probably felt afterwards:

> We licked our own numbers! And when they sent reinforcements to surround us, we licked those fellows too! We're better men than they are and we know it and they know it! But—moral!—don't ever stop to loot till you're sure the battle is all over.[35]

Apart from Conger's jaundiced view of the Midwestern volunteer's attitude towards Southern private property, he also offered a perceptive analysis of Grant's motives:

> The chief interest at Belmont lies in its being the first of a series of blows struck by Grant against an enemy capable and desirous of striking back, the series which ended at Appomattox. Strategically—in a narrow sense—it was difficult to justify; tactically foolhardy, yet psychologically a necessity. Up to this time, both in Kentucky and Missouri, the Confederates had had the initiative. Now Grant seized it and kept it.[36]

In effect, Grant had disobeyed orders, made a strategically ill-advised attack, was repulsed with heavy losses, and still came out smelling like a rose. In the words of Jean Edward Smith, "Grant was making his own luck."[37] To Northern troops (as well as the Northern press), Grant had attacked against long odds, personally been in the thick of things, inflicted heavy loss, and managed to break out after having been outnumbered and surrounded, the latter achievement being a first for a Federal force during Civil War combat.[38] Above all, as Grant recorded in his memoirs, "The National troops acquired a confidence at Belmont that did not desert them throughout the war."[39]

The rest of the month was spent by each side trying to put their best spin on what happened. The day after the battle, Grant issued congratulatory orders to his men, comparing them favorably to veterans of the Mexican War.[40] To St. Louis headquarters he reported that "Pillow was on the field & is reported killed."[41] This was wishful thinking, although on the other side Polk had initially heard that Grant was killed as well.[42] These rumors were probably a reflection of the ferocity of the engagement, considerable from most accounts. Writing to C.F. Smith, Grant exaggerated enemy casualties and underestimated his own (the Confederates initially did the same, inversely), adding, "The victory was complete."[43] With similar hyperbole, Grant wrote his father, "There was no hasty retreating or running away"[44]—not in Grant's sight, perhaps.

Even more inaccurate was Grant's claim (maintained until his dying day) that the battle of Belmont achieved the strategic objective of preventing Confederate troop detachment to other sectors.[45] It has since been proven that the overly cautious Polk never once considered doing this; on the other hand, it was certainly a reasonable assumption at the time, given Frémont's offensive and the dispersion of Grant's own forces. Moreover, after Belmont this defensive Confederate posture spread throughout the region. In the long run, Grant's alleged aim was accomplished. Perhaps the most telling comment, however, came from an anonymous Confederate P.O.W. After the battle an Illinois volunteer asked him if he still thought Southerners were better soldiers than Northerners, and the P.O.W. remarked, "Oh, we don't mean you Westerners. We thought this morning when you were approaching that we never saw such big men in our lives before. You looked like giants."[46] Thus the Federals achieved the great psychological victory that Grant had been seeking.

Grant did make one big policy change after Belmont. He now saw fit to negotiate with the Confederates regarding wounded and prisoners, and wrote to Polk in this regard.[47] After later meeting Grant downriver under a flag of truce,[48] Polk wrote to his wife, "I confess I was not much impressed with him [Grant]; I think him rather second rate...."[49] Such underestimation would prove to be a consistent pattern for most Confederate leaders during the early years of the war. Four days after his army had been battered at Belmont Landing, Polk literally suffered from shell shock when a cannon exploded near his person at Columbus on November 11.[50] This threw the Confederate high command into even more confusion, although during Polk's convalescence his earlier submitted resignation was rejected by Jefferson Davis, who by now may have thought that Gideon Pillow needed watching. The same day that Polk was laid low at Columbus, Major General Henry Wager Halleck was named the new commander of Federal forces in the West.[51] One of his first jobs was to try to reign in "the wild man of Belmont" (i.e. Commodore Shelby Foote)[52] now under his command.

Julia Grant arrived in Cairo about this time to give her husband much-needed cheer and moral support. Her lasting impression of the place was unfavorable: "I remember how high and angry the river was and how desolate Cairo seemed...." Meeting Commodore Foote, she was impressed by him as "a patriotic Christian gentleman." Above all, Julia now for the first time saw Grant as a general leading an army: "How proud I was ... witnessing the reviews and hearing the bands play 'Hail to the Chief' as *my* General rode down the columns inspecting!"[53] A normal spousal reaction, to be sure, and yet one cannot imagine military bands playing "Hail to the Chief" in the aftermaths of Bull Run or Wilson's Creek. This army had not been demoralized.

Regarding the soldiers themselves, Julia's sharp eye for detail is once again revealing. After the reviews, she describes a typical scene:

> When all was over, those gallant brave heroes would crowd around our ambulance to pay their respects with a bow or a smile, asking how we were pleased with the review. I always answered, with the greatest enthusiasm, that nothing could be more interesting, more thrilling, than to see these columns of brave men in motion. There was poetry in every move. No pageant has ever thrilled me or given me such intense interest as did those at Cairo and Bird's Point. We were always escorted back to headquarters by half a dozen or more of these gallant, brave men.[54]

Once again I am struck by the attitude of Grant's troops immediately after a very sanguinary and at best ambiguous engagement—delight in public visibility, pride of accomplishment, and voluntary respect for their commander's wife.[55] Any Confederate sympathizer who witnessed these spectacles probably had good cause for concern. No wonder Cairo appeared desolate; its numerous Southerner-sympathizer residents had likely cleared out by then.

While the remainder of the month was spent by participants in the events of November trying to process what had transpired, there was a curious coda. On November 18, in a letter to Colonel Oglesby, Grant describes the detaining of the Federal steamer *Platte Valley* en route to Cape Girardeau from Cairo by Confederate partisans commanded by Jeff Thompson. Writing his memoirs many years later, Grant appears to have remembered this particular incident, elaborating that a Confederate attempt was made to capture him after it became known through spies that Grant intended to make a trip to Cape Girardeau. As Grant noted, however, "something transpired which postponed my trip,"[56] and despite repeated demands from the disbelieving Southern officer who was supervising the search,[57] Grant was nowhere to be found on board. The Confederates then settled for taking prisoner two Federal officers on leave plus two alleged Northern spies,[58] but were disappointed at not being able to bag the highest ranking Union officer in that sector. Fate once again had protected Grant, this time from becoming a Confederate P.O.W. It seems as though another direct result of the battle of Belmont was that Grant was now a marked man in the eyes of the Confederacy. Another possibility is that Jeff Thompson was going for a little payback after Grant's repeated attempts to intercept him.

CHAPTER 9

December 1861:
Winter Quarters

It was among the great misfortunes of the Confederacy that the beginning of the war saw one of its worst commanders, Gideon Pillow, face off against the North's very best—Ulysses S. Grant.[1] It was doubly unfortunate that Pillow and many of his colleagues misinterpreted the result of Grant's probing raid at Belmont as a great Confederate victory, creating a greater sense of false confidence that would come back to haunt them three months later at Fort Donelson.[2] Military historian Thomas Connelly opined, "The victory at Belmont also fortified Gideon Pillow's belief in himself as a great strategist and tactician. Had Pillow been in a position where he could do no harm, his super-inflated ego would have mattered little." In reality, the battle of Belmont had placed the western Confederate forces in a fossilized defensive posture that perfectly accommodated Grant's blitzkrieg style of warfare. Even Pillow's long-suffering superior at Columbus, Leonidas Polk—though less foolish than his pretentious subordinate—became deceived as to Grant's future intentions. As Connelly emphasized, both Polk and Albert Sidney Johnston were now convinced that Columbus was the immediate Federal objective: "Through a series of events which were initiated in November [i.e., the battle of Belmont], Polk became totally immobilized in his Columbus fortress."[3] By the month of December, three weeks later, the long-term strategic effects of the ambiguous engagement were completely manifested. In effect, western Confederates were still overconfident, but now with even fewer good reasons for being so.

More damaging to the Confederacy than being misled and overconfident was the newly enhanced morale of Federal troops at Cairo. Belmont was the first sizeable battle of the war that was not a crushing defeat for Union forces. It was a technical defeat, perhaps, but one in which a Federal army deliberately attacked a Confederate target, sustained and inflicted frightening casualties, escaped after being surrounded and outnumbered, and managed to retreat with a minimal semblance of order. Above all, a Federal commander (Grant), though making many mistakes, demonstrated both physical bravery and cool-headedness while winning the confidence of his troops—another first. As such, Belmont could arguably (if not accurately) be described as a successful diversionary raid. Even though the intended diversion—protection of Oglesby's detachment—proved fallacious in hindsight, it was certainly a reasonable perception for Grant or any competent commander to have had at the time.

Above all, while the intended diversion was unnecessary, another kind of diversion was ultimately provided—putting Confederate forces stationed along the northern Mississippi Valley into a defensive mentality. Of overriding importance was that Federal troops engaged at Belmont emerged with increased, as opposed to decreased, confidence, while Confederate forces, who had only a few days previous been dreaming of conquering Missouri, were now content to occupy their "Gibraltar"[4] at Columbus. Jean Edward Smith summed up the result by writing, "In retrospect, the fruits of Belmont seem clear. Grant gathered momentum, while the Confederates settled into a defensive posture."[5] Thomas Connelly again: "Although the battle was little more than a heavy skirmish, it had importance consequences. It badly frightened Polk, for he interpreted it as the beginning of a campaign against Columbus."[6] Arthur Conger added, "With Belmont the tide turned, though this was not at first evident."[7] Thus Grant and the Federals gained the initiative.

The end of the momentous year 1861 saw opposing western forces at Cairo, Illinois, and Columbus, Kentucky, warily stare at and parry with each other, mostly at a distance. On the very first day of December, Confederate gunboats left a calling card at Cairo by firing upon Fort Holt, the furthermost Federal outpost downriver, but then quickly retreated when this fire was returned and Foote's gunboats went in pursuit. As Grant humorously chronicled, "Bishop Major General Polk's three gunboats made a Sunday's excursion up to see us this evening...."[8] Later that same week, Grant returned the compliment by sending Oglesby's column out on another raid to Belmont, this time to spike cannon that had been reported there. Upon arriving at Belmont in the evening, however, all the disappointed troopers found were grasshoppers and the lights of Columbus flickering across the river.[9] More serious was a widespread rumor that the Confederates intended to launch an all-out attack against Cairo on December 13, causing Grant to have his soldiers sleep under arms.[10] This, too, proved to be a false alarm, although Pillow was urging such a move at the time.[11] In reality, Polk and Johnston were busy fretting over how best to defend southern Kentucky against a possible Federal offensive that would all too soon materialize. After a lot of hemming and hawing, Polk finally sent a large detachment to Bowling Green on December 24.[12] This proved to be almost as big a mistake as occupying Columbus in the first place, since the Federals had no immediate plans for attacking Bowling Green. It did, however, set into motion high-level discussions (involving Grant) that eventually led to the Fort Donelson campaign and the complete loss of this region by the Confederates in less than two months. In effect, the extensive debating and pondering by Johnston and Polk simply resulted in a self-fulfilling prophecy—to be driven completely out of Kentucky and a good part of Tennessee as well.

The complete shakeup of the Federal military command in early November (after Frémont's dismissal) resulted in a new triumvirate of personalities overseeing Grant's movements. The most important of these three would be Major-General and army administrator *par excellence* Henry Halleck, who was Frémont's immediate replacement in St. Louis. Halleck's new colleague in Louisville was Major-General Don Carlos Buell, who replaced William Tecumseh Sherman after his temporary breakdown in October. Overseeing everyone from Washington, D.C., was Major-General George McClellan, who had snubbed Grant back in May, and who was now at the pinnacle of his reputation following the near bloodless capitulation of West Virginia to the North in late 1861.[13] Beginning in November and continuing through December, these three bickered amongst themselves over coordinating Union efforts in Kentucky and Tennessee. This infighting, however, set the stage in a rather unlikely, if not miraculous, fashion for the Fort Donelson campaign soon to be spearheaded by Grant, C.F. Smith, and Commodore Foote. All it needed further was a little encouragement from the Confederate high command (which it then received with the shift to Bowling Green), plus the persistence of Grant and his field officers.

The relationship between the desk soldier Halleck and the combat veteran Grant began on an inauspicious note in mid–December. Having obtained a shipment of Confederate prisoners from St. Louis that were supposed to be exchanged with Polk at Columbus, Grant then received a forged message from headquarters that the prisoners were impostors and should be returned to St. Louis, rather than exchanged. Instantly complying with this, Grant later learned the truth and with an injured sense of dignity had his wrists slapped by Halleck for being too gullible.[14] Gullibility was precisely the kind of reprimand that Grant was most sensitive to, given his pre-war failures and reputation. Though Halleck had his doubts about Grant, he also received favorable reports from his inspectors in Cairo, and may have wondered as well how much his own office was to blame. No sooner had Grant been rebuked by headquarters, Halleck then wisely extended his subordinate's command authority to include C.F. Smith at Paducah, Kentucky.[15] After things were straightened out, Grant wrote a letter to Polk calling the whole affair a "wicked hoax" and came surprisingly close to apologizing for his actions.[16] Reflecting a considerably mellowed attitude towards civilians passing between the lines, Grant recorded on December 23 his strikingly enlightened view that "On the old principle that it is better that ninety-nine guilty persons should escape than that one innocent person should suffer, we may be deceived some times."[17] It has been remarked that in today's modern world the opposite belief seems to be more fashionable.

As for Grant's relations with his subordinates, December 1861 was marked by a fascinating but rarely commented-upon episode involving the court-martial of Michael Lawler, colonel of the "brawling"[18] 18th Illinois Regiment. A number of grievances were brought against Lawler by his junior officers, including one that he may have improperly executed a soldier under his command guilty of murder, rather than turn the accused over to the proper civil authorities.[19] This charge, however, appears to have been an afterthought to the main complaint, which was that Lawler had appointed a Catholic chaplain for the regiment when in fact the Irish Lawler was the only Catholic amongst them. When this was respectfully pointed out to Colonel Lawler by his men, he seems to have responded by ignoring them. Thus Grant found himself appointing a tribunal over an officer who had been among those recommending Grant for his first commission only seven months previous. The result of this farce was that Lawler was found guilty with a recommendation for dishonorable discharge, but Halleck overruled the verdict and had Lawler immediately reinstated.[20] Obviously, a lot went on behind closed doors. Grant, for his part, provided a good character reference for Lawler shortly before Halleck rescued him. Previously Grant had personally written to President Lincoln, recommending that a Catholic chaplain (Father Hugh Quigley) be appointed for the army at large to serve those who felt uncomfortable with the nearly exclusive number of Protestant regimental chaplains.[21] Nothing ever came of this either, except perhaps that Lawler, who would go on to earn an enviable combat record, seems to have learned the limits of his own authority. The middleman between Lawler and Grant during these squabbles was General John McClernand, who sided with Lawler but mainly aggravated Grant by not being able to deal with the problem himself.

Concurrent with the Lawler court-martial was McClernand's inability to shield Grant from the irrepressible Captain William J. Kountz. Kountz had recently been appointed assistant quartermaster by George McClellan and was sent, along with his steamboat fleet and an inflated sense of self-importance, down the Ohio River with St. Louis as his ultimate destination. Stopping at Cairo en route, Kountz proceeded to criticize everything he saw in terms of government supply contracts and made numerous recommendations for changes in a rather forceful manner. McClernand, who met Kountz first and was quite impressed, passed his laundry list on to Grant, who was not so impressed. Almost as aggravating to Grant as Halleck's accusations were Kountz's charges of inefficiency. Writing to Kountz on December 21, Grant first gave him a cease and desist order until his official authority could be confirmed, then delivered the worst possible insult that he could think of: "To say the least you have acted in a manner displaying great ignorance...." This apparently offended Kountz as intended because from that moment on he remained a constant thorn in Grant's side. Professor John Y. Simon wrote that Kountz's "reputation for quarrelsomeness, obstinacy, and meddling counteracted his expert knowledge of steamboating."[22] Kountz then made the even greater mistake of alienating Julia Grant, who wrote that he was "always malignant."[23] Predictably, Grant had not heard the last of Captain William Kountz.

More remarkable is that Grant's planning and preparations for the first great Federal offensive of the war (Fort Donelson) were carried on while he was simultaneously occupied with these various distractions. Not the least of these was his second-in-command, the political general John McClernand, who was unwilling or unable to deal with them himself. To repeat, Grant tended to hold his junior officers more accountable than the volunteers themselves, and McClernand may have been one the earliest victims of Grant's displeasure in this regard. These headaches included fending off the pugnacity of a self-appointed watchdog steamboat captain plus the ongoing court-martial of an intransigent Irish-Catholic colonel.

In spite of these distractions, Grant primarily spent the month of December 1861 establishing winter quarters for his troops at Cairo and preparing, as he put it, "for the long struggle which proved to be before them."[24] Foremost among these tasks was responding to allegations made by the *Chicago Tribune* on December 12 that supply contracts in Cairo were rife with corruption. Grant immediately dispatched his adjunct William Hillyer to investigate the charges, and the day after Grant had told Captain Kountz to mind his own business on December 12, Hillyer returned to corroborate the allegations made by the *Tribune*, Kountz, and others. Although blindsided, Grant immediately recommended and cooperated in the full investigation which followed.[25] Some of the dishonest contractors then retaliated by leveling allegations of drunkenness against Grant.[26] The only direct evidence of Grant's contact with alcohol during this period was on December 4 when he apologized to headquarters for allowing 80 barrels of whiskey to be shipped south through his command post. Grant wrote to St. Louis that he was not opposed to sending whiskey south—in fact, he favored it—but was concerned that the barrels might contain other contraband.[27] Unfortunately for Grant, however, the exposed price-gougers were not the only persons complaining about Grant's lack of sobriety during the first week of December.

On December 17, a Cairo visitor from Galena wrote a letter to Congressman Washburne, expressing his concern that Grant had been "drinking very hard" and that someone should alert John Rawlins to the fact. Washburne was all over it. On December 30, Rawlins wrote a lengthy and passionate reply to Washburne defending Grant, explaining away what had been witnessed, and concluded with: "I pledge you my word for it, that should General Grant at any time become an intemperate man or an habitual drunkard, I will notify you immediately, will ask to be removed from duty on his staff (kind as he has been to me) or resign my commission." The same day that Rawlins responded to Washburne, however, William Bross of the *Chicago Tribune* wrote a letter to then–Secretary of War Simon Cameron, who then sent it to President Lincoln, stating the *Tribune* had concrete evidence that Grant had been "inebriate" early in the month.[28] This would have been about the same time that the 80 barrels of whiskey had landed in Cairo, subsequently forwarded south by Grant.

And where was Julia during this time? In point of fact, it appears that she was not in Cairo until after December 7. Having left Cairo for St. Louis on November 23, Julia, according to a letter from Grant to his father on November 27, would not return for "a couple of weeks." As specified by later allegations (discussed in the following chapter), Grant's alleged binge had taken place between December 5, when he rode a boat to Columbus under a flag of truce, and December 7 in Cairo. There is also a gap in Grant's known correspondence on December 7, with a flurry of activity (six letters) on the following day. As for Julia's return to Cairo, all we have is Grant's letter to her ("My Dear Wife," signed "Dode") on December 9, when she left Cairo en route to Covington, Kentucky. Grant, who sounds like he had allowed himself to be buried in paperwork, promised to see her and sent the letter from his office by messenger to wherever Julia was preparing to depart from in Cairo. She quickly responded by writing of her sadness in being separated and urged him to join her.[29] In retrospect, the whole episode now reads like a typical case of two separated and lonely lovers trying to reconnect.

Despite these trials, the end of 1861 saw Grant primarily grappling with economic problems of supply. These tedious hurdles tend not to be of much interest to students of military history, but still helped to prepare the future lieutenant-general for effectively dealing with the same crucial issues (but on a much larger scale) one year later in Mississippi.[30] The chicanery and hoodwinking at Cairo may have been embarrassing but at least Grant attempted to deal with it. This is in bold contrast to the nearby Confederate force under Jeff Thompson, which was steadily melting away, due in part to expired enlistments but more the result of desertions caused by lack of supplies.[31] While Thompson was a talented leader of guerilla fighters, he left much to be desired as a quartermaster. In fact, Thompson's idea of economic supply for his marauding party appears to have been random confiscation of goods from the very same civilians who supported his cause, occasionally tossing them some Confederate script as compensation. Given this contradiction, it is no wonder that Federal officers such as Colonel Oglesby became exasperated with the anti-government attitude of the local populace.

In short, during the winter of 1861-1862 not much was accomplished at Columbus; in Cairo, however, significant strides were made preparing Grant's army for the challenges that lay ahead. While Confederate and Union high commands bickered amongst themselves, Grant minded his "shop" at Cairo. Although problems and difficulties seemed endless, there were measurable gains, not the least of which was a confident, disciplined and well-equipped fighting force led by an aggressive and experienced group of officers. The only question remaining was how to most effectively deploy this force so as to avoid the disasters and setbacks thus far experienced by the North. The new year of 1862 would begin with one of the most riveting campaigns of the war, and one whose precise origins still appear mysterious, even after reviewing the dispatches 144 years after the fact. Leading it would be the odd little man who had been tending his brother's storefront in Galena back in mid–April. As Colonel Conger wrote, "From the time of this consolidation of the Cairo and Paducah districts, Grant takes his place as the commander of the vanguard of the Federal main column in the west."[32]

CHAPTER 10

January 1862:
Cairo Dogs of War

... our people have proven themselves to be the most formidable in war of any nationality.

—Grant[1]

President Abraham Lincoln began the new year by unsuccessfully badgering Generals Henry Halleck and Don Carlos Buell into launching a coordinated offensive in the West, just as he was urging George McClellan to move forward in the East.[2] As early as November 27, Buell had in fact made a written recommendation for a flotilla movement up the Cumberland and Tennessee Rivers.[3] With his friend McClellan trying to shield him, Buell had been bickering with Halleck over various matters for nearly two months and now, with McClellan on sick leave and Lincoln pressing, Buell specifically asked Halleck to order gunboats up the rivers.[4] Halleck, however, was full of excuses[5] why this could and should not be done quite yet, prompting a baffled Lincoln to write "it is all very discouraging."[6] Afterwards, when word reached Halleck that Buell and McClellan were plotting to have his troops transferred to their own sectors, he acted with decisiveness and cunning, ordering (on January 8) a massive demonstration against Columbus on the Mississippi River and Fort Henry on the Tennessee River.[7] Ostensibly, this was to deter any additional concentration of Confederate forces at Bowling Green, Kentucky, but Halleck seems to have ordered the move mainly because he was in danger of his troops being drawn away by McClellan and Buell. To thwart this, he had to keep them busy.[8] An interesting side note is that Grant, as authorized by Halleck, wrote his own intentionally misleading press releases, reporting that his forces were on their way to Nashville.[9] Halleck, it appears, even at this early stage in the war, recognized that Grant had a flair with words.

After a few days of delay due to weather and transport problems, Grant sent C.F. Smith south up the Tennessee River to scout out Fort Henry, while Grant himself (with McClernand) moved towards Columbus. In addition to this reconnaissance, Commodore Foote steamed Grant and his staff right up to the approaches of Columbus, encountering only feeble resistance. Despite miserable traveling conditions, Grant was personally involved in all of these maneuvers, and by mid–January had formed an even lower opinion of Confederate abilities to resist all-out onslaughts aimed at selective weak points.[10] Moreover, he correctly surmised that General Polk had by then sent away many of his best troops to Bowling Green and replaced them with raw, ill-equipped state militia. As for C.F. Smith's assessment of the poorly conceived and half-complete Confederate forts on the Tennessee River, he reported on January 21, "I think two iron-clad gunboats would make short work of Fort Henry."[11]

Before planning any grand military campaigns, however, Grant had to deal with a tough fight right in his own front office at Cairo. As Grant prepared to advance south upriver on January 14, he ordered the arrest of steamboat Captain William Kountz, with whom he had clashed the previous month. After Kountz had arrived in Cairo unannounced, he began pointing accusatory fingers at everyone over matters of efficiency before getting clearance with Grant. In a letter written to St. Louis headquarters the same day, Grant gave his detailed version of what happened:

> In making this move I found myself much embarrassed by deficiency in the Quarter-Masters Department. Capt. Kountz who was recently sent here as Master of transportation, from his great unpopularity with river men, and his wholesale denunciation of everybody connected with Government here as thieves and cheats[12] was entirely unable to get crews for the necessary boats. I was compelled to order that boatmen, if they declined serving voluntarily, should be put aboard the boats and made to serve as prisoners. Many expressed a willingness to serve if I said so but would not work under the Captain, and others left the city, as I am informed, solely to avoid the possibility of having to serve under his direction. He seems to have desired to be placed on duty here for no other purpose than to wreak his revenge upon some river men who he dislikes, and to get into the service of Government a boat in which he has an interest, either as owner or a former proprietorship not yet settled for. He has caused so much trouble and shown such a disregard for my orders that I have been compelled to order his arrest. I would respectfully ask that he be ordered to another field of duty.[13]

Julia Grant in her memoirs gives more or less the same account but adds that Kountz had raised such a ruckus at Cairo headquarters that Grant retreated into a back room just to escape from him, whereupon Rawlins physically threw Kountz out of the building. Then Kountz spread word about town that Grant was a drunk, for which he was promptly incarcerated.[14]

Grant seems to have initially tolerated Kountz, attributing his rancor to over-zealousness of duty, but a few days earlier had warned C.F. Smith that "although the Capt. may be a very good Steamboat man he knows but little of Military etiquette and I am afraid will never learn."[15] It appears that for the normally tolerant Grant, charges of corruption were bad enough, but public accusations of drunkenness proved to be too much. It also appears that Grant thought the best way to shut Kountz up and keep him out of the way during a critical period in the war was to throw him in jail. Three days later on January 17, Kountz wrote a letter directly to the new Secretary of War, Edwin Stanton, stating to the effect that he had been jailed for exposing corruption, incompetence, and immorality, then soon afterwards Kountz stirred up his Pennsylvania neighbors in a similar manner.[16]

Kountz, who had been arrested while John McClernand was absent, wrote of McClernand to his Pennsylvania congressman on January 26: "I have been supported by Genl. McClernand who is a very worthy indestryous & good man but his hands has been tied." The very same day, Kountz filed extensive and detailed accusations that he and others had witnessed Grant completely intoxicated on December 6–7, charges that Grant himself then personally forwarded to St. Louis headquarters.[17] Early December was the approximate time that a Galena visitor and *Chicago Tribune* reporter claimed to have seen Grant drinking, which raised concerns. It is not difficult to surmise that McClernand's cordial relations with Kountz probably irked Grant and further contributed to their poisoned relations and ultimate breakdown in trust. Thus Captain Kountz, though not of historical importance himself, becomes a relevant figure in relation to studies on Grant's alleged alcoholism as well as his troubled relationship with General John McClernand, a relationship that would eventually terminate during the Vicksburg campaign.

Near the end of the month, on January 29 (the eve of Halleck's authorization to attack Fort Henry), Kountz asked McClernand to intercede for him, demanding that he be charged and tried. In immediate response, Grant specified "Disobedience of Orders," "Disrespect to his Superior Officer" and "Conduct wholly subversive of good order and Military discipline," then referred to whole matter to McClellan, probably knowing that would be slowest way to achieve a resolution.[18] On the other hand, Kountz had managed to create plenty of enemies besides Grant. The same day that Grant arrested Kountz (January 14), Halleck received a petition signed by no fewer than 19 officers under Grant's command (McClernand was a notable exception), plus the person who had originally referred Kountz to McClellan, all asking that Kountz be replaced with the man who had been his predecessor. Almost as damaging was a second petition published in the newspapers around the same time and signed by 31 professional boatmen in the Cairo area, all condemning Kountz as someone who was impossible to work with. It appears Captain Kountz, whether he was right or wrong, was in no position to point fingers.

Kountz, however, was not the only one making trouble. On January 1, while trying to light a fire under his commanding generals, President Lincoln read and endorsed the December 30 letter from William Bross of the *Chicago Tribune* raising questions about Grant's fitness for command. Lincoln wrote,

"Bross would not knowingly misrepresent," and referred the matter to Washburne for investigation. But Washburne had already investigated, thanks to an earlier tip-off from a visiting Galena resident, and had received a forceful reply from John Rawlins in defense of Grant. Now it was Washburne versus the *Tribune*, and neither apparently backed off, because on January 14 (the same day that Kountz was arrested and Halleck received the petition against Kountz), the *Chicago Sunday Tribune Magazine* published a feature article titled "A New Lincoln Letter." Written by one Robert Anderson, the article alleged that Grant was a flat-out drunk, plus took a swipe at his wife Julia: "Until we can secure pure men in habits and men without secesh wives with their own little slaves to wait upon them, which is a fact here in this camp with Mrs. Grant, our country is lost." It appears that Julia was in Cairo not soon enough to prevent Grant's drinking but just long enough to offend some perceptions of how a proper Unionist wife should appear. Following hard on the *Tribune* criticism of Grant's leadership at Belmont, the roots of these new allegations appear to be in that Bross was treated shabbily by Grant—allegedly drunk—when he visited Cairo back in early December.[19]

Returning to military matters, Commodore Foote (in concert with C.F. Smith) urged Grant in the aftermath of their reconnaissance to visit St. Louis headquarters for the purpose of selling an attack on Fort Henry to General Halleck.[20] Grant requested to see Halleck, and, as he later wrote, "The leave was granted, but not graciously."[21] The endorsements of Foote and Smith surely counted for everything, at least in terms of securing Grant an audience. General Smith's reputation in the regular army was nearly unimpeachable (see Chapter Six) and he was esteemed by Halleck as well. Regarding Commodore Foote, Shelby Foote (no relation) wrote, "None ... was more distinguished, more experienced—or tougher—than the man assigned to flag command." Also crucial was that Commodore Foote, like Grant, strongly believed in the then-novel concept of combined army-navy operations.[22] The basic idea was that Grant's troops would attack on land while Foote's gunboats fired from the river. It seems incredible that there was ever a time in which coordinated land-amphibious maneuvers were not conventional military wisdom, but in early 1862 such strategy was not part of the written playbook. Grant, Foote, and Smith saw the potential, though, and a limited but clear-cut Federal success in November 1861 at Port Royal, South Carolina, involving gunboats and marines probably fueled their enthusiasm.

Also motivating this fearsome trio was absolute contempt for the enemy in their front, and there was reason for this. For starters, the attention of the Confederate high command was elsewhere. As Thomas Connelly observed, Albert Sidney Johnston "became absolutely certain that Buell was the only threat to Middle Tennessee, even though he knew that General Henry W. Halleck's army was in western Kentucky and that of General George H. Thomas in eastern Kentucky." Worse for the Southerners, "Not only did Johnston center his attention on Buell, but he also believed that when Buell moved, the advance on Nashville would come through central Kentucky."[23] The result was that Johnston was over-focused on Bowling Green while Polk remained sedentary in Columbus, both ignoring the glaringly weak condition of the river forts in between them, and repeated warnings from their own subordinates.[24] Arthur Conger concurred in Connelly's assessment, asserting that Polk's cluelessness and inertia at Columbus laid the true foundation for the Confederate disaster that was about to follow.[25]

The first fruits of Confederate detachment from reality came on January 19, as Grant was wrapping up his reconnaissance, when a Federal army under Brigadier General George Thomas scored its first clear-cut and large-scale victory at Mill Springs in southeastern Kentucky. For the Federals, this triumph came out of left field both literally and figuratively. Thomas, a native Virginian, was expected by many to go with the Confederacy, but instead chose loyalty to the Union.[26] Sent out by Buell (upon Lincoln's urging) to probe the Confederate right in Kentucky, he was rashly attacked by an equal-sized force under the command of Generals George Crittenden and Felix Zollicoffer.[27] Then Thomas proceeded to do what he would do well throughout the war— halt, draw a line, and wait for the enemy to come to him. The overconfident Southerners elected to attack during a pelting rainstorm, and were completely repulsed with over 400 casualties, including the death of Zollicoffer.[28] Those Confederates not killed, wounded, or captured during the engagement were lost during the retreat thanks to Crittenden's failure at properly managing the supply train. The remaining Confederate force scattered to the winds and had it not been for bad weather and impassable roads, it is generally agreed that Thomas with his victorious Federals could have pushed right through eastern Tennessee to Knoxville.[29] Thus while Johnston and his subordinates were focused on Bowling Green, eastern Kentucky was lost at Mill Springs. Then Johnston continued to ignore the hammer blow that was about to descend from Cairo.

Although the battle of Mill Springs had limited, direct strategic importance outside of eastern Kentucky, it had significant indirect consequences. At about the same moment Grant made his request to visit St. Louis, Halleck learned of Thomas' victory. Because his mistrusted rival Buell would receive credit for the success of Thomas, Halleck probably was beginning to overcome his legendary cold feet. Using the endorsements of Foote and Smith as an excuse, Halleck condescended to allow an interview to Grant, who departed for St. Louis on January 23.[30] Nevertheless, the first face-to-face meeting between Grant and Halleck was unproductive if not hostile, or at least it seemed that way at the time. Grant wrote, "I was received with so little cordiality that I perhaps stated the object of my visit with less clearness than I might have done, and I had not uttered many sentences before I was cut short as if my plan was preposterous. I returned to Cairo very much crestfallen."[31] If Grant was really crestfallen, however, he did not let it show. A St. Louis acquaintance, Dr. Joseph Brinton (later to join Grant at Fort Donelson), later recalled being hailed that same evening by Grant, who showed no signs of disappointment, as the two were in attendance at a somewhat disreputable theater establishment.[32] Halleck, in fairness, and whatever his shortcomings may have been, also had a flair for the dramatic. When the ladies of St. Louis who were in sympathy with the Confederacy began wearing red and white rosettes as a show of solidarity, Halleck ordered that red and white rosettes be passed out to town prostitutes, then made sure they received ample newspaper publicity for wearing these.[33]

With Grant's proposal seemingly rebuffed, another unexpected event then occurred, one even more surprising than the recent Union success in the field. On January 27, President Lincoln issued his "General War Order No. I," directing that McClellan, Buell, and Halleck immediately assume the offensive, specifically including in his mandate "the Army and Flotilla at Cairo."[34] Recognizing this opportunity, Grant repeated his request to assault Fort Henry on January 28, this time in writing and in tandem with Commodore Foote, who clamored for battle.[35] While Halleck was probably still recovering from the Presidential mandate to advance, plus Commodore Foote's rambunctious endorsement of the plan, Grant wrote a follow-up request on January 29, ending the dispatch with perhaps more tact than he had previously shown in St. Louis: "The advantages of this move are as perceptible to the General Commanding the Department as to myself, therefore further statements are unnecessary."[36] In spite of this multi-directional pressure, however, Halleck still seems to have needed one additional reason to give Grant and his colleagues the green light.

That additional reason had in fact already arrived two days earlier on January 27, when it was reported General P.G.T. Beauregard, Confederate hero of Fort Sumter and Bull Run, along with 15 regiments were en route from Virginia to reinforce Johnston's western army. This was the same day that Lincoln had issued his Presidential mandate for everyone to advance simultaneously.[37] The part about Beauregard being sent west was true, since he had been driving Jefferson Davis and everyone else crazy with a megalomaniacal Napoleonic complex that rivaled McClellan's. The part about the 15 Virginian regiments, however, was a false rumor started by a Confederate deserter. In the words of Arthur Conger, "Thus, as often happens in war, was precipitated through a 'soldier rumor' repeated by a deserter one of the most important campaigns in bringing about the reestablishment of the Union."[38] Even Halleck, one of the most cautious generals of the war, was now under irresistible pressure to authorize an offensive. This he did on January 30, ordering Grant to take Fort Henry, and later adding the imperative "with the least possible delay."[39] I wonder whether Grant would have ever been given the chance to move forward without this extraordinary convergence of factors during the last week of January 1862.

In the words of Jean Edward Smith, "Telling Grant to move with the least possible delay was like lighting a short fuse to a charge of dynamite."[40] Bruce Catton further observed that "Halleck's order to go ahead and take Fort Henry hit Grant's headquarters with galvanic effect." Junior officers broke out in spontaneous wild celebration before Grant told them to calm down lest the enemy get wind of their intentions.[41] On January 31, even before receiving his final instructions from Halleck, Grant wrote to Smith that their task force would be launched in three days.[42] This last-minute correspondence between the two has the all the air of two excited conspirators anxious to implement their plans before being prevented from doing so. Thus were unleashed Grant's formidable "Cairo dogs of war," to borrow the phrase of Colonel Conger.[43]

To repeat, had it not been for the incredible convergence of multiple circumstances—direct pressure from Lincoln, Halleck's suspicion of Buell and jealousy over the victory of Thomas, crucial endorsements from C.F. Smith and Commodore Foote, Grant's dogged persistence, the impatience of Grant's own men, the incompetence and neglect of the Confederate high command, and above all, the fantastical false rumor that finally put the ball into motion— one could argue that the Federal movement against Fort Henry and Fort Donelson would have never begun or at least would have been disastrously delayed. The absence of any single factor may have persuaded the famously hesitant Halleck to scotch Grant's historic offensive, or doom it with tardiness. Perhaps it is more accurate to say that the precise origins of the campaign remain a mystery except to those who insist on simple and easy answers to the hows and whys of history.

CHAPTER 11

February 1862:
Fort Donelson

*There was no time during the rebellion when I did not think, and often say,
that the South was more to be benefited by its defeat than the North.*

—Grant[1]

During the first days of February, as the Union task force at Cairo fever-
ishly prepared for its historic offensive, Grant wrote dispassionate letters to
Leonidas Polk in Columbus on the subject of prisoner exchanges.[2] Grant's
flotilla (which included approximately 15,000 troops) began to embark on February 2 under cover of night and, as noted by Jean Edward Smith, "Almost
miraculously, Confederate spies in Cairo and Paducah flashed no warning to
Fort Henry."[3] This was especially stunning since a *Chicago Tribune* reporter had
sent off dispatches announcing the move even before the force had left.[4] It was
as if the Confederate high command wanted to believe there was no problem,
but as Thomas Connelly observed, "Johnston's apparent disinterest in the Fort
Henry situation marked the beginning of the collapse of his leadership."[5]

Meanwhile, south upriver on the east bank, an under-gunned and under-
manned Fort Henry sat totally exposed. One British observer wrote that Fort
Henry's poorly constructed and maintained artillery were more dangerous to
the men who fired them than the targets they shot at.[6] As for the raw infantry
that manned the so-called works, many were ill-equipped with outmoded 1812
muskets and squirrel guns. This hodgepodge arsenal was about to face off
against Commodore Foote's ironclad gunboats.[7] The uneasy commander of
Fort Henry was the competent but luckless General Lloyd Tilghman, who
back in September fled from Paducah after Grant's army raced to that point
faster than Confederate forces.

By February 4, the Federals were approaching the fort. Grant, in keeping with his custom, conducted a personal gunboat reconnaissance to see how
close he could get before being fired upon. After getting quite close with no
response, the gunboat on its return was barely missed by a Confederate artillery

shell. This fortuitous shot not only spared Grant, but alerted him as to where it would be safe for his troops to disembark.[8] Around this same time, a nervous Henry Halleck in St. Louis dispatched General William Tecumseh Sherman to assume backup command at Cairo, and the brilliant, highly regarded Colonel James Birdseye McPherson to keep an eye on Grant's alleged drinking habits.[9] As with Halleck's earlier attempt to send watchdogs (Commodore Foote and General C.F. Smith), both Sherman and McPherson were soon to be won over by what they were about to witness. Writing to Julia the same day, Grant offered assurance: "I do not want to boast but I have a confident feeling of success."[10]

It would be pleasing to write that the successful Union assault on Fort Henry resulted from a heroic infantry charge; unfortunately, there was no charge at all. In fact, there was no infantry. While Foote's gunboats pounded the fort, Grant's two troop columns on either side of the river, instead of surrounding the fort, became hopelessly bogged down in the Tennessee winter mud.[11] Meanwhile, almost all of the 3,000-plus Confederate garrison had broken in panic and retreated to Fort Donelson before the Federals could cut them off. By then a furious gunboat artillery barrage had silenced Fort Henry.[12] On February 6, fewer than 100 prisoners, including Tilghman, surrendered before the Federal infantry even arrived.[13] Confederate Captain Jesse Taylor, who stayed with Tilghman, remembered that Grant stuck up for him after Taylor refused to give information to a hostile Federal interrogator: "Grant ... impressed me as a modest, amiable, kind-hearted but resolute man."[14] Brimming with overconfidence, Grant telegrammed St. Louis headquarters that "I shall take and destroy Fort Donaldson [sic] on the 8th...."[15] Then to Julia he wrote, "Fort Henry is taken and I am not hurt."[16]

The following day (February 7) as Grant reconnoitered the roads to Fort Donelson, the Confederate high command, including Johnston and Beauregard, met in Bowling Green, Kentucky, to assess their options. Earlier, upon his arrival in Columbus, Beauregard had urged a strike against Grant in Cairo, but the post–Belmont defensive mentality of Polk and Johnston still prevailed. Now Beauregard recommended that Grant be attacked from Fort Donelson, but Johnston was more worried about Buell's huge army creeping towards them from the north.[17] Even at this early stage in the war, Beauregard appears to have sensed that Grant was the true threat. In fact, whenever Beauregard was not involved in the decision-making process, the western Confederate high command seems to have been mainly characterized by bovine stupidity.

Although military historians are in disagreement over what was going through the minds of Johnston and his subordinates (the record is fragmentary), a few general observations can be made. In less than two weeks, Johnston made (or assumed responsibility for) a remarkable series of catastrophic errors with respect to the river forts. First, he ignored the problem despite many warning signs, not the least of which was Grant's ferocious buildup at

Cairo. Then, after gunboats pulverized Fort Henry, Johnston rejected Beauregard's sensible suggestion to concentrate and attack Grant. Next, Johnston wrongly concluded that Fort Donelson could not stand up to the gunboats and elected to retreat. These mistakes alone were enough to lose most of Tennessee, but Johnston was not through making bad choices. After allowing Gideon Pillow (of all people) to persuade him that Donelson could be defended if sufficiently garrisoned,[18] he dispatched a huge infantry force to that point, not to attack Grant but to defend the fort, thus instantly converting Donelson from a potential staging area into a huge trap.[19] Then, ensuring failure, he placed the fort under the divided command of Pillow and John Floyd, possibly the two most incompetent Confederate generals in the West, and from whom innumerable additional errors would emanate.[20] All of these missteps were bonuses for Grant and appear to have been based on the breathtaking fallacy that Grant's army would be afraid to assault a heavily reinforced Fort Donelson; instead they would choose, reasoned Johnston, to pivot west and attempt flanking the Confederate garrison at Columbus, Kentucky. In the words of Confederate Colonel John S. Mosby, "A greater blunder was never committed in war...."[21]—quite a statement coming from one who saw most of the major engagements in the East through Appomattox.

As for Grant, after conducting a second reconnaissance on February 9 and learning that Floyd and Pillow would be in command at Donelson, he decided the Federals should attack immediately and that speed was of the essence. In his own words, "I felt that 15,000 men on the 8th would be more effective than 50,000 a month later."[22] Foote's gunboats had just completed a "victory lap" (Professor Smith)[23] by spreading terror as far south as Florence, Alabama,[24] and had then steamed back north and prepared to repeat their shock and awe tactics, this time against Fort Donelson on the Cumberland River. To his sister Mary, Grant wrote excitedly the same day, "...G.J. Pillow commands at Fort Donaldson [sic]. I hope to give him a tug before you receive this."[25]

At a council of war on February 10, Grant announced the decision to immediately assault Donelson. That same day he wrote a frantic letter to Congressman Washburne in Washington, pleading, "For God's sake get the Senate to reconsider General Smith's Confirmation. There is no doubt of his loyalty & efficiency. We can't spare him now."[26] Although C.F. Smith had been promoted to Brigadier back in August, he was not yet confirmed because of his questioned loyalty. Part of the reason for this was that Smith, while in charge at Paducah, had used a soft touch with Confederate sympathizers. For this (plus a spat with other Union officers) Smith was criticized by the *Chicago Tribune*, just as they had recently attacked Grant (see Chapter 10).[27] Smith, for his part, merely remarked, "They'll take it back after our first battle."[28] Possibly helped by Grant's urging, Smith was finally confirmed on February 14, one day before he was destined to lead one of the most important infantry charges in American military history.

On February 12, Grant's army abruptly turned east and marched on Fort Donelson. Thus, instead of moving away from the Confederate buildup, Grant advanced directly towards it. Military historian Thomas Connelly wrote that Johnston was "severely jolted," "staggered," and "never seemed to recover from the shock of Grant's move on Donelson."[29] J.F.C. Fuller was even harsher on Johnston, claiming that the earlier loss of Fort Henry "upset his balance," leaving him "bewildered" and "paralyzed." Fuller wrote that Johnston "had not the mental training to see things in the proper tactical perspective" and then damningly labeled him "a very common type of brave and stupid soldier."[30] Connelly added that the success of the gunboats and dismal performance of the Federal infantry at Fort Henry also worked to Grant's advantage in that it helped to further delude his opponents as to the relative strength of each service branch.[31]

On February 13, just as John Floyd arrived to assume command at Donelson, the Federals began their investment. While morale among the Confederates was low due to lack of provisions and a jealously divided command, corresponding morale within the Union army was high. Grant reportedly joked with soldiers who had been wounded during the initial skirmishing and spoke allegorically of hunting bear, to their great amusement.[32] On February 14, the gunboats launched their anticipated attack, but to everyone's surprise, they were repulsed with heavy loss, including the wounding of Commodore Foote. This result was due to the higher placement of the fort on a bluff and its superior armament. Even this setback, however, worked to Grant's advantage as the dreaded gunboats drew attention away from the simultaneous land buildup of the Federals. A crucial part of Grant's strategy was his correct assessment that Floyd would submit to Pillow's judgment, foolishly allowing Grant's army to throw a cordon around them. After circumvallation was completed on the afternoon of February 14, Floyd and the Confederates, according to Thomas Connelly, "For the first time ... seemed to realize that the threat to Donelson was on the land side."[33]

When it finally dawned on the Confederates that they were under siege, their reaction was one of valor unsupported by planning or discipline. Grant himself was worried about supplies, and rode off on the morning of the 15th in response to the bedridden Commodore Foote's request to visit him while the army held the fort at bay. A few hours later, as Grant departed from Foote's flagship, a shaken John Rawlins arrived and informed Grant that the Confederates were attempting a breakout to the south. Apparently a strong north wind had concealed the sound of gunfire to all but those in the immediate vicinity. Early that morning the Confederates punched a hole in the south Federal lines (in the direction of Nashville), but in so doing charged right into the teeth of two experienced regiments commanded by Colonel Richard Oglesby, one of which belonged to Colonel John Logan, who had played a key role at Belmont.[34] Though successful, the Southerners could not have chosen a thicker barrier to have hurled themselves against. With respect to supplies, Grant noted that "the enemy relieved me from this necessity.... I had no idea that there would be any engagement on land unless I brought it on myself."[35] Then, with the road to Nashville now wide open, Gideon Pillow did what only Gideon Pillow would have done—he ordered Confederate forces to retreat and reorganize, thinking they could now depart at their own leisure.[36]

During this crucial lull, Grant arrived back on the scene, having ridden seven miles on his favorite stallion Jack,[37] no mean feat in the rugged, soggy terrain surrounding the fort. Personally riding along the lines, Grant exhorted his men to gather ammunition and prevent the enemy from escaping.[38] Demoralized confusion instantly turned into energized resolve. Instructing officers to counterattack upon his signal all along the line, Grant then rode back to C.F. Smith, stationed on the idle northern side of the fort, and ordered the newly confirmed Brigadier General to immediately charge. As Jean Edward Smith put it, Grant's former West Point commandant "had been waiting for such an order all his life."[39] Cartridge boxes were filled, bayonets fixed, drums rolled and volunteers formed into lines. For good measure, Grant ordered gunboats that were still serviceable to offer encouragement for the infantry by lobbing shells at the fort.

Thus, before the Southerners could reap the harvest of their morning success, they found themselves under pressure from all directions at once. In the face of such fanaticism, the Confederates grudgingly gave ground. Bruce Catton observed, "The Middle Westerners who made this attack remembered it as long as they lived."[40] Not only were positions south of the fort retaken, C.F. Smith's successful charge to the north breached the opposing rifle pits and by the end of the day Northern guns were staring down into the fort itself. As at Belmont three months earlier, Grant's cool decisiveness at a critical moment had turned the tide, only this time it was the Confederates who had attempted to cut their way out, and failed.

By the following day (February 16), Floyd and Pillow realized the game was up, but neither was willing to surrender their persons. Floyd was rightfully fearful of a treason trial, because of his prewar role as Secretary of War, for shifting arms to the South, and he commandeered the last transport ship out of Fort Donelson as stunned Confederate guardsman watched. Gideon Pillow, having sworn "Liberty or Death" en route to the fort, now (to borrow the phrase of historian James McPherson) chose liberty by stealing away on a small boat.[41] Grant's sharp comment later was that Pillow had nothing to fear because Grant believed he was more useful to the North fighting for the Confederates than as a prisoner of war.[42] Left to formally surrender Fort Donelson was Grant's old West Point friend Simon Bolivar Buckner, who was among over 12,000 Confederates now trapped inside.[43]

Responding to a request for terms, Grant, after consultation with a belligerently victorious C.F. Smith, quickly wrote out one of the most famous communiqués in military history: "No terms except an unconditional and immediate surrender can be accepted. I propose to move immediately upon your works. I am sir; very respectfully your obt. Servt. U.S. Grant Brig. Gen."[44] After a miffed Buckner was forced to accept, the Northern press quickly had a field day with Grant's eloquence and before long, schoolchildren were memorizing his "Unconditional Surrender" speech,[45] equating the initials "U.S." with his own name. This calls for a brief digression.

Ulysses S. Grant was not Grant's real name; that is to say, he had been born and christened Hiram Ulysses Grant. As the reluctant young cadet entered West Point, he was terrified of the acronym "HUG" and allowed himself to be mistakenly registered as Ulysses S. Grant, with the wrong assumption that "S" stood for Simpson, the maiden name of his mother and the first name of his younger brother. Grant's creative classmates, though, promptly dubbed him "Uncle Sam," and later "Sam" for short, whereby he was eventually known as Sam Grant to his colleagues.[46] Many years later the whole thing worked to Grant's advantage. After Donelson, his new first initials ("U.S.") gave his name tremendous cachet with the troops, the public, and the press.

In the wake of the surrender, Grant suddenly found himself with the largest capture of prisoners to date in American history, as well as being a household name. Viewing the dead and wounded, the ever-literate Grant was overheard to quote Robert Burns: "Man's inhumanity to man makes countless thousands mourn."[47] After ordering both Union and Confederate wounded to be tended,[48] Grant offered Buckner money (which was declined) as a gesture of appreciation for the kindness shown to him many years before. Though Buckner, as an officer, would soon be exchanged, many of the Confederate prisoners taken at Donelson would eventually be sent to Camp Douglas in Chicago, where their sufferings would continue.[49] Thousands (many with unknown names) would later be interred at Oakwoods Cemetery in Chicago, where a controversial monument to their memory still stands in the midst of an African-American neighborhood. Visiting the monument on Memorial Day, 2006, the author noticed that among the dead officially listed are 29 Confederates representing six of his eight maternal surnames.[50] These included Private T.M. Gray of the 37th Georgia Infantry (possible kinsman to my great-great-grandmother, Harriet Jane Gray) and Private F.M. Cash of the 55th Georgia Infantry Regiment (possible kinsman to my great-great-grandmother, Mary Cash). Though the 37th Georgia and the 55th Georgia were not present at Donelson, others buried with them certainly were. One ponders what all of their fates would have been had it not been for the career of Ulysses S. Grant.

Donelson was the first nail in the coffin of the Confederacy, and it was a big one. Historians have been unanimous in declaring Grant's victory one of the most important of the war, both strategically and psychologically.[51] Grant himself reflected, "The news of the fall of Fort Donelson caused great delight all over the North. At the South, particularly in Richmond, the effect was correspondingly depressing,"[52] while Julia proudly noted "The country simply went wild."[53] Northern church bells rang out and the press went into a frenzy—one month after the *Chicago Tribune* had criticized Grant's lack of sobriety, another paper now declared that any sober man found on the streets after dark should be arrested as a traitor.[54] Shelby Foote wrote that "The shame of Bull Run was erased,"[55] and Jean Edward Smith added, "The effect on morale in Dixie was devastating."[56] J.F.C. Fuller quoted Colonel Henry Stone, who was a severe Grant critic:

> The exultation throughout the North-West ... the consternation in the insurgent regions ... were not surpassed, if they were equaled, by those of three years later, when Petersburg was captured and Richmond abandoned. The hilarity at Chicago, and the panic at Nashville, cannot be described.[57]

Perhaps the biggest tribute came from Lincoln, who told intimates, "If the Southerners think that man for man they are better than our Illinois men, or Western men in general, they will discover themselves in a grievous mistake."[58] Another poignant remark came from Sherman, who later wrote to Grant:

> At Donelson, also, you illustrated your whole character.... Until you won at Donelson, I confess I was almost cowed by the terrible array of anarchical elements that presented themselves at every point; but that victory admitted a ray of light I have followed since....[59]

Bruce Catton summed up the result with: "Fort Donelson was not only a beginning; it was one of the most decisive engagements of the entire war, and out of it came the slow, inexorable progression that led to Appomattox."[60]

Northern euphoria and Southern gloom were justified. Not only was an entire Confederate army put out of commission, large amounts of soon-to-be Federally occupied territory in Tennessee ceased to exist as Confederate recruiting grounds. Within two weeks the "Gibraltar" at Columbus, Kentucky, which had been impervious to the Federals for nearly six months, was abandoned to avoid being enveloped like Fort Donelson.[61] Within nine days, Nashville would become the first Confederate state capital to fall into Federal hands. Possibly the greatest aftershock of Grant's triumph, however, was that it had a tremendous chilling effect on potential European support for the Confederacy.[62]

The fall of Nashville provides an interesting and somewhat humorous coda to the benchmark engagement at Fort Donelson. Grant to his dying day believed the war in the West could have been concluded with a rapid advance, but that "Providence ruled differently" in that the Federal high command insisted on moving slowly.[63] Commodore Foote, though wounded, supported an immediate push and was disgusted when this was forbidden.[64] Within three days, however, Grant's forces had pushed southeast up the Cumberland River to Clarksville, which promptly surrendered. On the same day (February 19), he was promoted to Major General of Volunteers by President Lincoln. In triumph he wrote to Julia, "Is father afraid yet that I will not be able to sustain myself?"—nevertheless adding, "I was extremely lucky...."[65]

As Grant's forces paused at Clarksville within tantalizing distance of Nashville, Don Carlos Buell cautiously inched towards the state capital on land, believing that Johnston intended to make a stand there. On February 23, a citizen delegation from Nashville arrived at Clarksville unannounced, informing Grant that Johnston had evacuated their city and pleaded with him to spare their property.[66] Soon afterward, one of Buell's divisions, led by the profane and physically imposing Brigadier General William "Bull" Nelson, steamed into Clarksville, ostensibly to provide support in the great battle that Buell believed to be imminent.[67] Grant elected to put a gleeful Nelson and his division to work by sending them cruising up the Cumberland to occupy Nashville, where he arrived the next day. In offering reasons for this unorthodox move, Grant wrote to Julia:

> I want to push on as rapidly as possible to save hard fighting. These terrible battles are very good things to read about for persons who lose no friends but I am decidedly in favor of having as little of it as possible. The way to avoid it is to push forward as vigorously as possible."[68]

As a result of this initiative, on February 25, as Buell's army sat on the north side of the Cumberland across from Nashville, it was confronted with the mortifying and humiliating sight of one of its own divisions occupying the city on the opposite bank.

Angrily, Buell wrote a complaining letter to C.F. Smith, exasperated by Grant's placement of Nelson and expecting Johnston to attack when in fact Johnston was in the process of retreating all the way south to Decatur, Alabama.[69] To aggravate matters further, Grant personally traveled to Nashville three days later, where his modest, respectful manner made a favorable impression on the locals, but he also succeeded in completely antagonizing Buell during a face-to-face encounter.[70] Buell later retaliated by ordering the division of C.F. Smith away from Grant to resist the phantom Confederate counterattack, an order that the obedient Smith called "nonsense."[71] The net effect of this farce was that relations between Grant and Buell were permanently strained.

Jean Edward Smith wrote, "The nature of Grant's greatness has been a riddle to many observers. The evidence begins with the assault on Fort Donelson."[72] Smith again: "One of the tests of military greatness is the ability to recognize and respond to opportunities presented." Another test of military greatness is incredible luck, and Grant had it in spades. Nine months earlier, Grant did not even have a commission; now he was the most prominent of Union war heroes.

CHAPTER 12

March 1862: America's Most Wanted Man

Grant's monumental campaign against Fort Donelson tends to be treated like an afterthought by historians,[1] when in fact there was perhaps no victory more important for the Union—not Gettysburg, not Vicksburg, not even Shiloh. Admittedly, in terms of casualties or destruction, Donelson was a relatively minor engagement; in terms of tactical military strategy, however, the ramifications of Grant's success on the Cumberland River were immeasurable. Most important of all, the negative psychological effects on the Confederacy and corresponding uplift in Northern morale exceeded anything that would transpire until 16 months later at Vicksburg and Gettysburg, if even then. Nevertheless, Fort Donelson is not a household name and even among Civil War buffs it tends to be grudgingly discussed. Perhaps the reason for this neglect is that the battle was such a resounding Northern victory with very little for Southern apologists to be proud of[2]; plus it was at this very moment in time that Ulysses S. Grant, former assistant store clerk from Galena, Illinois, was suddenly catapulted onto the stage of world history. So sudden was this prominence that some harried journalists felt a need to fabricate physical descriptions of the new American hero that were quite at odds with reality.[3] One detail the press did manage to get right was that Grant smoked a cigar during the engagement, prompting admirers to barrage him with gifts of stogies.[4]

As recent Federal gains in the West were punctuated by another victory at the battle of Pea Ridge in Arkansas during the first week of March, Grant—much to his surprise—found himself the target of ire from his own Federal superiors. The beginnings of this administrative fire in the rear went back to early February, when Halleck, Buell, and McClellan discussed taking over Grant's field command even before his forces began putting a stranglehold on Fort Donelson.[5] Then, after a dramatically victorious Grant became the darling of the press and made Buell look foolish at Nashville, Halleck became outraged when communications between him and Grant went silent during late February and early March. This interval appears to have been the result of Confederate sabotage, and it was not until March 5 that Grant first learned he had incurred Halleck's displeasure.[6] It was on this day Grant received a telegram from Halleck admonishing him for unresponsiveness and notifying him that he had been relieved of his command.

While Grant was busy re-equipping his victorious army and anxiously fretting as to how he might exploit their recent success, the winds of intrigue were rapidly working against him. On March 3, Halleck had wired McClellan:

> I have no communication with General Grant for more than a week. He left his command without my authority and went to Nashville. His army seems to be as much demoralized by the victory of Fort Donelson as was that of the Potomac by the defeat of Bull Run. It is hard to censure a successful general immediately after a victory, but I think he richly deserves it. I can get no returns, no reports, no information of any kind from him. Satisfied with his victory, he sits down and enjoys it without any regard to the future. I am worn-out and tired with this neglect and inefficiency. C.F. Smith is almost the only officer equal to the emergency.[7]

That very same day McClellan authorized Grant's arrest, after wrestling an endorsement from Secretary of War Stanton. It is impossible to resist the impression that Halleck, McClellan, and Buell were having major fits of jealous rage. Sherman later wrote that Halleck worked "himself into a passion" over the whole affair.[8] Rather than risk arresting the hero of Fort Donelson, however, Halleck then chose to add fuel to the flames by writing again to McClellan on March 4, further justifying his displeasure:

> A rumor has just reached me that since the taking of Fort Donelson General Grant has resumed his former bad habits [read: drinking]. If so, it will account for his neglect of my oft-repeated orders. I do not deem it advisable to arrest him at present, but have placed General Smith in command of the expedition up the Tennessee. I think Smith will restore order and discipline.[9]

Grant would have probably been better off if Halleck had arrested him as opposed to spreading more rumors about his drinking problems.

As Grant sourly reflected in his memoirs, "Thus in less than two weeks after the victory at Donelson, the two leading generals in the army were in correspondence as to what disposition should be made of me, and in less than three weeks I was virtually in arrest and without a command."[10] The fall of Fort Henry in early February not only aroused the enmity of Grant's superiors, it also reignited the drinking controversy made public by the *Chicago Tribune* in January. On February 10, the incarcerated Captain William Kountz wrote again to Secretary of War Stanton demanding a hearing. Two days earlier, unsigned charges against Grant, even more lurid than the ones originally submitted, had been placed in the Kountz file. These included Grant's "Getting so drunk that he had to go up stairs on all fours," "Visiting a Negro Ball ... and becoming drunk," consorting and getting drunk with "Harlots," losing his sword and uniform while drunk, getting drunk and then vomiting all over a ship during Flag of Truce negotiations with the enemy, getting publicly drunk after he had banned the sale of liquor around Cairo, and playing cards with secret service money.[11] A month later, however, after Grant had been reinstated, Kountz seems to have gone on the defensive. On March 13, Kountz resigned his commission. Then on March 16, Grant wrote to Julia, "You warn me against Capt. Kountz. He can do me no harm. He is known as a venomous man whose hand is raised against every man and is without friends or influence."[12] In a letter dated March 17, C.F. Smith came to Grant's defense (rather equivocally) by stating that his drinking habits were "unexceptional."[13] On March 24, the *Cincinnati Gazette* reported that the charges of Kountz were "sprung from personal feelings."[14]

The momentum change in favor of Grant is traceable to March 7, when Grant, in response to his censure, offered his resignation.[15] At this crucial point his guardian angel, Congressman Elihu Washburne, once again came to the rescue. After being notified of the spat between Halleck and Grant, Washburne got Lincoln personally involved; Lincoln, on March 11, ordered Halleck to either open an investigation or stop insinuating.[16] By this time, however, "Old Brains" had come to his senses. This was after communications had been fully restored and it slowly dawned on both Halleck and Grant that each had not been receiving the other's telegrams. Accordingly, Grant was officially reinstated on March 10, and when Halleck received Lincoln's ultimatum he informed everyone that things had been satisfactorily resolved. That same day, Lincoln offered Halleck a carrot as well as a stick by appointing him western commander-in-chief, thereby stripping McClellan of that authority. When Grant offered again to resign on March 13 after belatedly receiving one of Halleck's outdated, angry dispatches, Halleck replied, "You cannot be relieved from your command. There is no good reason for it.... Instead of relieving you, I wish you, as soon as your new army is in the field, to assume the immediate command & lead it on to new victories."[17]

The whole experience left a bitter taste with Grant for the rest of his life. Bruce Catton wrote that "it unquestionably left a scar on Grant, injuring him emotionally more than anything else that happened in all the war."[18] His reward for winning the biggest Union victory to date, aside from a symbolic promotion to Major General of Volunteers, had been a bewildering slap on the wrists from his commanders (Halleck and McClellan) and more public accusations (by Kountz) of drunkenness. On March 11, the day after he had been reinstated, Grant wrote to Julia, "...you may rely upon it that your husband will never disgrace you nor leave a defeated field."[19] The last bit about Grant promising, in effect, to die with his boots on provides some insight into his state of mind less than one month before receiving his most severe test as a field commander. Writing to Julia a little later in the aftermath of these allegations, when not complaining about the "Abolition press,"[20] Grant declared that "I want to whip these rebels once more in a big fight and see what will be said [in the papers] then."[21] His wish was about to come all too terribly true on the banks of the Tennessee River, but the press would continue to be uncomplimentary even after this.

As the Federal high command humiliated Grant and toyed with the idea of arresting him in early March, the Confederate high command was busy making far deadlier plans for the new Northern hero-of-the-moment. Thomas Connelly soberly observed, "The effects of the collapse of the Nashville myth of invincibility, of the first battle lost in Tennessee, and of the first surrender by a Confederate army all combined to produce in the people of the Heartland both fear and a loss of confidence in Johnston,"[22] adding that "When Nashville fell in 1862, panic gripped the slaveholders of the Mississippi."[23] If Ulysses S. Grant was in "virtual arrest" after Fort Donelson, Albert Sidney Johnston had recently seen his career and public reputation plummet to a new all-time low. About the only person who seemed to still believe in him was his long-time friend and admirer, Jefferson Davis. As a stunned and perplexed Johnston rushed south from Nashville with his demoralized, disorganized forces, the irrepressible General Pierre Gustave Toutant Beauregard assumed command of other Confederate forces now in the process of concentrating at the crucial railroad hub of Corinth, Mississippi.[24] This was approximately 20 miles southwest of the Tennessee River and state line. Immediately north on the west bank was a point called Pittsburg Landing, located near a Methodist log meeting house known as Shiloh, a Hebrew word meaning "Place of Peace."

Beauregard had the ego of a Gideon Pillow but also something to back it up. The successful Confederate strategist of Fort Sumter and Bull Run viewed himself as the Napoleon of the South, and set out with energy and clarity of purpose to stabilize a position in the West as Johnston's situation unraveled. The purpose was admirably simple: concentrate at Corinth and destroy Grant.[25] In January and February, Beauregard—with good instincts— had urged Johnston and his less-than-brilliant underlings to go after Grant, first at Cairo and then at Donelson, but to no avail. Now, with disasters multiplying around them, everyone seemed ready to listen. Though outranking Beauregard (as well as everyone else), Johnston readily complied with the Creole's stern recommendation to unite at Corinth by a risky and circuitous rail route through three states.[26] Meanwhile, every available able-bodied man (and at least one woman)[27] willing to bear arms for the Confederacy from Tennessee, Louisiana, Mississippi, Alabama, and beyond poured into the overwhelmed and astonished town of Corinth. By the time Johnston and his army finally arrived in late March, the rallying Confederates had achieved what may have been the largest concentration of shock troops (nearly 44,000) to date in American history.[28] Johnston then surprised everyone by offering supreme command to Beauregard (who declined), possibly out of chivalry but more likely due to the massive loss in confidence that Johnston had recently experienced.[29]

One can argue that the Confederate strategy against Grant was not personal; rather the obvious military thing to do was to strike back at the Federal juggernaut rolling up the Tennessee Valley and that Grant just happened to be the lead element of that advance. Postwar Southerner accounts of this planning process are not surprisingly reticent in admitting such a mentality against one who later became the greatest living hero of the Union. The unprecedented force soon to be unleashed at Shiloh was motivated by a logical need to attack before Grant's isolated army could be reinforced by Buell's Army of the Ohio coming down from Nashville. Surviving bits and pieces, however, suggest there was more than cold military stratagem at work. Twenty-three years later, when Grant was on his deathbed, Beauregard was invited by a Chicago journalist to write a short piece on the man he had faced off against in the spring of 1862. Beauregard responded with, "Let him die in peace, & may God have mercy on his soul. G.T. Beauregard cannot comply with your request...."[30] Beauregard's later acrimony is better understood in light of his Napoleonic public image having been permanently shattered by Grant during the epic struggle now unfolding in southwestern Tennessee.

As for Johnston, Beauregard's administrative skill and energy at Corinth had slowly awakened him to the possibility of recovering his lost reputation with one single, overwhelming blow. This strike would be surgically aimed at Johnston's main tormentor (Grant), whose army by late March was congregating around Pittsburg Landing and Shiloh Church, waiting for the torpid and pouting Don Carlos Buell to join them in a joint push against Corinth. It was a classic case of the hunter about to become the hunted. Although there are some indications that Johnston was still clinging to a defensive mentality as late as March 22 (when he rendezvoused with Beauregard at Corinth), this was surely beginning to change. The very act of joining up at Corinth admitted the possibility of an offensive move, and when confronted with the massive Confederate host now assembled there, Johnston no doubt began to take heart. When he first arrived, according to eyewitness Alfred Roman, "A shade of sadness, if not despondency, rested upon General Johnston's brow."[31] Less than two weeks later, however, Johnston would be cheerfully and personally leading his new army into combat despite an entreaty from Beauregard to call the whole thing off. Moreover, during late March a letter was dispatched to Johnston, written by none other than Robert E. Lee, strongly urging him to hit the Federal advance before it consolidated.[32] Thus, in a very real sense, Grant and Lee were strategizing against each other in the spring of 1862, even before the latter had assumed command of the Army of Northern Virginia. Lee, like Beauregard, felt an instinctive need to first crush Grant above all other priorities.

On the Ides of March, 1862, William Tecumseh Sherman and his Federal scouting party arrived at Pittsburg Landing on the west bank of the Tennessee River. This was less than 10 miles south upstream from Savannah, where an ailing C.F. Smith[33] had taken to his sickbed (from which he never rose) a few days earlier. Fittingly, the ground for the first truly horrible battle of the war was personally chosen by one of the first and few men who predicted that it would be a horrendous war throughout. Still considered by many to be out of his mind, Sherman had been given a second chance by Halleck after his breakdown the previous fall and recently been inspired back into action by Grant's lightning victory at Donelson. In simple terms, Shiloh was a triangular defensive position.[34] Though this campsite would place the back of the Federal army against the river, it was a river exclusively controlled by Union gunboats. The flanks consisted of the river itself and a deeply ravined tributary while the approach was one long, rolling, wooded, and uphill climb, culminating in the bluff at Pittsburg Landing. Sherman chose well, though (probably to overcompensate for his alarmist reputation) he emphatically told everyone there would be no attack made right up until the point that bullets started whizzing around his head on the morning of April 6. Grant himself arrived in person at Savannah on March 17 to confer with C.F. Smith, the same day that Sherman reported on his recent reconnaissance and choice of campsite.[35]

Grant seems to have been under the not-unreasonable impression that he was chasing a disorganized mob, now supposedly preparing for a siege at their chosen ground in Corinth. Grant's greatest delusion, however, and one probably shared by most Northerners, was that the anticipated battle would be the last "big lick,"[36] when in fact it would the first of many big licks over the next three years. As for numbers, everyone on both sides knew that the other was gathering and where, but only the Confederates appear to have accurately known the strength of their enemy. Grant's combat force would total approximately 40,000 by the end of the month (before the arrival of Buell and others would more than double that number), while rumors of Confederate strength at Corinth variously reported figures of 20,000, 40,000, 50,000, and even fantastical ones like 80,000 or 100,000.[37] While it appears that Grant's own estimate was accurately closer to the lower end of the range, he mistakenly believed the Southerners continued to be completely demoralized after their defeat at Donelson, with their swelling numbers at Corinth being further discontented by supply shortages.[38] Like everyone else involved in this fateful campaign, Grant was laboring under a massive set of false assumptions. Among other things, the Confederate generals, as well as their rank and file, had not yet begun to fight.

To say that Grant was completely misled and content to be a sitting duck at Pittsburg Landing, as some historians have suggested, however, is way off the mark as well. On March 23, he wrote a dispatch to C.F. Smith, reiterating the need for Federal offensive tactics: "I am clearly of the opinion that the enemy are gathering strength at Corinth quite as rapidly as we are here, and the sooner we attack, the easier will be the task of taking the place."[39] The failure of the Federal army to entrench the Shiloh campsite, though going against the book that Halleck or Buell would have followed, was the result of joint recommendations to Grant from his lieutenants, who included no less a trio than Sherman, Smith, and McPherson. None of them saw or wanted to see what was about to be hurled at them, and indeed what would be hurled at them was one of the riskiest and ultimately doomed endeavors in military history.

As Grant's army reposed around Shiloh Church in late March, almost all believing that the action would be some 20 miles away at Corinth, a small incident occurred that further drew Grant's attention away from the possibility of enemy attack. The ever-boisterous and ambitious John McClernand, whose command was now stationed at Shiloh under the wing of Sherman, threw a tantrum after learning that recently confirmed Brigadier General C.F. Smith now outranked him. Grant, who only seven months earlier had superceded the political general Benjamin Prentice (now present for duty at Shiloh as well) in the same manner, was, to put it mildly, unsympathetic.[40] Grant responded to McClernand's anger by first ignoring him, then reprimanded McClernand over reports that his troops had carried off local slaves for their own use.[41] On the eve of the first major blood bath of the war, Grant was still capable of preferring the property interests of slaveholders over complaints of a troublesome subordinate.

The vast majority of Confederate soldiers assembled in Corinth at the end of March 1862 were not slave owners. Most were poor farmers, including the author's ancestors who were there. They primarily came out to repel an invader, but may also have been deluded by dreams of military glory and encouraged by incompetent leaders who were blinded by a vision of the future wildly at odds with realities of the present. How some things never change! All eight of the maternal surnames in the author's family would be represented at the battle of Shiloh in regiments from Alabama and Georgia alone.[42] For example, Private Thomas W. Rape, kinsman to his great-great-grandmother Martha Hannah Rape, was assigned to Girardy's Washington Battery, later known as the 22nd Georgia Battalion, Heavy Artillery. Private Rape would survive the war and make no apologies for his life, so far as anyone knows; on the other hand, it is fairly certain that the things he and thousands of others were about to witness around Shiloh Church were not what he had expected, nor been told to expect. It is known, however, that Private Rape (described as a "faithful soldier" by a comrade-in-arms) elected not to re-enlist after his term expired immediately following the historic battle that was about to rage.

CHAPTER 13

April 1862: Shiloh

The troops on both sides were American, and united they need not fear any foreign foe.

—Grant on Shiloh[1]

Grant, often labeled a butcher by his critics, wrote that "Shiloh was the severest battle fought at the West during the war, and but few in the East equaled it for hard, determined fighting."[2] Many historians have agreed with this assessment and suggested that the severity of combat may have been influenced by an awareness of the high stakes involved. Jean Edward Smith: "Shiloh was a watershed.... The losses were stupefying.... Grant's victory ... doomed the Confederate cause in the Mississippi Valley."[3] Participants such as Sherman agreed that it was "one of the most important [battles] that has ever occurred on this continent."[4] Addressing his victorious troops, Grant went even further: "...in importance of results, but few such [battles] have taken place in the history of the world."[5] Remarkably, these comments in retrospect do not come off as hyperbole. Nevertheless, as with most important events, controversies and misconceptions surrounding Shiloh are legion. Grant again: "The battle of Shiloh, or Pittsburg landing, has been perhaps less understood, or, to state the case more accurately, more persistently misunderstood, than any other engagement between National and Confederate troops during the entire rebellion."[6] Modern commentators frequently concur. James Lee McDonough reflected, "The battle of Shiloh probably has more hard questions associated with it than any battle of the war."[7] Bruce Catton was more poetic: "Shiloh casts a long shadow, in whose dusk it is hard to see the precise truth."[8]

Disagreements over what exactly happened and why begin even before a vast Confederate host left their fortifications in Corinth, Mississippi, on April 3 in a determined attempt to surprise and crush Grant's invading army. General Albert Sidney Johnston, after weeks of prodding from Beauregard and others, made the decision to attack on April 2 after learning that Union reinforcements under General Don Carlos Buell had begun their trek from

Columbia, Tennessee, to link up with Grant at Pittsburg Landing.[9] Buell's long-overdue movement, however, appears to have been motivated by the initiative of one his subordinates. While Buell dilly-dallied over how to build a bridge, General William Nelson, who had earlier rushed his division to Nashville upon Grant's urging (and to Buell's consternation), seems to have had a premonition after learning that Grant's force was encamped exposed on the west bank of the Tennessee. Correctly deducing that the Confederates would strike while Grant's back was against the river, the boisterous and glory-hungry Nelson ordered his men to double-time south, while Buell reluctantly tried to catch up.[10] Thus it is a chicken-and-egg type of problem as to whether the Confederates or the Federals initiated a mass movement that would eventually see over 100,000 troops engaged.

The Confederates were also slow off the mark. Though only 20 miles from their objective, it took Johnston's army three days to get into position due to bad weather, bad planning, and bad execution. By April 5, Beauregard, now convinced that Buell had surely arrived and the Federals entrenched, lost heart and urged Johnston to abort the attack that he had planned and previously advocated. Johnston's famous reply, "I would fight them if they were a million,"[11] reflected his determination to hit Grant regardless of strategy. Then Johnston wrote out a pep talk for his troops, contemptuously referring to the Federals as "agrarian mercenaries."[12] This would prove to be a fatal underestimation of his opponents. Thus, on the same day (April 5) that General George McClellan's Army of the Potomac invaded Virginia, the Confederate Army of the Mississippi deployed to engage Grant's unsuspecting camp around Shiloh Church.

The Confederate battle plan on the dawn of April 6 deserves brief comment because this too has been disputed. It appears that Johnston's original idea was to turn the Federal left flank away from the river and drive them northwest against the ravines of Owl Creek. Johnston's deployment (delegated to Beauregard), however, was in Napoleonic echelon formation,[13] designed to push the Federals straight into the river or turn either flank, depending on the opportunity. Both plans were flawed because of rugged terrain and the inability of volunteer troops to perform complicated maneuvers during the heat of combat. The predictable result was total chaos at an early stage with all reserves committed on both sides. The surprise achieved against the Federals, though not complete, was stunning. Perhaps Arthur Conger put it better when he noted, "No modern general-staff intelligence section could be forgiven for the total ignorance which existed in each army concerning the other."[14]

The great battle that both sides claimed to have been seeking was now upon them. Comprehensive accounts have been given by other commentators far more vividly than this one could ever do. Those seeking a more detailed, blow-by-blow account of the swirling, kaleidoscopic violence during those three days of April should refer to the works of Shelby Foote, Bruce Catton, Wiley Sword, James Lee McDonough, Larry J. Daniel, and others. In a nutshell, Day One saw the Confederates push the Federals to the brink of destruction before the Northerners were saved by nightfall and stubborn resistance, along with twists of fate that any novelist would have difficulty concocting. On Day Two, after finally being reinforced by Buell, Grant boldly counterattacked and drove the outnumbered but still-defiant Confederates back to their Day One starting point, from which the Southerners began retreating to Corinth. On Day Three, a feeble pursuit by the exhausted Federals ended abruptly when an enraged Nathan Bedford Forrest charged his steed right through Sherman's startled command and somehow managed to escape after being wounded, the last casualty inflicted during the battle. By the time the guns fell silent, the Confederacy's supreme bid to wipe out U.S. Grant had failed.

Although a detailed narrative is outside the scope of this study, a few general observations are appropriate. The severity of the contest is attested to first and foremost by the number of killed, wounded, and missing—well over 20,000[15] and about equal on both sides. While precise figures are not available, the casualty rate for those involved during the first day of fighting may have exceeded that of Sharpsburg/Antietam, the bloodiest documented day in American history. These casualties were more than all previous Civil War battles put together and more than in all previous American wars *combined*.[16] Among the dead were Confederate general-in-chief A.S. Johnston, the highest-ranking American officer ever killed in combat, Confederate General A.H. Gladden, and Union General W.H.L. Wallace.[17] Union General Benjamin Prentice was captured. Other participants included two future U.S. presidents (Grant and James Garfield), one former U.S. vice-president (Confederate General John Breckinridge), the Confederate governor of Tennessee (Isham Harris), and, also among the slain, the Confederate provisional governor of Kentucky (George W. Johnson).[18] As Bruce Catton put it, "The concentrated fury of the fighting had been appalling, and it left its mark for all the rest of the war."[19]

The psychological blow delivered against Grant's surprised Federals was as serious as it could have been short of terminal. Many a terrified Northern soldier for the first time beheld the Confederate battle flag, brought in by Beauregard especially for the occasion. In describing Day One, the Spartan eloquence of Confederate infantryman Sam Watkins ("We were crowding them") remains unsurpassed. Watkins had more to record, however, with a view from the ground level:

> I had heard and read of battlefields, seen pictures of battlefields, of horses and men, of cannon and wagons, all jumbled together, while the ground was strewn with dead and dying and wounded, but I must confess that I never realized the "pomp and circumstance" of the thing called glorious war until I saw this. Men

were lying in every conceivable position; the dead lying with their eyes wide open, the wounded begging piteously for help, and some waving their hats and shouting to us to go forward. It all seemed to me a dream; I seemed to be in sort of a haze, when siz, siz, siz, the minnie balls from the Yankee line began to whistle around our ears, and I thought of the Irishman when he said, "Sure enough, those fellows are shooting bullets!"[20]

This was in front of the infamous "Hornet's Nest"[21] commanded by General Prentice which held the Union center until late in Day One, when it was surrounded and forced into surrender by a Confederate artillery barrage—till then the largest recorded in American history. On the Federal right, Sherman, who saw the worst of all three days, later wrote to his wife, "The scenes on this field would have cured anybody of war."[22]

And what of Grant? After hearing the din of cannonade and musketry while sipping morning coffee upstream at Savannah, he announced that the "ball was in motion"[23] and hailed a steamer south to Pittsburg Landing, where he arrived around 8:30 A.M. as the battle reached full fury. Two days earlier, while on reconnaissance, Grant's horse had slipped in the same mud that was bogging down Johnston's army en route, injuring his leg so badly that during the fight he rode with a crutch strapped to his saddle.[24] This later fueled rumors that he had been drinking at the time of attack but Grant's actions that day were not those of a drunkard. Grant did suggest in his memoirs that he easily could have been completely incapacitated by his fall if not for the soggy ground that he fell upon.[25] Had he been bedridden it is safe to say that the results of the contest would have been different. In addition to sobriety, Grant brought to the field of Shiloh crucial personal qualities for which he would later be legendary—determined poise and businesslike imperturbability.[26] Jean Edward Smith, a former military man, observed that "a general imparts attitude to an army" and this is precisely what Grant contributed at Shiloh to those under his command.[27]

Grant arrived on the scene wearing a sword—somewhat unusual for him—and the scabbard was soon struck by a piece of flying shrapnel that later caused the sword to break off.[28] By incredible contrast, Johnston, while leading a charge against the Hornet's Nest, had an artery in his calf severed by a minié ball of indeterminate origin and bled to death before anyone knew what was happening. Compounding this unlikely scenario, Johnston was hit in a leg reportedly rendered insensitive from sciatica—the result of a duel during his younger days—and appears not to have realized that he was hurt until fainting.[29] He reportedly died with a tourniquet in his pocket, having sent away his personal surgeon to tend Federal wounded and with those around him uncertain what to do.[30]

Writing to Julia on April 3 (the same day the Confederate army left Corinth) Grant remarkably predicted "the greatest battle fought of the War" would soon take place.[31] As at Belmont, however, this was not the battle that

Grant had anticipated. The Federals were hemmed in with their backs against the river, but this time they controlled the river with gunboats.[32] The immediate goal was not to escape (as at Belmont) but to survive the first day and then decide whether to escape (that is, retreat) or to counterattack and gain back what had been lost. By the end of Day One, after tremendous bloodletting, a Federal defensive triangle had been reduced in size by more than half, but still held, and the shortened lines were now stronger and reinforced with artillery.[33] The concentrated decibel levels of Federal cannon and gunboats around Pittsburg Landing that stopped the final Confederate assault were considered by some to be the loudest ever heard during the course of the war.[34]

The infantry on both sides fought with unprecedented valor. Much has been written on the estimated one-quarter of Grant's troops who fled to the rear at the first sound of gunfire; not enough has been written about the other three-quarters who, against all odds and expectations, stayed to resist and take casualties. According to the Confederate playbook, the panic of the Federal "agrarian mercenaries" should have been much greater, and the final assault should have been made by late morning rather than as the sun was going down after their own exhausted army had been badly cut up. Johnston's prediction that they would water their horses in the Tennessee River by noon was a reflection of this mentality.[35] The Confederate advance was slow mainly because large numbers of Federals fought back. Arguably, Shiloh was lost to the Confederacy the moment that three-quarters of the raw Federal volunteers chose to stand instead of run away. Confederate carnage in Sherman's sector alone testified to this determination. Perhaps it was lost at the Hornet's Nest, or perhaps it was lost when Federal troops under General Stephen Hurlbut offered chaotic, at times even suicidal resistance that delayed the Confederate encirclement of Prentice and Wallace. Thus the courage of Grant's "Egyptians" and other state volunteers parried if not equaled that of their opponents.[36] One could argue that because of the initial rout, Northern valor on that first day of Shiloh was of a very special and rare kind, partly attributable to the *esprit de corps* and confidence of victory that had been instilled by their field officers and commanding general. As for the Southerners, their courage on the second and third days while facing defeat was no less amazing—a defiant and orderly resistance in many ways more disciplined than their wild, fragmented attack on Day One.

Union victory at Shiloh was also attributable to superior leadership. After the initial shock, it is hard to find fault with the decisions and movements of Grant and his core staff, which included Sherman, McClernand, W.H.L. Wallace, Prentice, Hurlbut, and McPherson. Above all, a surprised and ill-prepared Grant was still victorious over a Confederate army that had over a month to prepare. As for Confederate leaders, despite undaunted physical bravery and impressive paper credentials, they could do little right before Beauregard ordered a withdrawal on Day Two. Their success till then was attributable to unscripted bravery in the ranks.[37] Blame for exhaustion, confusion and looting that hampered the Confederate advance ultimately rested with their officers—this certainly was Grant's view in the case of volunteer troops. In the words of Arthur Conger, the Confederate high command "ceased to function."[38]

Among the Confederate leaders present, Beauregard was probably the best of the bunch, which is to say he was merely competent. Those who should have been in charge—men like Forrest, Morgan, Cleburne, and Bowen—were still fighting in the ranks at this early stage in the war, unlearning the outmoded lessons of pre-rifled musket tactics inherited by their superiors. Above all, most labored under the colossal false assumption that all Federal "agrarian mercenaries" would run after the first shot. Given the overwhelming surprise achieved, the determination of the Confederates, their probable numeric superiority on Day One,[39] and Grant's initial absence, micro-tactics such as echelon formation or unit coordination became secondary factors. Beauregard's recommendation to postpone on April 5 may have represented a premonition of Confederate failure. Though his stated reasons—lack of surprise, etc.—were specious in hindsight, the real reasons may have been too terrible to say out loud; namely, the best efforts of the Confederate army simply would not be good enough to prevail. For similar reasons, it was psychologically necessary for him to later believe that a great victory had been won, given the unspeakable price paid. Not only was Beauregard's decision to disengage on April 6 wise, his call for retreat on April 7 probably saved his army from annihilation. Nevertheless, Beauregard later became the designated Confederate scapegoat, and remains so—undeservedly in one sense, yet perhaps a fitting legacy for one who masterminded the first truly terrible encounter fought between American armies.

J.F.C. Fuller correctly noted that Johnston's generalship was "nominal" and "of the most meager order" while it was Beauregard who exercised "actual command."[40] Grant himself had a low opinion of Johnston's judgment,[41] clearly implying that the battle could have been won by the Confederates with better leadership. Many subsequent military historians, such as Thomas Connelly, have shared this assessment.[42] Johnston threw his life away leading a charge against the Federal left which, though successful, was still not nearly enough to break the Hornet's Nest, let alone drive the Union line into the river. Nevertheless, in spite of all miscalculations, Johnston came close to success. Grant put it best, writing skeptically that "*Ifs* defeated the Confederates at Shiloh."[43]

Grant's subordinates earned fame as well. Sherman, who went into the battle widely believed crazy and insisting there was no danger, emerged with a steady demeanor resembling sanity, as well as an immunity to true accusations that he had been taken completely by surprise. The effect of Shiloh on

Sherman appeared psychologically beneficial and enabled him to become Grant's most reliable lieutenant.[44] The greatest Confederate failure was on the Federal right, where Sherman skillfully managed troops after finally coming to his senses when a young orderly next to him was shot dead. According to Grant, the Confederates tried to turn the Federal right flank several times and referred to this as "the key to our position."[45] The brave though incompetent John McClernand, stationed next to Sherman, did the Union a big favor that day by fighting under Sherman's wing and doing more or less what he was told. The sacrifice of William Wallace,[46] Benjamin Prentice and their men at the Hornet's Nest was awe-inspiring, towards the end holding off possibly 10 times their number.[47] The greatest Southern success was achieved on the Federal left, but this too was at tremendous cost, including the death of Johnston, and the generalship of Stephen Hurlbut[48] in this sector against superior numbers has never received its proper due.

Among the endless controversies surrounding Shiloh was the precise role played by Buell, whose forces arrived late on April 6 and, along with a tardy division under General Lew Wallace,[49] enabled Grant to successfully counterattack. The myth that Buell "saved the day" on April 6 has been thoroughly debunked by modern historians, along with a persisting misconception that Beauregard blew an opportunity to overrun the Federals at dusk. Even with reinforcements, it is questionable whether anyone but Grant had the will to use them, as opposed to retreating, which is apparently what everyone else wanted to do.[50] Buell was horrendously late to begin with (in a sense instigating the battle), and arrived in time only thanks to Nelson's lead sprint; then after arriving, Buell behaved in a dazed and petty manner according to many who observed him.[51] More than one historian has observed that Buell's fresh army was outperformed on Day Two by Grant's battered troops, particularly those under Sherman.[52] Grant later defended Buell's character but questioned his abilities with volunteer soldiers, as opposed to career professionals.[53]

As a maimed but unrepentant Confederate army retreated to Corinth on April 8, Grant (along with others), found himself disabused of numerous misconceptions. The conventional wisdom of a 90-day war had vanished, Grant noting that "I continued to entertain these views until after the battle of Shiloh."[54] When it was over, he "gave up all idea of saving the Union except by complete conquest."[55] For Grant, the only saving grace was that "[t]he result was a Union victory that gave the men who achieved it great confidence in themselves ever after."[56] On the Confederate side, the favorite general of Jefferson Davis had been killed and the reigning Southern hero (Beauregard) had been toppled.[57] Thomas Connelly: "More than a battle was lost. Beginning with the retreat to Corinth, Beauregard's influence began to decline..."[58] James Lee McDonough reminded us that "If the Confederates had won ... Grant and Sherman ... would probably have been ruined."[59] With an eye on the big picture, Craig Symonds pointed out that a Federal defeat at Shiloh "would not only have changed the momentum in the western theatre but Grant also never would have emerged as the man who captured Vicksburg, saved Chattanooga and led the Overland Campaign."[60]

The last three weeks of April 1862 were anticlimactic by comparison, as almost anything would be. General Henry Halleck arrived at Pittsburg Landing on April 11 to take personal command of the bloodied but still-growing Federal army.[61] Consequently, on April 23, Grant wrote to Julia that he was "no longer boss."[62] Two days later, on April 25, General C.F. Smith, whose key role during the Fort Donelson campaign in February (which inspired the Confederate counteroffensive) helped catapult Grant into celebrity, succumbed to complications from a fluke leg injury sustained back in March. On April 27, Grant reached his 40th birthday. One year earlier he had been slumming around as a civilian in Springfield, Illinois, trying to get someone to notice him; now he was among the best-known and most controversial of all Union generals, having won two of the most important battles of the war within two months.

It was at Shiloh that the great national tragedy first unfolded.[63] Historian James McPherson observed that "Shiloh launched the country onto the floodtide of total war,"[64] while Bruce Catton noted that "people began to feel the tragic impact of what had in truth been the bloodiest battle yet fought in the New World."[65] J.F.C. Fuller added that "its moral influence on the South was crushing."[66] On April 29, 1862, three weeks after the event, New Orleans—the largest city in the Confederacy—surrendered to the Federals, many of its sons having gone to Shiloh and a significant number never coming back.[67] New Orleans author George Washington Cable famously wrote, "The South never smiled again after Shiloh."[68] Perhaps the most appropriate words, however, were written three centuries earlier by the French humanist Montaigne: "And so as we often say, rightly, events and their outcomes depend, especially in war, mainly on Fortune, who will not submit to our reasoning nor be subject to our foresight...."[69]

CHAPTER 14

May 1862: Disgrace

As a traumatized nation tried to process what had happened around Shiloh Church in April, a pensive and abject Grant found himself at the center of a media frenzy. Though the battle is now recognized by historians as a watershed Union victory, this realization was very slow in coming due to the shocking loss of life and limb that had accompanied it. America had finally lost its innocence, or at least was forced to confront reality, and many reacted with hysteria while searching for someone to blame.[1] "U.S." Grant made a good, easy target. By May 1, critical reactions of press, public, and politicians were in full swing. The official tag line was that Grant was a drunken incompetent and imbecile butcher who should be cashiered. Typical phrases included "criminal negligence," "shameful neglect," and "the neglect of one man."[2] This was little more than two months after the press had hailed him as "Unconditional Surrender" Grant. In the field he had been effectively demoted to second-in-command while General Henry Halleck personally supervised the Federal advance on Corinth, delegating responsibilities to just about everyone except Grant. While deflecting criticism of his subordinate in public, Halleck wrote privately to General Ethan Allen Hitchcock in Washington that "Grant is absolutely disgraced and dishonored."[3] Thus, in the words of J.F.C. Fuller, "Grant passed into eclipse" during the spring of 1862.[4]

At this point it is worth remembering that Grant had received his commission less than a year previous thanks to a fluke progression of circumstances. Since that time he had rapidly evolved (with Congressman Washburne's help), from Colonel to Brigadier to Major-General of Volunteers, spearheading the first successful Northern campaign of the war, fighting the bloodiest battle (by far) in American history, and transforming from a complete nobody into a public hero, then into a public scapegoat, all within a matter of months. If he seemed a little dazed and confused during this stage of his career, it is understandable. On May 2, after the initial press salvo paused to catch its breath, Washburne rose on the floor of Congress and delivered a passionate defense of his designated protégé. Washburne pointed out, lest anyone forget, that Grant—with Shiloh, Donelson, Belmont, and the Mexican War under his belt—now had one of the most experienced and enviable combat records of any living American.[5] Thinking in these same terms, President Lincoln displayed crucial good sense when confronted with belligerent and insistent demands for Grant's removal. After listening to one of his own constituents vent, Lincoln matter-of-factly replied, "I can't spare this man; he fights."[6] In comparison to the lethargy and ineffectiveness of other Union generals, Grant's perceived shortcomings no doubt appeared quite manageable.

With regard to his critics, Grant stoically refused to respond. The day after Washburne's speech, however, several Northern papers printed a letter that he had written to his father Jesse Grant in which he tried to explain his thought process at Shiloh. Jesse then forwarded the letter to the press thinking that he was doing his son a favor.[7] In this communiqué, intended only for his father, Grant seemed to waffle, on one hand arguing that "we could not have been better prepared," while a few sentences later maintaining, "I did not believe, however, that they intended to make a determined attack."[8] Predictably, this unwanted publicity only added fuel to the flames, and Grant was extremely put-out with his father's misguided efforts.

To Julia during the early part of the month he variously wrote, "I have been so shockingly abused that I sometimes think it almost time to defend myself," but that ultimately "the best contradiction in the world is to pay no attention to them [the papers]."[9] When the storm first hit in late April, Grant expressed his naïve hope that the press would go easier on him once they got their facts straight:

> I hope the papers will let me alone in the future. If the papers only knew how little ambition I have outside of putting down this rebellion and getting back once more to live quietly and unobtrusively with my family I think they would say less and have fewer falsehoods to their account. I do not look much at the papers now and consequently save myself much uncomfortable feeling....[10]

While Grant had stopped reading the newspapers, he was obviously concerned that his family and particularly his wife had not.[11] In his view, there was not much else to do but hunker down. His stress during this time, however, is best reflected by the unusual (for him) gesture of writing his Methodist clergyman in Galena, the Reverend J.H. Vincent, lamenting, "It has been ... my very bad luck to have attracted the attention of newspaper scribblers."[12] Bruce Catton aptly summed up this period by writing that "Grant rode out the storm, but for a while the waters were rough."[13]

Meanwhile, the wheels continued to turn back in Washington. After delivering his Congressional harangue in defense of Grant, Washburne—in true political style—decided to double-check his facts, after-the-fact, that is. On May 16, Galena native John E. Smith, now a colonel serving under Grant and an eyewitness at Shiloh, reported in to Washburne. Smith, as a fellow townsman never known to be overawed by Grant or to flatter him unnecessarily, verified that the army had been totally surprised by the Confederate attack ("we were astonished"), but then admitted, almost grudgingly, that Grant had indeed been sober the entire time. Others who had been on the scene confirmed similar impressions—not the least of whom was Sherman—and Grant himself wrote a personal letter of explanation to Washburne on May 14.[14]

Washburne, now with both the truth and self-interest on his side, renewed his best efforts to protect Grant from newspapers that were not about to apologize for anything. None other than Joseph Medill, powerful editor-in-chief of the *Chicago Tribune*, wrote personally to Washburne on May 24, warning him for his own good not to try to shield his protégé too much. Shiloh, Medill maintained, "was a most reprehensible surprise followed by an awful slaughter.... The soldiers are down on him."[15] It is true that many people who lost friends and loved ones at Shiloh hated Grant for the rest of their lives. On the other hand, it is also true that many Federal soldiers who survived soon realized that they had indeed won the battle, and in fact now preferred to fight rebels under Grant's controversial leadership as opposed to digging ditches for Henry Halleck while being laughed at by the Confederates.

Another ramification of Shiloh, though rarely commented upon by historians, is that Grant's already fragile relationship with General John McClernand grew much worse. McClernand initiated a new round of hostilities by writing a personal letter to Lincoln, whom he had known on the Illinois court circuit, in which he harshly disparaged Grant's leadership.[16] The final straw for McClernand may have been that after the battle Grant reprimanded him for allowing his troops to fire their weapons indiscriminately even after the enemy was long gone. The fact that McClernand (promoted to Major-General after Donelson) had recently disputed the seniority of Grant's now-deceased mentor, General C.F. Smith, probably stuck in Grant's craw as well. Then throughout the month on May, with time on his hands,[17] Grant bickered with his unruly subordinate over McClernand's slowness to obey commands, a trait that Sherman noticed and was irritated by as well.[18] McClernand, for his part, may well have been miffed that Washburne's profuse Congressional praise of Grant forgot to mention that he too had an impressive combat record that included Shiloh, Donelson, and Belmont.

While Grant's rapport with McClernand continued to deteriorate, his friendship with Sherman grew by leaps and bounds. Comparing Sherman's reaction to press criticism with Grant's following Shiloh is a delightful study in contrasts. Whereas Grant kept a stiff upper lip against false accusations that he had been drunk, he consequently seemed to pay for it even more. Sherman, on the other hand, in response to very legitimate criticisms that he been taken totally by surprise, lashed out with spirit against the pundits, in effect silencing them. Never at a loss for words himself, Sherman also enlisted the powerful help of his Senator brother and banker/attorney in-laws—the Ewings—who made impassioned retorts against any reporter or politician who dared to second-guess Sherman's conduct. This lack of timidity was buttressed by the fact that no soldiers—even those whom he had recently court-martialed for cowardice—could deny that during the battle no one placed his life on the line more than Sherman, who emerged wounded and with bullet holes through his clothing.

In a dramatic gesture of solidarity with Grant, Sherman became livid when Benjamin Stanton,[19] the lieutenant governor of Ohio (Sherman's native state as well as Grant's), went public with criticism, referring to Grant's "blundering stupidity and negligence." Sherman shot back with an uninhibited letter lumping Stanton together with others whom Sherman classified as "intelligent cowards," accused Stanton of misappropriating funds intended for the troops, and then signed off with "Shame on You!"[20] In another one of several broadsides, Sherman placed the blame for all the media hoopla on "scoundrels who fled their ranks"—many of whom were from Ohio regiments—and now needed to divert public attention elsewhere.[21] In Sherman's view, the robbers were the ones crying thief. The end result of this P.R. barrage was that Sherman emerged with what nowadays would be called higher approval ratings, versus Grant, who committed the same mistake at Shiloh (being surprised) and came within a hair's breadth of having his career ended.

By the time the Federal army, now re-equipped, reinforced, and reorganized with some 120,000 troops, began its ponderous advance on Corinth in early May, Grant had been relegated to a figurehead, and not a very popular one at that. Grant was like a fish out of water. In his memoirs he wrote, "For myself I was little more than an observer."[22] On May 11, Grant again offered his resignation to Halleck, who refused it. Halleck wrote back, "For the last three months I have done everything in my power to ward off the attacks which were made on you."[23] This was being less than candid (as Grant would later learn), since Halleck had in the recent past floated the idea of replacing Grant, and would continue to do so for some time.

The slow Federal movement was in complete contrast to the lightning-war tactics favored by Grant. Halleck, in the words of J.F.C. Fuller, "literally dug his way" to Corinth.[24] Another historian with military credentials, Jean Edward Smith, wrote that "the Union army inched forward like a glacier."[25] Grant himself described the campaign as a moving siege.[26] The precise rate of advance was 20 miles in 30 days, or two-thirds of one mile per day, with the Federals digging and fortifying on every one of those days. General John "Black Jack" Logan, who had seen the heaviest fighting in all of Grant's campaigns from Belmont to Shiloh, was heard to remark, "My men will never dig another ditch for Halleck except to bury him."[27] Another good contrast to Halleck's rate of movement was Confederate General Stonewall Jackson, who on May 8 launched his legendary (and still studied) campaign in the Shenandoah Valley in which his men out-marched, outfought, and outsmarted no fewer than three Federal armies simultaneously converging on them.

As the Federals approached the Confederate fortifications at Corinth with over a 2–1 advantage in numbers,[28] they surrounded the town on three sides. At this moment, Grant chipped in with a suggestion to his superior that the encirclement be completed. According to Grant, "I was silenced so quickly that I felt I had suggested an unmilitary movement."[29] Halleck, for his part, believed that the Confederates were about to unleash their phantom hordes in a counterattack, and that, in any event, it was more important to occupy the town than to fight a battle. Therefore, he would give the Southerners a chance to retreat. As Jean Edward Smith put it, Grant's "instinctive recognition that victory lay in relentlessly hounding a defeated army into surrender had yet to gain a place in Union strategy."[30] Moreover, in the words of Bruce Catton, "Halleck underrated Grant, but so did almost everyone else."[31] When Grant's still-loyal staffers finally realized that their wagon was hitched to a fallen star as long as Halleck was around, they tried to suggest to anyone who would listen that Grant be sent east, but nothing came of this.[32] It may have planted the idea, however, for sending John Pope to Virginia after George McClellan's spectacular failure there in early June.

Back in Corinth, Beauregard and the Confederates, now somewhat reinforced but still with less than half the number of their approaching adversaries, licked their wounds and considered their options. At Shiloh they had failed to throw back or even stop the advance of the first large Federal army to penetrate the Southern heartland. Now, with no help from Richmond forthcoming, a decision had to made whether to fight once more against long odds or to withdraw and postpone the match for another day under more favorable circumstances. Beauregard wisely chose the latter, although he was careful not to tip off the Federals, or even Jefferson Davis for that matter, as to his intentions.[33] On May 30, as Halleck braced for the counterattack that he told everyone was coming, the Confederates completed their evacuation of Corinth, utilizing the escape route left to them by the Federals. Trains were heard rolling in and out from the south, and Halleck—with encouragement from his new man-of-the-hour John Pope—believed the trains meant a Confederate buildup when in fact it meant a pullback. Union scouts then inched forward to discover a completely deserted town garrisoned only with "Quaker" log cannons and dummy soldiers—some with smiles painted on their faces—along with derisive placards posted on selected buildings. Anything useful had been carried off or destroyed. Earlier in the month, Grant had written to Julia that "I think the hard fighting in the West will end with the battle of Corinth,"[34] and it may well have been so if a battle had in fact taken place. As it was, much was left to be settled, not the least of which was permanent possession of Corinth by Union or Confederate forces (see Chapter 19).

To the end of his life, Grant felt that the aftermath of Shiloh, like Fort Donelson, represented a lost opportunity to quickly dispose of the western Confederacy. He believed, perhaps correctly, that a two-day campaign commenced immediately after Federal reinforcements arrived at Shiloh would have resulted in the capitulation of Corinth, possibly even saving all of the bloodshed that followed over the next three years.[35] As for his troops, there is evidence that the fall of Corinth was, for them, an empty victory. Grant remarked, "They could not see how the mere occupation of places was to close the war while large and effective rebel armies existed."[36] Bruce Catton observed that it was during this period that the western Federal army, thanks in no small part to Grant's leadership, was beginning to think of itself as unbeatable,[37] and confirming Grant's own observation that their confidence had grown, just as his own personal confidence as a general was bottoming out.

Regarding the siege of Corinth itself, one is reminded of Grant's priceless anecdote from his days as a young officer during the Mexican War. One evening while camped in the middle of nowhere near the Texas border, Grant's green regiment was terrified by the loud, howling sounds of what they were certain was a wolf pack about to devour them. Their lieutenant—a Hoosier who apparently was familiar with these things—sternly ordered Grant to accompany him on a reconnaissance. While crawling towards the howling beasts, clutching their weapons, the grinning lieutenant asked Grant how many wolves he thought were in the pack. Grant opined that there were probably about 20 of them. Upon reaching the site of the canine uproar, they beheld a grand total of two wolves, sitting on their haunches.[38]

CHAPTER 15

June 1862: The Occupation of Memphis

The fall of Corinth, Mississippi, represented the first culmination of an epic campaign begun by Grant four months earlier from Cairo, during which the Union reversed the war tide and made its first major leap towards restoration. Grant himself went from being an obscure and unlikely brigadier at the outset of the campaign to national prominence and controversy. During this short time frame, the border states of Missouri and Kentucky became relatively secured, huge portions of Tennessee, Louisiana, and Mississippi fell to the Federals, including the major cities of Nashville and New Orleans, and the pivotal battles of Fort Donelson and Shiloh had been fought. Four months later (see Chapters 18 and 19), the Confederates would make a forlorn, final attempt to regain what had been lost, but this effort was also destined to be foiled by Grant and his lieutenants.

The beginning of June 1862 saw General Henry Halleck fail to win universal accolades for marching his gargantuan army unopposed into an abandoned Corinth. Northern papers variously classified the Federal triumph as barren and anticlimactic, or praised Beauregard for successfully escaping to Tupelo with his army and supplies intact.[1] Rather than pursue Beauregard, Halleck opted to build mammoth fortifications around Corinth which, according to Grant, were never used.[2] Then he dispersed his forces in every direction, attempting in vain to guard all strategic points in the Mississippi region against partisan fighters and a deeply resentful civilian population. Forced to twiddle his thumbs under Halleck, Grant had time to observe and size up the few local civilians that were still hanging around. On June 3, he wrote to Julia: "All hardships come upon the weak, I cannot say inoffensive, women and children. I believe these latter are worse rebels than the soldiers who fight against us."[3] Beauregard used this gift of time from Halleck to rest and recondition his army back into formidable fighting trim. Meanwhile, in Richmond, the ever-deluded Jefferson Davis, angry that Corinth went down without a fight, rewarded Beauregard's professional skill and good judgment by cashiering him. On June 17, Braxton Bragg, the man responsible for wasting half a day ordering bayonet charges against the Hornet's Nest at Shiloh, was named by Davis as the new general-in-chief for the western Confederate armies.

Soon after Corinth fell, Sherman learned from casual conversation with Halleck that Grant had requested and been given leave to return home.[4] Finding Grant sitting alone in his tent and packing, Sherman asked why the departure and was quietly told by Grant that Sherman knew the reason why. At this moment most people would have said something like "Sorry to see you go, we'll miss you, and good luck." Sherman, however—never known as a hand-holder and going against his style—seems to have been moved, or perhaps, unlike those less perceptive, simply realized what the Federals were about to lose. Marshalling his formidable powers of verbal persuasion, the future terror of Georgia and the Carolinas compared himself to Grant as a case example. Before Shiloh, colleagues and public, following the lead of newspapers, had all labeled him as "crazy"; now, he was in "high feather" after a single engagement. If Grant stayed and hung in there, a similar "happy accident" might change his fortunes, whereas if he went home, things would continue to move along without him. Grant, probably surprised that anyone cared, and who by now surely had a full appreciation for the vicissitudes of fortune, told him he would think about it.[5] On June 6, Sherman received a note from Grant informing him of his decision to stay and Sherman wrote back elatedly, reminding Grant that his earlier victory at Fort Donelson was "more rich in consequences than was the battle of Saratoga...."[6] Soon afterwards, Grant wrote to Julia, praising Sherman at length, especially his performance at Shiloh, adding, "I have never done half justice by him."[7] Thus had it not been for Sherman's forceful arguments—with seemingly little for him to gain at the time—Grant may well have gone back to being an assistant store clerk during the spring of 1862.

On June 6, the same day that Grant told Sherman of his decision, the city of Memphis fell to the Federals, further consolidating their control of the northern Mississippi Valley.[8] This also created an immediate need for military occupation, and Grant was selected to oversee the unwelcome job. In addition to being one of Halleck's many map points to be guarded, Memphis was behind the front lines and probably seemed like a good place to exile his currently out-of-favor subordinate. Nevertheless, Grant seems to have put on a good face by viewing it as an opportunity to command an army once again and perhaps do something useful in the process, as well as a chance to be closer to his wife. This was not quite the "happy accident" that Sherman hypothesized, but it was a major improvement, putting some physical distance between Grant and a superior with whom he would always have a severe personality conflict.

After some minor delays, Grant set out for Memphis on June 21. True to form, he preferred to ride on horseback the 100-odd miles from Corinth with a small escort (a dozen troopers), rather than take the train.[9] Riding out into the countryside, perhaps reflecting on Halleck's pie-in-the-sky attempt to guard thousands of miles of supply lines, Grant noticed that the locals were not exactly feeling the ravages of war:

> The crops around me looked fine, and I had at the moment an idea that about the time they were ready to be gathered the "Yankee" troops would be in the neighborhood and harvest them for the benefit of those engaged in the suppression of the rebellion instead of its support.[10]

The idea of "total war" against civilians was, by increments, slowly gaining acceptance, especially after the horrors of Shiloh and other battles that would soon follow. By the end of the year, total war would become a full-blown reality in Mississippi.

Also en route to Memphis, Grant narrowly avoided capture. While he was being given water at the home of a Tennessee Unionist, a nosey Secessionist neighbor dropped in to visit and upon hearing Grant's name looked at him as if he were the devil incarnate. At this point, his host, overruling objections from his wife, discouraged Grant from staying for dinner. Not fully comprehending the danger he was in, Grant rode blissfully off, only later learning about the sequel of events after arriving in Memphis.[11] The nosey neighbor had made a beeline for the nearest secret Confederate detachment in the neighborhood, led by Colonel William H. Jackson. Jackson's cavalry first sprinted to the house, and finding Grant's party gone, raced to the nearest crossroads where he learned that Grant had passed 45 minutes before. Jackson reasoned that he could not close the gap with Grant so close to Memphis and gave up in disappointment. According to Grant, at that very moment, his party was less than a mile further down the road, sitting under a tree, separated from their weapons, and taking a break, having been earlier rebuffed (for their own good) as dinner guests. The coda to this remarkable incident is that after the war, Jackson, while being paid a friendly visit by Grant, confirmed these details and told his former opponent that he was now glad there was no capture made. Grant wrote that he was glad too.[12] Within a matter of weeks, Grant had barely avoided, first his own resignation from the service, and then becoming a prisoner of war.

Grant arrived in Memphis on June 23 to find most of the city ignoring its Federal occupiers, with Confederate sympathizers "governing much in their own way."[13] These citizens were "thoroughly impressed with the justice of their cause" and thought that the Yankee occupiers even secretly agreed with them.[14] Within a week after beginning his new assignment, Grant had another spat with Halleck over communications, but this time it was via telegraph and he emerged with dignity intact, winning a small battle of written words. After Halleck insinuated that Grant had been ready to "stampede" based on false rumors of nearby enemy strength, Grant correctly pointed out that Halleck was misreading his maps and added, "Stampeding is not my weakness." Halleck replied with "...Nor did I suppose for a moment that you were stampeded...."—as much of an apology as Halleck was capable of giving.[15] Grant's telegram skirmish with Halleck overlapped still more problems he was having with General John McClernand, now among those within his new command district. The end of June saw a repeat of the previous month in that McClernand once again was slow in movement and fast with excuses when being ordered about.[16] Then Sherman, as in the previous month, noticed the same behavior.[17] It appears that after Shiloh, the overly ambitious McClernand saw his chance to eclipse Grant (just as John Pope had recently done), and therefore began to routinely question the organization of command, utilizing every opportunity to drive a deeper wedge between Grant and Halleck. This would eventually backfire, and his behavior in June was a precursor of what would later go down between the two men during the Vicksburg campaign.

Grant's experiences with the civilian population in Memphis were better than those with military colleagues, but still with a fair amount of aggravation. In his memoirs, Grant recalled that most citizen requests brought to his attention were reasonable but that others were not, and listening to the latter tended to take up most of his days. A sampling of the these included complaints that local churches had been "defiled" by Union chaplains preaching from the pulpits, and that all past Memphis debts to the Northern states should be cancelled because of the rebellion. Regarding one attorney who made this claim, Grant wrote, "His impudence was so sublime that I was rather amused than indignant."[18] Startlingly, in a private letter to Julia, Grant laid a good part of the blame for Southern intransigence on Northern abolitionists who kept making trouble by whipping up Confederate sentiment against them.[19]

Grant may have been onto something, because it was indeed during this precise moment in history, and at this exact place, that true emancipation began. Although most of us were taught in school that the slaves were officially freed by President Lincoln's Emancipation Proclamation in the fall of 1862,[20] the de facto process actually began earlier that same year. When Grant's Cairo dogs of war punched their way up the Tennessee and Cumberland Valleys back in February, this was the first time that a Federal army had successfully penetrated the Southern heartland. Until 1864, similar efforts in the East only resulted in Federal armies being sent reeling back whence they came by Robert E. Lee, Stonewall Jackson, and others. In the West it was different, and slaves in this part of the country suddenly found themselves with the option of running to Federal troops for protection, or in some cases, simply refusing to follow their own masters who were fleeing further south as the Yankees advanced. This had even become a minor point of discussion during the surrender of Fort Donelson, as Grant and his perplexed Midwestern farm boys suddenly found themselves in possession of human contraband.

For the Federals, the obvious short-term solution was to confiscate the private property (i.e., slaves) of rebels for public (read: army) use. Regarding this decision, Bruce Catton rightly observed:

> Once this took place, slavery was doomed. What happened in western Tennessee in the middle of 1862 was important, not just because it meant unlimited woe for plantation owners and ordinary farmers, but because the Western soldiers had, in effect, ratified the Emancipation Proclamation before it was even written. They did this by instinct rather than by thought. Back of Grant, Sherman and the others was the vast, still shapeless body of enlisted men, whose emotions were beginning to be dominant for the entire war.[21]

Catton's remarks on this subject are profound and deserve to be quoted at length. Grant's "Egyptians" were not abolitionist crusaders; in fact, most of them were probably outright racist. Moreover, based on letters, many appear to have been totally unimpressed with what they saw of the agricultural antebellum South, and felt no qualms about confiscating anything that they needed.[22] Catton again:

> The soldiers who helped to create the new policy were not reflecting any reasoned change in sentiment about the rights or wrongs of slavery. Most of them came from areas which detested abolitionists, and the sentiment back home had not changed appreciably.[23]

In this sense, the "total war" that Grant and Sherman later made famous began not with plundering foodstuffs, burning down buildings, or destroying infrastructure, but with appropriation of Southern slave labor. This, noted Catton,

> ... marked the beginning of a profound shift in Army opinion. Not only were the soldiers beginning to believe in hard war; they were seeing slavery as the justification for this belief, were blaming it for the war itself, and were coming to feel that slavery must be stamped out along with the rebellion, as if the two were indeed different aspects of the same thing.[24]

Contrary to popular myths perpetuated by fictions such as *Gone with the Wind*, many slaves seemed to prefer being teamsters and cooks and menial laborers for their new masters in blue, as opposed to remaining on the plantation. To this writer's mind, it is one of the supreme ironies of history that the first emancipated slaves in this country were freed (so to speak) by Federal troops who, in all likelihood, had been dead opposed to the idea of emancipation less than a year previous.

A bit of personal family history will help to underscore this point. The author's great-great-grandfather was one William E. Dozier, who, along with his first cousin, Ezekiel Alexander Dozier, were fairly wealthy men with property holdings in Columbia County and Wilkes County, Georgia. The Doziers stood in contrast to my other poor, sharecropping Southern ancestors, and this accumulated wealth was in no small part due to the slaves that they owned. During the war and Reconstruction, all of this changed—thanks to U.S. Grant and his "Egyptian" volunteers. With the Southern economy devastated and no more slave labor, their fortunes waned and my great-great-grandparents appear to have died during the war (the record is sketchy). My great-grandmother, Rebecca Dozier, along with her siblings, ended up living with her married older sister.[25] It was here that Rebecca eventually married (down to) one of my poor sharecropper ancestors, Private Frederick A. Cox of the 37th Georgia Infantry. I prefer to believe that Rebecca, who was a young teen-ager during the war, never learned to turn her nose up at those less fortunate than herself.

Returning to June of 1862, with emancipation in its infancy and Grant dealing with jealous colleagues (along with surly Memphis citizens), guns were being fired in the East—lots of them. General Robert E. Lee, replacing a wounded Joseph Johnston, was named commander-in-chief of the newly christened Army of Northern Virginia by Jefferson Davis. As George McClellan's Federal army crept inch by inch towards Richmond at a pace that would have made even Henry Halleck impatient, Lee studied his lethargic opponent like a cat ready to pounce. By conventional wisdom, Lee had been a questionable choice because of his prewar opposition to secession and his inability the previous year to rescue John Floyd from his own incompetence in West Virginia. Lee, however, had appearance and bearing, which counted for everything in the eyes of Davis. He also had military genius, and many Federals were about to go to their graves because of it. During the last week of June (June 25 through July 1), Lee—though heavily outnumbered and outgunned—launched a series of audacious, pounding blows known as the Seven Days, sending McClellan's shell-shocked Federals skedaddling back to the friendly confines of Washington, D.C. The staggering casualty numbers on both sides were comparable to those of Shiloh, but Richmond had been saved and Northerners found themselves up against a new and frightening adversary in Robert E. Lee.

As McClellan's reputation was being permanently damaged by this fiasco, it was decided in Washington to bring a western general, preferably from Illinois, first as an advisor and then to replace McClellan. John Pope was selected. An indignant Julia Grant recorded the event in her memoir with disdain,[26] but Grant did not even see fit to mention it in his. At the time he was too busy sitting at his desk in Memphis listening to complaints about church pulpits being defiled. Having previously encountered Pope, first making patronage offers in Springfield, then as a lax disciplinarian in Missouri, and finally as an inept strategist in Corinth, Grant probably knew what to expect. As for Pope, he bounded off to join his new army, lamely christened the Army of Virginia, and convinced of his own destiny. This he would meet soon enough in the person of Lee. As for Grant, the comparatively quiet time in Memphis would eventually work to his advantage. Military historian Arthur Conger observed:

The importance of this period in the evolution of Grant the strategist cannot be overestimated ... if we consider him as destined to command all the armies of the United States two years later, we can see how fortunate it was that he should have been given periods of relative inactivity for study and reflection, when he did not have his entire mind occupied each day—as it had been from the time he reached Cairo onward—with petty details appertaining to a purely local situation.[27]

In other words, other Union generals would fail and fade into oblivion while Grant was given a unique opportunity to watch and learn. His pubic disgrace, bad though it was, fell short of ending his career and would end up boosting it in the long run.

CHAPTER 16

July 1862:
Reunited with Family

Memphis was the first large Southern city that Grant was ordered to supervise during the course of the war. Although he had earlier witnessed the occupation of Nashville and few people had greater appreciation of widespread Confederate sympathy in places like St. Louis, this was the first time that all the problems landed right on his desk. One such problem was that a significant number of Memphis citizens had previously or occasionally borne arms against the North as their mood dictated, but also, at least for the time being, were otherwise just ordinary people trying to get by and live their lives. Regarding this class of offenders, Grant wrote in his memoirs that he chose to more or less look the other way because "I deemed it better that a few guilty men should escape than that a great many innocent ones should suffer."[1] This admirable attitude—so seemingly out of place in today's modern world—deserves praise, if not wonder and astonishment. That Grant opted for such a magnanimous policy during the nation's bloodiest and most bitter period of civil strife is more remarkable still. Whatever Grant's faults may or may not have been—drunkenness, bigotry, butchery—for this one virtue alone he should be extolled by history.

While amnesty towards former Confederate combatants would become one of Grant's hallmark traits, this same kind of leniency did not extend everywhere; in fact, non-combatants tended to get the worst of it if they stepped out of line. One such example was the local press. On July 1, after a warning to the editors had been ignored, Grant ordered publication of the *Memphis Avalanche* to be suspended in the wake of articles alleging outrages committed by the city's Federal occupiers.[2] Having been recently burned himself by the Northern press, Grant was probably in no mood to receive similar treatment from Southern journalists. Another example occurred on July 3 when Grant issued a proclamation that government property damage caused by rebel guerilla activity thereafter would be paid for by taxes levied against wealthy citizens who refused to swear loyalty to the Union.[3] Most controversial of all was a July 10 proclamation by Grant that expelled from Memphis all families having members currently serving in the Confederate army or government.[4] This last item drew a threatening letter of protest from Grant's old adversary, the guerilla partisan leader Jeff Thompson. Rather than personally respond, Grant had one of his new sub-commanders, the Indiana lawyer-turned-brigadier general Alvin Hovey, write a reply to Thompson. The gist of Hovey's response was that Tennessee Unionist families were the real victims in Memphis—not Confederates—and that if Thompson intended to do anything about it then he would have to do better than the Confederate army did at Fort Donelson and Shiloh.[5] This entire exchange made quite a contrast from the previous year in which Thompson successfully embarrassed general-in-chief John Frémont after the latter issued his heavy-handed and ineffective proclamation in St. Louis.

Memphis, having been forced back into the Union less than a month previous, was compelled to celebrate the Fourth of July 1862 with fireworks. In the midst of his proclamations against defiant newspapers and civilians, Grant showed up for the festivities dressed like a well-to-do Southern planter.[6] With him were his wife and children. Julia Grant in her memoirs proudly reminded readers that two of their young children—Nellie and Fred—were born on July 4, and recorded that the kids thought the fireworks were exclusively for their birthdays. This may have been a reflection of how sparse local turnout was. According to Julia, birthday girl Nellie remarked of the show, "Why, this is very kind of the rebels."[7] If nothing else, Grant succeeded at Memphis, as he did at Nashville and other places, in defeating resident preconceptions of how "U.S." Grant should look and act.

Also in early July, during the aftermath of spectacular Federal failure along the Virginia peninsula, the "happy accident" that Sherman had earlier wished for Grant now occurred. On July 11, Henry Halleck was named new general-in-chief for all Union armies, and was ordered to report immediately to Washington. This move was made in tandem with an empty-headed and puffed-up John Pope being allowed to take the field against Robert E. Lee and his lieutenants. In the West, however, the unexpected move would produce serendipitous benefits for the Federals. In the words of historian J.F.C. Fuller, "Halleck's promotion to Washington was almost an act of Providence ... his removal from the West set Grant free."[8] Halleck, upon his elevation and transfer, taciturnly ordered Grant to move his headquarters from Memphis to Corinth. Grant was not given a clue as to why or what was going on.[9] Although he was still technically second-in-command in the West, Grant was not Halleck's first or even second choice to be his replacement. Initially, Halleck had asked Secretary of War Stanton if the President wanted to name his successor. "Why not Grant?" may have been the unwelcome response (this is a surmise). Then Halleck offered the job outright, along with a huge promotion, to a surprised Colonel Robert Allen, who, fortunately for Grant, declined, telling an incredulous Halleck that he was already overwhelmed by his duties as chief quartermaster,[10] which had also been the young Lieutenant Grant's job during the Mexican War.

Thus on July 13, Grant, with his family accompanying him, set out for his new assignment filled with uncertainties. Traveling retrograde, first by steamer north up the Mississippi to connect with the railroad at Columbus, Kentucky,[11] Grant peacefully passed through the citadel town that had so defiantly resisted Federal occupation only five months before. This was also where his raid on Belmont had ended ambiguously seven months previous. In addition to the satisfaction this must have brought, Grant was surely thinking of his family's comfort and safety by taking them to Corinth roundabout via boat and rail. This was especially true given his near escape from capture by Colonel Jackson's Confederate cavalry only a few weeks earlier, back in June.

The Grant family arrived in Corinth on July 15, where they would stay together another month. This would be a crucial (yet infrequently remarked upon) period in Grant's rebounding career. Restored to an important command post racked with problems, along with jealousy and mistrust among the Federal commanders (Sherman excepted), Grant would begin his slow climb back to triumph and national prominence with his wife and children by his side on a daily basis. For a person like him, the benefit was huge, and it was not something that had been planned in advance—it just happened. In addition to emotional stability, Grant was able to eat well and had gained 15 pounds since the grueling Shiloh campaign and its aftermath. This was due exclusively to Julia, who catered to his tastes.[12] She also kept him away from alcohol. Julia herself many years later recalled their dramatic nighttime arrival in Corinth, with thousands of Union troops sitting around campfires and singing "John Brown."[13] The image, whether real or partly imagined, is appropriate given that the man who would eventually lead the Federals to victory was now back commanding an army in the front lines after an imposed three-month hiatus.

While stationed in Corinth, the Grants did not live in barracks; in fact, they were quite commodiously situated. This was the result of a confiscation. To repeat, Grant's lenient attitude toward ex–Confederate soldiers did not extend to non-combatants. One such unfortunate individual was Francis Whitfield, a Corinth plantation owner whose daughter described him as "one of the hottest rebels around here." Mr. Whitfield, it appears, made the double mistake of being discovered as a Confederate informant and then showing no remorse. After refusing to take a loyalty oath, Mr. Whitfield was expeditiously shipped north to Federal prison camp on July 17 while his plantation was converted into Union headquarters.[14] Julia, who had a real taste for the antebellum lifestyle and appreciated such things, described the house in her memoirs:

> The General's headquarters were in a handsome and very comfortable country house, situated in a magnificent oak grove of great extent. The house was a frame

one, surrounded by wide piazzas, sheltered by some sweet odor-giving vine—
Madeira vine, I think. On the grounds were plantain, mimosa, and magnolia
trees. A wide walk extended around the house. It was like a garden walk without
sand or pebbles in it, only the mold or earth. It was kept in fine order, as it was
sprinkled and raked morning and evening.[15]

Later, an angry Whitfield accused the Grants of carrying off his furniture.
These charges, however, were later personally investigated by that fearless,
Yankee-hating warrior, Nathan Bedford Forrest, who determined the accusa-
tion to be unfounded (see note 14).

After settling in with his family, Grant got down to business. The first
order was to dismantle the cumbersome fortifications around town that Halleck had built in June and replace these with more practical ones that could
be defended with fewer troops.[16] The problem was a very real one since the
magnificent 120,000-strong Federal army that marched into Corinth back in
May had now been scattered to the four winds by Halleck. After Grant returned
to Corinth, even more troops were detached to reinforce Don Carlos Buell,
whose forces were creeping tentatively southeast towards Chattanooga, Tennessee. As Jean Edward Smith wrote, the Federals now "were dispersed from
hell to breakfast."[17] Grant was now responsible for guarding the critical railroad junction of Corinth, the recently conquered Memphis on the Mississippi
River, and everything in between, from the likes of Nathan Bedford Forrest
and John Hunt Morgan. This daunting if not impossible task forced him, for
the first and only time in his career, to think in defensive terms.[18]

One of Grant's first decisions was to send to Sherman to Memphis (with
Stephen Hurlbut as adjunct), where he would prove to be a highly effective
though somewhat draconian military governor. McClernand was sent to Jackson, Tennessee (which lay roughly equidistant and north of Memphis and
Corinth), to guard the backlines. It is hard to resist the impression that Grant
was putting McClernand out of the way as punishment for his recent conniv-
ing, similar to the way in which Halleck had recently exiled Grant to Memphis. To assist with the defense of Corinth and environs, Grant now had
under his command Major-General William Rosecrans, who the previous year
had played a key role in helping George McClellan to secure West Virginia,
and now took over the Federal troops left behind by the recently departed
John Pope. Rosecrans would soon prove his mettle as a combat commander
during some of the most desperate fighting seen in the western theater. Unlike
Sherman, however, he would also prove to be constantly at odds with Grant
over military strategy and ultimately incompatible with him in terms of personal temperament.

On July 22, taking careful note of Halleck's dispersals and the indecisive
movements of Buell, General Braxton Bragg moved his rejuvenated Confederate army via railroad out of Tupelo and towards Chattanooga (via Mobile
and Atlanta), eventually beating Buell to that strategic point before the latter

realized what was happening. Alerted to Bragg's movement through the daring cavalry reconnaissance of a promising but pugnacious colonel from Ohio named Philip H. Sheridan,[19] Grant quickly telegraphed a warning to Buell that was to no avail.[20] Meanwhile back in Corinth, Grant braced for what he correctly sensed would eventually come his way in the form of yet two more Confederate armies assembling in his sector under the separate commands of Generals Sterling Price and Earl Van Dorn.[21] By July 30, Price had pushed to Holly Springs, about 40 miles from Corinth, but when Grant requested permission from Halleck to go after this menace, he was discouragingly told above all to be prepared to reinforce Buell.[22] This maneuvering in late July marked the embryonic stage of a pivotal fall campaign in which the Southerners would seek to recapture not only Corinth, Mississippi, but regain the entire states of Tennessee and Kentucky as well.

As anxiety mounted over the Confederates' recent seizure of initiative, military tensions also grew in Memphis under Sherman's watch. Part of the reason for this problem was that not long after the Federal occupation began in June, a booming illicit trade opened up between local cotton dealers—supposedly loyal to the Union—and Northern speculators who paid for merchandise in gold and silver. This hard currency would then be swiftly funneled South and put to use for the Confederate war effort. Apolitical civilian profiteers got rich fast while rebel government coffers were replenished. Noticing this robust commerce, many a Federal officer (and some enlisted men as well) reacted by deciding that they too wanted a piece of the action. Unionists who did not want to get their hands dirty had to watch the whole thing in dismay. Grant succinctly observed that "It was also demoralizing to the troops."[23] It was also free enterprise at its most unregulated and had the full support of Washington politicians.

Nevertheless, on July 25, Grant, with the backing of both Sherman and McClernand,[24] ordered that the purchase of cotton with gold and silver be prohibited. The next day, in a letter written to Brigadier General Isaac Quinby, stationed at Columbus—the entry point for Northern profiteers—Grant specified that all suspicious baggage should be checked for gold and silver currency, and that "Jews should receive special attention."[25] Grant's proclamation was countermanded by his superiors within a matter of days. On July 31, Grant vainly vented his frustration in a letter to U.S. Treasury Secretary Salmon P. Chase. After pointing out that all communications in his sector had been strained to the breaking point due to behind-the-lines partisan activity, his army was now called upon to protect the commerce of their enemies. As to the Northern speculators who were involved, Grant in so many words called them traitors and, more euphemistically, "a class of greedy traders."[26]

That would not be the end of it. This embarrassing episode in late July represented a clear precursor of Grant's infamous "obnoxious order" against the Jews in Memphis six months later, after the first push against Vicksburg came to naught (see Chapter 21). One may try to excuse Grant with the obser-vation that he suddenly had a lot on his plate, especially with newly inspired Confederate armies resolved to take back everything that his army had won for the Federals during the first half of the year. On the other hand, the failed entrepreneur from Galena once again displayed his insecurity when it came to business matters. Grant may have been the victor of Shiloh, but regulating free market trade in Memphis was a different kind of fight. He was better at leading armies into battle than he was trying to rein in unregulated capital-ists. The only thing that can be said in Grant's favor regarding the Memphis cotton trade is that he was far from alone in his attitudes. Indeed, his frus-trated attempt to clamp down on unscrupulous commerce, however misguided, probably put a damper at least on officers under his own command who were engaged in these activities as middlemen. His anti–Semitism may have even made him more popular with the troops, most of whom shared this preju-dice.

As a field commander, however, Grant continued to grow and master his trade. The situation he inherited at Corinth during the summer of 1862 would have surely been the downfall of many a lesser-gifted general. Regarding this situation in northern Mississippi and western Tennessee, military historian Arthur Conger perceptively observed that "here was almost a repetition of that when he [Grant] first went to Cairo, though on a larger scale with regard to both forces and territory." Not quite one year previous Grant had found him-self stationed in Cairo, Illinois, facing a strong enemy with roving bands of partisan rangers on both flanks and surrounded on all sides by resentful, unco-operative civilians. Colonel Conger elaborated:

> Grant, again as he had done at Cairo, learned to distinguish the points essential to be occupied from those which were not so; to study how to make the most of every unit under his command; to guard his broad front, on the defensive—than which there is no better training, particularly for a commander with an aggressive disposition.[27]

Over the next three months, the little rumpled man from Galena would prove superb at this activity, although for him it was a new kind of challenge. Hav-ing his beloved family at hand in a comfortable setting during the first six-week phase of this period did not hurt, either. For that, Grant could be grateful to the defiant Francis Whitfield for lending his plantation to the Federal cause. Meanwhile, to the east, other inferior-led Union armies would soon find themselves being chased halfway to the North Pole.

CHAPTER 17

August 1862: "The Most Anxious Period of the War"

The cause of the great War of the Rebellion against the United States will have to be attributed to slavery.

—Grant[1]

In Grant's *Personal Memoirs* he recalled receiving orders on August 2 to the effect that he was to now handle rebels "without kid gloves" and to "live off the country" whenever necessary.[2] Although Grant appears to have been conflicted on these two points at this earlier stage of the war (especially with respect to the first item), these new directives reflected a growing sense of tension across the board as Confederate forces both East and West began mass movements to regain lost territories. Though back in charge of Federal operations in the Mississippi Valley, Grant felt highly constrained as his troops continued to be dispersed within his department, or worse, completely taken away from him and sent to other sectors. Grant did not even feel secure in his job and wrote to his father on August 3 that he expected to be eventually replaced by Halleck's friend, General Ethan Allen Hitchcock.[3] The backlash and stigma of Shiloh had far from subsided. Overall, Grant spent the month of August dealing with contraband (both human and otherwise) within his lines, and shoring up troop discipline in preparation for what he correctly anticipated would soon happen.

In the same letter to Jesse that Grant expressed pessimism over his own future, he wrote, "I have no hobby of my own with regard to the negro, either to effect his freedom or to continue his bondage."[4] This well-documented early apathy of Grant towards slavery was in complete contrast to his father's stern disapproval of the institution, which surely had contributed to strained relations between the Grants and their Dent in-laws. It is important to recall at this point in history that President Lincoln's Emancipation Proclamation would be issued in less than two months. This landmark declaration would follow in the immediate wake of Grant's victorious western armies appropriating slave labor for their own purposes, along with the bloodiest recorded day in American history, soon to be played out in September along Antietam Creek, near the town of Sharpsburg, Maryland.

Grant's stereotypical and ambiguous attitude towards the slaves makes an interesting comparison with that of President Lincoln, especially during this same time frame. As Grant's baffled Midwesterners received first hand exposure to the evil, preconceptions gradually shifted from outright prejudice and ignorance to a kind of instinctive pragmatism. Less than nine months previous, on November 27, 1861, in the aftermath of Belmont, Grant had written to his father these extraordinary sentences:

> My inclination is to whip the rebellion into submission, preserving all constitutional rights. If it cannot be whipped in any other way than through a war against slavery, let it come to that legitimately. If it is necessary that slavery should fall that the Republic may continue its existence, let slavery go. But that portion of the press that advocates the beginning of such a war now, are as great enemies to their country as if they were open and avowed secessionists.[5]

For students of emancipation, this has a familiar ring. Abraham Lincoln is quoted as saying, "If I could save the Union without freeing *any* slave I would do it, and if I could save it by freeing *all* the slaves I would do it; and if I could save it by freeing some and leaving others alone, I would also do that."[6] Had Grant read Lincoln's speech? No, because Lincoln was replying to a Horace Greeley editorial from August 22, 1862,[7] nine months and three weeks, respectively, after Grant's letters to his father in which he expresses a similar idea. Was Lincoln copying Grant? Certainly not; on the other hand, Lincoln—the consummate politician—was in tune with Northern opinion, which was well-embodied by men like Grant and those serving under him. Nevertheless, emancipation would be proclaimed one month later, at which point it would become a war both to restore the Union and to abolish slavery.

It is worth repeating that Grant and his army of unwitting liberators were probably beginning to realize that the time had come for emancipation, though they may not have cared to say it aloud. In a letter to his sister Mary on August 19, Grant hints at the seismic shift then occurring and his own role in the process: "Their [the slave owners'] *institution* [the slaves] are beginning to have ideas of their own.... I don't know what is to become of these poor people in the end but [it is] weakening the enemy to take them from them."[8] The very fact that Julia Grant discovered the troops singing *John Brown* around campfires when she first arrived in Corinth is highly suggestive of an attitude adjustment. These boys had not originally signed on to be freedom fighters; however, with Shiloh now behind them and everyone realizing that much, much more hard fighting lay ahead, it may have been psychologically necessary for them to convert what had been a purely political struggle into a crusade against slavery. Those among them who still thought otherwise could at least agree that it was better to confiscate rebel contraband for menial labor while they themselves did the fighting.

In early August another event occurred, the long-term repercussions of which are still being hotly debated amongst the most eminent Grant scholars (see Chapter 27). On August 8, Grant wrote an order for Sherman in Memphis. With barely disguised, angry glee, Grant directed him to immediately arrest and incarcerate journalist Warren P. Isham of the *Chicago Times*.[9] The *Times*, widely perceived as a Copperhead paper, plus one with a very wide circulation (especially among Federal troops), had recently published a sensationalist story by Isham (who was also the brother-in-law of the paper's editor), writing under the pen name of "Shiloh."[10] The story, which was completely fabricated, reported that a fleet of Confederate ironclads had smashed through the Union blockade in and around the vicinity of Mobile Bay. The legendary Sylvanus Cadwallader,[11] who would eventually become Grant's sidekick as a result of this story, gave a perfectly believable explanation for Isham's behavior, as well as the motives of the *Chicago Times* in publishing such a controversial piece:

> It delighted in seeing how near it could approach the line of actual disloyalty without incurring the penalty. Mr. Isham was considered one of the most brilliant correspondents in that department, but was never sufficiently careful and guarded in his statements. He had been cautioned by General Grant once or twice before this against giving such free range to his imagination. This last offense was that of sending off for publication a "cock and bull" story about a fleet of rebel iron-clads at Pensacola, which he claimed to have received by "grapevine" telegraph through the Southern Confederacy."[12]

Grant, as I have noted, was not well-disposed towards journalists at this point in his career, and neither was Sherman. In the words of Cadwallader, "The order could not have been placed in the hands of a more willing officer in the department."[13] On August 17, Sherman wrote a jocular letter to Grant, proudly noting the rough treatment that he had given to Isham. After rejecting all of Isham's appeals, Sherman derided his use of the pseudonym (his "false name") "Shiloh" and blandly wrote to Grant that "I regard all these newspaper harpies as spies."[14] Grant, for his part, to the end of his days expressed what could be interpreted as admiration for the way in which the Southern Confederacy effectively silenced all media opposition within its controlled boundaries during wartime.[15] To make an example out of Isham and to vent their own frustration, Grant and Sherman had him locked up and the key thrown away until Cadwallader came to his rescue a few months later. The *Chicago Tribune* (a competitor of the *Chicago Times*) of course applauded the action.[16]

In retrospect, poor Warren P. Isham was in the wrong place at the wrong time. Tensions were running high and someone had to pay for it. By mid–August, Grant, who often had his wife and children near his person while fighting was going on, decided that it would now be safer for them to leave Corinth. Writing to Mary Grant on August 19, he explained, "Things however began to look so threatening that I thought it best for them to leave."[17] Shortly before Julia's idyllic six weeks together with her husband had ended, she correctly sensed espionage taking place about headquarters, specifically noticing a man who later proved to be a double agent.[18] Everyone seemed to know that the uneasy post–Shiloh interlude of peace was about to end, as indeed it would.

In addition to being parted from his family and clamping down on loose-cannon reporters, Grant was still having to cope with the ever-more-difficult General John McClernand. Having temporarily put McClernand out of the way in Jackson, Tennessee, Grant had to deal with a new spat after sending a contingent under General Edward Ord to nearby Bolivar, Tennessee. McClernand took exception to another Union general operating within what he perceived to be his fiefdom and protested sharply. On August 17 Grant wrote a cool reply in which he reminded McClernand that the latter commanded troops and not territory, and that it was Grant himself who commanded all of the troops. McClernand whined back defensively on the following day that Grant's reminder was "a boast of authority uncalled for anything I have said or done."[19] Curiously, a week later on August 25, Halleck ordered Grant to send McClernand back to Springfield, Illinois, for the purpose of raising more volunteers, an activity that McClernand the politician and speech-giver excelled at.[20] While the need for more troops in this dispersed sector was very real and pressing, the opportunity to remove McClernand from the zone of combat by Halleck and Grant was a bonus. For the first time since the war began, the two West Pointers (Halleck and Grant) truly saw eye-to-eye on something—McClernand's liability in the field.

On the other end of the spectrum within Grant's department was the talented up-and-comer, Major-General William Rosecrans, who had now become Grant's new point man facing Confederate forces in Mississippi. A lively correspondence between the two generals transpired during this period, with Rosecrans eventually being stationed at the railroad town of Iuka, Mississippi, about 25 miles southeast of Corinth. It was here that Grant correctly surmised trouble would first hit. Acknowledging the need to temporarily think in defensive terms, Grant wrote to Rosecrans on August 17 that "we will have to draw in our horns a little for the present, and spread again when we can."[21] Rosecrans, for his part, displayed at a very early stage his reluctance (unlike Sherman) to follow the strict letter of Grant's orders, such as his questioning of troop distributions at the beginning of the month.[22] In August of 1862 there was every reason to believe that Rosecrans would one day supercede Grant in command, given his talent and ambition. Grant himself seems to have recognized it and at this point was more intent on using Rosecrans' abilities to the Federal advantage, rather than holding him back as, say, Halleck had done to Grant. Julia Grant, though extremely jealous of her husband's reputation, acknowledged, "I liked Rosecrans too. He was handsome and brave, and I liked him also because the General did."[23]

The Federals needed all the ability they could get. On August 18, the Federal garrison at Clarksville, Tennessee, surrendered to a Confederate raiding party after it had been duped into believing they were outnumbered. Commanding the garrison was Colonel Rodney Mason, who, after having fled the field at Shiloh in disgrace, successfully played on his superior's compassionate nature by persuading him to allow Mason a command post way behind the front lines. Mason's premature capitulation was later recalled by Grant as being "among other embarrassments" that occurred at the time.[24] Though Clarksville was quickly retaken by Federal reinforcements after the raiders made tracks, this incident underscored the need to have competent officers such as Sherman to guard and maintain order in critical points like Memphis.

Grant's biggest problem during this period, though, was that his sector was currently viewed by Washington and the public as—to borrow a phrase from Sam Watkins—a side show to the big show, or to be more precise, a side show of a side show. Generals, politicians and public were focused on operations in Virginia or perhaps in Buell's fumbling eastern Tennessee campaign. By mid–August, Grant was ordered to sent yet two more divisions to reinforce Buell, who was then scrambling to catch up with Bragg's Confederate army racing north from Chattanooga. This left Grant at Corinth with barely enough troops to hold his own against forces led by Price and Van Dorn in the Mississippi Valley. Grant to his last days maintained, "The most anxious period of the war, to me, was during the time the Army of the Tennessee was guarding the territory acquired by the fall of Corinth and Memphis and before I was sufficiently reinforced to take the offensive."[25] As the month of August wound down, he found himself dealing simultaneously with troop shortages, runaway slaves, hostile news reporters, subordinates who were incompetent and/or uncooperative, double agents in his own headquarters, and gathering Confederate forces that were preparing once again to give him their best shot.

On August 28, Bragg's 30,000-strong army began its rapid trek north from Chattanooga to the Kentucky state line and beyond, while the ever-tentative Buell raced to catch up. The audacious Confederate strategy was to link up with forces under General Kirby Smith, which simultaneously began a sprint out of Knoxville, Tennessee, towards Lexington, Kentucky. Meanwhile, it was expected that Sterling Price would bring up his troops from the West by bowling over his now thinned-out opposition in Mississippi. These combined armies would then wreak havoc upon the Ohio Valley after defeating Buell, that is, if he dared to engage. Such a plan could do more than regain lost Confederate territory—it could win the war for the South. Cities such as Louisville and Cincinnati were not exactly abolitionist hotbeds, as Ohio Valley natives like Grant, Sherman, and Sheridan knew all too well. One problem with Bragg's grand plan was that it seriously overestimated rebel sympathy in a state (Kentucky) that the previous year had voted itself neutral only to be invaded by Confederate armies a few months later. Another flaw was that Bragg seemed to ignore what Grant was capable of bringing to the mix, Shiloh having apparently taught the western Confederate general-in-chief nothing in this regard. In the words of historian Charles Bracelen Flood, "[T]he Confederate high command underestimated what he [Grant] could do with the reduced Union forces he still had with him."[26] Bragg may have been better off allowing Buell to build his own railroad all the way to Chattanooga. Nevertheless, the Confederate movement at the end of August generated panic and consternation in the North, and would eventually succeed in ending for all practical purposes the Civil War career of Don Carlos Buell.

As bad as things now were in the West, in the East they had become critical. On August 29th and 30th, as Bragg and Smith's armies began their rapid push north, the Battle of Second Manassas[27] was fought in northern Virginia. A prelude to this had been the Battle of Cedar Mountain, Virginia, fought on August 9, in which a recklessly aggressive Federal army under General Nathaniel Banks had been given a sound thrashing by Stonewall Jackson. Now at Manassas, with the impetuous John Pope given a chance to show what he could do with a large field command, the Federals were handed their bloodiest defeat to date. Over the course of two days, Confederates under Robert E. Lee, Stonewall Jackson, and others took turns using Pope's hapless and mismanaged Army of Virginia as a punching bag. By the time it was over, the Federals had suffered some 16,000 casualties and their survivors were straggling back to Washington. Rather than pursue the beaten enemy into its citadel, however, Lee opted to launch a full-fledged Northern invasion of his own, hoping to draw the prey once more out of its den. Thus the end of the month saw not one, but two concerted Southern offensives into Union territory, Maryland and Kentucky, respectively. The latter was planning to be reinforced by a successful movement in Grant's sector. More than one historian has rightfully called this period the high tide of the Confederate war effort, though it occurred only three months after Grant's victory at Shiloh and McClellan's near approach to Richmond on the Peninsula. These three months were also Grant's most inactive period during the entire war, except for the first seven months before Belmont, which represented a similar interval of Federal failure and setbacks.

One hypothetical question naturally poses itself: what if Grant had been brought east to fight Lee rather than John Pope in August of 1862? As much as I admire Grant the soldier, I think the end result would have been similar for the Federals, though probably less disastrous. The Ulysses S. Grant of August 1862 was not the Grant of April 1864. He was probably just not ready at this point to face off against Lee, Jackson, and company. The ancient historian Plutarch tells us of how, in his opinion, Julius Caesar had to first defeat the Gauls before he was ready to wage war against Pompey, much the same way an expert wrestler must sometimes retire and develop his skills before challenging a champion. The same idea likely applied to Grant at this point in time. Vicksburg, Chattanooga and the West still had to be won before Richmond could fall. One thing that can be argued with more confidence, however, is that had Grant been in Buell's place, the climactic battle for the West in 1862 would have been fought around Chattanooga in August, rather than hundreds of miles north at Perryville, Kentucky, in October. Then again, the "what ifs" of history are relevant only to those who are interested in not repeating the mistakes of the past.

CHAPTER 18

September 1862: Acoustic Shadow at Iuka

... many loyal people despaired in the fall of 1862 of ever saving the Union.
—Grant[1]

On September 2, Henry Halleck ordered Grant to send yet another division from Corinth to the aid of an embattled Don Carlos Buell in Kentucky, this time one under General Gordon Granger, which included the services of recently promoted Brigadier General Philip H. Sheridan. As a surprising new campaign unfolded in eastern Tennessee and Kentucky, Buell finally realized that Braxton Bragg had completely outmaneuvered him and was racing north to terrorize anything in his path. The month of September 1862 would see most of east-central Tennessee temporarily fall back into Confederate hands without a single shot being fired. Meanwhile in the East, Robert E. Lee's victorious army would march into Maryland looking to deliver a knockout blow to the Union cause. President Lincoln, Henry Halleck, and all Union sympathizers were understandably mortified at these unexpected developments.

Buell, with Northern politicians beginning to call for his head, now had to do more than merely catch up with Bragg—he had to outrace him to the Ohio River. Accordingly, Granger's division was ordered directly to Louisville and departed from Corinth on September 4. Grant noted that Granger and Sheridan beat Buell to Louisville (though they had a much greater distance to cover) and had the city fortified before their commander even arrived. At this point in his career, Sheridan was more interested in fighting high-profiled battles, possibly in defense of his home state (Ohio), rather than (supposedly) sitting idle with Grant, who was still under a cloud after Shiloh. With respect to Sheridan's hurried, unsentimental departure, Grant wrote, "I felt a little nettled at his desire to get away and did not detain him."[2] Grant and Sheridan would meet again a year later under completely different circumstances at Chattanooga.

While Bragg and Kirby Smith continued to make Buell look inept in Tennessee (much the way Grant had done the same to Albert Sidney Johnston earlier in the year), the Southerners were once again guilty of making superficial assumptions. Though a bumbler himself, Buell now had some good subordinates in people like Sheridan (and later General George Thomas), plus a large, well-supplied army that was capable of tenacious fighting under inspired leadership. More egregiously, the attitudes of Bragg, Smith, Price, and Van Dorn toward Grant in Corinth are difficult to fathom, even in hindsight. Writing euphorically to Price in early September, Bragg ordered him to advance and said that he expected Price and Van Dorn to defeat Sherman and Rosecrans at their leisure, then to meet Smith and himself in the Ohio Valley.[3] The lack of reference to Grant (who commanded Sherman and Rosecrans), is striking. One is tempted to conclude that Bragg still could not admit to himself that he had been whipped by Grant at Shiloh, preferring instead (like many other deluded Confederates) to blame Beauregard for not ordering a miraculous *coup de grâce* on Day One of that controversial battle. In his mind, Grant was apparently just another Yankee bureaucrat to be ignored—and a drunken one at that—certainly not the equal of Bragg's direct opponent Buell.

Bragg was not the only Southerner having trouble thinking straight. On September 13, Sterling Price, with hundreds of square miles of unoccupied terrain to choose from, opted to occupy Iuka, Mississippi, in effect daring Rosecrans to attack him.[4] Jean Edward Smith observed, "It was a strategic miscalculation of the first magnitude."[5] Grant had been tipped off the week before that Price and Van Dorn were on the move, presumably to join Bragg, and was only surprised that Price offered himself up as an easy target before he and Van Dorn linked up.[6]

On September 14, Grant wrote a noteworthy letter to Julia in which he accurately forecasted events to occur over the next month: "I am concentrated and strong. Will give the rebels a tremendous thrashing if they come...."[7] Though now reduced in strength to fewer than 50,000 troops in his department,[8] Grant had these skillfully distributed under able commanders and waited for the Confederates to make mistakes, which they were prompt in doing. In the same letter to Julia, Grant promised:

> You will see the greatest fall in a few weeks of rebel hopes that was ever known. They have made a bold effort, and with wonderful success, but it is a spasmodic effort without anything behind to fall back on. When they do begin to fall all resources are at an end and rebellion will soon show a rapid decline.[9]

A bit of an overstatement, perhaps, but not too far off the mark. The high tide of the Confederacy would be receding within a matter of weeks, if not days. Grant's skill as a department commander would play a significant though infrequently remarked upon role in the process, and in many ways his was the most impressive performance among many involved in the Federal high command.

Meanwhile, in the East, as Grant prepared to intercept Price, events moved towards a similar but far more sanguinary climax. On September 9, George McClellan was restored to command and inject morale into the beaten, cowering Federal army then sheltering itself in Washington, D.C. Concurrently, Robert E. Lee prepared to launch his first all-out invasion of the North. By September 15, Harpers Ferry, Virginia, had been taken back by the Confederates and Lee's army was marching through Maryland doing its best to provoke McClellan into the field. After an intercepted message, however, tipped McClellan off as to the Army of Northern Virginia's scattered deployment, Lee suddenly found himself near Sharpsburg, Maryland, being confronted by a huge Federal army that outnumbered him nearly 2–1.

Rather than gracefully retreat, and in a move typical of his poker-faced and unpredictable nature, Lee coolly faced about and offered battle to the Federals, fooling a timid McClellan into believing that the opposing armies had comparable numbers. On September 17, 1862, came the bloodiest documented day in American history. When it was over, nothing had much changed except for some 23,000 dead, wounded, and missing Americans scattered along Antietam Creek. After the two maimed armies glared at each other across the battlefield for another day, the Southerners began an unmolested retreat back to Virginia. Allowing himself once again to be intimidated would soon cost McClellan his job for a second time, and permanently at that.

Fighting in this pointless massacre were many of my ancestors. On the Confederate side, two of my great-great-grandfathers were present at Sharpsburg, Private Burl Washington Nail of the 27th Georgia Infantry and Private Thomas J. Cox of the 13th Georgia Infantry, the latter emerging disabled for life with a leg wound.[10] The vast majority of my Confederate veteran forefathers, though mostly from Georgia, had signed up to fight under Lee in Virginia, partly because they themselves had ancestral roots in the East and also because this was where the "big show," as Sam Watkins coined it, was taking place. As Northerners and Southerners unsuccessfully tried to invade each other's territory in the East during the first three years of the conflict, however, tangible, long-term results were manifesting in the West. Little did my ancestors probably know at the time that the war was really being decided in the West, although few people would come to this realization until the following year, and many have yet to come to it.

On the very same day that the guns of Sharpsburg/Antietam were roaring, Grant wrote a uniquely combative letter to his father Jesse, with whom he had been displeased for some time on a number of accounts. Responding to what appears to have been a laundry list of fatherly requests, Grant began by releasing a fair amount of pent-up frustration: "I now have all my time taxed. Although occupying a position attracting but little attention at this time there is probably no garrison more threatened today than this...." Then came the unpleasant part, Grant having heard that Jesse had been trying to defend his son's reputation by disparaging fellow Union officers:

I would write you many particulars but you are so imprudent that I dare not trust you with them; and while I am on this subject let me say a word. I have not an enemy in the world who has done me so much injury as you in your efforts in my defense. I require no defenders and for my sake let me alone....

Then Grant pointed out, rather unfairly,[11] that his reputation seemed to be the worst around Cincinnati, which lay opposite the Ohio River from Covington, Kentucky, where his father lived. Finally, he rebuffed Jesse's request to put in a word for a friend's appointment, telling him he had nothing to do with such things (again not true), although in fairness Grant may have been trying to minimize the sort of influence peddling he had always despised, especially with regards to family. Grant signed off this extraordinary letter with "My love to all at home."[12] The very same day (September 17), he wrote to his sister Mary, asking her to peruse the enclosed missive he had just penned to their father and explaining, "I have not been very well for several weeks but so much to do that I cannot get sick."[13] This was also several weeks after Julia and the children had departed from Corinth and he was likely feeling lonesome.

Grant's "so much to do" was no exaggeration, either. In response to Sterling Price's move on the chessboard of northern Mississippi, Grant had begun his own maneuvering towards Iuka on September 16. For this engagement, however, Grant intended to trap Price in a pincer movement between forces delegated to Generals Rosecrans and Ord, while Grant himself remained in nearby Burnsville directing traffic. Rosecrans was to move west and then south of Iuka and engage Price, with Ord to join in the attack from the north upon hearing the sound of guns.[14] On paper it was a good plan. Grant arrived in person at Burnsville on September 18, while Rosecrans continued his flanking maneuver against Price. Ord drove back the advance elements of Price's Confederates from the other direction and then prepared to charge the moment Rosecrans arrived.[15] One Illinois soldier remembered that at this time Rosecrans would have won a popularity contest among soldiers, but Grant was still well-liked even though he had been derided by the press all year, except in the brief aftermath of Fort Donelson.[16] For example, on his way riding to Burnsville, Grant went off the road to avoid spattering his own troops with mud, which was later remembered and appreciated.[17]

After an inexplicably slow approach to Iuka by Rosecrans, he ran headlong into the Confederates during the late afternoon of September 19, and a small but fierce battle began, resulting in the Federal advance being stopped dead in its tracks. At this crucial moment, instead of rushing in with reinforcements, Ord and Grant heard nothing because of strong northerly winds, creating a so-called acoustic shadow in which nearby gunfire could not be heard from the opposite direction. This was obviously something that no one had anticipated. At Shiloh, Grant had been jarred from his morning coffee by the sounds of distant battle; at Iuka, within a few miles of the action, no one heard anything and it was assumed Rosecrans had not been able to attack before dark. By the time Grant and Ord learned otherwise, it was the middle of the night. As Grant, Ord, and Rosecrans all finally converged into Iuka on the morning of September 20, they discovered that Price's army had slipped away between them on the other road leading south out of town, one that Rosecran neglected to guard.

Thus Sterling Price, with the help of an acoustic shadow and the oversight of Rosecrans, lived up to his reputation as an elusive "old woodpecker,"[18] that is, difficult to trap. The Federals suffered the majority of the more than 1,300 casualties in the engagement, but the Confederate movement north to reinforce Bragg had been successfully blocked. On September 20, Grant issued a congratulatory order to the troops in which he praised both Rosecrans and Ord for their contributions.[19] Privately, however, Grant wrote, "I was disappointed at the result ... but I had so high an opinion of General Rosecrans that I found no fault at the time." Adding to Grant's disappointment was the ordered transfer of General Thomas's division to Buell in Kentucky on the very same day that Rosecrans was fighting outside of Iuka.[20] This represented a final reduction in Grant's forces around Corinth with the decisive battle for that place yet to be fought.

The battle of Iuka makes an interesting comparison to that of Wilson's Creek the previous year, in which Federal forces tried to surround the very same man—Sterling Price—in a similar manner, but suffered total defeat and were driven from the field. Unlike Wilson's Creek, the troops engaged at Iuka were mostly veterans; particularly on the Federal side, the men and officers were of a much higher caliber. The Union commander (Grant) was not personally leading either wing of his force, unlike Nathaniel Lyon who died in the fighting at Wilson's Creek,[21] nor was he overextended or unsupported. Instead of being presented with an opportunity to drive the Federals from the field, Price realized that he was being slowly hemmed in by superior numbers and, with good judgment, chose discretion as the better part of valor.

Though failing in some of his objectives—namely, to bag Sterling Price— Grant did his job at Iuka and did it under unforeseen and difficult circumstances. Military historian Arthur Conger summed up Grant's mixed achievement:

> The plan failed wretchedly ... but the failure taught Grant another vital lesson— that methods successful with a regiment or a brigade are by no means necessarily so with a division or an army corps; also, that there is no more assurance that a major-general ... will always do the right thing under stress than there is that a major will do it.[22]

Grant was no more suited by temperament to run an army by remote control through Rosecrans than he was to be second-in-command under Halleck. Nevertheless, he gave it his best effort and probably came out the wiser for it.

Part of the reason that the battle of Iuka was hardly noticed at the time and has been scarcely noticed since is what happened three days later. Contemplating the senseless slaughter that had taken place at Sharpsburg, President Lincoln wisely decided to give the battle itself and the entire war a whole new meaning. This he did by issuing the Emancipation Proclamation on September 22, freeing all slaves in any state still in rebellion as of January 1, 1863. A civil war over states' rights was thus instantly transformed into a holy war against human slavery. Lincoln's decision would quickly change the character of the struggle by making it even more desperate and determined than it had previously been. The Proclamation would also no doubt influence the no-holds-barred fighting in the West that took place at Corinth and Perryville the following month. Sharpsburg/Antietam, though horrendous in scope, was still an indecisive battle in and of itself; however, the truly decisive struggle now unfolding in the West was just gearing up.

Southern reaction to emancipation was pretty much what one would expect—mostly one of hysterical outrage. Specific Confederate reaction to events at Iuka was slightly more nuanced, though hardly less irrational. Having his grand push north stymied by determined and sophisticated Federal resistance, Sterling Price was now ordered by the overly ambitious Confederate General Earl Van Dorn to link up with his forces coming up from Vicksburg, this time to give Grant's forces a much harder shove than they had received at Iuka. In a sense, it was Shiloh all over again. There, rather than bypass a stubborn pocket of resistance in the Hornet's Nest to achieve their ultimate goal, the Confederates first had to stomp it out completely, thus losing the battle. Now, in a much wider field of operations, Van Dorn and Price opted to take back Corinth and crush Grant (along with Rosecrans) before meeting Bragg in the Ohio Valley. Had they been smart they would have gone around. This was a Hornet's Nest that would not be stomped out; in fact, there was more than one nest to it by design.

The end of September saw Grant race around his large department while trying to prepare his numerous subordinates for events that he once again accurately foresaw. On September 24, two days after emancipation was proclaimed, Grant was all the way back in St. Louis conferring with General Samuel Curtis, probably on what he could expect from Van Dorn, whom Curtis had defeated at Pea Ridge earlier that year. Then on September 26, Grant ordered that his own headquarters be transferred north from Corinth to Jackson, Tennessee, the very same place he had exiled John McClernand to only two months previous. This point on the map had now become the figurative Pittsburg Landing of the Mississippi region. If Corinth fell, then the Federals could regroup and make another stand, or if Buell was defeated in Kentucky, then Grant would be closer and more advantageously placed to rush into that sector. As at Iuka, Grant would once again try to orchestrate troop movements behind the front lines via telegraph. Finally, on

September 30, he rushed back to Corinth to meet with Rosecrans, to whom he had entrusted his front-line defense. He had given the job to precisely the right man, although the aftermath would once again be anticlimactic and his achievement underappreciated.

CHAPTER 19

October 1862:
The Battle of Corinth

*Mr. Jefferson Davis said in a speech, delivered at LaGrange, Mississippi,
before the secession of that State, that he would agree to drink all the blood
spilled south of Mason and Dixon's line if there should be a war.*

—Grant[1]

By 7:30 P.M. on October 1, shortly after arriving in Jackson, Tennessee,
Grant learned of a Confederate mass troop movement in northern Mississippi
led by Generals Earl Van Dorn and Sterling Price.[2] Their ultimate objective
being to move north and link up with Braxton Bragg's forces in Kentucky,
Van Dorn's harebrained scheme was to first feint north, then turn around
and launch an all-out attack south against the large Federal garrison at
Corinth, now under the immediate command of Major-General William Rosecrans.[3] By the time Grant realized on October 3 that the initial Confederate
target was Corinth, he was sending a steady stream of urgent messages to Rosecrans, exhorting him among other things to "Fight!"[4] This Rosecrans would
be forced to do that very same day as over 20,000 screaming rebels stormed
the outer works of Corinth against a similar number of forewarned and well-
entrenched Federals. This battle would not be another Shiloh in terms of surprise or lack of preparation.

While Rosecrans and his troops held on at all costs, Grant was thinking
in broader terms. After recovering from his surprise at the foolishness of the
Southern attack, and correctly anticipating that it would be repulsed, he
ordered another Federal force under General Edward Ord to race south and
block the Confederate retreat. This was still on October 3. By October 4, after
some initial gains the previous day, the Confederates began a full withdrawal,
having suffered over 3,600 casualties, including the death of General John
Martin.[5] In addition to being a good defensive fighter, Rosecrans benefited
from the special fortifications that had been built two months earlier by
Grant's order,[6] plus those constructed for the Confederates by Beauregard in

the spring. Halleck's impractical defense works dating from June, designed for a much larger army, were not a factor in the final struggle for Corinth.

On October 5, after learning that the Confederates had been completely repulsed and that Ord's smaller force was now engaging them, Grant urgently telegraphed Rosecrans and ordered him to "Push the enemy to the wall."[7] Rosecrans hesitated, however, having suffered himself over 2,300 casualties during the previous two days of fighting, including the death of General Pleasant Hackleman and the near-fatal wounding of General Richard Oglesby. After General Ord was also seriously wounded, Rosecrans belatedly tried to join in the chase while hauling a wagon train of supplies and initially taking the wrong road in pursuit.[8] By this time, though, the Confederates had effectively made good their escape.

At this point, relations between Grant and Rosecrans, shaky from the start and deteriorating since the battle of Iuka, went into a tailspin. Grant ordered Rosecrans on October 7 to discontinue his pursuit, now convinced that the right moment for annihilating the enemy had passed. Grant was legitimately concerned that by the time Rosecrans caught up, the Confederates would be defending a position of their choosing with no one nearby to rescue Rosecrans.[9] Observing events long distance from Washington, Halleck was perplexed by Grant's decision[10] and Rosecrans completely miffed. Rosecrans was also probably cognizant that for the second time in two months he had missed a clear-cut chance to destroy an opposing army. Nevertheless, Grant's cease-and-desist order was obeyed and in hindsight appears wise, if for no other reason than that no pursuit is usually better than a slow one. In any event, the battle of Corinth once and for all ended Confederate hopes of retaking that crucial point in the Mississippi region. It also had broader consequences that are generally underappreciated by students of the war, and were generally underappreciated at the time as well. One exception was President Lincoln, who sent a warm congratulatory message to Grant and soon promoted Rosecrans by giving him Buell's job in eastern Tennessee.

On the same day that Lincoln sent his telegram to Grant (October 8), the battle of Perryville, Kentucky, was fought. Though a complicated and indecisive engagement viewed in isolation, the net result was that Braxton Bragg's highly touted invasion of the North, which had begun so promisingly, ended with a full retreat back to southeastern Tennessee. A large Confederate army would never again set foot in Kentucky. A good part of this result was because of what Grant had accomplished in his sector at Corinth, most of which was conducted long-distance from Jackson, Tennessee. Bragg's approval ratings with his troops took a sharp nose dive and stayed there for the rest of the war, although he would remain in command of his less-than-admiring army for over another year. Among the Confederate rank and file, the indestructible Sam Watkins had nothing but negative things to say about Bragg in retrospect,[11] while offering at least some positives on every other commander that he served under during those four years. Bragg would keep his department much longer than he should have, solely through the influence of Jefferson Davis, who (unlike Abraham Lincoln) believed it was always preferable to have a general popular with Jefferson Davis, rather than popular with the soldiers. As for Grant, in his memoirs he repeated an old army joke about Bragg having quarreled with everyone in the service, including Bragg himself.[12]

In addition to blocking a formidable attempt by the Confederates to retake Corinth, Grant had prevented Bragg from receiving reinforcements in Kentucky, which played an important part in Bragg's ultimate decision to retreat. Moreover, Grant had accomplished this while still being able to send several of his own divisions to Buell that helped the latter to achieve numerical superiority. Not the least of these was the one including General Philip Sheridan, which put on the best combat performance among the Federals at Perryville. Those in the know (such as Lincoln) recognized that Grant had done his job skillfully, if not brilliantly. More recently, military historian J.F.C. Fuller summed up Grant's impressive recent progress as a strategist:

> Grant ... has been classed as a butcher and a bludgeon fighter, yet at Iuka and Corinth he showed a strategic grasp that is quite amazing.... In both, he cunningly planned to hold his adversary with one force, and to strike him in the rear with another ... he had grasped the great secret of the art of war, namely, how to develop offensive action from a defensive base, how, in fact, to generate mobility from protected-offensive power, marks him down as one of the most noteworthy generals of the age.[13]

Grant himself described the battle of Corinth as a "crushing blow to the enemy."[14] In recognition of these recent successes, Grant's command of his own department, which hitherto had been viewed as provisional and temporary, was finally confirmed on October 16. Grant was now officially out of his post–Shiloh doghouse, at least as far as Lincoln and Halleck were concerned.

Of course, there were other important factors contributing to Federal gains during the fall of 1862 besides Grant, not the least of which was Confederate stupidity. This was particularly the case with Braxton Bragg, who was unable to concentrate his forces, partly because of Grant and partly because his own troops were unnecessarily spread out across a broad front when the shooting began.[15] The Southerners were also overly concerned with making symbolic gestures, such as attempting to inaugurate a Confederate governor at Frankfort, Kentucky, thus separating Bragg's forces from those under Kirby Smith.[16] Smith, like many other Confederates, disdained to place himself under the immediate command of Bragg, further aggravating the problem. Bragg's "invasion" was essentially a large-scale raid in which the Confederates were inferior to their opponents in terms of supplies, organization and discipline.[17] Above all, the citizens of the Bluegrass State would not rally to the cause of any invading army, whether it be Confederate or Federal. As at Shiloh,

Bragg and his staff again conducted a major campaign while seemingly lost in a fantasy-world haze. In the end, Bragg was outmanned, outgunned, and outsmarted at Perryville. All he seemed capable of doing was to make a mad dash at the enemy, which in his mind he believed would have won the day at Shiloh five months earlier.

At Perryville, Bragg hardly even knew who he was fighting. At one point, he thought Grant was in Louisville when in fact he was in Jackson.[18] Once again, Bragg seems to have been reliving Shiloh. This kind of behavior made a dramatic contrast to Grant's evolution during the same time period. Perhaps the Emancipation Proclamation from two weeks earlier had psychologically unhinged Bragg and Van Dorn, or at least threw them off balance.[19] The fighting in early October had a frenzied quality to it, with the Confederates exhibiting far more valor than discretion. Among the four primary Confederate commanders, the only one with an understanding of the situation seems to have been poor Sterling Price, who deserved better and openly wept after the defeat at Corinth.[20] Price was no one's idea of a military genius, but at least he knew better than to hurl himself against a brick wall. Having earlier engaged Rosecrans at Iuka, Price also probably had a better appreciation of what the Confederates were up against.

On the Federal side, William Rosecrans emerged from the battles of Corinth and Iuka with laurels in addition to those he had won the previous year in West Virginia. Unfortunately, his relations with Grant had been permanently damaged, although as Bruce Catton noted, Grant seemed to be the only one bothered by the recent Confederate double escape.[21] What seems to have disturbed Grant more, as well as his staff (and even his wife), was that Rosecrans appears to have been spreading stories about Grant, or at least allowing those under him to do so. The unpleasant climax of this ill will came on October 21 when Grant and Rosecrans fired off a series of short, sharp telegrams to each other. On the surface, these exchanges dealt mostly with administrative matters such as arms distribution and command prerogatives, though reading in between the lines one gets a deep sense of other unspoken matters. Then Grant let the cat out of the bag by accusing Rosecrans of encouraging discord between their armies through his use of the media.[22] This last dig was not an idle accusation.

Two days before the aforementioned blow-up, Colonel Mortimer Leggett wrote an impassioned letter to John Rawlins, expressing outrage over the recent behavior of Rosecrans and his staff. The most egregious offense alleged was that the ambitious Rosecrans had retained something of a personal P.R. man in the person of one William Bickham, a reporter affiliated with the *Cincinnati Commercial.* Bickham, according to Leggett, was a satellite of none other than Lieutenant Governor Benjamin Stanton of Ohio, the same public official who had seriously bad-mouthed Grant after Shiloh and consequently earned a wrathful rebuke from Sherman (see Chapter 14). Lieutenant

Governor Stanton was continuing to spread rumors that Grant was an incompetent drunk and was described by Leggett as Grant's "bitterest enemy." Leggett concluded his letter to Rawlins with, "For Heaven's sake do *something* in this matter."[23]

Leggett was not the only one upset with Rosecrans. During the recent battles, Rosecrans had criticized the courage and performance of troops who were Grant's veterans from Fort Donelson and Shiloh, which did not endear him to them. Then John McPherson and Stephen Hurlbut, two of Grant's veteran commanders, became displeased with the professional conduct of Rosecrans, and spoke of this to Julia Grant when she visited headquarters in Jackson.[24] All of this seemed to be building up to a dismissal of Rosecrans by Grant, who was nonetheless reluctant to do so and seemed less outraged than his staff at the time. He was rescued from having to make this decision by Lincoln, however, who on October 23 cashiered Don Carlos Buell for his stodgy performance in Tennessee and Kentucky, and replaced him with Rosecrans, who reported immediately for duty in Cincinnati.

About the same time that Grant and Rosecrans were happily parting ways, a journalist with the unmistakable name of Sylvanus Cadwallader sauntered into the Federal camp at Corinth and flashed his credentials as the new war correspondent for the *Chicago Times*. This was the same newspaper that less than three months previous had its star reporter, Warren Isham, gleefully thrown into prison by Grant and Sherman after he had fabricated tales of Confederate naval prowess. Cadwallader, however, was no ordinary journalist; in fact, time would eventually prove him to be the Ernie Pyle of his generation. A former Douglas Democrat born in Ohio (like Grant), Cadwallader had settled in Milwaukee to run a local paper with his brother-in-law while freelancing with other larger publications such as the *Chicago Times*. He had been sent to Mississippi by the *Times* in his official capacity as their new man on the beat. Unofficially, his real mission was to get Isham out of jail.[25]

In his classic memoir *Three Years with Grant*, Cadwallader records that on his way to Corinth by train, he overheard troops with the Army of the Cumberland (under Rosecrans) bashing Grant with absolutely no inhibitions:

> Grant was used up at Belmont—he was drunk all day.... Rosecrans was the most brilliant officer in the west—Sherman was crazy—but Grant; well, he just now commanded a department; he never did amount to anything, and never would; he had been kicked out of the United States Army once, and would be again; he was nothing but a drunken, wooden-headed tanner, that would not trouble the country very long, &c, &c.[26]

This hearsay calls to mind Professor Smith's observation about a general imparting attitude to his army,[27] only in this case it applied to Rosecrans in a negative way. Cadwallader had nothing to say in his memoir about Bickham but plenty about the *Cincinnati Commercial* and its editor, Marat Halstead, whose hatred for Grant, according to Cadwallader, was implacable.[28] As for Rosecrans, Cadwallader opined, "General Rosecrans had been so unjust to Grant and his troops in the past that I decided to send a special correspondent with them, to see that newspaper justice was done them."[29] "Them" in this case referred to Sherman and his men under Grant's command, who were later sent to Corinth after the battle of Chickamauga in September 1863. Grant did not know it at first, but his own P.R. man had just walked in through the door unsolicited, and in the long run would prove to be a godsend.

In brief, Cadwallader quickly won over both Rawlins and Grant, using interpersonal skills that were (then and now) in very short supply—thoughtful tact and good manners. Cadwallader was not long in obtaining a pass from Grant to go more or less anywhere in camp anytime he felt like it. This unusual privilege marked the beginning of Grant's image rehabilitation with the public, although the process would be continuous over the next three years and not vanquish his critics until he reached the gates of Vicksburg seven months later. Cadwallader was probably the first reporter to realize that the best way to influence Grant was through his key adjunct, John Rawlins. For the present, however, Grant now had a much-needed coach in the arts of media relations. Perhaps he was inspired (or provoked) by the example of Rosecrans but did ten times better in the person of Cadwallader.

One of the first things that Cadwallader recorded in his memoir was that he was made privy to many of Grant's strategic plans. A basic "don't ask, don't tell" policy seems to have been adopted in his particular case—remarkable given that he was a journalist. Near the end of October, Cadwallader noted that a plan had been proposed by Grant and approved by Halleck to move against the Confederate citadel of Vicksburg, Mississippi. On October 26, Grant had wired Halleck the following suggestion: "With small reinforcements at Memphis I think I would be able to move down the Mississippi Central road and cause the evacuation of Vicksburg...." Thus with this sentence, almost casual in tone, began one of the most celebrated campaigns in military history, one that was to consume all of Grant's energies for the next eight months and mark the permanent turning point of the American Civil War. The following day, on October 27, Halleck wired back his approval, and Grant announced the plan to his staff with the *Chicago Times* correspondent in their presence.[30] This would not be the first time that Sylvanus Cadwallader would witness history being made.

J.F.C. Fuller noted that with the complete disappointment of Confederate hopes in the West during the fall of 1862, "Grant could once again begin to think offensively."[31] Grant could also allow himself to think offensively because Halleck and Lincoln, among others, were now allowing him to. It appears at this point in time even Halleck was beginning to appreciate the results that Grant achieved, whatever his other perceived shortcomings may have been. Fuller again:

... in the West strategy was beginning to take form round the person of one man—Grant. It was a most fascinating evolution, guided and nurtured by no single hand, by no means committee of directors, but compelled to take shape through force of circumstances....[32]

"Force of circumstances" is an appropriate phrase. Grant's unpredictable career, which had almost come to an abrupt halt back in June, first with contemplated resignation and then with near-capture, was now moving into its next unlikely phase. During the upcoming campaign against Vicksburg, Grant would transform himself from a successful though controversial general into something that was quite larger than life.

CHAPTER 20

November 1862: The First Vicksburg Campaign

... one of my superstitions had always been when I started to go any where, or to do anything, not to turn back, or stop until the thing intended was accomplished.

—Grant[1]

The town of Vicksburg sits upon a high bluff on the east bank of the Mississippi River, roughly equidistant between New Orleans and Memphis. Across the river are the bayous of east Louisiana and about 40 miles due east is the state capital of Jackson, Mississippi. Most modern tourists in Vicksburg, notwithstanding the national military park and numerous historical landmarks, have difficulty in appreciating that this friendly, unpretentious place was once the focal point of an epic struggle marking nothing less than the turning point of the American Civil War. Today the river makes a lazy bend on the south end of town, but in 1862 this was not the case—it made a hairpin turn on the north side of the city, thus preventing ships from gathering speed while passing downstream beneath the bluffs. Boats had to move slowly past Vicksburg, whether traveling north or south, and this had strategic consequences; in effect, one was forced to navigate past Vicksburg deliberately, under imposing heights commanded by artillery. God had created a natural bastion for the Confederacy, and by November 1862 it was about all that they still controlled of the river.[2] New Orleans and the lower Delta region had fallen to the Federals, and the upper valley region had also capitulated. All this had been mainly due to the efforts of Grant and his western armies.

Anyone who could read a map with intelligence knew at the outset of the war that control of the Mississippi Valley was essential. By late 1862, the area around Vicksburg was acknowledged by both sides as the most important point to be captured or defended. Lincoln himself declared "Vicksburg is the key" and that "The war can never be brought to a close until that key is in our pocket." Confederate President Jefferson Davis, with far less talent

146

for metaphor than Lincoln, maintained that "Vicksburg is the nail head that holds the South's two halves together."[3] The environs of Vicksburg also held immeasurable symbolic value to both North and South as the adopted home of Davis, whose Brierwood Plantation and brother Joseph's adjacent Hurricane Plantation were in the vicinity.[4] Davis and Southerners in general regarded Vicksburg as the new, impregnable "Gibraltar" of the West[5]; never mind that Columbus, Kentucky, had been described in identical terms only nine months earlier and was now a Federal depot. Objectives were straightforward: the South wanted to hold Vicksburg at all costs and the North wanted to take it. Grant may not have personally originated the plan to assault the town, but he was among those who immediately grasped its significance and was the first Union general to act upon this realization.[6] Unfortunately, the Federal Navy, with an inadequate number of Marines, had unwittingly made this job harder in July with a series of unsuccessful attacks, alerting the Confederates as to Union intentions before Grant even began his historic campaign, and thus encouraging greater fortification of that city's already formidable natural defenses.[7]

In the wake of Confederate setbacks during early October, Davis gave the western high command another shakeup. Earl Van Dorn and Sterling Price were effectively demoted to cavalry commanders. Van Dorn's unlikely replacement as the newly appointed defender of Vicksburg was 48-year-old General John Clifford Pemberton, a northerner by birth (from Philadelphia), but who married into a Virginia family and was a fervent believer in states' rights. Pemberton may have represented a step up from Van Dorn, but that was not saying much. Though a West Pointer, Pemberton had no combat experience to speak of plus a reputation for being difficult to deal with on a personal level. The reasons Davis made this fateful choice have always been somewhat of a puzzle to historians, but we are bold enough to offer speculation. The fact that Pemberton was a Yankee who fought for the Confederacy made him an exotic commodity, akin nowadays to something like a black conservative or a liberal Baptist. This quality, I think, ultimately proved irresistible for Davis. A man like Pemberton reassured Davis that his own political views were in the right.[8] Grant had a different take on it. As the Federal army later tightened its noose around Vicksburg, Grant sat around a campfire with his surprised, curious troops, and almost apologetically explained to them that Pemberton was "a northern man who had got into bad company."[9] As for relations between Grant and Pemberton, the first official exchange were cordial letters during late November regarding the transport of relief supplies for sick and wounded Confederate prisoners then being held at Iuka, Mississippi.[10]

Davis did manage (reluctantly) to do one thing right: on November 24 he appointed General Joseph Johnston as western general-in-chief to coordinate the efforts of Pemberton in Mississippi and Bragg in Tennessee.[11] Joseph Johnston was no relation to Albert Sidney Johnston, who had fallen at Shiloh;

in fact, the difference between the two was day and night. In short, Joseph Johnston was a highly competent though underrated military leader who was appointed by Davis only because there was no one else for him turn to at that moment. Davis was reluctant to bring in Johnston because possibly no two men in the Confederate States of America had more baggage between them. The roots of this conflict went back to their student days at West Point with a tavern brawl over a girl and continued at regular intervals thereafter, as Davis rose politically and Johnston militarily. Even their wives hated each other.[12] Nevertheless, everyone in the army recognized Johnston's talent, which played a role in the victory at Bull Run, in tandem with Beauregard. Johnston had been on the shelf for the last five months due to a serious wound suffered in Virginia during late May, causing him to be superceded by Robert E. Lee in the East. Now Johnston reported back for duty and he was desperately needed, although Davis would always be the last one to admit it.

Meanwhile, on November 2, Grant moved out from Jackson, Tennessee, to begin his first campaign against Vicksburg.[13] This expedition would be anchored along the Mississippi Central Railroad through the middle of the state. In the words of Shelby Foote, "Grant's mind had emerged from the tunnel it had entered after Shiloh."[14] The following day (November 3), Sylvanus Cadwallader was told by one of Grant's staffers that if he wanted to witness an active campaign, then he should immediately board a designated train and that "asking no questions, none would be asked."[15] Arriving in Bolivar, Tennessee, on November 4, Cadwallader found himself invited to sit down for breakfast with Grant and his officers. Table talk consisted exclusively of everyone chuckling over practical jokes being played on the rookie recruits by veterans. Then everyone mounted their horses and rode straight into LaGrange, Mississippi, that same day. At one point, Cadwallader rode next to Grant, who, rather than tell him how the war was going to be won, made small talk about farming. Cadwallader asked no questions.[16]

The Federal army spent a good part of the month in LaGrange while long lines of supply trains were organized. These lines extended all the way back through Mississippi, Tennessee, Kentucky, and beyond. Grant's "Egyptians," impatient with hunger, began to plunder the Mississippi countryside. On the way to LaGrange, Cadwallader witnessed these depredations and wrote a graphic story for his paper, which he regretted issuing after its dispatch. When the papers reached camp, he slinked around until buttonholed by Grant, expecting to be thrown in jail along with his colleague Warren Isham. Instead, Grant apologized for the behavior of his troops, explaining that there was no time for courts of inquiry. Grant also told Cadwallader that he could write anything that was true (unlike Isham had done), but that making predictions or reporting plans were not permitted.[17] Then Grant published a special field order against plundering and threatened punishment for anyone caught with dishonorable discharge and suspension of pay. A few days later,

Cadwallader ventured a suggestion to John Rawlins that Warren Isham had paid enough for his offense and should be released. Grant agreed and Isham was freed on November 12.[18] Thus within a month, Cadwallader accomplished his mission and was now an insider with Grant and his staff. Grant's extraordinary accommodation of Cadwallader may have been influenced by Rosecrans' continuing campaign of P.R. subterfuge in which he tried to build up his own reputation at the expense of Grant's troops. Grant wrote at length of this concern in a letter to Congressman Washburne dated November 7.[19]

Another reason Grant and Cadwallader may have hit it off was shared prejudice—specifically, anti–Semitism. Grant's attitude in this regard first manifested itself during his tenure at Memphis in June and July. Now with supply lines running all along the Mississippi Valley, illicit cotton trade seems to have received special attention from Grant, who viewed Jews as a class, or at least seemed to. Grant wrote to General Hurlbut on November 9, disallowing trading permits beyond Jackson, adding, "The Isrealites [sic] especially should be kept out."[20] The following day (November 10), Grant wrote this shocking missive to Colonel Joseph Webster:

> Give orders to all the conductors on the road that no Jews are to be permitted to travel on the Rail Road southward from any point. They may go north and be encouraged in it but they are such an intolerable nuisance that the Department must be purged from them.[21]

About the only thing that can be said in Grant's defense was that his prejudice was probably being fueled by bad influences around him. Not the least of these was Cadwallader himself, who later that month got into an altercation with a cotton dealer named D.W. Fairchild. This incident seems to have won more points in the eyes of Grant and Rawlins, who viewed cotton traders (read: Jews) as "a gang of thieves."[22]

A bigger headache for Grant, however, was coming from the hosts of runaway slaves swarming around the Federal camp in anticipation of official freedom on January 1. In this case (unlike the thorny mercantile issues of the cotton trade), Grant's genius once again revealed itself. On November 13, as Federal cavalry pushed on to Holly Springs, Mississippi,[23] in the face of token resistance, Grant summoned to his headquarters a young lieutenant by the name of John Eaton, Chaplain for the 27th Ohio Infantry Regiment. Eaton was a Dartmouth-educated seminarian who earlier in the war had done a short stint as a P.O.W., during which his Confederate captors were so impressed with him that he was allowed to preach non-political sermons to the Southerners. Now he was informed by Grant that he had been hand-picked to oversee the newly established Freedman's Bureau, in which emancipated slaves would be "compensated"[24] for their labor, particularly in regard to the harvesting of crops. This was obviously a job that no one wanted. Despite his own vehement objections of being unqualified, along with plenty of ribbing from Grant's staff,[25] Eaton went on to perform this role magnificently, earning from Grant praise as being "efficient"—typically the highest compliment he gave. After the war, Eaton then went on to distinguish himself as U.S. Commissioner of Education.[26]

The greatest threat to Grant during this time, however, came not from racial issues or even from the Confederate army, but rather in the form of Union General John McClernand. McClernand, the reader may recall, had been shipped back north in August to raise more volunteer troops (an activity he excelled at), and to get him out of everyone's hair at Corinth. McClernand, as a Democratic political general from southern Illinois, was viewed by all of the West Pointers as being an incompetent and dangerous burden,[27] even though he had survived some of the hardest fighting at Belmont, Donelson, and Shiloh. McClernand was also a personal friend of Lincoln, the two having practiced law together on the Illinois circuit. In late October, McClernand had secured an audience with Lincoln and Secretary of War Stanton in what Jean Edward Smith termed "one of the more bizarre episodes of the Civil War"[28]—bizarre, that is, to anyone unused to dealing with master equivocators such as Lincoln, Stanton, and Halleck. During this meeting, McClernand obtained written authorization to lead an independent expedition against Vicksburg with the new troops he had recruited. Even more alarming was that McClernand outranked Sherman at this point in the war and intended to take over Sherman's force then stationed in Memphis. Although McClernand was a lawyer, the combination of Lincoln, Stanton, and Halleck[29] would have made a formidable law firm itself, and McClernand was ultimately way out of his league.[30]

Lincoln's unorthodox move of endorsing McClernand's separate command probably had, like most of his other unorthodox moves, multiple purposes behind it. Foremost among these was that the Republican Party was about to get a black eye in the midterm elections on November 4[31]; therefore, continued Democratic, bipartisan support would be needed to prosecute the war—not to mention more volunteer troops. McClernand would be useful in these areas. Lincoln may have also been hedging his bets on Grant and/or trying to light a fire under him after his post–Shiloh funk. Nevertheless, a later account by Admiral David Porter of a meeting with Lincoln around this time leaves little doubt as to the President's strong sympathy with his former political crony.[32] Lincoln apparently had yet to recognize that Grant was far superior to McClernand as a military commander.[33] It was also probably through Porter that Grant first heard of McClernand's new mission while pushing forward in Mississippi.[34]

On November 10, while in LaGrange, Grant confronted Halleck with the following telegram:

> Am I to understand that I lay still here while an Expedition is fitted out from Memphis or do you want me to push as far South as possible? Am I to have Sher-

man move subject to my order or is he & his forces reserved for some special service? Will not more forces be sent here?[35]

On November 11, Halleck responded with "You have command of all troops sent to your department and have permission to fight the enemy where you please."[36] The general-in-chief, who had been continually at odds with Grant during the last year over just about everything, now finally showed solidarity with him; in fact, Halleck's finest moment during the war was probably reigning in McClernand. It also presents a case study in how a high-ranking officer can be disposed of by colleagues working in close concert with each other. This gave the green light to Grant, who, in the words of Shelby Foote, "considered himself unleashed."[37] On November 14 he ordered Sherman to move his army out of Memphis along a separate column to Vicksburg, thus keeping him out of McClernand's reach before the latter arrived on the scene.[38] The next day (November 15), he directed Sherman to meet him for a strategy session as both made a flying backtrack by rail to Columbus, Kentucky.[39]

Grant wrote no letters to his wife in November because she was either by his side or following in his wake with their son Jesse and her female slave Jule. Her own memoirs recall an amusing incident from LaGrange headquarters in which Grant asked Julia why she sat staring across the room at a stationary washstand:

> "Ulys, I don't like stationary washstands, do you?" "Yes, I do; why don't you?" I replied, "Well, I don't know." He said: "I'll tell you why. You have to go to the stand. It cannot be brought to you."[40]

He was obviously delighted in having her around and was ready to defend Julia from any criticism, even from his own father. On November 23, Grant wrote another angry letter to Jesse, this time rebuking him for a bad attitude towards his daughter-in-law:

> I am only sorry to say your letter and all that comes from you speaks so condescendingly of everything Julia says, writes or thinks. You without probably being aware of it are so prejudiced against her that she could not please you. This is not pleasing to me.[41]

It is possible that Jesse, among other things, questioned the wisdom and safety of Grant having his wife and child accompany him on an active military campaign. Though their presence helped keep Grant on an even keel (not to mention sober) during this critical period, events in early December would substantiate Jesse's concern for them.

On November 28, Grant left LaGrange and reached Holly Springs (at the Tallahatchie River) the following day, joining his army that had now gathered there. He commanded a force of over 70,000 troops (this included Sherman) that was advancing along several columns towards Vicksburg. Some 60 miles to the south at Granada and the Yalobusha River were Pemberton's

Confederates, who along with troops remaining at Vicksburg barely totaled 50,000.[42] Grant's next advance across the vast Mississippi countryside would be to the university town of Oxford. Grant was now poised to engage Pemberton under favorable circumstances and it would have been a battle to conclude the year-long campaign for the Mississippi Valley. By moving to Holly Springs, the Federals plunged deeper South than they ever had before, but the inherent flaw in Grant's deliberate advance was about to manifest itself.

CHAPTER 21

December 1862: The Beginning of Total War

No political party can or ought to exist when one of its corner-stones is oppo-sition to freedom of thought and to the right to worship God "according to the dictate of one's own conscience," or according to the creed of any reli-gious denomination whatever.

—Grant[1]

The month of December 1862 began with Julia Grant traveling (with her son and female slave) from LaGrange, Mississippi, to the Federal base at Holly Springs, where she hoped to join her husband. She arrived there only to find that Grant had left her a letter before moving south to Oxford, Mississippi.[2] While awaiting Grant's instructions to join him in Oxford, Julia was the house guest of Mrs. Pugh Govan, whose own husband served in the Confederate army.[3] Separated from Grant and most of the advancing Federal army, Julia found herself more or less tortured daily by the spiteful Southern women of Holly Springs. In her memoirs, she described how she was segregated from their company until summoned, then regaled with patriotic Confederate songs and invited to sing along. After declining this humiliation, she was lectured on the Southern loyalties of her home state (Missouri) and quizzed on the constitutional right of the Confederate States of America to secede from the Union. Poor cross-eyed Julia held her own but admitted, "I really was much grieved at my ignorance of these matters, but since then I have learned that even the chief justice is sometimes puzzled over the interpretation of this same Constitution."[4]

While Julia Grant was fending off attacks that rivaled anything Pember-ton's Confederate army would ever mount, her husband was about to make the biggest administrative blunder of his military career. This occurred on December 17 when Grant issued his infamous General Orders No. 11, begin-ning with "The Jews, as a class, violating every regulation of trade established by the Treasury Department and also Department orders, are hereby expelled from the Department."[5] Some apologists have tried to argue that this order

153

was not really written by Grant, or that "Jews" was a euphemism for "dishonest traders," but the hard truth is that Grant personally wrote the order and that he—at least at that time—equated Jews with dishonesty.[6] Grant's reputation in history will always be tarnished by this act far more than by his drinking habits; hence, the immediate and distant origins of General Orders No. 11 call for a brief digression.

As Federal supply lines stretched further than ever during early December, Grant found himself dealing with mercantile issues more than for any previous campaign, and for the first time, he was not up to the challenge. On December 5, writing to Sherman regarding a cotton trader variously identified as "Haas" or "Maas," Grant complained that cotton from the plantation of "Colonel" William H. Coxe in Holly Springs had been illicitly traded right under Grant's nose and that he intended to do something drastic about it: " ... in consequence of the total disregard and evasion of orders by the Jews my policy is to exclude them so far as practicable from the Dept."[7] Ten days later on December 15, the subject was still foremost in Grant's mind as he wrote to his sister Mary: "With all my other trials I have to contend against is added that of speculators whose patriotism is measured by dollars & cents. Country has no value with them compared to money."[8] This letter, otherwise optimistic in tone, also mentions that Grant's father Jesse had recently arrived in Mississippi, and that Jesse would soon be paying a visit (along with Grant's wife and son) in Oxford.

The reuniting of the Grant family in Oxford, however, turned into a highly unpleasant affair. While he was delighted as usual with the company of his wife and son, Grant's encounter with his father soured their troubled relationship even more than it had been previously. Specifically, Jesse Grant had brought along with him three businessmen, the Jewish Mack brothers of Cincinnati, for whom he had promised to secure a cotton trading permit from his son in return for a hefty percentage of the profits. For Grant, this was the final straw. His disappointed father, along with Julia and the Mack brothers, were all put on the first train headed back north.[9] Lieutenant John Eaton later recalled listening to Jesse complain on the train about wasted cattle hide.[10] Then, the same day that he issued General Orders No. 11, Grant wrote a nearly ranting letter to Assistant Secretary of War Christopher Wolcott in which he asserted that "Jews and other unprincipled traders ... seemed to be a privileged class."[11] Grant, the man who with little or no emotion could successfully command armies during the heat of battle, had completely lost his composure when his father tried to make him part of shady business deal. One is tempted to surmise that he tried to banish all Jews from his department in an attempt to rationalize the rough treatment he had just handed out to his father.

Regarding Grant's issuance of General Orders No. 11, a Jewish friend of the author remarked, "Let's hope he was drunk when he did it." Alas, Grant appears to have been perfectly sober—Julia was around, for one, as was John Rawlins. On December 13, a few days before he was joined by Julia in Oxford, Grant had written to assure her that a gift of bottled bourbon had been forwarded to Sherman, and furthermore that "Myself nor no one connected with the Staff ever tasted it."[12] Far more likely than inebriation, Grant was influenced by his many past failures in the private business sector, combined with the memory of Union soldiers recently fallen in battle. The incident itself was probably triggered by the stress of a family argument. The only persons resembling good influences around him in this regard were Julia and Rawlins, with the latter protesting strenuously against General Orders No. 11,[13] despite his own prejudices regarding the cotton traders. More typical was Grant's new sidekick, journalist Sylvanus Cadwallader, who caustically related that he personally knew of only one benevolent slave owner and one Jew serving in the army.[14] No doubt Grant's popularity with his officers and troops went up because of this act despite the severe public and political fallout, eventually leading to the revocation of the order in January.

Grant makes no mention of this disgraceful episode in his memoirs. After his death, however, Julia (to her credit) tackled it in hers, referring to Grant's proclamation as "that obnoxious order." In regards to the later forced revocation of the order, Julia claimed that "the General said deservedly so, as he had no right to make an order against any special sect."[15] One wants to believe that Julia was being straight with us, and there is some reason to think that she was. In addition to Grant's firm defense of religious freedom, he claimed on the final page of his memoirs that his deathbed well-wishers included Jews.[16] Even if none of this was sincere—and it is believed that most, if not all, of it was—it would be over-simplistic to view Grant's opinions on race and religion as anything but conflicted and ambiguous. In these qualities, he was very much a man of his time. Moreover, if he did in fact modify his views for the better as he aged, then he becomes a role model for us all.

On December 13, the same day that Grant assured Julia he had not opened any bottles of bourbon, the Army of the Potomac, under its newly appointed commander General Ambrose Burnside, suffered yet another terrible defeat, this time at Fredericksburg, Virginia. Burnside had ordered his troops to make an uphill assault against a fortified position manned by Robert E. Lee's determined veterans, and the results were predictable for everyone except Burnside and perhaps Lee, who was only surprised at Burnside's foolishness. For the fourth time in 18 months, a Federal attempt to invade Virginia had come to grief, this time at a cost of nearly 13,000 casualties. This senseless slaughter came closer to winning the war for the Confederates than most realized at the time, because immediately afterwards Lincoln's cabinet made a serious attempt to reorganize itself. This came with a Senatorial caucus that required all of Lincoln's considerable political savvy to ward off.[17] Had it succeeded, the results may have ultimately been Federal peace overtures and/or Lincoln's resignation.

While Lincoln and his supporters busied themselves trying to contain this political fire in the rear, Grant's army in Mississippi found itself dealing with the military equivalent. Coming like a divine rebuke two days after his General Orders No. 11, Grant learned that a large Confederate cavalry force under General Earl Van Dorn had gotten behind him and was rushing north. Immediately he telegraphed a warning to the officer in command of the Federal supply depot at Holly Springs, Colonel Robert Murphy, who when he received the message shrugged it off with hung-over irritation and went back to bed. On December 20, Van Dorn and his troopers, eager to redeem themselves after their devastating defeat at Corinth in October, stormed into Holly Springs, forced the unprepared Federal garrison to surrender, and proceeded to commandeer or destroy everything of possible use to Grant's army, the quantity of which was enormous. Long after the fact, Grant still referred to Murphy's conduct at Holly Springs as "disgraceful" and "most reprehensible," but in typical fashion for him, absolved the troops of cowardice and placed all the blame on the officers.[18] Grant not only cashiered Murphy, but had the Federal cavalry commander who allowed Van Dorn to get around them (Colonel Lyle Dickey) and another officer (Colonel Calvin Marsh) who allowed Van Dorn to escape, reassigned as well.[19]

The Federal setback at Holly Springs was bad enough, but the worst was yet to come. On December 10, Confederate General Nathan Bedford Forrest moved out with a small but intrepid cavalry force and spent the rest of the month making a shambles out of Federal communication and supply lines in western Tennessee and Kentucky.[20] In his memoirs Grant flatly stated that Forrest was the ablest cavalry commander in the West: "...for the particular kind of warfare which Forrest had carried on neither army could present a more effective officer than he was."[21] Few historians have disagreed with this assessment. Cadwallader, in his memoirs, elaborated on Grant's military respect for Forrest, a man who would later become one of the charter members of the Ku Klux Klan. Cadwallader wrote that Grant "stood in much dread" of Forrest because of the latter's unpredictability, and that whenever informed of enemy cavalry, Grant first wanted to know who was in command, typically making light of anyone other than Forrest. If it was Forrest, however, Grant "at once became apprehensive."[22] Between the activities of Forrest and Van Dorn, Grant's advance through northern Mississippi was no longer tenable, at least according to the conventional military wisdom of that time.

During his lightning raid on Holly Springs, Van Dorn had also come disconcertingly close to hitting the jackpot. Julia Grant, along with the two Jesses (Grant's father and son), had left town only a few days previous to join Grant in Oxford, before being transported back north after Grant's fit of anger. According to Julia, she later learned that, upon charging into Holly Springs,

General Van Dorn enquired as to her whereabouts and required much persuasion to be convinced that she had left. Then his troopers plundered all of Julia's possessions still at the boarding house, except for her personal baggage, which was surprisingly protected from the raiders in an honorable gesture by Mrs. Govan herself.[23] When Julia soon returned to Holly Springs, she was invited to stay at the Coxe plantation before moving on to Memphis. Upon scolding her slave Jule for misplacing "Master Jesse's silver cup," she was immediately presented with a crystal glass souvenir by the chivalrous Colonel Coxe.[24] One gets a sense that Julia was holding up Mrs. Govan and Colonel Coxe as civilized exemplars at a time when this sort of behavior was becoming increasingly unusual. Had the Grant family been captured by Van Dorn, one can only imagine what the effect would have been on Grant's judgment and subsequent Federal withdrawal from northern Mississippi. As it was, Grant surely got a bad scare, which may partly explain his tough discipline of the officers who were to blame for the fiasco, not to mention a new and severe attitude toward uncooperative civilians that was about to manifest itself.

It was in the immediate aftermath of December 20, 1862, that "total war," or war against civilians, became the new and terrible calling card of western Federal armies in the South. Grant vividly described this moment in history with barely concealed satisfaction over 20 years after the fact. The success of Forrest and Van Dorn quickly became public knowledge in Oxford, and gloating citizens apparently began taunting Grant about how his army was going to fight or retreat without any food or supplies. This proved to be a mistake. Grant's cold response was that men with "arms in their hands" could not be expected to starve, and since the Confederates had destroyed Union supplies, the Federals would now confiscate theirs. Horrified civilians were then advised to evacuate out of the path of the retreating army.[25]

Anticipating famine and want during their withdrawal, Grant and his troops instead encountered surplus beyond their wildest expectations. Although Grant had noted during his ride to Memphis in June that the Southern heartland appeared bountiful, he nevertheless "was amazed at the quantity of supplies the country afforded." Instead of starving, the Federals found themselves better supplied than from Holly Springs before the raid of Van Dorn, perhaps better supplied than ever—at the expense of Mississippi civilians, that is. Grant succinctly recalled that "this taught me a lesson...."[26] His successful quartermaster experience during the Mexican War[27] had thus far served him very well, and now Grant's skill at supplying troops took on a new, unheard-of dimension as his army was encouraged to live off the land of a hostile enemy. Not counting the suffering and displacement of Mississippians, Grant's retreat was from all accounts orderly and accomplished with minimal loss. Unlike Burnside's Army of the Potomac in the East after Fredericksburg, Grant's western soldiers retreated more in anger than in sorrow. This was far from being the first time during the war that the property of Southern civilians had been plundered by Federal soldiers, but it was the first time that it was done with official sanction and no apologies made.

In my family there is an outrageous legend that one of my female Georgian ancestors, wielding an unloaded shotgun, prevented General Sherman from personally plundering her house during the latter's "March to the Sea" in 1864 (almost every Southern family has a story like this). While there is no doubt that the historical basis for this anecdote is far less grandiose, it does represent a popular tradition in the South that everyone was justified in resisting the Federal invaders because they were no better than organized vandals. Listening to these stories, one would think that the war was all about Midwestern farm boys coming south just to steal chickens. Sherman, once again with typical foresight, had earlier during the Corinth campaign advocated to Grant a need for more harshness towards the Southern civilians:

> They cannot be made to love us, but may be made to fear us.... We cannot change the hearts of those people of the South, but we can make war so terrible that they will realize the fact that however brave and gallant and devoted to their country, still they are mortal and should exhaust all peaceful remedies before they fly to war.[28]

Grant's own later justification was that "The whole South was a military camp"[29] and needed to be treated as such by his invading army. Yankee depredations in the South may have been evil but would prove necessary in order to win. Moreover, Confederate excursions north of Mason-Dixon—or even south of Mason-Dixon—were not known for maintaining their own supply lines, then were justified by the perpetrators as retaliation. Two wrongs, however, did not make a right, and the new Grant-Sherman philosophy represented, if nothing else, a firm grip on the realities of warfare, modern and otherwise.

As Grant's retreating Midwesterners cut their barbaric swath through the Mississippi countryside, Pemberton's army was now racing back in the opposite direction from Granada to Vicksburg. Sherman's separate Federal column was still advancing remorselessly south along the Mississippi Valley towards Vicksburg, completely unaware of Grant's inland retreat to the east, thanks to all communications between them being severed by Forrest and Van Dorn.[30] While Van Dorn's raid on Holly Springs was achieving its purpose, Vicksburg was visited for a rally by its favorite adopted son, Jefferson Davis, accompanied by new western general-in-chief Joseph Johnston on December 21–22.[31] Publicly everyone was all smiles and cheers but privately Johnston was critical of both Pemberton's fortifications and the decision of Davis for manpower distribution in favor of Mississippi at the expense of eastern Tennessee.[32] Johnston was also unhappy because, as noted by historian Thomas Connelly, "There seemed good cause for Johnston's belief that the government deliberately gave him a nominal command with little power, but with heavy responsibilities."[33] Returning to Jackson, Mississippi, on December 26, Davis and Johnston addressed the state legislature, with Johnston being more enthusiastically received. This was an ominous sign because, as Shelby Foote noted, "Apparently the general was more popular than the Chief Executive, even in the latter's own home state."[34]

Meanwhile, Sherman's expeditionary force rushed to what they believed was Grant's support at Vicksburg when Grant at that very moment was in fact retreating north. What Sherman encountered instead on December 29 was a now-concentrated and entrenched Confederate army under the personal command of Pemberton. Worse for Sherman, the defenders of Vicksburg were fighting behind strong fortifications at Chickasaw Bluffs, located north of the city and overlooking an approach that was carpeted by swollen bayous extending east from the Mississippi River. It was in many ways similar to the impregnable position at Fredericksburg, Virginia, that Burnside had foolishly attacked 16 days earlier. Unlike Burnside, however, it took Sherman only about 1,800 casualties (in two hours) before realizing that he was attempting the impossible. He called off the attack and ordered a retreat back upriver to the Federal outpost at Milliken's Bend, located north of the Yazoo River on the west bank of the Mississippi.[35] Thus ended in a whimper Grant's first Vicksburg campaign.

Sherman's repulse at Chickasaw Bluffs was particularly frustrating because upon the return of his force to Milliken's Bend, he was greeted by newly-arrived General John McClernand and was immediately ordered to hand over his command. Sherman's blind dash at Vicksburg in cooperation with Grant had been motivated by their joint desire to avoid McClernand and the continuing saga of his independent authorization from President Lincoln. Sherman had not only taken his own men with him to Chickasaw Bluffs but also those volunteers recently raised by McClernand. For this purpose he had rushed back to Memphis on December 8 and, in accordance with Grant's orders, taken over the new troops before McClernand arrived on the scene. Grant himself later explained, "I doubted McClernand's fitness; and had good reason to believe that in forestalling him I was by no means giving offence to those whose authority to command was above both him and me." Then, on December 18, just before chaos erupted in Grant's sector, he was ordered by Halleck to include the en-route McClernand in the overall Federal advance. "This," Grant remarked, "...interfered with my plans, but probably resulted in my ultimately taking command in person."[36]

Grant, however, was about to be cut off from the outside world and Sherman had already left Memphis. By the time that Sherman was underway, all communications between Grant and the outside world had been severed—courtesy of Van Dorn and Forrest—and Grant could no longer change what had been set in motion. Bruce Catton marveled, "By an odd coincidence, this interruption of communications came just when it would be most damaging to the aspirations of General McClernand."[37] After marrying his young second wife on December 23, a perplexed McClernand (with bride in tow) arrived via steamboat in Memphis on December 28, only to find that his new army had moved on without him.[38] That he later found it and asserted his rank over Sherman in early January did not change the big picture substantially, except perhaps to fill an already overly-conceited McClernand with an even higher opinion of himself than was justified.

Although the year 1862 ended on this sour note for Grant, it had still been a year in which large parts of the western Confederacy ceased to exist, thanks mainly to Grant's efforts at Fort Donelson, Shiloh, and Corinth. At the beginning of the year, Grant had been just another Union Brigadier General with a questionable reputation after fighting the battle of Belmont. Now, the first abortive Vicksburg campaign, seemingly so futile at the time, would yield several long-term benefits for the Federals. In addition to throwing (and keeping) the Confederates in a defensive posture, Grant had learned the crucial lesson of an army living off the land, a lesson that would play such a devastating role in Federal strategy for the rest of the war. In addition, Grant's most destructive rival, the political adventurer John McClernand, had been contained with unlikely, concerted help. Finally, Confederate forces at Vicksburg seemed to enter into another new phase of false confidence and blindness that would contribute to their complete undoing over the next six months.

CHAPTER 22

January 1863: The Second Vicksburg Campaign

New Year's Day 1863 began with the nightmarish battle of Stone's River being fought near Murfreesboro, Tennessee. By the end of January 2, General William Rosecrans, now with his own independent command, had led the Federal Army of the Cumberland to a hard-fought victory over Braxton Bragg's Confederate Army of Tennessee. This was achieved with no small help from the division under General Philip Sheridan, whose services had been diverted away from Grant's army the previous summer, and had played a similar key role at Perryville in September. Also similar to Shiloh, by the time the Confederates began their retreat, Union forces had been so damaged by the three-day engagement that it probably did not have the will to pursue, even had Rosecrans ordered it to do so. The end result of Stone's River was that the Federals maintained a firm grip on east-central Tennessee, and perhaps even more problematic for the Confederates, for the second time in four months Bragg's leadership suffered a severe loss in confidence among his troops and subordinates.[1]

The stalemate in eastern Tennessee had more than indirect consequences for Grant's second Vicksburg campaign. Though technically victorious at Stone's River, Rosecrans and his army still left the impression with friend and foe alike that they needed all the help they could get. This meant that large reinforcements were unlikely to come Grant's way. It also meant there was still a possibility that Grant may have been called upon to send reinforcements to Rosecrans. Unlike Pemberton at Vicksburg, Bragg was trying to gain back what had been lost (however ineffectively) in his sector, and in terms of priorities had the support of his immediate superior, General Joseph Johnston. Jefferson Davis, though, saw things differently and demanded that a good portion of the western Confederate Army remain in Mississippi. Accordingly, few troops were diverted from either side. Much of the Confederate force would be haplessly consumed over the next six months while trying to oppose some of the most brilliant and surprising military maneuvers in history. At the beginning of January 1863, however, Grant found himself isolated in the northern part of the state and temporarily cut off from outside communications. Telegrams, on the other hand, would be very soon in arriving, beginning with a directive from President Lincoln to make right something Grant had made wrong the previous month.

On January 4, Grant was ordered by General Henry Halleck from Washington to revoke his infamous General Order No. 11, in which he attempted to expel all Jews from his department. This was only 18 days after the order had been originally issued. Since that moment, a delegation from Paducah, Kentucky, led by businessman and civic leader Cesar Kaskel, had arrived in Washington and was granted a personal audience by President Lincoln. Lincoln greeted Kaskel with the words, "And so the children of Israel were driven from the happy land of Canaan?" Without missing a beat, Kaskel responded, "Yes, and that is why we have come to Father Abraham's bosom, asking protection." An impressed Lincoln replied with "And this protection they shall have at once."[2] After the revocation was endorsed by Halleck, he explained to Grant that the issue was not "Jew peddlers" but rather Jews as a class, many of whom were serving in the Federal army and the vast majority of whom were not creating any mischief. Even more serious for Grant's public image was a congressional resolution to censure him for issuing the order, which was narrowly defeated 56–53 in the House. This result was thanks in large measure to yet another vigorous defense of Grant by Congressman Elihu Washburne.[3] Grant was, in turn (at least according to Julia in her memoirs), grateful to Washburne at the time for this help,[4] in addition to the many other previous assists received from his omnipresent political benefactor.

Back in Mississippi, Grant regrouped his forces at Holly Springs, their supply base having been destroyed in late December, and completely unaware that Sherman's attempt to assault Vicksburg directly from the north had come to grief at Chickasaw Bluffs on December 29. On the same day (January 4) that Halleck directed Grant to revoke General Order No. 11, Sherman handed over his command to General John McClernand, who had finally arrived at Milliken's Bend on January 2, accompanied by his new bride and filled with fantasies of military glory. Though privately galled at being forced to stand down, Sherman put on a good face and prepared to manipulate, with surprising effectiveness, his dimwitted new commander. The previous day (January 3), Admiral David Porter wrote to the ailing Commodore Andrew Foote (whom Porter had superceded) that "McClernand has just arrived and will take command. Sherman, though, will have all the brains."[5] Porter, like most of his colleagues in both service branches, was no fan of McClernand and was deeply concerned over his potential negative impact on the Vicksburg campaign. In tandem with Sherman, Porter prepared to direct McClernand's fitful nervous energy into constructive channels, at least until the local Federal command structure could be improved. This improvement would not occur until Grant arrived on the scene personally.

The first project that Sherman and Porter used to occupy the attention of McClernand was a raid against the Confederate garrison stationed at Arkansas Post, about 50 miles northwest of Vicksburg along the Arkansas River. This combined land and amphibious assault was successfully completed on January 11, with army and navy working together seamlessly as a team. Meanwhile, Grant had left Holly Springs for Memphis on January 9, having only recently been made aware of Sherman's repulse at Chickasaw Bluffs some 12 days earlier. Arriving in Memphis on January 11, Grant now learned of the new side movement into Arkansas and complained to Halleck that McClernand had gone off on a "wild-goose chase."[6] Soon, however, Grant realized that the whole thing had been Sherman's idea to keep McClernand busy and then changed his tune, especially after becoming cognizant that the raid had eliminated a potentially dangerous outside threat to their Vicksburg operations. As a result, Sherman had simultaneously succeeded diverting the attention of McClernand and accomplishing a bona fide military objective. Grant may well have been more grateful to Sherman for his incredible energy and foresight than to Washburne for warding off a political censure from the House of Representatives.

Grant's premature outburst against McClernand, instead of angering Halleck, met with approval. Both Grant and Halleck—two professional West Point soldiers—were highly mistrustful of the political general who continued to show little or no efficiency when left to his own devices. On January 12, Halleck wired Grant, "You are hereby authorized to relieve General McClernand from command of the expedition against Vicksburg, giving it to the next in rank or taking it yourself."[7] In the words of Jean Edward Smith, "For Grant, Halleck's telegram was a godsend."[8] On January 13, Grant wrote to General James McPherson that he now intended to take command in person,[9] even though this went against his original plan, which was to utilize Sherman's skills independently.[10] By now Sherman and Porter urged Grant to take command in person as well, in order to relieve them of having to baby-sit for McClernand. Thus Grant's direct command for one of the greatest campaigns in military history resulted not from his own design, but rather from the political ambition of an inept subordinate. Accordingly, that same day (January 13) Grant from Memphis ordered all troops under McClernand to return from Arkansas Post back to the environs of Vicksburg. This was only two days after the Confederate garrison there had been suppressed by McClernand's expedition under the combined guidance of Sherman and Porter.

By January 16, Grant was steaming south from Memphis. On January 17, he and McClernand met face to face at the appropriately named port town of Napoleon, Arkansas. It was probably here that it dawned on McClernand for the first time that his "independent" command was to be no more independent than any other in Grant's department. At this conference, which included Sherman and Porter, Grant later wrote that he was firsthand witness to everyone's mistrust of McClernand, that he considered this mistrust to be "an element of weakness," and that he felt "great embarrassment about McClernand."[11] Still not quite ready to assert his authority, Grant then immediately returned to Memphis and began preparations to personally lead the Vicksburg expedition at the end of the month. McClernand, perhaps sensing that the carpet was about to be yanked out from under him, whined in a letter to President Lincoln about the "clique of West Pointers who have been persecuting me for months."[12] Lincoln, however, was no longer willing to overrule Halleck in this matter, especially now that more troops had been levied. That these volunteers had been levied by McClernand himself may have been viewed by his distrustful colleagues as "mission accomplished," as opposed to McClernand leading these same volunteers into combat himself. Writing in smooth, Lincolnesque language, the President informed McClernand that he would not back him up: "You are doing well—well for the country, and well for yourself—much better than you could possibly be if engaged in open war with General Halleck."[13] This was sound advice that McClernand would never heed.

Grant himself wrote to Halleck on January 20 that he had no faith whatsoever in McClernand's leadership. This opinion placed emphasis on Grant's not being alone in his assessment, which was shared by Sherman and Porter:

> I regard it my duty to state, that I found there was not sufficient confidence in Gen. McClernand as a commander; either by the Army or Navy, to insure him of success. Of course all would cooperate to the best of their ability but still with a distrust. This is a matter I made no enquiries about but it was forced upon me. As it is my intention to command in person, unless otherwise directed, there is no special necessity of mentioning this matter, but I want you to know that others besides myself agree in the necessity of the course I had already determined upon pursuing. Admiral Porter told me that he had written freely to the Sec. of Navy on this subject, with the request that what he said might be shown to the Sec. of War.[14]

Grant's reference to Porter is yet another example of the full support from the navy that he received throughout the war, first from Commodore Foote, and now under his appointed successor. Porter, though completely different in personality and background from Grant, had first met the controversial but unassuming department commander in December, and was highly impressed by Grant's straightforward single-mindedness of purpose with respect to Vicksburg.[15] This was in polar opposition to Porter's outspoken negative view of McClernand as a vainglorious fool.

One week and one day later, on January 28, Grant traveled to Young's Point above Vicksburg, having made final arrangements for supplies and logistics with his designated legatee in Memphis, General Stephen Hurlbut. Though anecdotal in nature, novelist-historian Shelby Foote's account of Grant's arrival perhaps best captured the typical reaction of Federal troops unfamiliar with their commander's low-keyed style and minimal indication of rank: "There's General Grant," an Illinois soldier told a comrade as they stood and watched his unceremonious arrival. "I guess not," the other replied, shaking his head. "That fellow don't look like he has the ability to command a regiment, much less an army."[16] Admiral Porter, for one, was relieved, writing to Secretary of Navy Gideon Welles on the same day, "General Grant is here now, and I hope for a better state of things."[17] Setting up his floating headquarters on the steamer *Magnolia*, Grant also allowed, rather incredibly, his favorite journalist Sylvanus Cadwallader to have a private room on the same boat, thus once again giving this fated reporter a front-row seat for the historic campaign that was about to unfold.

Cadwallader's ability to get preferential treatment was uncanny and appears due mainly to his formation of a close relationship with Grant's heavily relied-upon adjunct, John Rawlins. Cadwallader first described in convincing fashion the high level of security that was constantly maintained around the *Magnolia*, then how he was informed privately by Rawlins that he would be allowed exclusive access, not to mention his choice of unoccupied state rooms and meal service.[18] One must infer from these unusual privileges that Grant and Rawlins felt Cadwallader had more than good P.R. to offer them in return. This probably included sympathetic company and a potential buffer against the many public detractors who would soon redouble their efforts against Grant, especially over the next three months.

The moment for Grant to assert his rank over McClernand had finally arrived as well. Responding to a letter from McClernand later characterized as "a reprimand" and "highly insubordinate," Grant wrote back on January 30 that he was now officially commanding the expedition in person, over McClernand and everyone else, and in accordance with Halleck's earlier authorization. Then on January 31, Grant formally issued the symbolically numbered General Order No. 13, assigning McClernand to oversee the symbolically numbered 13th Army Corps.[19] On a less symbolic level, Grant was opting for the classic and time-proven strategy of keeping his most troublesome subordinate close at hand where he could be carefully watched, if not completely controlled. Those whom he trusted—Sherman, McPherson, and even the officially unbeholden Admiral Porter—were given indirect license to operate further afield; they were also no longer under McClernand's dangerous authority.

If wrangling with McClernand required great finesse, Grant's anticipated engagement with the Confederate army at Vicksburg would necessitate the employment of all his accumulated experience, skill, and endurance as a soldier. Writing to Julia on the last day of January, Grant, after earlier warning her that he would not be returning to Memphis anytime soon, confided that "Vicksburg will be a hard job."[20] This assessment would prove entirely correct, unlike McClernand's ridiculous and alarming prediction to Porter that

Vicksburg could be taken in a week. Threshold difficulties included weather and topography. Before any battles could be fought, the Federals had to first find a way toward the Mississippi citadel. In addition to the high bluffs upon the river, the only other dry ground in the immediate area was located east and south of the city. Everything else consisted of tributary rivers, bayous, swamps, canals and lakes—all now in the process of swelling far beyond their usual capacity. This was due to heavier rains than normal, even for the winter season in Mississippi.

Compounding these threshold difficulties was that Grant had to work within very defined limits, both in regards to his allocated manpower and the number of available transport ships. In short, he did not outnumber the enemy. This problem was somewhat offset, however, by the wide dispersal of Confederate forces over a vast Mississippi landscape, and even more countered by a divided and dysfunctional leadership structure. Jefferson Davis not only disregarded Joseph Johnston's prioritization of eastern Tennessee, he then later discouraged Johnston's preference for concentration of these forces for striking back against Grant. The idea of surrendering an inch of Mississippi real estate in order to beat an invading army was apparently a concept that Davis never learned when he attended West Point, or afterwards, for that matter. On the Federal side, Grant's gathering army around Vicksburg would have been greatly enhanced by any outside help, whether this came from eastern Tennessee or elsewhere.

No more outside help was coming. McClernand's new levies had already arrived and had been deployed. To the south, combined Federal land and naval operations had been stymied at Port Hudson, Louisiana, due in no small part to the timid and inept leadership of General Nathaniel Banks. Banks had been one of three Federal commanders defeated by Stonewall Jackson in the Shenandoah Valley during the previous year, and would go on to earn a reputation for mediocrity (at best) during the course of the war. So ineffectual were Federal efforts at Port Hudson that Banks, despite receiving help from his peerless naval colleague Admiral David Farragut, may have been content simply to prevent the Confederates from sending reinforcements to Vicksburg. Halleck from Washington felt a need to advise Grant that no one had any faith in Banks; therefore, he should expect to be pretty much on his own.[21]

As Grant's second Vicksburg campaign unfolded over the next five months, any impartial historian—amateur or otherwise—must be struck by the unlikelihood of how it unfolded. Things rarely (if ever) went as planned for either side. The first Federal attempt to take Vicksburg, so promising in its beginnings and sound in its conventional planning, had ended abruptly in confusion and retreat. Now the Union army faced an entirely new set of problems and variables that few had foreseen. The excruciating difficulty of what Grant and his army were about to accomplish should never be underestimated by those studying it in hindsight, although more often than not this is precisely what many military historians tend to do. The ultimate achievement is typically viewed as being the result of a scientific process, or worse, as something inevitable. The first step—that of forming a viable strategy—would perhaps be the hardest. Twenty years later in his memoirs, Grant recorded that at this point in time, "The real work of the campaign and siege of Vicksburg now began."[22]

CHAPTER 23

February 1863:
Bogged Down, Literally

General John McClernand had not quite given up trying to break free from Grant's higher authority. Like a petulant child, McClernand fired back an angry letter to Grant on February 1 after being preemptively ordered to take his place among the Federal corps commanders facing Vicksburg. With his scope of command now specifically limited, McClernand wrote to Grant with indignation, "I protest against its competency and justice." Then he demanded that the whole matter be submitted to General Halleck, Secretary of War Stanton, and President Lincoln, although McClernand agreed to do as he was told in the meantime. This was necessary, he lectured Grant (with startling chutzpah), because the Federals needed to keep a united front in the face of the enemy.[1] By insisting upon this appeal to higher authority, however, McClernand was really bluffing and blowing smoke, since Lincoln had earlier written to tell him that he would not back McClernand up in a dispute with Halleck.

Grant immediately called McClernand's bluff. Before punctually forwarding copies of their correspondence to Washington—this was still February 1—Grant wrote a cover letter in his most formidable, professional manner, explaining:

> If Gen. Sherman had been left in command here such is my confidence in him that I would not have thought my presence necessary. But, whether I do Gen. McClernand injustice or not, I have not confidence in his ability as a soldier to conduct an expedition of the magnitude of this one successfully. In this opinion I have no doubt but I am born out by a majority of the officers of the expedition though I have not questioned one of them on the subject. I respectfully submit this whole matter to the Gen. in Chief and the President. Whatever the decision made by them I will cheerfully submit to and give a hearty support.[2]

Grant by now must have known that Halleck was going to support him, if nothing else, out of his respect for Sherman, who loathed serving under McClernand. The worst-case scenario for Grant and Sherman was that Lincoln would once again change his mind and overrule Halleck. This did not come to pass, though, nor did Lincoln see fit to respond to McClernand's final written protest.[3]

Once again, Lincoln's better judgment had prevailed at a crucial moment, despite the earlier encouragement that he had given to McClernand for an independent expedition, and in spite of the long history of the two men together in Illinois politics. McClernand did have cause to be miffed that the large volunteer force he had recently raised and sent south would now be subject to Grant's ultimate authority; on the other hand, it did not take a crystal ball to see what was coming. The irascible political general was probably just as upset at no longer being the sole decision-maker, not to mention having been embarrassed in front of his new second wife. Grant had now firmly taken over the reins, and this control was not symbolic or illusory: later in the month, when McClernand tried to suggest a repeat of his recently successful excursion into Arkansas, Grant quickly nixed the idea.[4] From now on, the exclusive focus of the expedition would be on capturing Vicksburg itself.

Complete focus would indeed be required. With heavy rains and the Mississippi winter season turning the low ground occupied by the Federals into one big morass, problems multiplied. Hundreds of troops, eventually thousands, began to die of every known variety of swamp illness, and many others deserted in order to avoid this fate or simply out of boredom and impatience.[5] They had not signed up to spend the winter in a bog. Direct, head-on assault against Vicksburg by land and/or river—as demonstrated by Sherman in December at Chickasaw Bluffs—would result in, at best, a Pyrrhic victory or, more likely, a pointless sacrifice of men and material. Numerically, Grant's army was at its peak and in enemy territory with no reinforcements coming, plus a possibility that they themselves would be called upon to send reinforcements east. The only tactical advantage enjoyed by the Federals was that their gunboats controlled the river, but even this control was not absolute, as the month of February would underscore. Perhaps the only real advantage enjoyed by Grant—one that he seems to have appreciated at the time—was that the Confederate command structure, besides being stridently overconfident, was divided and, with a few notable exceptions, breathtakingly inept.

A persisting myth among students of the war is that Grant's grand strategy to take Vicksburg was conceived full-blown at the outset of the campaign like Minerva springing from the head of Jupiter. Grant himself wrote after the fact, "From the moment of taking command in person, I became satisfied that Vicksburg could only be turned from the south side."[6] Be that as it may, the next two months would be consumed with activities designed to find shortcuts for the transport boats needed to bring troops across to the east bank of the Mississippi, and what Grant did after he finally got them there can only be attributed to inspiration of the moment. Perhaps his most controversial decision at the beginning of February, at least one that went against the conventional wisdom of the day, was to not order a retreat to Memphis, since from there another campaign could be launched across north central Mississippi, one that could be conducted mostly upon dry ground. Grant, despite his West Point training, had thus far been sustained by the political good graces of Lincoln and Washburne, and by now perhaps had a much fuller appreciation for the political aspects of warfare. This was in opposition to his most able lieutenants, such as Sherman and McPherson, who would favor such a retreat right up to the moment that Grant committed his army to a far more unconventional course. Recognizing that any perception of retreat at this point would be politically disastrous for the Union, Grant decided that the only political option was stay and find a way into Vicksburg or die in the attempt. As he later wrote in his memoirs, "There was nothing left to be done but to *go forward to a decisive victory*."[7]

A more likely scenario for the development of Grant's successful and complex strategy at Vicksburg is that it developed gradually and organically, piece by piece, over the course of the next three months. This kind of open-minded, experimental approach was in keeping with Grant's style throughout the war: try everything, see what worked, and then exploit whatever did. In February 1863, this meant putting all available manpower to work in an attempt to create a water route bypassing Confederate guns and also leading to dry ground. In hindsight Grant claimed that he never felt much faith in these experiments but believed them necessary as a diversion for the enemy, the Northern public, and his own troops, at least until the harsh elements of Nature offered other alternatives.[8]

To assist in this task, Grant had at his disposal two of the army's finest young engineers, General James McPherson and the newly arrived Colonel James Harrison Wilson. The day after Grant assumed personal command of the expedition at Young's Point, Wilson quickly sized up the big picture and advised chief-of-staff John Rawlins that Grant should opt for the plan he eventually adopted. This first involved running the fleet directly downstream and then, with whatever got through, shuttling the army over to the east bank, south of Vicksburg. Before then, the troops should move south along the west bank as best they could, beyond the range of the Confederate guns. Grant reportedly listened to the proposal and made no response.[9] This plan, too, carried enormous risk. Even assuming the fleet could get through, once through it would probably not be able to get back upstream against both the river current and enemy artillery.

Grant decided to at least try other alternatives before staking all on a single throw of the dice. In sum, he chose to risk accomplishing nothing for a few months, rather than immediately risking everything, or worse, politically risk going back to Memphis. This decision was a far cry from the impatient combat soldier who had hurled himself against Belmont Landing less than 15 months earlier, and reflected a significant maturing process that had taken place in Grant during that time. It was also not the type of decision that a commander could loudly broadcast to his subordinates—it had to be internalized, something that Grant had always been good at. As military historian J.F.C. Fuller phrased it, Grant's officers "could only help him by being kept in the dark."[10] Perhaps the experiments would succeed but more likely they would not. The Federals could only try while waiting for the Mississippi waters to recede in the spring. It was a truth too depressing to say out loud.

Large quantities of ink have been expended by historians (and even by Grant himself) in the minute description of the multiple canal projects attempted by the Federal army during the winter of early 1863 at Vicksburg. I do not intend to join this distinguished company. Jean Edward Smith best summed up the Herculean Federal effort to create no fewer than five different water shortcuts to their objective with: "For the next ten weeks Grant busied himself with a variety of halfbaked schemes to divert the Mississippi from its main channel and provide an alternative water route to flank Vicksburg's defenses."[11] Three of these attempts were on the west side of the river and two were on the east, north of the city. All were eventually foiled by weather, mud, and rapid Confederate countermeasures that often were more bemused than alarmed in attitude.

As early as February 4, Grant was expressing a loss of faith in the first of these canal routes, a short bypass around the western bend of the river north of the city.[12] First the river current would not cooperate, or rather the canal was improperly designed by its original Confederate builders, failing to take advantage of the current. Confederate artillerists were clever enough, however (once they realized what was being done), to adjust their guns so that this canal became nearly as dangerous for the Federals as the river itself. About the same time, Grant authorized work on a monumentally longer canal route that would be safely out of enemy range, beginning at Lake Providence, Louisiana (to the northwest). The scope of work, however, was unrealistically large to begin with, but Lake Providence did serve as a convenient place for Federal officers to take recreational pleasure cruises while work was in progress. Simultaneous with the Lake Providence boondoggle, to the east of the river and north of Vicksburg, the Federals blew out the levees along the Yazoo River, causing the entire Mississippi tributary system north of Vicksburg to flood. This created even more wet ground and less dry, but the thought was to take advantage of the high water and give the Federal navy more room to maneuver.[13] Organized expeditions along these enhanced waterways in March (see Chapter 24) would prove to be mini-fiascos. During February, however, these at least offered a forlorn hope for Grant's forces while other setbacks both big and small were being experienced. Grant at one point even lost his dentures to the river when a servant accidentally tossed them overboard.[14] Regarding the various failed Federal projects during this frustrating stage of the campaign, J.F.C. Fuller put the best spin he could on them by opining,

"...though all failed in their object, they undoubtedly formed admirable training for Grant's army, hardening and disciplining the men, in fact turning
them into salted soldiers."[15] I would add that digging ditches and battling
swamp fever also probably made them more eager to fight the Confederates.

While the army was busy "hardening and disciplining" itself, the navy
was conducting its own series of experiments. These mainly consisted of seeing whether it was at all feasible to run the Confederate batteries above the
river on the bluffs of Vicksburg. It rather surprisingly proved to be the case
with enough speed or armament. Grant also noticed that these successful
runs "produced the greatest consternation among the people along the Mississippi from Vicksburg to the Red River."[16] Almost as soon as the navy began
to think it a routine assignment, however, the Confederates succeeded in dis-
abling and capturing two of these ships in quick order—the famed lightweight
ram-steamer *Queen of the West*, and, more problematic for the Federals, the
formidable ironclad gunboat *Indianola*. Grant blamed the loss of the *Indianola*
on its captain and crew trying to accomplish too much by going upstream with
a heavy barge in tow against a small fleet of makeshift Confederate vessels,
which included the recently captured and repaired *Queen of the West*. While
the Southerners rejoiced at these gains, Grant became convinced that a large-
scale run past the bluffs, properly planned and organized, could make it
through with acceptable losses.[17]

Confederate possession of one of the Federal navy's proudest ironclads
could have posed a serious problem for Grant. Admiral Porter remedied the
situation, however, in very unlikely fashion. On February 26, Porter floated
downstream a quickly constructed dummy craft that looked very much like
an enlarged version of the prototypical and legendary Federal ironclad *Monitor*. Panicked Confederates, including those aboard the *Queen of the West*, fled
before the approach of the unmanned raft, as artillery shots passed mysteriously through their target with little or no effect. Downstream, work crews
trying to repair the *Indianola* heard rumors of the attacking monster and hur-
riedly decided to blow it up rather than surrender their prize. Soon after this,
when Porter's giant theatrical prop became stuck in the mud not far from
shore, the first Confederates with the courage to approach it discovered not
an invincible warship but only a painted inscription reading "Deluded people, cave, in."[18] While these antics seemed of little importance at the time, it
is probably significant that the *Indianola* was not repaired to be later used by
South against Porter's fleet. While Grant and Porter were very different in
many ways, both shared a love of the theater, and this incident marked a noteworthy use of Porter's dramatic talent during the war.

The greatest arts of illusion, though, were being exercised by the news
media on both sides of the conflict. While the Confederate press alternatively
carped and barked, Northern papers fought amongst themselves over market

share and news scoops. Grant in his memoirs noted with humorous understatement that "wars produce many stories of fiction," and with barely disguised frustration that "I would like to see truthful history written."[19] The stunningly successful access gained to Grant by Sylvanus Cadwallader of the *Chicago Times* seems to have been predicated (at least in part) on Cadwallader's comparatively truthful reporting, whatever his other faults may have been. In early February, Cadwallader learned that General Stephen Hurlbut in Memphis had suppressed the circulation of his paper, but by February 13 had persuaded Grant (via Rawlins) to revoke Hurlbut's order. Without attaching any blame to Hurlbut—a veteran of Shiloh and one of Grant's most loyal subordinates—Cadwallader in his memoirs explained that the original ban had been the result of Federal officers in Memphis being whipped into a frenzy by rival papers jealous over the *Times'* burgeoning circulation.[20] Grant, in a diplomatic letter to Hurlbut, wrote almost apologetically that whatever Copperhead lies were being printed by the *Times* (presumably, not written by Cadwallader himself), these would only be amplified by a departmental suppression.[21] In effect, Grant wrote, it would bring only more publicity to try to stop it; nevertheless, Grant would change his tune in March when local papers began to violate his other principal injunction against Cadwallader—giving advance notice of Federal military movements.

On February 14, the day after Grant ordered Hurlbut to lift his ban of the *Times*, Grant wrote to Julia that he believed the only real threats to his campaign were desertions and bad press, as opposed to Confederate resistance.[22] Before Grant had exempted Cadwallader's employer from censure, however, Sherman had been busy making an example out of another errant journalist. In late December, Henry Knox of the *New York Herald* had smuggled himself into Sherman's army, despite the latter's ban against noncombatants. Then Knox attacked Sherman in print for his performance at Chickasaw Bluffs, and among a number of factual errors also repeated the refrain that Sherman was mentally imbalanced. Sherman, who hated all reporters to begin with, responded by arresting Knox. On February 1, Knox tried to make amends by writing a groveling apology to Sherman, who, rather than being mollified, had Knox ingloriously court-martialed and expelled from the department on February 5. Knox would then loudly appeal his case to President Lincoln and the Northern public.[23] Although Grant was not yet involved in the case, he would later become so and once again demonstrate his growing sophistication at dealing with the press.

Kenneth Williams wrote that "Grant's winter before Vicksburg was one of the great testing periods of the war...."[24] Physical endurance and patience were strained and both would eventually be pushed to their limits. If February had been a bad month for Grant, though, March would prove to be horrendous. As Mississippi winter flood levels peaked, Federal hopes around Vicksburg seemed to be drowned in the process. All of the hard work put into the canal projects was about to unravel amidst widespread frustration. Now an exasperated Northern press would get into the act, and Grant's accumulated enemies at all levels would make one final effort to conspire for his removal.

CHAPTER 24

March 1863:
Steele Bayou Expedition

By early March, flooding along the Yazoo River was cresting as a result of seasonal rains and Federal sabotage of the levees. The Yazoo, along with its tributaries, the Tallahatchie and the Yalobusha, plus numerous bayous and swamps, offered the prospect of a Federal combined land and naval assault against Vicksburg from the northeast. Such an attack would (in theory, at least) bypass the bluffs and get the troops on a dry, firm footing. Naval superiority was (usually) a clear-cut Northern advantage that Grant always took advantage of if possible. The first of these hopeful expeditions converged on a strategic point where the Tallahatchie and Yalobusha flowed into the Yazoo River, only to find a hastily constructed Confederate stronghold, surrounded on all sides by water and dubbed Fort Pemberton by its defenders.

Fort Pemberton was commanded by none other than General Lloyd Tilghman, who had been captured by Grant at Fort Henry, Tennessee, the previous year, and since exchanged back into the Confederate service. Tilghman was now determined to redeem his military reputation and more or less did just that. In three separate amphibious attacks on March 11, March 13, and March 16, the Federals made absolutely no headway, being severely limited by the burgeoning flood plain that they had been so instrumental in creating. After inflicting few (if any) casualties and suffering numerous ones in return—including their fleet commander, who suffered a nervous breakdown—the Federals had to admit that they were stymied and withdrew.[1]

Immediately in wake of this dramatic failure, the apex of Federal hopes in the Yazoo sector came with Admiral Porter commanding his flagship gunboat in person along the flooded Steele Bayou towards Vicksburg. He was supported by Sherman's infantry, who were being transported not far behind. On March 15, Porter and Grant personally reconnoitered the entrance to Steele Bayou and on March 16 the expedition set out with high hopes. Sylvanus Cadwallader, once again an eyewitness, sarcastically described this slow advance with mock foreboding, as if Napoleon were marching across the steppes of Russia to meet his fate. The Federals at first encountered no rebels, but plenty of threatening wildlife in a Paleozoic environment that any sensible person would have avoided at all costs. Cadwallader memorably nails his description of Steele Bayou: "Not a plantation or clearing broke its dreary solitude for forty miles. Birds, fish, snakes, turtles and alligators were the only living things we saw while traversing its gloomy labyrinths."[2] After getting through this formidable natural barrier, Porter then ran right straight into Confederate special forces, some 4,000 strong, who were eagerly waiting for him.

To stop an ironclad in the bayou, the Confederates had merely cut down a lot of trees. Then, once lured into the trap, Porter realized that trees were being cut down behind him as well. Any Federal shipman who dared to poke his head out of a porthole became sport for sophisticatedly positioned sharpshooters. It was payback time for the dummy ironclad trick that Porter had played on the Southerners back in February. Miraculously, Porter found a local freedman—typically ignored as non-persons in the eyes of many Confederates—who heroically escaped through the swamp and somehow managed to deliver an SOS to Sherman. In response to Porter's abject plea for help, Sherman's infantry waded forward and drove back the Confederates long enough so that the ironclad could backpedal out of trouble.[3] After getting over their amusement at the navy's plight, Federal troops were mainly disgusted by the whole affair. On March 22, the ill-fated Steele's Bayou expedition was officially abandoned.

Reporter Cadwallader was not impressed with Admiral Porter's performance during this nor any other episode in the war. Long afterwards he wrote:

> At the risk of being thought dogmatic, and of standing alone in this opinion, I pronounce him [Porter] by all odds the greatest humbug of the war. He absolutely never accomplished anything if unaided. He bombarded Vicksburg for months; threw hundreds of tons of metal into the city; never hit but one house and never killed a man. The Confederates laughed at him.... Add to this that Porter was vain, arrogant and egotistical to an extent that neither can be described nor exaggerated and you have his caliber completely.[4]

If this were not enough, he then accuses Porter of riding Grant's coattails to fame throughout the war, but acknowledges that Porter "possessed many polite accomplishments"—a backhanded reference to the admiral's love of theater and high culture.[5] David Dixon Porter is generally held in higher esteem than this, but it is certainly true that the Steele Bayou expedition was not his finest moment. Furthermore, he owed his survival that day to Sherman's efficiency plus the personal bravery of a Mississippi freedman.[6]

In spite of all this, Grant was not quite through experimenting. Back on the west side of the Mississippi River, it had finally dawned on everyone that the gigantic Lake Providence canal project would not be completed before doomsday. During the process, however, Grant and his engineers noticed that another, intermediate canal route might be created, running roughly between Duckport, Louisiana, to the north and New Carthage, Louisiana, to the south. This would be shorter and more practicable than the Lake Providence route, but also longer than the first canal that had been thwarted by poor design and new Confederate artillery placement. The only problem with the new route was that it depended upon high water to be navigable, and by late March, the Father of Waters—"perverse to the ways of man," in the words of Jean Edward Smith[7]—had finally begun its annual receding process. What should have been the first plan all along came to grief because everyone had been too slow in recognizing its merit.

Long after these events, Grant noted philosophically and perhaps with a bit of self-justification that his five attempts to cut a shortcut to Vicksburg, if nothing else, kept the enemy guessing as to his intentions. The Confederates may have been fooled, but the Northern press was not. By mid–March Grant was weathering the most relentless media storm that he had experienced since Shiloh. It began with the papers giving lurid and not entirely inaccurate accounts of sickness and death in the Federal camps and makeshift hospitals along the Mississippi.[8] After the navy was foiled along the Yazoo Pass, criticism intensified. Despairingly, the *New York Times* reported that Grant was now "stuck in the mud of northern Mississippi, his army of no use to him or anybody else."[9] Even the brother of Congressman Washburne, now serving in Grant's army under General McPherson, wrote confidentially, "The truth must be told even if it hurts. You cannot make a silk purse out of a sow's ear."[10] Another Federal officer wrote, "This winter is, indeed the Valley Forge of the war."[11] Historian James McPherson described the dreary situation in the fewest words: "For two months Grant's army had been floundering in the mud."[12]

Rumors also began to circulate that Grant had fallen off the wagon, and these appear to have been not entirely unfounded. Julia was not with him and neither was Rawlins for at least part of the time. On March 15, General McClernand, still chafing at Grant and the West Pointers who had taken away his volunteer army, wrote President Lincoln to vouch for the character of Captain William Kountz ("an honest and reliable gentleman"). Kountz, the reader may recall, had been one of the loudest witnesses against Grant's sobriety during late 1861 and early 1862, before he had been incarcerated and then (it seems) encouraged to resign from the merchant marine. On the back of McClernand's letter to Lincoln was an undated and unsigned note, possibly in Kountz's handwriting, reading: "[O]n the 13th of March 1863 Genl. Grant was Gloriously drunk and in bed sick all next day. If you are averse to drunken Genls I can furnish the Name of officers of high standing to substantiate the above."[13]

Having been outwitted through regular army channels, McClernand was now apparently seeking to regain control of the Vicksburg expedition by having Grant sacked. That someone of McClernand's limited abilities should have risen to such a high rank was nothing unusual; that he now outranked men like Sherman, McPherson, and even other political generals such as Benjamin Prentice, continued to present a major problem for Grant. During this same period, Prentice was in command of the adjacent Federal district in eastern Arkansas. Available correspondence shows that he and Grant worked smoothly together despite having earlier butted heads on the issue of rank[14] and Prentice's division having been sacrificed by Grant at Shiloh. This stands in sharp contrast to Grant's relationship with McClernand which, though by now irretrievably hostile, was still far from bottoming out.

As for William Kountz, the pesky steamboat captain had decided to attempt reviving his war career by badgering Secretary of War Stanton, who finally wrote that he should report for duty to McClernand. Cautiously, Kountz wrote McClernand for clearance, and received this (as a river superintendent) on March 12, one day before Grant was allegedly making a spectacle out of himself, and three days before McClernand wrote Lincoln his insinuating letter. At this point, things could have easily spun out of control, March 13 also being one of the days that a Federal assault against the swampy Fort Pemberton had been repulsed and immediately prior to Porter and Sherman's ill-fated Steele Bayou expedition. Once again, however, vigilant chief-of-staff John Rawlins stepped in to fill the breach. Getting wind of Kountz's presence, Rawlins wrote McClernand a pointed letter on March 16 asking if Kountz had indeed returned. McClernand responded evasively on March 17 that Kountz had been there, but later departed on a steamer headed north.[15] Kountz, it appears, sized up his new surroundings around Vicksburg and decided to beat a quick retreat.

One could infer many things from this curious and obscure episode. Rather than engage in lengthy and idle speculation, however, I will merely postulate a single, likely scenario. Specifically, McClernand and Kountz, like many other vain and foolish schemers throughout history, may have suddenly realized what they were getting into, and the powerful individuals they were up against. Consequently, they decided the whole thing was a no-go. Kountz ran for cover (perhaps with McClernand's encouragement), and McClernand waited for his next opportunity to trap Grant in a moment of weakness. This moment of opportunity would in fact present itself before the Vicksburg campaign was concluded, but the end result would be that McClernand, rather than Grant, was the one given an embarrassing discharge from the service.

Between the concurrent aspersions made against Grant by McClernand, Kountz, Halstead, and all the others, something was bound to happen. Although Lincoln had, against all odds, resisted removing Grant from command, the decision was made to open a secret (or not so secret) investigation into the allegations of drunken incompetence. The first phase of this investigation consisted of sending to Vicksburg Adjunct General Lorenzo Thomas, the same man who, less than two years earlier, had filed away into oblivion

Grant's pathetic written request to be made a colonel in the regular army. Thomas was ordered west by Stanton on March 25, officially to inspect the new African-American regiments currently being organized around Memphis,[16] but unofficially to take a look at Grant's headquarters near Vicksburg. By this time, though, Thomas had no doubt formed a somewhat higher opinion of Grant and, more importantly, like his colleague Halleck, was surely inclined to close ranks around a fellow army professional such as Grant, regardless of fault.

Accordingly to Cadwallader, General Thomas arrived in Memphis and dallied there under the pretense of being fascinated with the new black regiments.[17] This was in fact a good pretense, since history was being made by these particular outfits, with men being transformed from slaves to contraband to freedmen to laborers to soldiers, all within the span of about one year. It was also an experiment that Grant, becoming more and more strapped for manpower, wholeheartedly approved of. In her memoirs, Julia—who was also in Memphis at the time—recalled her indignation when learning of Thomas' presence, and his "secret" mission to relieve her husband of command. She also claimed that Grant later told her that he was aware of Thomas' supposed objective and, rather incredibly, that he and Thomas were in cahoots.[18] Although by doing this Thomas effectively declined to do the dirty work of Washington politicians regarding Grant's alleged misbehavior, it only postponed the final showdown, since another, much more formidable messenger of intrigue would be dispatched by President Lincoln himself to the Vicksburg theater during the following month.

Grant probably realized by this time that he needed family support, and the first thing he did was to summon his excited 12-year-old son Fred to Vicksburg. As early as March 3, he had written to Julia on this subject, alluding to possible quarrels with his father over the matter.[19] Jesse Sr. was no doubt still recovering from the shock of their all being nearly captured by Confederates back in December, and Julia was probably concerned as well. It is not hard to surmise that Grant was hoping that, with his son around, homesickness would not easily overtake his better judgment. On March 29, Fred arrived at camp and would stay with his father throughout the duration of the campaign. The following day (March 30), a delighted Grant wrote to Julia that Fred had arrived and that "I never enjoyed better health or felt better in my life than since here."[20]

On March 27, two days before Fred's arrival at the Federal camp, his father had written to Julia and confided to her his military situation: "I am very well but much perplexed. Heretofore I have had nothing to do but fight the enemy. This time I have to overcome obstacles to reach him. Foot once upon dry land on the other side of the river I think the balance would be but of short duration."[21] The same intrepid army and determined commander that had been victorious at Donelson and Shiloh and Corinth were thus far baffled by the topography and climate of Vicksburg. This perplexity, though, would prove to be temporary.

In his memoirs, Grant gives a tortuously detailed description of the local geography, tedious to the casual reader but providing insight into Grant's successful generalship.[22] Whoever conquered Vicksburg would need an aptitude for complex topography, and Grant was just such a person. The first evidence of this ability can be seen from Grant's student days at West Point, where he created a series of striking watercolor and pen-and-ink landscapes under the tutelage of Robert Weir, who, in addition to being a distinguished artist himself, also taught the famous James Whistler.[23] Grant's little-known artistic talent—which easily translated into military cartography—is surprising to behold, just as his literary talent was to those who first noticed it only after his death. In this sense, he was like Stonewall Jackson, perhaps the greatest tactician produced by the war and one known for being a quick study of geographic problems.

On March 20, as frustration with the Vicksburg campaign was reaching peak level, Halleck wrote to Grant, reminding him that "The eyes and hopes of the whole country are now directed to your army.... In my opinion the opening of the Mississippi River will be to us of more advantage than the capture of forty Richmonds."[24] No one was more aware of this than Grant, and he was working on it. Military historian Arthur Conger, among others, relates the well-known story of an officer's party on board the *Magnolia* at Milliken's Bend and how an oblivious Grant sat apart, intensely studying maps. When the congenial General McPherson told Grant to lighten up and offered him a drink, Grant declined whiskey but asked for cigars and told McPherson that he would have things figured out by the time he had smoked them.[25]

Grant's casual remark did not mean that he would have a grand, inflexible plan for taking Vicksburg—"inflexible" does not appear to have been in his vocabulary, for that matter. What Grant's comment to McPherson probably meant was that he would soon have all the variables mastered and be prepared to use them to the best Federal advantage as opportunities presented themselves. Typically, Grant again kept the details to himself, for he likely knew that once these were known, the reaction from even his most loyal subordinates would be one of alarm and from Washington, outright approbation. Nevertheless, on March 29, Grant sent forward troops under his most untrustworthy subordinate, General McClernand, to New Carthage, Louisiana, located south of Vicksburg on the west bank of the Mississippi, to await further instructions. There would be no more attempted shortcuts or ditch-digging, and the first move of the ultimately successful plan had now been made. Months of unbroken frustration for the Federals was about to change.

CHAPTER 25

April 1863:
Running the Gauntlet

While morale in the Federal army began to sink under the weight of multiple hardships and setbacks in early April, the Yankee press was just getting warmed up. Kicking into high gear was Grant's indefatigable critic Marat Halstead, editor of the *Cincinnati Commercial*, who, among other accomplishments, had done so much to permanently poison relations between Grant and General William Rosecrans during the Corinth campaign. Now, when not exhorting his underlings to slam Grant publicly in print, Halstead devised a political attack showcasing the evil, creative genius for which he was known. Writing "privately" to his friend, Secretary of Treasury Salmon Chase, on April 1,[1] Halstead really went to work on Grant, labeling him

> ... a jackass in the original package. He is a poor drunken imbecile. He is a poor stick sober, and he is most of the time more than half drunk, and much of the time idiotically drunk.... Grant will fail miserably, hopelessly, eternally.[2]

These are just excerpts. Predictably, Chase showed the letter to Lincoln. At this point in the war, though, Lincoln was probably grateful to still have generals, alcoholic or otherwise, who had not yet been defeated in battle. He responded to Chase's alarmism with yet another one of his firm resolutions: "I think Grant has hardly a friend left, except myself.... What I want, and what the people want, is generals who will fight battles and win victories. Grant has done this and I propose to stand by him."[3]

Chaplain Lieutenant John Eaton, now overseeing the Freedman's Bureau courtesy of Grant, was also in Washington about this same time. He later related his famous story of witnessing a congressional delegation that approached Lincoln, demanding that Grant be sacked for drunken behavior. To this intense political pressure, Lincoln responded that they should find out Grant's brand of whiskey so he could give it to his other generals.[4] Lincoln in March of 1863 may not have been as fully appreciative of Grant as he would soon become, but he was not about to be railroaded into cashiering a man merely for perceived moral shortcomings. This defense of Grant represented a repeat performance for Lincoln, following the public outcry after Shiloh during the previous year. Halleck also held firm. Grant, to the end of his life, was appreciative, writing in his memoirs, "With all the pressure brought to bear upon them, President Lincoln and General Halleck stood by me to the end of the campaign. I had never met Mr. Lincoln, but his support was constant."[5] It is not idle speculation to suggest that, had it not been for the unique genius of Abraham Lincoln, the Civil War career of Ulysses S. Grant would have come to an inglorious political termination on at least two occasions, both before his great triumph at Vicksburg had been achieved.

The Confederates had no Abraham Lincoln; in fact, the term "Confederacy" was (and is) often interpreted by its apologists as an excuse to believe anything they want to, or to not think at all. April 1863 would be a month that vividly underscored this shortcoming, as Confederate politicians and military leaders, bloated with overconfidence and self-importance, would proceed to spectacularly misinterpret the every move and intention of Grant and his Federal task force at Vicksburg. This effect was no doubt intended by Grant, who seems to been all too aware of the lack of imagination in his adversaries; nevertheless, the Southern chain of command, beginning at the front with General John Pemberton and running all the way up to President Jefferson Davis, must ultimately bear at least partial responsibility for the complete collapse of Confederate fortunes that was about to transpire over roughly the next 10 weeks.

On April Fool's Day (the same day that Marat Halstead wrote his smearing letter), Grant, along with Sherman (and Grant's son Fred for part of the distance), accompanied Admiral Porter on a gunboat reconnaissance up the Yazoo River. After taking one look at Hayne's Bluff, the least imposing approach to Vicksburg from the north, Grant decided it was out of the question and informed Porter of his decision the following day.[6] The only sure way to take Vicksburg without huge losses, in Grant's opinion, was from the south. This meant marching down the west bank of Mississippi and crossing the river somewhere below the city. Both would have to be done in the presence of the enemy, one of the riskiest of all military maneuvers. Jean Edward Smith noted, "Grant's plan was breathtakingly simple but fraught with peril at every step."[7] When Sherman and Grant's other subordinates got wind of this decision, almost all of them objected. Conventional military wisdom demanded that the army and navy retreat to Memphis and begin another overland campaign in north-central Mississippi, as had been attempted the previous November and December.[8] Grant would have none of it. Unlike his otherwise highly competent staff, he understood politics—the same politics that had raised him from nothing to his current fortune and more than once sustained him when nothing else would. Northern voters and politicians demanded a forward advance, and to do otherwise risked the entire war effort. Military historian J.F.C. Fuller acknowledged Grant's exceptional insight:

"Grant clearly saw, however, the political danger of a retrograde movement, which outbalanced any strategical advantage accruing from the northern route...."[9] On April 3, Grant wrote with stoic confidence to Julia, "I am doing all I can and expect to be successful."[10]

Almost immediately after Grant had made the most controversial decision of his career, a government agent arrived in the Federal camp on April 6 who had the power to make or break him. His name was Charles Dana, and he was not your everyday, run-of-the-mill bureaucrat.[11] Trained as a journalist and former managing editor of the *New York Tribune*, Dana embodied a rare combination of intellectual accomplishments and physical courage.[12] If Sylvanus Cadwallader was the Ernie Pyle of his generation, then Charles Dana was the Edward R. Murrow. Recognized for his talents by the Lincoln Administration (which he admired), Dana had been retained by the War Department and sent to the West by Lincoln and Stanton to investigate allegations against Grant which were now reaching a crisis. This became necessary after General Lorenzo Thomas, who had been earlier sent for the same purpose, stubbornly lingered in Memphis—according to Cadwallader, due in large part to his intense personal dislike for Stanton.[13] Like Thomas, Dana was given a phony mission (to inspect military payroll), but his real job was to observe Grant's behavior and report back to Washington.[14] Historian Kenneth Williams aptly describes Dana as a "Very Important Person."[15]

As was the case with General Thomas, advance word of Dana's "secret" mission quickly filtered back to Grant's headquarters before Dana even arrived at camp. The very first countermeasure appears to have been chief-of-staff John Rawlins telling Grant's young Illinois protégé, Colonel James Wilson, to sit down so that Rawlins could tell him the facts of life regarding their commanding officer:

> Now I want you to know what kind of man we are serving. He's a Goddamned drunkard, and he's surrounded by a set of Goddamned scalawags who pander to his weakness. Now for all that, he is a good man, and a nice man, and I want you to help me in an offensive alliance against the Goddamned sons-of-bitches.[16]

After delivering this harangue, Rawlins presided over a general staff meeting, to which the omnipresent Cadwallader was invited. At this huddle, the initial reaction to Dana's foretold coming was voiced by Grant's chief-of-artillery, Colonel William Duff, who unhelpfully suggested that they all greet Dana by tossing him into the Mississippi River. Duff, according to Cadwallader, was in fact one of Rawlins' "Goddamned scalawags" who enabled Grant's drinking habits.[17] Following this outburst, Rawlins coolly reprimanded Duff's crude advice and proposed that the opposite tack be taken with Dana—that is, treat him like a king. The "wisdom and tact" of Rawlins prevailed, noted Cadwallader, who always believed (as does this writer) that John Rawlins has never received his full due for the indispensable role that he played in Grant's ultimate success.

When Dana arrived in camp on April 6, he received a near-hero's welcome. Dana was presented with his own personal horse, his own tent, his own bodyguards, and his own meal service. Cadwallader recorded the end result: "Dana was not long in becoming an enthusiastic admirer of Gen. Grant's military ability, and remained his staunch friend until the war ended." Making this admiration and friendship easier for Dana was his being genuinely impressed with everything he saw, as Grant's army made final preparations for its historic offensive. Cadwallader again:

> Mr. Dana was also shrewd enough to see that much which had been urged against Gen. Grant was untrue, or unjust, and undoubtedly thought it would be unwise to remove him from command on the eve of important movements, or in the middle of a campaign.[18]

Cadwallader took no personal credit for what was possibly the greatest P.R. coup in military history; all credit was given to Rawlins. Nevertheless, there can be little doubt that the Ohio-born freelance reporter had paved the way over the last six months for Grant and his staff's learning how to better cope with potentially hostile newspapermen. These, as Grant had earlier written to Julia, were a bigger threat to the Vicksburg campaign than the Confederate army. It was a lesson that some of his most able subordinates—such as Sherman—never learned.

It is important to note at this point that the new approach of Grant and Rawlins to the news media consisted of more than mere obsequiousness. It was an approach that reflected a sophisticated and nuanced selectivity, if not always rational consistency. The very same day that Dana arrived in camp (April 6), Grant gave effective marching orders to Henry Knox of the *New York Herald*, who had recently returned after being court-martialed for bad behavior and banished from camp by Sherman back in February. Knox mistakenly believed he had vanquished Sherman by winning over public opinion and getting Lincoln to overturn Sherman's decision. Grant set him straight, first in writing[19]; then he pulled Knox aside and told him the real score—once again, this is according to Cadwallader, who delighted in recalling the ups and downs of his journalistic colleagues. First, Sherman was too valuable for Grant to antagonize him over "so trifling a matter." Second, if Knox chose to stick around and Sherman responded by doing something rash to him, Knox should not bother running to Grant for protection. After this one-sided conversation, Knox took the first steamer headed back north.[20] Then a few days later on April 9, in a similar vein but with no pretense whatsoever, Grant summarily ordered General Hurlbut to suppress the *Memphis Bulletin* and to arrest its editors. Their offense had been one of the taboos spelled out earlier by Grant to Cadwallader; namely, giving advance, printed notice of anticipated Federal troop movements.[21]

April 6 was also a red-letter day for Grant in that he invited Julia to come down from Memphis and join him.[22] Julia wasted no time and humorously recalled their reuniting near Vicksburg:

> I had hardly said "how do you do" before I began to make suggestions, asking the General, "Why do you not move on Vicksburg at once? Do stop digging at this old canal. You know you will never use it.... Move upon Vicksburg and you will take it." The General was greatly amused and inquired if I too had a plan of action to propose. Of course I had. "Mass your troops in a solid phalanx at a point north of the fortress, rush upon it, and they will be obliged to surrender." He said, smiling, "I am afraid your plan would involve great loss of life and not insure success. Therefore I cannot adopt it. But it is true I will not use the canal. I never expected to, but started it to give the army occupation and to amuse the country until the waters should subside sufficiently to give me a foothold and then, Mrs. Grant, I will move upon Vicksburg and will take it, too. You need give yourself no further trouble."[23]

Obviously, Julia Grant was made of sterner stuff than her husband. Fortunately, for the Federal infantry in front of Vicksburg, Grant had already decided upon a less bloody, though in many ways far riskier approach.

Julia had been brought down to witness the next, crucial phase in Grant's plan. Porter's fleet of gunboats and transports would attempt to run the Confederate batteries along the bluffs of Vicksburg, the object being to get Federal troops across the river somewhere downstream. After warning Grant that once the fleet was downstream it could probably not be brought back up, Porter made thorough preparations for his most famous exploit of the war. On the evening of April 16, about the same time a Vicksburg gala ball celebrating its own supposed invincibility was in full swing, Confederate artillery suddenly erupted in a frantic barrage that could be heard 60 miles away.[24] Porter's historic running of the gauntlet was observed by just about everyone stationed at various points along the river, including Julia, her son Jesse (who was on the knee of Colonel Wilson), and even Mrs. John McClernand.[25] Allowing Minerva Dunlap McClernand onto the observation deck of the steamer *Henry von Phul* with Julia was probably a very skillful political move by Grant, just as it was for him to give General McClernand command of the lead army advance. Having Colonel Wilson baby-sit for young Jesse Grant was also good domestic policy, no doubt. By the time all of the noise and smoke had subsided, nine of Porter's 10 ships, including all of his gunboats and barges, had gotten through with minimal casualties. The Federal army and navy were now both below Vicksburg. The following day, Julia and young Jesse Grant returned to St. Louis, but Fred Grant remained with his father.[26]

After the tumultuous passing of the Federal fleet under Vicksburg, the Confederates should have guessed that something was afoot; instead, they reacted with arrogant indifference. Up until April 16, Pemberton had informed his superiors that he believed a frustrated Grant would soon retreat back to

Memphis and be sending part of his troops to Rosecrans' army in eastern Tennessee. Pemberton also expected to send part of his command to Bragg in the same sector to counter this anticipated move. Now, instead of showing flexibility, the Confederate high command engaged in wishful thinking. The purpose of the move, they thought, was to limit Confederate naval operations south of Vicksburg. Grant was still going to retreat, as far as they were concerned. The only adjustment Pemberton made was to inform Joseph Johnston that he now would not be able to send Bragg as many reinforcements as previously thought.[27] Pemberton would cling to this delusion for yet another two weeks.[28]

Part of the reason the Confederates would not face up to reality is that Grant had arranged for a series of diversions to baffle them. The first of these was the famed cavalry raid led by Colonel Benjamin Grierson, which plunged into northern Mississippi on April 17, the day after Porter's gauntlet run. As Jean Edward Smith wrote, Grant was "tired of being victimized" by Confederate cavalry raids and had decided to borrow a leaf from their playbook.[29] Grierson, an unlikely pony soldier, had previously been a small-town music teacher and, as a boy, had been kicked in the face by a horse. Combining speed and audacity that would have done Nathan Bedford Forrest proud, Grierson's raiders raced straight south, behind Vicksburg, all the way through Mississippi, not stopping until they reached Baton Rouge, Louisiana, some two weeks later. In between they created havoc and confusion, winning every skirmish in the process.[30] Discounting Grant's retreat through northern Mississippi the previous December, Shelby Foote wrote: "It was Grierson who first set the example of what might be done in the interior of the enemy's country without any base from which to draw supplies."[31] In point of fact, it was the first time that such a strategy had been deliberately planned in advance, and would prove to be a terrible forerunner of what was about to come. Sherman called Grierson's raid "the most brilliant expedition of the war," and Grant wrote with satisfaction to General Halleck that "Grierson has knocked the heart out of the State."[32]

Grant was so pleased with the success of Porter's run and the Confederates' lack of appropriate response while Grierson was on the loose, that he decided to try it again. This time, on April 22, six steamers and a dozen barges made the attempt, and although Vicksburg gunners by now had more practice with moving targets on the river, only one steamer was sunk and once again casualties were surprisingly light. With Porter's naval shipmen downstream, civilian crews had balked at manning the second, unarmed expedition, so General John Logan pressed into service any infantry from his brigade who had previous river experience. Their success, as Professor Smith remarked, demonstrated that "once again luck was on Grant's side."[33] The primary purpose of the second, improvised run was to bring down additional supplies for the troops, which former quartermaster Grant (unlike many of his colleagues) was ever so conscious of and attentive to during the entire course of the war.

During the two days before the supply barges made it through, Grant wrote to his wife and father in a manner that suggested he was settling his affairs. On April 20, he gave Julia detailed instructions regarding business matters at home[34]; then, on April 21, he wrote to Jesse. Like many letters to his father, there is a sense of tension in this missive, although no scolding as on other recent occasions. Grant seems mainly concerned about justifying his acts for both Jesse and posterity in general, possibly because rumors of his unconventional strategy were beginning to filter back north. To his father, Grant insists, "I have no idea of being driven to do a desperate or foolish act by the howling press.... I want, and will do my part towards it, to put down the rebellion in the shortest possible time.... I beg that you will destroy this letter."[35] Grant's repeated references to the press are a reminder that he did not trust his father in this regard, given the leaks and interventions that had occurred during the previous year in Cincinnati.

On April 24, Grant arrived downstream to join his expedition and scout out the formidable Confederate defenses surrounding Grand Gulf, Mississippi, on the east bank of the river south of Vicksburg. Three days later, on April 27, he celebrated his 41st birthday. Two years previous he was an unknown civilian. One year previous he was the newly designated scapegoat for (till then) the bloodiest battle ever fought on the American continent. Now Grant was poised to lead his veteran army on one of the most spectacularly successful campaigns in military history. One year later he would be Lieutenant-General and arguably the most powerful man in the country. As one contemplates Grant's unprecedented career arc within the space of a mere 36 months, it is apparent that in late April 1863 around Vicksburg, Mississippi, some titanic force of nature was about to be unleashed, the source of which Grant himself seems to have never really understood—nor anyone else for that matter.

On the same day as his birthday (April 27), Grant respectfully requested Sherman to make a massive demonstration in front of Hayne's Bluff to the north of Vicksburg. Having taken careful note of Confederate susceptibility to feints—Grierson's raid, in particular—Grant now decided to use more of a good thing. His letter to Sherman, perhaps utilizing reverse psychology, apologized to his media-hating colleague for the way in which newspapers would likely interpret the demonstration as a defeat.[36] An indignant Sherman, however, exclaimed to his staff, "Does General Grant think I care what the newspapers say?"[37] Sherman then responded to Grant, telling him that the inherent risk of Grant's plan (which Sherman had opposed) now demanded that Sherman fully cooperate and a demonstration was now essential. Next, he went on one of his memorable rants against journalists, referring to them as "sneaking croaking scoundrels" that should be scorned more than the Confederates.[38] Sherman's demonstration and pretend-retreat were then flawlessly executed on April 29 as Grant's other land and naval forces congregated along the west bank of the river south of Vicksburg. The desired effect was achieved. Between the feints of Sherman and Grierson, Pemberton was "flummoxed" (Jean Edward Smith)[39] and "completely bewildered" (J.F.C. Fuller).[40] Responding energetically to Sherman's theatrics, Pemberton recalled troops that had recently been detached and sent south as a safeguard, thus leaving the path in front of Grant nearly wide open.[41]

While Sherman and Grierson were distracting the Confederates, Grant was keeping the troublesome John McClernand busy as well. Once again on his birthday (April 27)—the same day he "persuaded" Sherman to threaten Hayne's Bluff—Grant sternly ordered McClernand's 13th Corps to prepare for an all-out move against Grand Gulf, the nearest fortified Confederate position on the east bank of the river.[42] On April 29, as Sherman put on his performance to the north, Porter's fleet engaged in a near-pointblank artillery duel with the batteries at Grand Gulf, only to come away with a realization that the Confederate position was impregnable. Grant's original plan had been to ferry his army across at the nearby town of Rodney and then quickly reduce Grand Gulf.[43] Now, after Porter's naval repulse, he knew that sending McClernand's corps in directly would be suicide. It was at this moment that Grant made the first of a series of snap decisions characterizing his movements over the next three weeks. These improvised decisions would, in hindsight, win the war for the North.

Just as Porter's flagship had been rescued by an African-American messenger the previous month at Steele Bayou, Grant's army now received crucial intelligence from another former slave who mysteriously arrived on the scene. A few miles below Grand Gulf on the east bank was the town of Bruinsburg, Mississippi. Here, according to the runaway and not widely known, was dry, level ground upon which an army might land without opposition. On April 30, Grant's army was transported by Porter's navy across the Mississippi River to Bruinsburg. The crossing went without a hitch. Fuller wrote, "Four months of ruse and feints, of wrestling with swamps, bayous and forest, of labours seldom equaled in war, were the mists which covered this landing. Pemberton had been completely misled...."[44] In the words of Shelby Foote, Grant "showed the flexibility that would characterize his planning throughout the various stages of the campaign which now was under way in earnest."[45] Concurring with this assessment, Jean Edward Smith later wrote that Grant was "demonstrating the flexibility that had become his hallmark."[46] Charles Bracelen Flood put it even more succinctly: "Grant was always a man to follow up an opportunity."[47]

Eyewitnesses to this place and time later recalled seeing a different Grant than they had previously known. Bruce Catton summarized the documented record with: "None who had known him in the previous years could recognize him as being the same man.... From this time his genius and his energies seemed to burst forth with new life." Federal officers on the scene later wrote, "There was no nonsense, no sentiment; only a plain businessman of the republic, there for one single purpose of getting that command across the river in the shortest time possible."[48] Once over the river, Grant continued to supervise in person, exhorting his troops simply with, "Push right along."[49] Part of Grant's apparent transformation was due to a sense of relaxation, as he tried to explain the aftermath of the river crossing many years afterward:

> When this was effected I felt a degree of relief scarcely ever equaled since. Vicksburg was not yet taken it is true, nor were its defenders demoralized by any of our previous moves. I was now in the enemy's country, with a vast river and the stronghold of Vicksburg between me and my base of supplies. But I was on dry ground on the same side of the river with the enemy. All the campaigns, labors, hardships and exposures from the month of December previous to this time that had been made and endured, were for the accomplishment of this one object.[50]

Yankee ingenuity had now done all it could do—from this point on the fate of Vicksburg (and of the Federal Union) would be decided by Grant's leadership in the field and the naked valor of his "Egyptian" infantry. As Shelby Foote memorably wrote, "The showdown was unquestionably at hand."[51]

CHAPTER 26

May 1863: Champion Hill

I cannot think of the bloody hill without sadness and pride. Sadness for the great loss of my true and gallant men; pride for the heroic bravery they displayed.

—Union Brigadier General Alvin Hovey[1]

The first week of May 1863 began with a shattering rout of Federal forces at Chancellorsville, Virginia. The Confederate Army of Northern Virginia under Robert E. Lee, though outnumbered nearly 2–1, decimated the invading Army of the Potomac led by Union General Joseph Hooker, in a battle widely and rightfully viewed as Lee's tactical masterpiece. By the time the guns fell silent on May 6, some 30,000 Americans were casualties (approximately 17,000 of which were Federals). Although Stonewall Jackson—perhaps the greatest tactician of them all—had been mortally wounded by friendly fire near the end of the engagement, Lee's veterans had achieved their most spectacular victory in the field.[2] Marse Robert himself had now acquired a reputation both at home and abroad for invincibility, not entirely undeserved given his recent accomplishments. After two years, umpteen different generals, and a ghastly price paid in both blood and treasure, the Federals were no closer to taking Richmond than they had been when hostilities first commenced. At this point in the war, Unionists may well have decided it was time to throw in the towel had in not been for gains in the West, thanks mostly to the efforts of Ulysses S. Grant. Moreover, even as the battle of Chancellorsville opened, Grant had begun in earnest his own campaign around Vicksburg, Mississippi, that was destined to become his own crowning achievement from a military strategic standpoint.

Having now crossed over to the east bank the Mississippi River below Vicksburg after six months of labor and frustration, Grant's army found itself immediately confronted at Port Gibson by a small Confederate force ably led by General John Bowen. Bowen was a Georgia-born West Pointer who later settled in Missouri and had been (unlike many others) a friendly and respectful neighbor of Grant's during his Hardscrabble Farm days. Now on May 1,

Bowen and his men found themselves facing the vanguard of the Grant's Federal advance, and though offering stubborn resistance, could not overcome a 4–1 disadvantage in numbers,[3] nor the pent-up frustration of Grant's veterans. After each side sustained over 800 casualties,[4] Bowen prudently retreated north to the river citadel of Grand Gulf and sent out word that the Federal army was there and not a half dozen other places it was rumored to have been, thanks to Grant's many recent feints and ruses. After this small victory, Grant wrote to Admiral Porter, "Our day's work has been very creditable," noting with some satisfaction that Bowen's fellow–Georgian, Confederate General Edward Tracy, had been killed in the fight.[5]

By May 2, Pemberton finally realized the Grant's army had crossed below Vicksburg.[6] This was over two weeks after their movement had begun from the north. By the time Sherman raced down to join Grant, the Federals had concentrated nearly 40,000 troops. Pemberton had about 30,000 regulars, but these were scattered across central Mississippi, in an attempt to defend all points simultaneously.[7] Grant at this moment enjoyed an approximate 25 percent technical advantage in manpower, but this advantage would have quickly disappeared if Confederate reinforcements had been brought in from Bragg's inactive sector (versus Rosecrans), not to mention from Louisiana (versus Banks), from Arkansas and the trans–Mississippi, or, for that matter, from the overwhelmingly hostile civilian population of Mississippi itself. In any event, Hooker had enjoyed nearly a 100 percent advantage in manpower at Chancellorsville, and in the end was lucky to have escaped alive. As Lee was beginning his rout of Hooker at Chancellorsville, Pemberton at Vicksburg received conflicting orders. President Jefferson Davis ordered him to hold a particular place (Vicksburg), while General Joseph Johnston ordered him to concentrate his forces and defeat Grant's army.[8] This would not be the last time during the Vicksburg campaign that Johnston's sound advice would be drowned out by a majority of fools.

Meanwhile, at Grand Gulf, rather than directly assault a nearly impregnable fortress, Grant opted for a flanking maneuver by having McPherson's corps race around northeast to Hankinson's Ferry. By the time this was successfully accomplished on May 3, Bowen had to choose between waiting for Pemberton to rescue him or trying to join Pemberton.[9] Bowen wisely chose the latter, somewhat to the annoyance of Pemberton, who never seemed to grasp the futility of Bowen's situation, and who was out of his element except when fighting behind fortifications. That very same day Pemberton received a reminder from Johnston that it was imperative to unite his army and beat Grant.[10] Bowen's withdrawal had facilitated this, but Pemberton seems to have interpreted Johnston's repeated directive by hunkering down at Vicksburg and waiting for Grant to come to him. With the fall of Grand Gulf, Port Gibson, and environs, the Federals now had a solid foothold on Mississippi soil to the south of Vicksburg.

Almost as soon as Grand Gulf was under Federal occupation, Grant seems to have made another change of plans. Originally intending a straight-ahead push against Vicksburg, he now opted to move east and first remove the threat of Pemberton's receiving any reinforcements from that direction. Conventionally, this entailed a long supply train running back to Grand Gulf and the river, but even getting supplies to that point was a very nebulous affair with Confederate guns still commanding the bluffs of Vicksburg. Grant therefore broke with conventional wisdom and decided to have his army live off the land, although he did not immediately inform Halleck and Washington of his intent.[11] Another factor influencing this bold move was notification on May 3 from General Banks at Port Hudson that Federal reinforcements would be slow in coming (if they came at all).[12] As if in confirmation of his new resolve, Grant learned soon afterwards that the latest supply tugboats trying to run the gauntlet past Vicksburg had been mostly sunk, although one of these had been filled with newspaper reporters, bringing unconcealed joy to the media-hating Sherman when he heard about it.[13] Grant also admitted that, by making this decision, he would necessarily lose communication with Washington, which would be an additional advantage in a campaign to be largely decided by speed and stealth.[14]

Overeager Northern sympathizers and Southern apologists have often credited (or discredited) Grant as being the first modern general ordering his army to live off the land during the Vicksburg campaign, but this is an over-simplification. More accurately, during the war he was the first one (long before Sherman in Georgia) to consciously and unapologetically employ it as part of an offensive infantry movement. He had been forced to do it during his retreat from Oxford the previous December, and Grierson had recently done it during his two-week cavalry raid through Mississippi. For that matter, Grant's former commander Winfield Scott had successfully done it during the Mexican War, and long before him, the conquistador Hernando Cortez, also in Mexico. Now it was Grant's turn to take advantage of this strategy at the expense of Mississippi civilians, most of whom supported the Confederacy and were no more than rebels in the eyes of Grant's soldiers. On May 7, Grant issued both a congratulatory order and a pep talk to these troops: "Other battles are to be fought. Let us fight them bravely. A grateful country will rejoice at our success, and history will record it with immortal honor."[15] A few days earlier he had written to Julia, "This army is in the finest health and spirits,"[16] and on May 9, wrote to her again, "No army ever felt better than this one does nor more confident of success. Before they are beaten they will be very badly beaten."[17] To Halleck he wrote that his army consisted of "well-disciplined and hardy men, who know no defeat, and are not willing to learn what it is."[18] This proved not to be idle boasting. Grant knew his army and within three weeks the boast would be sealed in blood across the landscape of central Mississippi.

Joining the Federal army at Grand Gulf for its sendoff were Grant's original political benefactors Congressman Elihu Washburne and Illinois Governor Richard Yates,[19] as well as those who would accompany the expedition, including Charles Dana and *Chicago Times* correspondent Sylvanus Cadwallader. Last but not least was the 12-year-old Fred Grant, who rode alongside Dana.[20] No one yet knew exactly what was in store. On May 6, Grant wrote Halleck with a forlorn request that Rosecrans make a demonstration to prevent Bragg from detaching troops.[21] On May 9, Joseph Johnston, still ailing from his Virginia wounds, was ordered by Jefferson Davis to Mississippi in person, which Johnston soon complied with. On May 10 (the day Johnston set out), Grant responded to complaints from the ever-dissatisfied John McClernand that his transports were inadequate, pointing out among other things that McClernand already had more wagons than any other division.[22] The bad timing of McClernand's protest was impeccable, given that Grant was making last-minute preparations for a rapid movement that would depend on wagon supplies more as a ruse than a backup. Towards this end, final arrangements were made for a limited supply train that in the end would do more to further deceive his adversaries than to feed his huge mobile force.

Finally, on May 11, Grant wrote to Halleck what he intended to do, and signed off with, "[Y]ou may not hear from me again for several days."[23] Then Grant cut off from his base of supplies and communications, knowing that it would take Halleck several days at least to get him a reply message. When Halleck did hear about it, he countermanded the decision just as expected, but Grant was long gone by then.[24] All of Grant's subordinates were alarmed as well, excepting perhaps the dense McClernand, but beginning with the most loyal ones such as Sherman.[25] Just as Grant's staff had opposed his recent move south, they were now disconcerted by a maneuver that went against all the books. As before, however, and once again with the exception of McClernand, all cheerfully obeyed the unorthodox commander they had attached their fortunes to. Part of McClernand's new disgruntlement may have been due to his corps no longer having the honor of the lead advance. Now the highly competent McPherson and Sherman were given the lead while McClernand was assigned rear-guard duty with his cherished and cumbersome wagon train. As for the lead divisions, they proceeded to commandeer the bounty of the Mississippi countryside. Military historian J.F.C. Fuller wrote that "Grant's tremendous energy electrified his men,"[26] while the attitude of the army was best summed up in one sentence written by a private in a letter to home: "We live fat."[27] As for the reaction of the Confederate high command, Fuller added that Grant's "plan completely bewildered Pemberton"[28] because, although Pemberton had anticipated Grant might move east towards Jackson, he did not anticipate Grant cutting loose from his supplies and moving with such rapid, uninhibited alacrity.

Within one day, McPherson's spearheading column had reached the Mississippi hamlet of Raymond, located less than 20 miles southeast of Jackson. There they found a single Confederate brigade of perhaps 5,000 troops skillfully led by Texas-born General John Gregg. At first Gregg thought they were facing a small Federal raiding party, but after slowing McPherson's advance, Gregg's brigade then absorbed the full fury of the Federal attack and, in order to survive the day, was forced to make a beeline back to Jackson.[29] The fight had been short but sharp. Casualties at Raymond were approximately 400 for the Federals and 500 for the Confederates.[30]

Grant at this point was at Fourteen Mile Creek, not far behind. On the evening of May 12, after the battle of Raymond had been reported, Cadwallader relates an interesting incident. Lodging within the tent of artillery chief Colonel Duff (the same man who had earlier suggested that Charles Dana be tossed into the river), a surprised Cadwallader saw Grant enter. With hardly a word or glance being exchanged, Duff gave Grant several swigs of whiskey from a stashed canteen. Grant then unceremoniously retired. This was the first time, Cadwallader later wrote, that he had ever seen Grant drink. It would not be the last, not even during this campaign. According to Cadwallader, the whiskey had come from a barrel procured by none other than Governor Yates himself. Chief-of-staff Rawlins was of course unaware of the situation.[31]

Joining McPherson, then leapfrogging over him, was Sherman's division, and the two pushed on towards Jackson through a driving rainstorm on May 14. Joseph Johnston had arrived in town the day before from his leisurely journey west only to find Gregg's defeated brigade digging in with hastily organized reinforcements and trying to make a stand against the oncoming Yankee hordes. Sherman and McPherson's troops, enjoying a 5–1 advantage in numbers, hit the Confederates head-on and sent them staggering back through Jackson.[32] Johnston quickly sized up the situation, realized the game was up, and ordered what was left of his command to evacuate. Sending an urgent message in to Pemberton, Johnston stressed the need to link up and added that a strike against Grant's imagined supply line would be advisable in the meantime. Neither Johnston nor Pemberton knew there was no Federal supply line, but at least Johnston realized that Pemberton was doing no one any good by being holed up in Vicksburg. Grant and Sherman entered Jackson in person on May 14, making it the third Confederate state capital to fall, at a cost of 300 Federal casualties.[33] The two others—Nashville and Baton Rouge—had surrendered due mainly to Grant's exertions in 1862. Everything in Jackson happened so fast that many citizens were either unaware of the Federal occupation or expressed an uppity indifference towards the Northern invaders. Of the Federal soldiers, Bruce Catton wrote that by this point they "were whooping with joy" and that "[t]he men were beginning to realize that this campaign was something special ... they were being led with cold audacity." Confederate POWs recently brought in from the East admitted to their captors that "they were not fighting New York troops."[34]

Perhaps the most surreal incident involved a Confederate cloth factory that Grant and Sherman entered with curiosity but then left in ashes. In his memoirs Grant related that factory operations were still in full swing as he and Sherman were ignored by the mostly-female workforce. After watching for awhile tents labeled "CSA" rolling off the assembly line, Grant ordered the place cleared and Sherman's men to torch it.[35] This was not the beginning of Sherman's career as an arsonist (he had done it before), but it may have been the first time that Grant gave him such a directive. Soon, much of the city was in flames, although the origins of these fires appear not to have been exclusively Federal. That evening, Grant spent the night at the Bowen House hotel, reportedly in the same room that Johnston occupied the night before.[36] Charles Dana also caught up with Grant to show him a telegram from Secretary of War Stanton, confirming Grant's full authority (and responsibility) to conduct the campaign.[37] Stanton's message may have been a subtle reminder for McClernand to behave now that the ball was in motion.

Loss of the state capital finally stirred Pemberton into motion, but with fits and starts. He also once again treated Johnston's orders as if discretionary. Detaching from Vicksburg a mobile force of approximately 23,000, Pemberton headed east but made destruction of Grant's illusory supply line his primary objective, rather than finding Johnston, who would have immediately assumed head command. Fuller noted, "At this time the situation of the Confederate forces was a ludicrous one," with Johnston retreating northeast, Pemberton moving southeast, and Grant's victorious army in between.[38] Worse for the Confederates, Grant had intercepted a copy of Johnston's orders to Pemberton and knew what they were up to, more or less, for Pemberton was not yet trying to find Johnston in earnest, but was looking for a supply train that did not exist. By the time Pemberton figured things out and changed direction, Grant had also changed direction and was now moving west. The formerly rear and now lead Union division under McClernand, along with some 30,000 Federal troops, was coming up fast and bearing down hard upon their would-be pursuers.[39] Instead of concentrating forces with Johnston, Pemberton found himself outnumbered, off-balance, and being hit sideways. Thus the stage was set for the single most key and decisive battle of the American Civil War.

Champion Hill is one of the highest topographical points in the region and is named after a family that still owns property there. Indeed, most of the battlefield remains private property, and represents a perfect contemporary case study in the conflict between those private interests and historic preservation. On May 16, 1863, one of the most important battles in history transpired at this place, yet one that is not a household name and was relatively small in scale. In addition to the rugged Mississippi landscape which made any offensive military operation tedious, the wooded neighborhood around Champion Hill was, as Grant later wrote in his memoirs, "difficult to penetrate with troops, even when not defended."[40] Remnants of this thick, tangled landscape can still be seen as one drives down the back roads, and despite the beautiful Mississippi countryside, an inexplicable aura of sadness still pervades around this particular location.

When Pemberton's mobile force realized they were being stalked by an elite Federal army looking to deliver a knockout blow, they summoned all of their courage and prepared to defend themselves. They were immediately greeted by a crack Union brigade under General Alvin Hovey, who wasted no time in storming the Confederate position. Hovey was a former lawyer and, like many of his troops, hailed from Indiana. Like Grant, he politically began life as a Democrat, but unlike Grant, switched to the Republican Party before the war in 1858.[41] Hovey's troops represented the lead element of McClernand's entire corps, which came up fast on Hovey's left but then, per McClernand's orders, paused as Hovey began his assault. To their right, General Logan's brigade (under McPherson) raced beyond the hill and took up positions which, unbeknownst to them at the time, blocked the only escape route for Pemberton's army. Meanwhile, defenders of the hill could not withstand Hovey's charge and completely gave way until the Federals found themselves in possession of the summit. Before Hovey's brigade could be reinforced, however, they found themselves in the crosshairs of a deadly counterattack led by Grant's friend and former Missouri neighbor John Bowen (with his mostly Missouri troops), who was about the best possible man for the job. One of Hovey's brigadiers later described this phase of the battle as "one of the most obstinate and murderous conflicts of the war."[42] The result of the counterattack was that Hovey's division steadily melted away as it was stubbornly driven back down the same hill gained only a few moments before.

The reader must forgive the author if he shrinks from presenting the battle of Champion Hill in all of its melancholy detail or resorts to oversimplification in this brief account. Contemplating the waste and tragedy of war ultimately suggests that there are never any winners—only losers—and this is not what we want to believe. As Bowen's veterans drove Hovey's veterans from the hill, Hovey called out in every direction for reinforcements. Grant, still exasperated 20 years after the fact, recalled repeatedly ordering the adjacent McClernand to send help, and repeatedly being ignored.[43] McClernand instead believed that his inactive troops were about to be attacked (they were in reality facing token opposition)[44] and, incredibly, ordered the beleaguered Hovey to send *him* reinforcements. When it became clear that McClernand would do nothing, Grant ordered Logan's troops to come back around, thus abandoning (what later became obvious) a position that cut off the enemy's retreat.[45]

Grant arrived in person at the front during this key moment—both for the battle and the entire war—just as Hovey's survivors were retreating. His reported reaction was typical for him and momentous for all those engaged:

"Hovey's division are good troops.... If the enemy has driven them, he is not in good plight himself."[46] Grant then ordered his own counterattack with whatever was available, and that happened to be Union brigades under Logan and General Marcellus Crocker, who had double-timed to the front on their own initiative. Crocker was another one of Grant's best field commanders, but (like Rawlins and Grant's late brother Simpson) was dying of consumption and would not long survive the war. According to Grant, "His weak condition never put him on the sick report when there was a battle in prospect, as long as he could keep on his feet."[47] Champion Hill would be Crocker's last official engagement, and when ordered to attack, his troops drove back Bowen's weary Confederates, who had been given no reserves by Pemberton to call upon. The final blow came during the disorganized Confederate retreat, now made feasible with the roads opened, when Confederate General Lloyd Tilghman was killed by a Federal cannonball.[48] It had been Tilghman who two years previous was chased from Paducah by Grant, then surrendered to Grant at Fort Henry in 1862, and now, more recently, repulsed the Federals at Fort Pemberton in March. His last direct encounter with Grant in the field, however, proved fatal.

Many commentators have remarked that the battle of Champion Hill was unusual in that such a crucial engagement involved surprisingly few troops, that even fewer of these were absolutely engaged, and that the total casualties (more than 2,400 Federal—about half from Hovey's shattered brigade—and more than 3,800 Confederate)[49] were relatively small by Civil War standards. In this sense it was comparable, say, to the battle of Midway during World War II. The aftershocks were no less significant. Joseph Johnston, upon learning the result, ordered Pemberton to immediately evacuate Vicksburg and, yet again, to link up with his forces. It was like talking to a brick wall. Pemberton preferred to literally obey his commander-in-chief Jefferson Davis and hold Vicksburg at all costs.[50] Part of Pemberton's army, however, thought otherwise and raced to join Johnston, thereby avoiding capture at Vicksburg. Among the Confederates who fought at Champion Hill was Corporal Joseph Henry Nail of the 56th Georgia Infantry, first cousin to the author's great-great-grandfather. In fact, all eight of the maternal surnames of the author's family were represented in Georgia and Alabama regiments alone at Champion Hill (as at Shiloh). The performance of these regiments has sometimes been criticized by historians, but the fact is, with exception of Bowen, Tilghman and a few others, they were very badly led against the very best that the Federal army could throw at them.

Champion Hill was the turning point of the war. On the scene was Charles Dana, who immediately dubbed it "a great and momentous victory."[51] Historian James McPherson judged it "the key battle of the campaign"[52] while Jean Edward Smith observed that "Champion Hill sealed the fate of Vicksburg. What appears so stark in retrospect is that the battle turned on a dime."[53]

I would add that this was true despite the mediocrity of Pemberton's leadership. The Confederates were not outfought at Champion Hill; they were out-generaled. After all of the back and forth, it was Grant who held the winning hand. Also noteworthy were his fabled written communication skills, as Grant dashed off no fewer than nine letters to five sub-commanders during that memorable day.[54]

Cadwallader was on the scene too. Together with Joseph McCullagh of the *Cincinnati Commercial*, he decided to coin the name of the battle Champion Hill. This decision was made despite Grant, Dana, and others referring to Baker's Creek, which was located in the same vicinity. Cadwallader then got the scoop on McCullagh as his story was published first in the *Chicago Times*, and hence claimed credit for the name by which history will remember the place. Cadwallader only regretted not consulting Grant first, who felt that he had earned the right to name it,[55] but history can be grateful that Cadwallader's good journalistic instincts prevailed. Cadwallader also noted with awe the rapidly moving Federals as they lived off the land, writing, "The army is absolutely nomadic"[56]—a fair comment on Grant's pillaging and light-traveling "Egyptian" infantry.

The following day (on May 17), the demoralized, retreating Confederates tried to make a stand at the Big Black River. As the opposing armies collided, an advancing Grant and his staff suddenly and unexpectedly found themselves exposed to enemy fire, but, as Cadwallader recalled, "providentially no one was hurt."[57] Then a staff messenger from Halleck in Washington finally caught up with Grant (after six days), ordering him to call the whole campaign off so that General Banks in Louisiana could be reinforced. As Grant told the uncomprehending messenger that Halleck would no longer give such an order, he heard an uproar and turned to see an unordered charge being made against the Confederate line by Union General Michael Lawler.[58] Lawler's brigade had been both embarrassed and chafing at the bit ever since learning that their commander McClernand had left Hovey in the lurch at Champion Hill. Stripping off his coat, the fiery Irishman led his men in what Cadwallader described as "the most perilous and ludicrous charge that I witnessed during the war."[59] Everyone was surprised, especially the Confederates, most of whom either broke and ran or were captured. After the rout was over, the Federals had suffered 200 casualties and the Confederates nearly 1,800.[60]

The road to Vicksburg was now wide open. Grant's army had fought and won five battles in 17 days, marched some 180 miles and inflicted approximately 7,200 casualties while suffering 4,300 themselves.[61] By May 18, Vicksburg was besieged. Grant's unorthodox, counterclockwise movement across central Mississippi was described by Colonel Arthur Conger as "a campaign as brief and brilliant as is to be found in military annals,"[62] while Fuller called it "one of the most elaborate and successful surprisals ever effected in war."[63] Perhaps the biggest compliment came from Sherman, who had opposed the entire concept, yet cooperated in it. Upon reaching the bluffs north of Vicksburg that had defied him only three weeks previous, Sherman told Grant, "Until this moment I never thought your expedition a success. I never could see the end clearly until now. But this is a campaign. This is a success if we never take the town."[64] President Lincoln, hearing the news, concurred: "Whether General Grant shall or shall not consummate the capture of Vicksburg, his campaign from the beginning of this month ... is one of the most brilliant in the world."[65] Grant himself voiced modesty and, referring to the once impressive Confederate army now bottled up inside of Vicksburg, "We were fortunate, to say the least, in meeting them in detail."[66]

On May 19, Grant's Federals tried to take Vicksburg by storm. By this time they were charging into some of the most formidable fortifications yet constructed during the war, and the Confederates were fighting for their lives. Contrary to most expectations, the Union advance was brought to an abrupt halt with heavy losses. Two days later (on May 21), as the Federals caught their breath and consolidated, Grant rode up to inspect the front. Meeting a glance from one of his seemingly indestructible infantrymen, Grant heard a single word uttered: "hardtack." The same cry was immediately taken up all along the line. Although the soldiers had lived well off the countryside, they had been short on bread, and felt only this was needed to achieve final victory. Grant then told his cheering troops that hardtack was on its way, which it was.[67]

Now supplied and concentrated, Grant determined that his army would make another all-out assault on May 22. It was a mistake. When the smoke cleared, nothing had been gained, and the Federals had lost almost as many troops (over 3,200) during the last three days in front of Vicksburg, as they had during the entire three weeks preceding.[68] Grant took full responsibility for the blunder, but tried to justify it with the aggressive spirit of his troops and their impatience towards siege warfare.[69] Perhaps this was necessary to keep his sanity. Many of the heroes who had won the war at Champion Hill and elsewhere now lay dead in front of the works at Vicksburg, including perhaps the young men who had cried out "hardtack" to Grant the day before. Grant did throw some well-earned blame, however, at his nemesis John McClernand, who at a critical moment during the second assault repeatedly urged reinforcements rather than withdrawal. Grant, in spite of his better judgment, sent these men in and regretted it the rest of his life. When informed of the result, according to Cadwallader (who brought the bad news), Rawlins exploded in profanity and Grant did a quiet burn.[70] Two days later (on May 24) Grant vented his anger in a letter to Halleck:

> General McClernand's dispatches misled me as to the real state of facts, and caused much of this loss. He is entirely unfit for the position of corps commander, both on the march and on the battlefield. Looking after his corps gives me more labor and infinitely more uneasiness than all the remainder of my department.[71]

McClernand, for his part, probably realizing by now that he was the most unpopular man in the army, blew up at the young Colonel James Wilson when handed one of Grant's orders. After Wilson threatened to beat his superior to a pulp, however, McClernand changed his tune, and by doing so succeeded in amusing Grant, probably for the first time ever.[72]

Cadwallader, like almost everyone else, had formed a low opinion of McClernand by this time. Having witnessed up close the second assault on Vicksburg, he relates the tragic account of one colonel serving under McClernand. According to Cadwallader, when the order came to renew the assault, the colonel pronounced the endeavor suicide, handed over his personal effects with instructions they be delivered to his wife, charged with his men, and was immediately shot dead. Summarizing the fiasco, Cadwallader wrote that May 22 was "a fair sample of Gen. McClernand's victories."[73] In his memoirs, Grant stopped just short of admitting that the second attack was a mistake, but viewed McClernand as exasperating the loss.[74] In the end, it was Grant's own fault and he knew it.

To Halleck on May 24, Grant wrote that "The fall of Vicksburg ... can only be a question of time."[75] Soon after Grant had been persuaded by recent events to "out-camp the enemy,"[76] Cadwallader relates yet another remarkable story. As the Federals began to build their own fortifications around Vicksburg, there was one particular spot that Grant's men (by now, with justification) dreaded exposing themselves to enemy fire. In response, Grant, without apparent emotion, escorted the detail squad to this same location and personally supervised the work as bullets whizzed around them, wounding several. This was the only example, Cadwallader, wrote, of Grant ever displaying what he termed "foolhardy bravery,"[77] coming in the aftermath of the May 22 assault. By now, surely no one better than Grant realized that Union victory at Champion Hill, Vicksburg, and the war as a whole, came at immeasurable cost. This is also no doubt why he later dedicated his own memoirs to "the American soldier and sailor."

CHAPTER 27

June 1863:
The Siege of Vicksburg

As catastrophic for Pemberton's army as was Grant's string of victories and circumvallation of Vicksburg in May, in the long run it proved to be even more devastating for the Confederacy as a whole. In early June of 1863, the seemingly indestructible Army of Northern Virginia under Robert E. Lee began a northern offensive that would eventually culminate at Gettysburg, Pennsylvania.[1] The impetus for Lee's rash gamble came directly from the pressure that Grant was applying around Vicksburg. On May 15–16, the same days that the battle of Champion Hill was developing and being fought, Lee met with Jefferson Davis and his cabinet. The Federal sacking of Jackson, Mississippi, on May 14 had prompted this emergency session to determine whether reinforcements should be sent to the Mississippi theater. Lee, rather than weaken the defense of his native Virginia, advocated a decisive blow against Washington (via Pennsylvania) that would force a peace. Thus Gettysburg would probably never have been fought had it not been for Grant's Vicksburg campaign. Shelby Foote aptly described May 16 (the date of Champion Hill and the second cabinet meeting in Richmond) as "a critical day for the young republic."[2] Now, as spring turned into summer, Lee marched north while Grant engaged in siege warfare.

As the heat of the Mississippi summer began, Vicksburg found itself surrounded and, for all practical purposes, cut off from the outside world. Only a few weeks before it had been widely considered invincible, a Gibraltar of the West. Now, its inhabitants were living underground and starving. Some of the most notable moments of the siege were provided by a female Irish immigrant turned Federal soldier, Jennie Hodgers, alias Private D.J. Cashier, of the 95th Illinois Regiment, who, when not verbally taunting the besieged Confederates from the Union ramparts, was making a daring escape from their hands after having been briefly captured.[3] Other than side attractions such as this, however, the month of June provided no excitement comparable to the 22 days of nearly nonstop combat witnessed in May. Pemberton's defeated, demoralized Confederate army now huddled behind its breastworks, little comforted by the casualties it had inflicted on the Yankees, particularly in front of those very same works. Mainly, it no doubt wondered how they had come into such a plight, blamed Pemberton, and hoped for a miracle in the form of Joseph Johnston. On the Federal side, civilians, politicians, reporters, suppliers, and massive reinforcements flooded in from the North. Along with this circus, a number of highly significant events took place behind the scenes, beginning with Grant himself as he cruised up and down the Yazoo River on June 6–7.

Responding to remote rumors of a Confederate relief force under Johnston in the vicinity of Satartia, Mississippi, Grant set off by steamboat with a small escort, under the pretense of making a reconnaissance. This was the beginning of what Shelby Foote termed "a two-day bender"[4] for Grant, and marks the most controversial episode in the controversial and long-running debate over Grant's alleged alcoholism. For some, great American heroes do not have drinking problems. I, on the other hand, subscribe to the view that Grant was indeed an alcoholic, and am not alone in this view. Among biographers who acknowledge Grant's frailties, Jean Edward Smith, with understated delicacy, noted, "The evidence is overwhelming that during the Vicksburg campaign he occasionally fell off the wagon. Grant was a binge drinker."[5] Other modern commentators as diverse as Shelby Foote and William McFeely have agreed on this point. Foremost among Grant's many colleagues and contemporaries who did the same was his friend and admirer General Sherman, who long after the war wrote:

> We all knew at the time that Genl Grant would occasionally drink too much—he always encouraged me to talk freely of this & other things and I always noticed that he could with an hour's sleep wake up perfectly sober & bright—and when any thing was pending, he was invariably abstinent of drink.[6]

Rather than catalogue the seemingly endless reported instances of Grant's overindulgence—many of which may well be myths—we will endeavor to briefly overview the issue. Then we shall critique various reports surrounding the Yazoo River incident to the best of our abilities.

The best modern clinical study of this issue has been made by Professor Lyle Dorsett of Wheaton College in 1983. Dorsett begins his article with, "Until the problem of Grant's drinking is openly, objectively, and clinically examined, his character will be shrouded in obscurity"; furthermore, "It is my thesis that Ulysses S. Grant was an alcoholic." Dorsett then classifies Grant as a classic binge drinker who could function amazingly well in spite of his affliction: "Many inflicted with alcoholism are binge drinkers. They hold down jobs, pursue demanding careers, support families, and go for extended periods without a drink. When they do imbibe they take more than a few social drinks. Usually they get drunk."[7] After giving his diagnosis, Dorsett recites a long list of characteristics common to both alcoholics and Grant's background.

Some of these include that Grant's grandfather and son were alcoholics, that Grant began drinking as a child, that his drinking was noticed during the Mexican War and later forced him to resign from the army, and that Grant briefly joined the Sons of Temperance (a forerunner to AA).[8] With respect to the Civil War, Dorsett notes:

> It makes more sense to see Grant a frequently quiet, moody and depressed man who did not understand himself and what was happening to him.... Actually, rather than seeing the approaching war as a great tragedy that saddened him, the evidence suggests that U.S. Grant saw it as an escape hatch from his troubles.[9]

Surprisingly (or perhaps not), Dorsett concludes that Grant's particular type of alcoholism made him a better field commander: "Paradoxically, Grant was the great military leader President Lincoln so desperately needed, in part, because he suffered from alcoholism. The disease had such an impact on Grant's personality that it became a factor in Grant's military success ... because he had absolutely nothing to lose, Grant could brush aside caution."[10] Such a prognosis lends weight to Lincoln's apocryphal joke that his other generals needed Grant's brand of whiskey.

In spite of constant "Joe Johnston to the rescue" rumors, the Vicksburg siege represented a relatively inactive period for Grant, the type of which was known to set off his drinking problems, especially when he was separated from his wife. Before Grant had embarked on his "reconnaissance" up the Yazoo River on June 6, his personal watchdog John Rawlins had apparently noticed demons coming to the forefront, and wrote him a stern letter of warning that did not come to light until after Rawlins' death.[11] Grant then seems to have escaped Rawlins' watchfulness by steaming some 50 miles up the Yazoo under the pretense of seeing what Johnston was up to at Satartia. Most of what posterity has been told about Grant's Yazoo bender comes from the pen of Sylvanus Cadwallader, whose work was not written until some 30 years later (by which time he was raising sheep in secluded northern California), and not published until 1955. Predictably, Cadwallader has since been vilified or embraced—I choose the latter.

In brief, Cadwallader claimed that after steaming up to Satartia himself on June 6, his boat (the *Diligence*) met Grant's approaching steamer on the return trip, by which time Grant was roaring drunk. Grant then jumped on board the *Diligence* and ordered it to turn around and go back to Satartia. Then Grant planted himself in the ship's barroom. Noticing the general's escort was too timid to do anything, Cadwallader resolved to save Grant from himself. First, Grant was lured out of the barroom and the key was "conveniently lost ... in a safe place." Next, Cadwallader locked Grant in a room, and defying angry threats from the hero of Vicksburg, kept him there until he fell asleep. The escort had been cowed into submission by far-from-idle threats that Cadwallader would otherwise report to Rawlins, whom they all feared. Upon reaching Satartia, Grant initially insisted on leading his small band into a town "filled with desperadoes and rebel sympathizers." After everyone else refused to go on shore, Grant then announced that he would mount his horse and ride overland all the way back to Vicksburg. This command was also ignored, and the steamer started back downstream, arriving at Hayne's Bluff the morning of June 7.[12]

By this time, Grant seemed to be sobering up when Cadwallader discovered that another supply of whiskey had been procured from on shore. Grant then ordered the boat to take him back to headquarters near Chickasaw Bayou as he proceeded to re-medicate himself. Fearful of what the world would see when Grant arrived back at Chickasaw Bayou, Cadwallader persuaded the steamboat captain to make it a very slow return trip, during which all liquor onboard was made inaccessible. Unfortunately, yet another steamer came along while Grant's boat was idling, allowing Grant to jump ships, joining an officer's party there in full swing. Cadwallader managed to chase Grant down, persuading him to leave the festivities with a lie that his escort was waiting for him.[13]

Upon reaching shore after dark, the still-intoxicated Grant called for his trusty warhorse "Kangaroo," whom he had originally found emaciated and wandering the battlefield at Shiloh. Rehabilitated, Kangaroo had been Grant's horse throughout most of the Vicksburg campaign,[14] and was named for a tendency to rear up before he dashed off. Combined with Grant's legendary equestrian skills, the two made a formidable pair. Particularly during Grant's lightning war tactics in Mississippi, Kangaroo had proven to be the perfect mount. Cadwallader recalled that Grant immediately put the spurs to Kangaroo and left everyone in the dust as he tore through the Federal camps, fortunate not to have been killed in the process. By the time Cadwallader caught up, Grant and Kangaroo were alone and going at a trot with Grant wobbling in the saddle. This allowed Cadwallader to hide them in a thicket and hail an ambulance in order to take Grant back to his tent.[15]

The finale to this farce came when Cadwallader found Rawlins and warned him what to expect. Grant greeted them cheerfully by stepping out of the ambulance and going to his tent as if nothing had happened. Cadwallader was then afraid that Rawlins would not believe him but was immediately assured to the contrary.[16] Thus Rawlins never personally witnessed any misbehavior, except for the prelude on June 5. As for Cadwallader, rather than being punished by Grant, he found his unique standing in the Federal camp raised to even greater heights.[17] If Charles Dana was Washington's eyes and ears, then Cadwallader filled the same role for Grant and Rawlins. As for Cadwallader's secret (and later unpublished) manuscript, he asserted that he did not want to jeopardize Grant's public reputation, and "[t]o speak the whole truth concerning Gen. Grant's periodic fits of intemperance has required all the courage I could summon to my assistance."[18] He also gives due credit to Rawlins and Julia Grant for protecting the general's reputation,[19] and heavily implies that Grant's intractable enemy Marat Halstead of the *Cincinnati Commercial* would have succeeded in having Grant disgraced had Vicksburg not surrendered as soon as it did.[20] I would only interject that Grant may have needed to go on a binge (and escape Rawlins) after his recent combat spree, particularly after his failure to take Vicksburg by storm on May 19 and May 22.

Charles Dana was also on board the *Diligence*. In his own memoir (published during his lifetime), Dana—by then even more concerned about protecting Grant's reputation than Cadwallader—flinched and balked at relating all the details. He merely states that Grant was "ill" and confined to his room at Satartia, but notes that upon returning to Hayne's Bluff, Grant asked Dana if they were still in Satartia.[21] Years after the fact, Cadwallader reminded Colonel James Wilson of the incident, who mentioned it to Dana. Dana responded to Wilson's gossip by denying that Cadwallader had been on board; yet, Cadwallader's paper the *Chicago Times* received a dispatch from Satartia on June 6 at 10 P.M. Wilson, for his part, had made a diary entry on June 7, 1863: "Gen. G. intoxicated!"[22] In the final analysis, one must pass judgment on Cadwallader's account. Embellishment of the facts and hyperbolic, journalistic self-aggrandizement? Surely. Total fiction? Very unlikely. Our own conclusion is based on the cumulative weight of circumstantial evidence. Were some of the stories about Grant's drinking due to malicious envy? Probably. Most of it? Possibly. All of it? We don't think so. On June 9, Grant wrote a letter to Julia—almost pathetic in tone—asking her to come down and join him at camp, which she was unable to immediately do. Later (on July 15), Grant again expressed to her his lonely feelings.[23]

Not long after Grant had made it seem through his behavior that he had a death wish, he caught another major break. While he was still brooding over the failed May 22 assault in a letter to his father on June 15,[24] a recent news release was inciting the profound anger of his staff against one of their own— General John McClernand. In the wake of the May 22 assault, in which McClernand's failings were so conspicuous, the wayward political general had copied the press on his congratulatory order in which his personal achievements were trumpeted at the expense of his colleagues, even hinting that he deserved credit for the impending surrender of Vicksburg. When General Francis Blair[25] saw it in the *Memphis Bulletin* of June 17 (a reprint from the *Missouri Democrat* of June 10), he showed it to Sherman, who called it "a catalogue of nonsense ... an effusion of vainglory and hypocrisy ... addressed not to an army, but to a constituency in Illinois."[26] Then Sherman forwarded it to Grant, both knowing that McClernand's public address was a direct violation of regulations which called for the immediate removal of any offender. In the words of Shelby Foote, "Grant had waited half a year for this"[27]—we would say longer, perhaps ever since Fort Donelson. Grant immediately wrote to McClernand, enclosed a copy of the article, and queried if it was really his. McClernand responded that it was.[28] Colonel Wilson, still spoiling for a fight with McClernand, volunteered to deliver the note at 2 A.M. McClernand, forcibly roused from bed, remarked to Wilson, "Well, sir, I am relieved." Wilson replied with, "By God, sir, we are both relieved!"[29] Accordingly, at 2 A.M. on June 18, 1863, Grant's arch-nemesis, General John McClernand, was finally cashiered.

Sherman's post-mortem on the affair was that "not an officer or soldier here but rejoices he [McClernand] is gone away."[30] Incredibly, instead of Grant's falling victim to his own notorious habits plus the intrigues of McClernand, Halstead, and countless others, it was now McClernand who was being sent home in disgrace. Perhaps he had served his purpose. Perhaps what kept Grant from going over the brink during the siege of Vicksburg was the thought that McClernand would probably succeed him if he did otherwise. McClernand vigorously appealed his dismissal by trying to blame his staff for the article, but was ignored with the exception of his old associate President Lincoln. Lincoln, however, with the wit for which he was famous, wrote to McClernand that generals are best judged by their own comrades in the field and that "he who has the right needs not to fear."[31] Less humorously, military historian Colonel Arthur Conger wrote:

> McClernand's career is a perfect illustration of failure through almost a single fault of policy. He appears to have been a man of force, of a certain degree of offensive spirit, of presence of mind, of initiative, and of constantly growing appreciation of military operations. But his success was tainted from the start by his failure to be personally loyal to his immediate superior and this was the direct cause of the wreck of his military career, from which even the best wishes and personal endeavors of the President in his behalf could not save him.[32]

Perhaps the final assessment of McClernand, though, should be given to Grant. In his memoirs, though detailing McClernand's foolishness in all of its detail, Grant still surprisingly concludes by praising his courage, sacrifice, and patriotism.[33] Nevertheless, at the end of the day, McClernand is a case study in self-destructive behavior.

By way of contrast, Grant had nothing but praise for Confederate General Joseph Johnston, as did most who fought against him or under him. By early June, as Lee marched north, all Confederate hopes at Vicksburg were focused on the miracle of Johnston rescuing them from the east. Grant called Johnston "one of the ablest commanders of the South" but one not in favor with Jefferson Davis or his cronies, and that was the rub.[34] Johnston's order for Pemberton to link up with him had been wise, in Grant's opinion.[35] In regards to Johnston's later Fabian tactics against Sherman in Georgia, Grant made the following extraordinary assertion: "Anything that could have prolonged the war a year beyond the time that it did finally close, would probably have exhausted the North to such an extent that they might have then abandoned the contest and agreed to a separation."[36] These are strong words that few Confederate leaders heeded, not even Robert E. Lee. Had they heeded them, the Confederacy certainly would have been no worse off than it eventually was.

Johnston's position by June was hopeless. By the time he had gathered a relief force of some 30,000 men, only about two-thirds of which were trained regulars, Grant had assembled almost 80,000 veterans surrounding Vicksburg and Pemberton with his 30,000 defenders.[37] The Federals had ramparts not only facing Vicksburg but facing east towards Johnston as well. Sherman and Blair were even sent out to probe for Johnston at one point. Witnesses suggest that Johnston was perhaps the only Confederate leader thinking straight at the time ("His mind was clear as a bell," wrote one officer).[38] As for Pemberton, the only option he ever considered was to hunker down behind fortifications and pray that Johnston could pierce through the combined armies of Grant and Sherman, reminiscent of Vercingetorix at Alesia against Julius Caesar. Had Johnston attacked, the result would have been the same as Alesia—probably worse, since Johnston had less than half of Grant's numbers, whereas the Gauls heavily outnumbered Caesar. Had Johnston attacked, the war would have probably ended even sooner than it did, because all Confederate defense of east-central Mississippi and Alabama would have collapsed in the event of his defeat.[39]

As Vicksburg starved, false rumors of its salvation from Johnston seemed to increase. This may have motivated Grant to increase the pressure in various ways,[40] one of which involved the explosion of an underground mine beneath the Confederate works on June 25. The attempted incursion by the Federals was a dismal failure, but the aftermath provided Grant and his infantry a chance to engage in a little crude, racist humor. During the explosion, a former slave named Abraham, working behind the lines, was blown sky-high but landed alive and in one piece amongst the Federals. Grant's delighted Midwesterners immediately set Abraham up as a freak show and made a neat profit by charging admission to curious gawkers. According to Grant, when asked how far he had been transported by the explosion, Abraham replied, "Dun no, massa, but t'ink 'bout t'ree mile."[41] To judge Grant's attitude towards race on this one pathetic incident, however, would be an oversimplification. During this period, Grant (unlike Sherman and many others) was giving enthusiastic support to the recent formation of African-American regiments. His support was particularly strong after June 7—also the last day of his Yazoo bender—when untrained and poorly armed black regiments stationed at Milliken's Bend (a supposedly quiet sector) played a key role in fending off an attempted Confederate raid from Arkansas. This raid had been intended to aid the relief effort for Vicksburg but, thanks to the heroic efforts of recently armed freedmen, achieved nothing.[42]

On June 25—the same day of the mine explosion—Grant requested and later received permission for the transfer of Captain Ely Parker to his command post. Parker was a fellow Galenan, an accomplished engineer, and a full-blooded Seneca tribesman. Later Parker would become Grant's advisor on Native American affairs (both during and after the war), and play an important administrative and symbolic role at the Appomattox surrender.[43] For the present, it seems, Grant wanted another good engineer (in addition to ones such as General McPherson and Colonel Wilson) to assist in the reduction of Vicksburg. The following day (June 26), another symbolic but barely noticed event occurred. Commodore Andrew Foote passed away in New York state after a long bout of ill health caused by illness, old age, and wounds sustained during (among others) Grant's Fort Donelson campaign the previous year. Though ably replaced by Admiral Porter, it had been Commodore Foote, along with the late General C.F. Smith, who had done as much as anyone to launch Grant's unlikely career into the public eye in 1862. It is a tragic irony that neither lived to see Grant's final triumph at Vicksburg, though Foote perhaps foresaw the event, which would occur about a week later.

The last week of June also saw another harrowing event for Grant, but one far removed from Mississippi. His son Fred, who had accompanied him throughout three weeks of nonstop combat, was subsequently sent north to recoup his strength. While Fred was staying at the home of his uncle and aunt (Julia's sister, Emma Casey) in Caseyville, Kentucky (along the Ohio River), Confederate guerillas made an attempt to abduct the boy. For whatever reason, Fred had that particular day rode into town with his uncle James Casey and was not at home when the guerillas came calling. Immediately, Mrs. Casey sent a servant to warn her husband and instructed him to put Fred on the first boat back to Cairo, Illinois, which was soon accomplished.[44] Neither Grant nor Julia were informed as to what had happened. The timing of this incident, coming on the eve of Vicksburg's surrender, raises a number of questions that are both fascinating and horrifying. Not the least of these is whether Fred Grant was safer with his father in a raging battle or staying near his grandfather and aunt in the guerilla-infested countryside of Kentucky. It had been only six months since Confederate cavalry had ridden into Holly Springs, Mississippi, and demanded to know the whereabouts of Julia Grant. In any event, Jesse Grant, Sr.'s worst nightmare for the safety of his son's family had been nearly realized while he was supposedly out of harm's way.

On June 29, Grant happily wrote to Julia that Fred had returned to camp with him, and that "[d]uring the present week I think the fate of Vicksburg will be decided."[45] This would prove to be an accurate assessment. As the Federal army tightened its death grip around Vicksburg, Joseph Johnston was preparing to create a forlorn diversion that would perhaps allow Pemberton's army to break out. But the Confederates inside of Vicksburg were too exhausted to do much of anything; in fact, they were famished. The day before (June 28), Pemberton had received a letter signed "Many Soldiers," the key sentence of which read, "If you can't feed us, you had better surrender...."[46] In contrast to the undernourished Confederates, Grant's army was living in the midst of plenty. In his memoirs, Grant recalled that family and friends of the Federal soldiers with good intentions would bring them snack packs, thinking that the troops were underfed. Ever since Grant had turned them loose on the Mississippi countryside, however, they had been living large, so much so that now the sight of poultry (compared to red meat), in particular, disgusted them. Of the visitors, Grant remarked, "They did not know how little the gift would be appreciated."[47] In addition to winning battles, former quartermaster Grant was keeping his troops well-fed. Now that Johnston appeared to be making hostile moves, Grant responded by preparing to make an even bigger all-out assault against the exhausted defenders of Vicksburg. He correctly sensed that the great moment of triumph, both for himself and the Federal cause, was now at hand.

CHAPTER 28

July 1863:
Major-General Grant

Nations, like individuals, are punished for their transgressions.

—Grant[1]

During the first three days of July 1863, as the siege of Vicksburg reached its climax, the eyes of the nation turned in the direction of Gettysburg, Pennsylvania. After a ferocious three-day contest, the battle ended on the slopes of Cemetery Ridge with one the most futile direct assaults in military history ("Pickett's Charge"). General Robert E. Lee's still proud but decisively beaten Army of Northern Virginia retreated back South, with many of the author's ancestors hobbling along in the ranks. Thus ended the Confederacy's desperate endeavor to force a peace—desperate because of what Grant had been doing in Mississippi. Although subsequent history has lavished most of its popular attention on the battle of Gettysburg, while assigning (at best) a respectful nod towards Grant's Vicksburg campaign, in truth it was Vicksburg that had caused Lee's Northern invasion in the first place.

There can be no diminishment of the signal victory at Gettysburg by the Army of the Potomac under General George Meade, except perhaps that Lee and his veterans may have gone into battle believing themselves invincible—not a completely unreasonable assumption given their past performance. Nevertheless, one must ask: what if Lee had prevailed at Gettysburg? Would the Confederates then have simply marched on Washington and forced a peace? Perhaps. Then again, maybe not. Maybe by this time the war had become more than, as Grant once put it, "the mere occupation of places." Was Gettysburg in fact the last, high-stakes gamble of a Confederate States forced into a rash response by Grant's efforts? At the very least, it appears that Lee was eventually undone, however indirectly, by Grant's relentless pressure at Vicksburg. Rather than reinforce Vicksburg, Lee (in typical fashion for him) had opted to risk everything on a single throw of the dice and had lost.

While battle raged at Gettysburg, Grant began preparations for another all-out assault against the fortifications of Vicksburg, projected to take place on July 6.[2] Not only had signs of weaknesses in the Confederate defense recently appeared due to famine and shortage of ammunition, Grant was also energized by yet another rumor that General Joseph Johnston's army to the east was about to create a diversion. This diversion would be for the purpose of allowing the besieged Confederates to break out and escape sometime around July 7.[3] It was in fact true that Johnston was preparing to make such a move, but by this time despair and fatigue had gripped the defenders of Vicksburg, who were in no physical or mental shape for offensive operations, and needed nothing short of a full-scale outside attack against Grant to save them. Nothing of the sort was forthcoming. As journalist Sylvanus Cadwallader noted, "The utter impossibility of supplying his army with necessary food had been a sufficient reason for Johnston's not falling upon Grant's rear and attempting to raise the siege."[4] In effect, Confederate strategy in both Mississippi and Pennsylvania was based on pipe dreams, and the bitter fruits of these delusions were about to be harvested in full.

Fortunately for the soldiers on both sides of the lines, Pemberton was receiving sensible advice from subordinates. Foremost among these was General John Bowen, Grant's friend and former Missouri neighbor, who had fought so gallantly for the Confederacy throughout the Vicksburg campaign. When Pemberton finally realized that he was possibly the last Confederate in Vicksburg who still wanted to hold out, he agreed to open negotiations with Grant, if nothing else to delay the inevitable. At 10 A.M. on July 3, white flags went up along the Confederate lines and the Federals were approached by Bowen, accompanied by Pemberton's aide-de-camp.[5] After an audience with Grant was refused, it was agreed that Pemberton and Grant could later meet and talk in no-man's land. In preparation for this meeting, Grant sent Pemberton one of his more famous notes, the heart of which read as follows:

> The useless effusion of blood you propose stopping by this course can be ended at any time you may choose, by the unconditional surrender of the city and garrison. Men who have shown so much endurance and courage as those now in Vicksburg, will always challenge the respect of an adversary, and I can assure you will be treated with all the respect due to prisoners of war.[6]

Although Grant and Pemberton had known each other in the old army, their reunion quickly became unpleasant. When Pemberton realized that it was Bowen rather than Grant who set up the conference, and that Grant was merely offering the same unconditional terms that he had given to Buckner at Fort Donelson, he responded "rather snappishly" (in the words of Grant) and started to walk away. At this point, Bowen once again came to the rescue by proposing that the two commanding generals take a short break while he and Union General McPherson discussed collateral terms. As Bowen and McPherson engaged in some diversionary posturing that accomplished nothing on the surface, this allowed Grant and (especially) Pemberton to cool off under a nearby oak tree.[7]

Pemberton finally came to his senses, by now possibly cognizant that Grant's threat of a full assault was no bluff and that such an attack was likely to succeed. Before the conference ended, it was agreed that Grant would submit final, written surrender terms before the end of the day. When Grant did this, its key, revised provision was prisoner parole as opposed to unconditional surrender and more than 30,000 Confederate POWs. Grant had reflected that it would be much easier to transport a few boxes of paroles than the largest number of prisoners ever taken during an American war (more than double the number at Fort Donelson). Moreover, the vast majority of these parolees would probably go home and never fight for the Confederacy again. After the clarification of some of Pemberton's rather vague terms with Grant's usual precise language, Pemberton agreed, and Grant was informed of this acquiescence shortly after midnight.[8] Vicksburg would surrender on July 4 (Independence Day), while unbeknownst to either party, Lee's army simultaneously retreated out of Pennsylvania. Pemberton later claimed credit for the July 4 timing of the surrender, ostensibly to obtain better terms, but Grant disputed this and there can be little denying that it was an added humiliation for the Confederates.[9] My own view is that the timing probably had little impact on Grant's offered terms, and that Pemberton's rank and file would have preferred another day be chosen. In any event, the long ordeal had finally ended and, after eight brutal months, nearly six of which showed no tangible Federal gains, Ulysses S. Grant had achieved his greatest victory, and one that is still studied at West Point to this day.

Among the countless and fascinating accounts of surrender ceremonies at Vicksburg on July 4, our favorite is one from a Southern woman who had endured all the hardships of the siege and was now eyewitness to the Federal army entering the city. Momentarily overcoming her prejudice against the Yankees, she recorded, "Civilization, discipline, and order seemed to enter with the measured tramp of these marching feet."[10] The good behavior of Grant's troops was truly remarkable, given that they had been tearing apart the Mississippi landscape for over a year. Confederate prisoners were treated with respect and provisions were shared. Southern civilians, much to their surprise, were offered a helping hand as well.[11] For the first time in a long time the Federals were not hell-bent on death and destruction. When Julia Grant later arrived, she noted that civilians were being fed, and that some of them even appeared grateful for it.[12] Grant's only personal plunder from the entire campaign seems to have been a horse from the nearby plantation of Jefferson Davis,[13] the horse probably coming out better for the bargain. A recurring theme in Grant's memoirs is that he felt more sympathy and leniency towards rebels who had fought and endured privations for their beliefs, than he did for Northern Copperheads and others who merely agitated.[14]

While President Lincoln had been sorely disappointed that Meade did not pursue Lee after beating him at Gettysburg, his jubilation at Grant's Vicksburg triumph was profuse and unequivocal. After announcing, "The Father of Waters again goes unvexed to the sea," Lincoln then sent a new signal to Grant's many previous critics and detractors on July 5 by proclaiming: "Grant is my man, and I am his the rest of the war."[15] Then Lincoln sat down and wrote the following letter:

MY DEAR GENERAL:

I do not remember that you and I ever met personally. I write this now as grateful acknowledgment for the most inestimable service you have done the country. I wish to say a word further. When you first reached the vicinity of Vicksburg, I thought you should do, what you finally did—march the troops across the neck, run the batteries with the transports, and thus go below; and I never had any faith, except in a general hope that you knew better than I, that the Yazoo Pass expedition, and the like, could succeed. When you got below and took Fort Gibson, Grand Gulf and vicinity, I thought you should go down the river and join Gen. Banks; and when you turned Northward East of the Big Black, I feared it was a mistake. I now wish to make the personal acknowledgement that you were right, and I was wrong.

Yours very truly,

A. LINCOLN[16]

Although Lincoln had agreed with the controversial decision to run the gauntlet, he—like Sherman and just about everyone else—had been alarmed when Grant cut loose from his supply line and moved against Jackson. Now Lincoln, like Sherman, found himself admitting to Grant that he had been mistaken. I am not aware of any other person who ever received simultaneous apologies from Abraham Lincoln and William Tecumseh Sherman. The most tangible evidence of Lincoln's appreciation, though, was expressed by immediately promoting Grant to Major-General in the regular army on July 7 (backdated to July 4), the highest rank then available to bestow. Before then, Grant had only been a Major-General of Volunteers. Perhaps the celebratory mood of the North was best expressed by that otherwise cynical and hardest-to-impress of all American historians, Henry Adams, who, in a subtle reference to Grant's drinking problems, wrote, "I want to get the whole army of Vicksburg drunk at my own expense. I want to fight some *small* man and lick him."[17]

The surrender of Vicksburg had a domino effect for the entire Mississippi region. On July 9, Confederate defenders of Port Hudson, Louisiana, received word of the surrender and, correctly deducing that they would soon be surrounded and overwhelmed, capitulated as well. Grant's first act after the surrender was to order Sherman's restless perimeter force to push east until Johnston's makeshift army had scattered to the winds. By July 16, Johnston had wisely elected to save his men and munitions for fighting another day and evacuated Jackson, which he had temporarily relieved from Federal occupation. On July 17, Sherman entered Jackson for the second time in little over a month, this time unopposed. On this occasion, however, none of the forbearance exercised at Vicksburg was extended. What little that was left in the state capital of Mississippi was pillaged and then the city itself was burned. Sherman's "bummers," who were beginning to cultivate their fearsome reputation as plundering arsonists, re-christened Jackson "Chimneyville" as they departed, and began their return journey to Vicksburg on July 23.[18]

Today, nearly a century and a half later, even Grant's harshest critics tend to fall silent while contemplating his Vicksburg campaign. The dean of scholars in this area, Edwin Bearss, has written that "Grant was the difference in the Vicksburg campaign,"[19] while Kenneth Williams simply proclaimed, "Vicksburg is Grant."[20] Others, such as historian F.V. Greene, have declared, "We must go back to the campaigns of Napoleon to find equally brilliant results accomplished in the same space of time with such small loss."[21] In terms of immediate cause and effect, historian James McPherson judged, "The capture of Vicksburg was the most important northern strategic victory of the war...."[22] Grant himself later wrote, "The fate of the Confederacy was sealed when Vicksburg fell."[23] This comes across as a bit of an overstatement, given that nearly two years of hard fighting, blunders, and near-misses still lay ahead for both sides; nevertheless, Vicksburg at the very least can be viewed as the true and decisive turning point of the war, not only for the things that resulted in Mississippi, but also for pushing Lee to fatefully march into Gettysburg as well. After a few pages of reflection, Grant himself added: "It looks now as though Providence had directed the course of the campaign while the [Federal] Army of the Tennessee executed the decree."[24]

Possibly the true brilliance of Grant's achievement was the manner in which he reduced the sluggish Pemberton with one arm, while holding at bay with his other the formidable Joseph Johnston. Moreover, Grant seems to have possessed both a thorough knowledge of his opponents and the capabilities of his own men. This is possibly one reason why he was so confident when others were not. Fighting in the heart of the enemy's country with limited resources, Grant was hampered by intrigue against him in Washington, in the press, and even from key subordinates such as John McClernand. One of his many great blessings was that he had yet to meet an opposing general who was really worthy of his talents. Competent officers such as Johnston, Forrest, Bowen, and Buckner were consistently made subordinate to the mediocrity of Jefferson Davis and his favorites, with consistently disastrous results.

Grant succeeded at Vicksburg by going against conventional wisdom, which surely would have failed; it also appears as though Grant was the only individual capable of doing what he did. Even more stupefying in retrospect is Grant's relatively short road leading up to this great accomplishment. Two months prior, almost everyone (with a few notable exceptions) wanted him cashiered. One year prior, he was sitting at a desk in Memphis listening to complaints about church pulpits being defiled. Less than 20 months previous, he had never led a body of men into combat. Less than 25 months before the surrender of Vicksburg, he did not even have a commission, nor apparent prospects for one. In the final analysis, the Vicksburg campaign, although deservedly one of the most studied chapters in all of military history, remains an inexplicable mystery—it should not have transpired and yet it did, with immeasurable effect on American and world history.

An apoplectic Jefferson Davis reacted to the capitulation of his adopted home state by lashing out against Joseph Johnston, one of the generals least to blame for the defeat and possibly the only one who had too much personal dignity to respond to such criticism. Davis, forgetting months of his own executive blunders, told his cabinet in Richmond that Vicksburg had been lost for "want of provisions inside and a General outside who wouldn't fight."[25] Then again, the irrational reaction of Davis was not an isolated occurrence in the South, or in the North, for that matter. Julia Grant astonishingly recorded that even after news of the surrender reached St. Louis, Confederate sympathizers there still seemed ignorant of the event and kept referring to the place as the "Rock of Gibraltar" without a single hint of irony.[26] Mary Chesnut recorded in her diary that she fainted upon hearing the news.[27]

Perhaps the most ungracious reaction, however, came from Pemberton. Regarding Pemberton's captured army, Grant had quickly deduced that parolees were preferable and POWs acceptable, but escapees (armed or unarmed) were neither. To Pemberton's embarrassment, some of his former troops preferred the brutality of Northern prison camps to the future prospect of being conscripted back into the Confederate army, and Grant would not force anyone to sign their paroles.[28] Then as Pemberton and his official parolees marched east to eventually rejoin their comrades and countrymen, most of them stole away into the countryside, never to bear arms again for the Confederacy. By the time Pemberton found Johnston in mid–July, reposing with his army still relatively intact, Pemberton's over 30,000 parolees had reportedly melted away to fewer than 2,000 over the course of two weeks.[29] As Cadwallader observed, "The wisdom of Grant's releasing them on parole was thus early proven."[30] Now faced with the humiliation of both defeat and the desertion of his once intrepid troops, Pemberton (like Davis) responded by placing blame on Johnston. When the latter greeted Pemberton with an outstretched hand, it was refused. After Pemberton gave a terse report, he and Johnston never saw each other again.[31] Johnston's future performance against Sherman's Federals in Georgia and the Carolinas would also improve from that moment on.

Upon joining her husband in Vicksburg, Julia Grant, with her keen eye for detail, records a number of interesting observations. Julia claimed that she had never witnessed an occupied Southern house being commandeered for Federal headquarters unless it was by invitation. Vicksburg, though, was different. As the Federal cavalry scouted out locations, a female visitor who had been trapped during the siege at the spacious mansion of Mr. and Mrs. William Lum made an ugly face at the cavalry captain, who immediately selected that particular house for Union headquarters. Julia records with unconcealed satisfaction, "The ladies were greatly alarmed and fled like a flock of partridges before the company as it marched in." She quickly adds, however, that Mrs. Lum expressed the family's thanks to the troops for sharing supplies, not to mention rental payments in the form of Federal greenbacks. Lastly, Julia humorously notes that Grant's Puritanical chief-of-staff John Rawlins was annoyed by the flirtatious manner in which some Southern women ingratiated themselves with the troops, although he himself would soon conspicuously fall victim to these same tactics (see Chapter 30).[32]

While Sherman was busy sacking Jackson, Grant wrote to General Halleck on July 18, suggesting that the next proper military step would be to move against Mobile, Alabama.[33] By doing do, Grant was staying true to his consistent view of the war, which was that the best way to minimize bloodshed and destruction would be to move quickly and forcefully against Confederate armies. Halleck, however—reverting back to his cautious attitude towards all of Grant's ideas—preferred another course. Specifically, this involved scattering Grant's victorious troops in various other directions as needed, particularly to the trans–Mississippi and Texas, along the Mexican border.[34] In overruling Grant's recommendation, Halleck had political support from Lincoln and others, who were concerned about potentially pro–Confederate French incursions into Mexico during that same period. This involved the ill-advised and ill-informed installation by Napoleon III of Archduke Maximilian on the throne as Mexican Emperor, as opposed to the popularly elected Benito Juárez as Mexican President. Grant himself noted long after the fact that this one incident was an exception to his strong belief that "France is the traditional ally and friend of the United States."[35] As Jean Edward Smith put it, Grant's proposed "expedition against Mobile was stillborn."[36] Although the Mexicans would eventually prove adept at handling the French themselves, trusting them to do so in the aftermath of Vicksburg was not the politically popular choice. As a result, Grant had little else to do except smell the roses and wait for the next crisis to develop in which his services would be needed.

CHAPTER 29

August 1863: "All Look Upon Us as Enemies"

In the two years since Grant had been appointed a Brigadier General through the political influence of Congressman Elihu Washburne, he had progressed from being a rather dubious and untested field officer to the unquestioned kingpin of all Union commanders. As recently as late April 1863—less than three months before the surrender of Vicksburg—he had been in serious danger of losing his job. If we are to believe half of what journalist Sylvanus Cadwallader wrote (and I do), right up to the moment of surrender Grant stood in very real jeopardy of being publicly disgraced over his reported drinking binges during the campaign. Now, all of this was suddenly behind him. By early August 1863, after celebrations over recent Federal successes at Vicksburg and Gettysburg had subsided, Grant was the man of the hour. Whereas Fort Donelson had introduced him to celebrity (and Shiloh quickly thereafter to notoriety), Vicksburg solidified Grant's preeminent standing as a military leader and, more importantly, silenced a good number of his critics. This was all a mere 27 months after he had been a complete nobody in Galena, Illinois. Although this study covers the 36-month period from his Galena clerkship to the moment he was appointed Lieutenant-General, Grant's nothing-less-than-miraculous transformation in the public eye really had transpired over a much shorter time frame, roughly between his signal victories at Donelson and Vicksburg—some 17 months in all.

Grant's entirely new status amongst his colleagues entailed receipt of much more flattery, but not always necessarily more power or influence. Secretary of War Stanton, one of Grant's greatest fair-weather friends, owned the distinction of being the first politician after Vicksburg suggesting that Grant be brought East to command the Army of the Potomac. This brainstorm, however, was quickly nixed by Grant's own modest reluctance (a trait that Washington politicians were not used to dealing with) and, more importantly, a very real concern over the feathers that might be ruffled by such a move. For example, Senator Henry Wilson of Massachusetts voiced anxiety that if Grant were brought to the East, he would likely be at the mercy of jealous intrigue within the army itself.[1] It was soon decided that Grant would stay where he was, but that his victorious army—by now acquiring a well-deserved reputation for success—would be redistributed to other sectors and under other generals as needed. By August 5, Grant was writing to Charles Dana, thanking him for his intercession which helped to prevent (or at least delay) Grant's eastern transfer.[2]

General Halleck in Washington had invited both Grant and Sherman to express their views on how the war should now be prosecuted.[3] Even before Halleck had made this gesture, however, Grant had recommended a campaign against Mobile, Alabama, and began making plans for this, not knowing that nothing of the sort would be allowed by either Halleck or President Lincoln, due to recent events in Mexico. It may even be that this anticipated rebuff motivated Halleck's out-of-character invitation for Grant to speak his mind. On August 11, Grant wrote to Halleck regarding the need to consolidate recent Federal gains in Mississippi and Louisiana:

> This state and Louisiana would be more easily governed now than Kentucky or Missouri if armed rebels from other states could be kept out. In fact the people are ready to accept anything. The troops from these states too would desert and return so soon as they find that they cannot be hunted down.[4]

Grant's allusion to his early activities in the border states underscored that these areas—unlike Mississippi and Louisiana—had not suffered the full privations of war and hence the latter would likely be more submissive, provided Confederate armies could be barred entry. Grant then repeats reports he had received that Mississippi citizens were trying to organize a movement bringing themselves back into the Union. Grant's opinion, however, was not universal in this respect, as we shall see in a moment.

Towards accomplishing this end, Grant expressed another opinion to Halleck that was not commonplace at that time, on the matter of African-American regiments: "The negro troops are easier to preserve discipline among than are the white troops, and I doubt not will prove equally good for garrison duty. All that have been tried have fought bravely."[5] Grant repeated his endorsement in a letter to President Lincoln on August 23: "I have given the subject of arming the negro my hearty support. This, with the emancipation of the negro, is the heavyest blow yet given the Confederacy."[6] Then, a week later (August 30) in a letter to Washburne, Grant elaborated on his opinion and tried to explain how he had changed his mind on the issue: "Slavery is already dead and cannot be resurrected. It would take a standing Army to maintain slavery in the South if we were to make peace today guaranteeing to the south all their former constitutional privileges." Then, at perhaps the most unfashionable moment he could have chosen, Grant admits to Washburne in the same letter, "I was never an Abolitionist, not even what could be called anti-slavery, but ... it became patent to my mind early in the rebellion that the North & South could never live at peace with each other except as one nation, and that without Slavery."[7] Over the course of two years, Grant—like many of his volunteer troops—had been forced to confront their conventional beliefs and come to see things in a different light.

Also over the course of two years, Grant's originally high opinion of fellow Galenan and chief-of-staff John Rawlins had gone up higher than ever, and with good reason. To Washburne, Grant forcefully stated that "Rawlins ... is no ordinary man ... some men ... are only made by their Staff appointments whilst others give respectability to the position. Rawlins is of the latter class."[8] It was Rawlins who ran the administrative shop, it was Rawlins who played bad cop when that was needed, it was Rawlins who told Grant when he was making mistakes such as General Order No. 11, it was Rawlins who brought Sylvanus Cadwallader into the fold, and it was Rawlins, along with Julia, who helped to keep Grant sober. The same man who had inspired the down-and-out ex-captain with his patriotic speech on April 16, 1861, was now Grant's right-hand man and soon to be a promoted Brigadier General in his own right. Rawlins' latest important service for Grant had been to give a presentation in Washington on July 30 before President Lincoln and his cabinet, one which both impressed the audience and cast a bad light on Grant's powerful political enemies such as John McClernand.[9] While Rawlins may never have been the "brains behind Grant" that some claimed, he was certainly an indispensable factor in Grant's rise to fame and influence, and it is difficult to imagine anyone else filling the same role.

Grant's opinions, both changing and informed by hard experience, were appropriate for a nation that was now questioning the constitutional meaning of states' rights, particularly with respect to the waning institution of human slavery. Around this same time, Julia Grant humorously noted in her memoirs that she confronted her father, Colonel Dent, with some of these issues. Julia asked, "Papa, why don't they make a new Constitution since this one is such an enigma—one to suit the times, you know. It is so different now." Colonel Dent responded with:

> Good Heavens! If Old Jackson had been in the White House, this never would have happened. He would have hanged a score or two of them, and the country would have been at peace. I knew we would have trouble when I voted for a man north of Mason and Dixon's line.[10]

Julia quickly added, "But dear papa was always pleased at any success of my husband and was immensely proud of him, notwithstanding his great sympathy with the South."[11] Grant expressed the firm and sensible conviction that "[i]t is preposterous to suppose that the people of one generation can lay down the best and only rules of government for all who are to come after them, and unforeseen contingencies."[12] He obviously believed that anyone who was incapable of changing their minds on any particular issue (as he himself had on more than one occasion) to be a fool.

By August 23, Grant had accompanied Julia and their children back to Cairo, Illinois, where Grant's campaigns had begun in late 1861. From there, Julia continued on to St. Louis, while Grant wrote to Colonel Dent ("Dent") on August 23, "I feel younger than I did six years ago."[13] This was a reference to 1857, Grant's miserably impoverished year spent in the St. Louis area. Then he returned downstream to Memphis, where two banquets were held in his honor on August 25 and August 26. The first event was sponsored by the board of trade and the second by the mayor and city council. This was the same group of people that Grant had had run-ins with the previous year over his attempted suppression of the cotton trade and, more successfully, his censorship of the press. At both events, Grant (from all accounts) turned his wine glass down and let others do the talking, most notably when his trusted legatee, General Stephen Hurlbut, read a brief statement of gratitude on Grant's behalf at the second banquet and received a standing ovation in response.[14]

Meanwhile, the war continued. In eastern Tennessee, Grant's rival, General William Rosecrans, along with his Army of the Cumberland, having contributed little if anything to the Federal victories at Vicksburg and Gettysburg, was now under heavy pressure from Washington and the War Department to advance. Rosecrans, still thinking conventionally, kept appealing for more rations and supplies, to which Lincoln deviously replied that the more he was sent, the more he seemed to consume. After all excuses and appeals had been exhausted, Rosecrans began his southward push against Braxton Bragg's Army of Tennessee (stationed at Chattanooga) on August 16.[15] By the end of the month, through skillful feints and maneuvering, Rosecrans was forcing Bragg to evacuate Chattanooga. This set the stage for the terrible battle that would be fought between the two armies the following month in northern Georgia.

In wake of the multiple Confederate disasters brought on in no small part by his own lack of foresight, Jefferson Davis proclaimed August 21 to be a day of national fasting and prayer.[16] Grant, who knew more about adversity before the war than did Jefferson Davis, had himself little but contempt for such displays. In his memoirs, Grant later wrote, "I would not have the anniversaries of our victories celebrated, nor those of our defeats made fast days and spent in humiliation and prayer; but I would like to see truthful history written."[17] Rather than celebrating, Grant wanted to attack Mobile, but Halleck officially put the idea to bed on August 6.[18] This too, may have been fortuitous for Grant because Jefferson Davis also had warned General Joseph Johnston that he thought Mobile would be the next Federal target.[19] While Davis no doubt blamed Johnston, Beauregard, or whoever else was at hand for the divine wrath that seemed to recently descend upon Confederate fortunes, his attitude was far from being unusual amongst his Southern compatriots, at least for those who were politicians or civilians rather than soldiers. After all, it is much easier to blame God, the devil, or others for any mishap, rather than one's own foolishness.

Along these lines, journalist Cadwallader preserved his impressions of Mississippi citizenry during the month of August for posterity, and they were not flattering. Recalling that Sherman had set out for Jackson in mid–July with hopes of discovering Union sentiment in the wake of recent Confederate defeats, he claimed that Sherman, upon his return, never harbored such fantasies again.[20] Cadwallader's observations are worth quoting at length, since these represent a snapshot of the time and place:

> I have conversed with hundreds of families between here and Jackson, and have not found one citizen who could properly be termed a Union man. Many profess a conservatism which in the opinion of the administration at Washington, is treason. Very many more attempt no reserve or concealment, but openly proclaim their attachment to their own government, while drawing rations and supplies from ours. All are intensely pro-slavery in feeling, and curse the Yankees for "stealing their niggers."[21]

These feelings, however, did not prevent the locals from seeking Federal protection and largess, though it did make them reluctant to lend a helping hand:

> The crowds that continually swarm hitherward from the Black river come to *claim* rations, protection, and other *rights* of citizenship; but are wonderfully reluctant to acknowledge or discharge the duties thereof. None join our army; none contribute in word or deed to the Federal Cause; all look upon us as enemies, even when asking for, and accepting, subsistence at our hands. Their manners are often insufferably insolent and insulting. I must reiterate that after long, close, and (I believe) impartial investigation, I can find none whom I believe to be truly Union men or women, in this entire region. If here, it has never been my fortune to meet them.... [22]

Grant, for his part, was less condemning and/or saw things that Cadwallader did not. For example, in a letter to Halleck he noted that some former Confederates had asked to join the Union army but were refused for security reasons.[23] Then again, these would-be volunteers were soldiers rather than civilians.

Cadwallader continued to vent. He claimed that Mississippian contemporaries of Jefferson Davis were a breed apart, different from other Confederates:

> In one particular the people of Vicksburg and vicinity differ widely from all other communities.... While cherishing the utmost bitterness and malignancy towards us, they nevertheless accept our favors and benefactions. They even come as cravens and sycophants to beg favors that were denied when insolently demanded. They lack honesty and sincerity in a markable degree. Elsewhere the citizens have submitted to our rule under protest (as a matter beyond their control) but have preserved their own self-respect, and often challenged ours. They were sometimes sullen and morose, but, if enemies, were openly and consistently so. Here no duplicity is too low; no cunning or treachery too base, to practice towards us. The people as a whole are the most ungrateful on the face of the earth...."[24]

This is pretty strong stuff, to say the least. Cadwallader's scathing judgment, however, did not seem to take into account the then-unprecedented devastation he witnessed in this part of the South. It is likely that few societies would have reacted much better under similar conditions. Places such as Nashville and New Orleans, after all, had not been reduced to nothing as had been central Mississippi.

As the month of August 1863 came to a close, Grant steamed down the Mississippi River to New Orleans, a route that he had personally helped open up to traffic through his recent Vicksburg campaign. In New Orleans he would confer with General Nathaniel Banks for reasons that are still shrouded in mystery. Bruce Catton marvelously described Grant's New Orleans adventure as "a trip whose real meaning he almost certainly could not have explained."[25] Perhaps the two Union generals wanted to secretly revisit Grant's idea for a Mobile expedition; more likely, Grant was just bored. Departing from Vicksburg on August 31, little did he or anyone else at the time seem to realize that Federal efforts in the West were about to meet with another major setback, and that Grant's services would once again be urgently needed to retrieve the situation. For Ulysses S. Grant, however, personal feelings of boredom could be even more dangerous than enemy gunfire.

CHAPTER 30

September 1863:
New Orleans

... accident often decides the fate of battle.

—Grant[1]

During the first 19 days of September, 1863, there is a highly unusual gap in Grant's otherwise voluminous and documented correspondence. The reasons for this gap are twofold. First—as incredible it may still seem so many years after the fact—Grant was given nothing in particular to do after Vicksburg had surrendered. After promoting him to Major-General, Grant's superiors in Washington and the War Department, if anything, seemed intent on keeping him on the shelf while other projects, such as securing the Mexican border and Rosecrans' evolving campaign in eastern Tennessee, received priority (read: transfer of Grant's troops). The second reason for the gap is that on September 4, Grant came as close to being killed as he ever did during the entire course of the war. After two years of fighting the Confederate army in hostile territory, the preeminent general of the North was almost done in by an unruly horse, possibly combined with his own indiscretion. This fluke incident occurred in New Orleans, and for the next several weeks, Grant was a semi-invalid.

Grant had arrived in New Orleans on September 2, and was given a hero's welcome by General Nathaniel Banks with nonstop receptions, banquets, and troop reviews. Julia was not with him (she was in St. Louis); neither was chief-of-staff John Rawlins. In New Orleans, Grant was surrounded by flatterers but not necessarily friends. By September 4, the day of his mishap,[2] he would have had either to have turned down numerous offers for spirits, or ... not. In his memoirs, Grant wrote that he was riding back to his hotel on a "vicious" horse on loan from General Banks, when the horse suddenly bolted and was then spooked by a bypassing train. Grant, true to his great equestrian form (sober or not), stayed in the saddle as the horse tried to throw its rider but instead toppled directly down upon him. Hitting the ground,

Grant was knocked unconscious and then carried back to his hotel. By the time he woke up, he was in bed with doctors hovering over him. Though no bones were broken, there had obviously been a concussion and one leg was completely incapacitated by swelling. Grant was forced to remain in bed for over a week afterwards, unable to move. When he finally could move a bit, he was carried in a litter to the nearest steamer and transported back to Vicksburg.[3] By then, it was mid–September.

Although no one seems to have said anything to Grant's face, rumors that his tumble in the Big Easy had been caused by drunkenness began to circulate almost immediately. What is particularly interesting in this case is that the Grant scandal-mongering of the post–Vicksburg era had a distinctly more discreet air about it. Now no one was screaming that the Union's greatest field commander should be cashiered. They talked about his drinking, some even wrote about it, but no one seems to have demanded any kind of retribution for it. Even Grant's long-standing enemies in the media, the army, and the capital appear to have been more concerned with the repercussions that public accusations against Grant would bring to their own credibility, as opposed to their previous and supposed citizen-like concern over how Grant's public behavior might reflect on the war effort. Perhaps they were more concerned about incurring Lincoln's displeasure, since the President had now declared that Grant was his man after defending him from previous onslaughts. When Grant had fallen off his horse before the battle of Shiloh, which from all appearances was not the result of being drunk, the press and his critics hollered and bellowed moral turpitude. Now that he had done it again after Vicksburg, and in all likelihood was not sober at the time, everyone was hush-hush or even in denial. Among those who recorded the incident as being the result of inebriation, perhaps the most damning was Grant's personal watchdog John Rawlins, who a few months later wrote to his fiancée that the New Orleans escapade was an example of Grant's falling off the wagon.[4]

Grant's mishap in New Orleans may have seemed like a near-disaster at the time, but in hindsight it brought Julia and John Rawlins back into the picture, which is exactly what Grant needed in preparation for what was about to happen. During Grant's absence, Sherman had been left in charge at Vicksburg, and on September 13, General Halleck from Washington ordered Grant to send Sherman and his men to reinforce Rosecrans in eastern Tennessee and northern Georgia. The order was repeated on September 15. Because of slowness in communications to the West, however, and possibly because of Grant's condition and convalescence, Halleck's order was not received until two weeks later, around September 27.[5] When it was finally received, the order was obeyed, but by that time the circumstances surrounding Rosecrans had completely changed. Had Sherman been immediately sent east, he and his troops may well have been caught up in the disaster that eventually visited Rosecrans and the Army of the Cumberland on September 20. Instead, Sherman found himself rushing to the timely relief of Chattanooga, rather than into an ambush.

On September 19, Grant finally wrote his first letter after nearly three weeks of silence. This was addressed to Halleck from Vicksburg, with Grant still unaware of Halleck's repeated and urgent call for reinforcements. Grant's letter had been prompted by Halleck's earlier invitation to comment on the big picture, and he had recently perused Sherman's quotable but harsh ruminations to Halleck on how the South should be reconstructed. Sherman took the hard line and referred to the proposed restoration of civil government as "simply ridiculous," thus implying that military government was the only way to go. For good measure, Sherman added that "I would not ... even meet them halfway."[6] Given this kind of attitude, Cadwallader may have been right in asserting that Sherman's revisiting the defeated landscape of Mississippi back in mid–July had helped to entrench his already conservative views on how far former Confederates could be rehabilitated. For Sherman, "rehabilitated Confederate" was an oxymoron.

Grant reacted to Sherman's intelligent pessimism in a manner that very few of his Federal colleagues would emulate. Picking up pen and paper from his bed in Vicksburg, Grant wrote to Halleck as follows:

> I have just read General Sherman's private letter to you, but do not fully coincide with the General, as to the policy that should be adopted towards these people. While I believe with him, that every effort, should be made, to fill up our thinned ranks, and be prepared to meet and destroy their armies wherever found, I think we should do it with terms held out that by accepting they could receive the protection of our laws. There is certainly a very fine feeling existing in the state of Louisiana, and in parts of this state, towards the Union. I enclose you copies of Resolutions sent me, by Citizens of both Louisiana and Mississippi, showing something of this feeling.[7]

Grant favored a carrot-and-stick approach, rather than just Sherman's big stick. As the most successful Union general of the war, Grant could of course afford to be magnanimous. On the other hand, this recommendation seems to have been true to his temperament. He believed that, given encouragement, Southerners (or at least many of them) would come back into the fold. Having family ties to the South (like President Lincoln and unlike Sherman), Grant also spoke with some authority on the subject. It was also a recommendation that Lincoln happened to agree with.

By the time Julia Grant arrived in Vicksburg in mid–September to nurse her horse-fallen hero, some changes had taken place since her stay the previous month. In fact, her anecdotes during Grant's period of convalescence are priceless. The first of these involved chief-of-staff Rawlins, who only a few weeks before had sternly denounced the impropriety of "rebel women" flirting with Federal officers in order to obtain supplies. He had even scolded Julia for cracking a joke about it. During the interim, Rawlins had become engaged to Mary Emma Hurlbut, governess at the Lum mansion that was used for Federal headquarters. While Ms. Hurlbut (no relation to the Union General in Memphis) was in fact a Connecticut Yankee with "secret" pro–Union sentiments, she had been living in the South for many years and had shared all the hardships of the Vicksburg siege with her employers, the Lum family. According to Julia's account, Rawlins (a widower himself) had been smitten by Mary Emma's modest demeanor—in effect, the manner in which she asked for the same favors that Rawlins disapproved of—and thus became the most prominent victim of the activities that he had been so loudly railing against.[8]

Mary Emma's tactics were child's play, however, compared to those of the widow Mrs. Eugenia P. Bass. As Julia recalled, she was one day approached by "a beautiful woman, tall and majestic as Juno," who politely requested an audience with the bedridden general. Overawed by this epitome of Southern gentility, Julia admitted Mrs. Bass, who then explained to the conqueror of Vicksburg that she had lost everything except for her dependents, including elderly former slaves that still had be fed and cared for. Grant's advice was for her to go directly to Washington for help. This Mrs. Bass did immediately, first marrying the admiring and well-to-do Italian Ambassador, Giuseppe Bertinatti, then winning a postwar petition for government restitution, a very rare victory of its type. Julia's subtle point in her memoirs was that Grant, immobilized by his New Orleans injury, was prone to the decorous but insistent importunities of Vicksburg females. Fortunately for him, Julia was the gatekeeper.[9]

Concurrent with Julia's intriguing tales of romance, the post–Vicksburg aura of Federal military ascendance was rudely shattered by events in northern Georgia. The very same day (September 19) that Grant was expostulating his views on Reconstruction to Halleck and still unaware of Halleck's orders for Sherman, the Army of the Cumberland, under Grant's old rival General William Rosecrans, was engaged in a huge and desperate battle around Chickamauga Creek, south of Chattanooga and the Tennessee state line. By the end of the following day (September 20), the Federals had been completely defeated and sent retreating back to Chattanooga. Although Grant was hundreds of miles away and had no knowledge or involvement in the events, the battle of Chickamauga was influenced, if not instigated, by Grant's prior activities. By the time it was over, some 37,000 Americans (the majority of whom were Confederate) were killed, wounded, or missing, making it the largest and bloodiest battle to date in the western theater.[10] After over two years of continuous defeat (since Wilson's Creek in August 1861), the western Confederate armies, with an assist from Robert E. Lee's Army of Northern Virginia, had its first great victory—costly though indisputable. Maimed and traumatized would not be inappropriate words to describe Federal forces after they escaped the battlefield and returned posthaste to Chattanooga.

Egged on by Washington and the example of Federal success in other sectors, a reluctant Rosecrans had spent over a month pushing and outmaneuvering Braxton Bragg's Army of Tennessee, until the Confederates resolved to deliver a determined counterpunch. This strategy was facilitated by a number of factors, including Rosecrans' being overextended due in no small part to his lack of skill in waging offensive (versus defensive) warfare. Another factor—one that proved to be decisive—was that Bragg was heavily reinforced during the battle by several corps from Lee's Army of Northern Virginia, led by Grant's friend and former West Point classmate, General James Longstreet. At the height of the engagement on September 20, Rosecrans—trying to revert to his defensive style during an offensive campaign—shifted a division to fill an illusory gap, and thereby created a real one. As fate would have it, Longstreet and his hardened veterans at that very moment charged though the newly-opened breach in the Federal lines. Recognizing the golden opportunity that had been handed to them, Longstreet's corps proceeded to roll up the Federal flanks like baseball tarpaulins.

While Rosecrans and his staff ran for their lives, however, Virginia-born Union General George Thomas, who had won the very first (albeit small) Federal victory of the war at Mill Springs, Kentucky, in early 1862, chose to stand and fight, thereby earning him forever the nickname "Rock of Chickamauga." Choosing a powerful defensive position at Snodgrass Hill, Thomas and his line succeeded in hurling back wave after wave of disjointed Confederate assaults, much the same way Benjamin Prentice had at the Hornet's Nest during Shiloh. As at Shiloh, Braxton Bragg was giving orders for the Confederates. While the Federals rallied around the steadiness of Thomas, the Confederate pursuit was slowed, thereby allowing Rosecrans and the rest of the Union army to escape to Chattanooga. At nightfall, Thomas and his courageous defenders, still standing firm, retreated and did the same. Nevertheless, the battle of Chickamauga ended with Federal forces besieged in Chattanooga, their backs against a river on low ground and surrounded on three sides by the newly victorious Confederate Army of Tennessee.[11]

Rosecrans had previously won at (among other places) Corinth and Stone's River, two of the more sanguinary battles of the war, and was unquestionably a general of comparative talent and ability, as American Civil War generals go. He also established, early on, a major personality conflict and inability to work in tandem with Grant. By the time he was given his own command in eastern Tennessee, Rosecrans was on the verge of being relieved by Grant (see Chapter 19), and according to more than one source, thoroughly deserved to be dismissed. One of these breaches of conduct involved his allegedly encouraging the press to attack Grant and, more egregiously, Grant's troops. His failure and rout at Chickamauga have subsequently provided endless fodder for military second-guessers, many of whom have even insinuated that the Roman Catholic religious beliefs of Rosecrans were to ultimately blame for his downfall.

Putting aside for a moment his tremendous bad luck at having made a single mistake at the worst possible moment in the battle, Rosecrans does not appear to have been nearly the same caliber of field commander as Grant. Given the tremendous responsibilities that he had assumed, it appears more likely that Rosecrans was eventually going to make just such a catastrophic error before Grant would have under similar circumstances. Chickamauga may have been decided by an "accident" but Rosecrans was still no Ulysses S. Grant. Overall, Rosecrans was by temperament a defensive fighter unsuited for speedy and aggressive offensive operations. Grant was of course the opposite, although his conduct at Shiloh and Belmont demonstrated that he could hold his own when an unexpected defensive situation arose. On more than one occasion, Rosecrans showed a lack of mastery over problems involving troop supplies and communications with fellow officers. These also happened to be specific areas that the former quartermaster and future literary memoirist, Grant, excelled at. Grant from his early student days also exhibited an unappreciated aptitude for geography and topography, whereas Rosecrans was known every once in a while to get his roads and directions confused. In the actual event of failure, Rosecrans (like most Civil War generals but, again, unlike Grant) had never known real adversity and reacted badly upon his first encounter with a serious setback. This was quite a different reaction from what Grant's had been at, for instance, Shiloh.

Finally, if William Rosecrans was no more ambitious or dishonest than Grant, he did a poor job of masking it to those around him; consequently (as in most such cases), the loyalty and cohesion of his subordinates suffered for it. By an early stage in the war, Grant enjoyed the unqualified allegiance of his core staff, which included people like Sherman who continued to disagree with Grant's decisions while still obeying his orders. The only exception to this tendency was General John McClernand, who was kept in check by the combined and coordinated efforts of Grant's staff and colleagues. Now, Rosecrans, through bad luck combined with his own personal shortcomings, had joined McClernand and other generals who were once ambitious to supersede Grant but now were out of the war.

Chickamauga signaled the effective end of Rosecran's Civil War career, just as John McClernand's bogus political self-promotion at Vicksburg had marked the end of his. Unable to psychologically cope with the magnitude of the disaster or his own flight from danger when others had stood firm, Rosecrans needed to be replaced before the entire army (and central Tennessee) were lost. President Lincoln, Secretary of War Stanton, and all Northern politicians appear to have had the same thought upon hearing news of the Federal defeat, which was to call in Ulysses S. Grant immediately. No one, however, seemed to be able to find or get through to him. Unlike Chattanooga, which had a direct pipeline to Washington, communications to Vicksburg were slow, roundabout, and continually disrupted by Confederate guerillas.

By the end of September, Grant was in Vicksburg and had somewhat recov-ered from his embarrassing sojourn to New Orleans, but other than hearing some disturbing rumors, he knew nothing of Chickamauga. Only a few days earlier he had received Halleck's order to send Sherman to Rosecrans. Now everything had changed. Grant was about to receive new orders that would launch him into his finale phase of transformation from an assistant store clerk into Lieutenant-General of the largest army in the world.

CHAPTER 31

October 1863:
Rebels in Blue Suits

Amid the men of Manhattan I saw you as one of the workmen, the
*   dwellers in Manhattan,*
Or with large steps crossing the prairies out of Illinois and Indiana,
Rapidly crossing the West with springy gait and descending the Alleghanies,
Or down from the great lakes or in Pennsylvania, or on deck along the
*   Ohio River,*
Or southward along the Tennessee or Cumberland rivers, or at
*   Chattanooga on the mountain top,*
Saw I your gait and saw I your sinewy limbs clothed in blue, bearing
*   weapons, robust year,...*

—Walt Whitman[1]

Regarding the condition of the besieged Federal army at Chattanooga in October 1863, military historian J.F.C. Fuller wrote, "It would be difficult to find a more perfect example of an army paralyzed by the inefficiency of its commander, who in this case had completely collapsed under the shock of defeat."[2] The Federal commander in question, General William Rosecrans, seemed (in the words of President Lincoln) "confused and stunned like a duck hit on the head."[3] There was good reason for this apparent despondency, given that the Federals had not only been defeated in battle, but were significantly outnumbered,[4] starving and, for all practical purposes, surrounded. The despair of Rosecrans after Chickamauga, however, compared unfavorably with the grim resolve of Grant during and after the first day of Shiloh. Charles Dana, who earlier observed the situation in Vicksburg under Grant, was now at Chattanooga and reported back to Washington in a near panic that Rosecrans intended to evacuate, causing alarm among both politicians and the military hierarchy.[5] Grant in his memoirs opined that had Rosecrans ordered a retreat, most of his army would probably not have survived the attempt.[6] Thus the situation in Chattanooga had many parallels with the siege of Vicksburg four months earlier, but this time with the roles reversed between Union and Confederate armies.

In response to this crisis, Grant was ordered on October 3 to report immediately to Cairo, where he would receive further instructions. By this time the War Department realized that communications between Washington and Vicksburg were so slow and vulnerable that it was advisable to first get their best general to a point where he could receive instructions quickly and then assess the overall situation. After finally receiving this communiqué a week later on October 10, Grant—still barely able to walk after his fall in New Orleans—set out from Vicksburg, with Julia accompanying him. By October 16 he was in Cairo,[7] where he was ordered to proceed posthaste by rail to Louisville, Kentucky, via Indianapolis, Indiana.[8] On October 17, as Grant's train was pulling out of the station at Indianapolis, it was hailed and boarded by Secretary of War Edwin Stanton. Two weeks after the original order had been issued, Grant was finally brought up to speed on the situation by Stanton as they traveled towards Louisville, arriving at the Galt House Hotel on October 18.[9] En route, Grant was formally assigned top command of the Federal war effort in the West. Then he was given the option of either keeping Rosecrans in charge at Chattanooga or replacing him with General George Thomas. Grant sensibly chose the latter.

At Louisville, Stanton received Dana's frantic warning about the intention of Rosecrans to retreat. When Grant returned to the hotel late at night after visiting local in-laws with Julia, he found himself accosted by what seemed like the entire hotel staff. Then he was hustled up to Stanton's room, where the disheveled Secretary of War brought Grant up to date. In his memoirs, Grant reflected that Rosecrans, in addition to being a pain when the two of them worked together in northern Mississippi, had (despite several requests and orders) given no help whatsoever to Grant during the Vicksburg campaign.[10] Now Grant was called upon to rescue Rosecrans and his army from destruction. Sending off a flurry of telegrams that would now be instantly transmitted, Grant ordered his new on-site commander General Thomas to "Hold Chattanooga at all hazards. I will be there as soon as possible."[11] Thomas responded with, "We will hold the town till we starve." Grant later recalled, "I appreciated the force of this dispatch later when I witnessed the condition of affairs which prompted it."[12]

While Federal response time to the developing crisis in Chattanooga may have been poor by modern standards, the Confederate failure to capitalize on its success could hardly have been worse. Racked by internal dissension after Chickamauga, the Southern high command was at war with itself first and the Yankees second. General Braxton Bragg, despite having recently won the only major Confederate victory in the West, was now widely blamed (justly or unjustly) for the failure to follow up on that victory. Grant's friend and former West Point classmate, General James Longstreet—on loan from Lee's army in Virginia—was mostly given credit for any gains that had been made to date.[13] Furthermore, Bragg, even in victory (which had been costly), remained as unpopular as ever with his troops, who also remembered major defeats recently suffered at Perryville and Stone's River. About the only person who still stood by Bragg was his old friend Jefferson Davis, who traveled personally to Chattanooga on October 9, hoping to reconcile his feuding generals.[14] A series of disastrous conferences and meetings ensued over the next week—these taking place while Grant was gradually making his way from Vicksburg to Louisville.

In addition to Bragg, most of the Confederate generals at Chattanooga were Grant's old adversaries—Leonidas Polk, Simon Bolivar Buckner, Frank Cheatham, Nathan Bedford Forrest, and others. Those not present in Chattanooga but working behind the scenes (against Bragg) were other recent Grant opponents such as William Hardee, P.G.T. Beauregard, and Joseph Johnston. The first victim of Bragg's spitefulness was Polk, who was banished to Atlanta after his dismal performance at Chickamauga. The first general to walk away in disgust by his own choice was (not surprisingly) Nathan Bedford Forrest, who, despite his ferocious reputation, considered the high expenditure of blood at Chickamauga to be pointless without an aggressive follow-up. Forrest had been putting up with Bragg's ineffectiveness since Shiloh, and when the latter tried to reassign Forrest's troopers to another command, it was the last straw. After browbeating his stunned superior with a laundry list of Bragg's failures and shortcomings, the larger-than-life cavalry leader threatened to kill Bragg if he did not stay out of his way. Then Forrest stormed out of camp, never to return and with no one daring to detain him.[15]

Present for the October 9 meeting with Davis and Bragg were three remaining corps commanders who all called for Bragg's ouster. These included Longstreet, Buckner, and D.H. Hill, joining a fourth, Polk, who urged the same, albeit long-distance. After this fiasco, which appears to have taken Davis completely by surprise, he offered Longstreet top command but (to everyone's surprise) this was declined. Instead, Longstreet recommended Joseph Johnston, causing Davis to bridle since he still irrationally blamed Johnston for the Vicksburg defeat. General William Hardee was also sounded out but demurred, perhaps sensing like Longstreet that the ship was beginning to irretrievably sink. Meanwhile, Beauregard was trying to send in suggestions to Bragg on how to salvage the campaign, but warning him not to mention his name to Davis, who would never agree to any plan that came from him.[16] Finally, Davis—in true Jefferson Davis style—decided to leave Bragg in command while transferring Bragg's numerous enemies to other sectors,[17] thus gutting the Army of Tennessee even further in terms of leadership and morale.[18]

The effect on the Confederate rank and file of Jefferson Davis' visiting Chattanooga was no less destructive and disheartening. While Davis and his generals bickered, the army starved. Tennessee infantryman Sam Watkins best described the angry mood widely shared among the troops:

Bragg, in trying to starve the Yankee out, was starved out himself. Ask any old Rebel as to our bill of fare at Missionary Ridge. In all the history of the war, I cannot remember of more privations and hardships than we went through at Missionary Ridge. And when in the very acme of our privations and hunger, when the army was most dissatisfied and unhappy, we were ordered into line of battle to be reviewed by Honorable Jefferson Davis. When he passed by us, with his great retinue of staff officers and play-outs at full gallop, cheers greeted them, with the words, "Send us something to eats, Massa Jeff. Give us something to eat, Massa Jeff. I'm hungry! I'm hungry!"[19]

With the departure of Jefferson Davis from Chattanooga in mid–October, the stage was now set for the momentous arrival of Grant on the scene.

Grant, leaving Julia behind, departed from Louisville, heading south by train on October 20. Rapidly passing through Kentucky and Tennessee,[20] he arrived first at Stevenson, Alabama, and then Bridgeport, Alabama, the following day on October 21. According to an eyewitness on the train, Grant rode alone, looking like a private soldier.[21] Bridgeport was only about 30 miles southwest of Chattanooga, but much farther over twisting mountain roads. At Bridgeport (also the nearest Federal supply depot to Chattanooga), all rail and river transit came to a halt. During the earlier layover at Stevenson, Grant had met with Rosecrans, who quickly departed from Chattanooga and was now headed back north. While debriefing Rosecrans, Grant noted that his former rival was now courteous and had an air of serenity after being relieved of his command.[22] It was an odd ending to an odd relationship, almost as if Rosecrans finally realized that he had been in over his head.

From Bridgeport, Grant (with bad leg and crutches) mounted his horse and, with a small escort that included Rawlins, began the final trek to his beleaguered destination. To this day, driving through the Cumberland Mountains to Chattanooga can be an iffy affair, but riding through on horseback in October 1863 was, from all accounts, a horrifying experience. Later Grant wrote to Julia that he traveled over "the worst roads I ever saw. A description of the roads over the mountains would give you no conception of them."[23] Rawlins was appalled as well, describing the trail as "the roughest and steepest ever crossed by army wagons and pack mules."[24] In addition to brutal terrain and weather, the road was littered with debris and dead, starved horses, sending a none-too-subtle message as to what lay ahead for all human beings in Chattanooga unless food was brought in sometime soon. These primitive conditions also no doubt allowed small parties such as Grant's to pass through without being detained by Confederate pickets. Two days after leaving Bridgeport, on October 23, a wet, hungry and tired Grant arrived at Chattanooga to assume personal command in the field.

At Federal headquarters, Grant was formally greeted by General Thomas and his chief-of-staff, General Joseph Reynolds, the same man with whom Grant was staying in Lafayette, Indiana, during early June 1861, when he first learned that he had been appointed a Colonel of Volunteers. After eating, Grant sat down by the fire and declined an offer of dry clothes. Lighting up a cigar, he received a status update from Thomas and his chief engineer, General William "Baldy" Smith. In short, breaking the siege at Chattanooga was a complicated problem. As summed up by Bruce Catton, "Geography was all-important,"[25] and this geography was complicated by a winding river, mountains, and surroundings that Grant later described to Julia as "one of the wildest places you ever saw...."[26] Grant compared Chattanooga to Vicksburg in terms of devastation and judged that Chattanooga was worse because of depopulation. As in Grant's other campaigns, there was a river (the Tennessee), but no Federal gunboats as the Confederates had cut off all traffic downstream. Massive reinforcements were poised to be brought in both from Sherman and General Joseph Hooker, the latter sent west from the Army of the Potomac and now waiting at Bridgeport; however, it made no sense to bring in anyone when there was nothing to eat. The first order of business, everyone agreed, was to establish what Grant termed a "cracker line" for supplies from Bridgeport.

Among Thomas' staff present that night was the young Captain Horace Porter, who would later vividly record his impressions of Grant for posterity. In particular, Porter took note of Grant's impressive writing skills, which were obviously well above what he had been used to seeing in a commanding general.[27] Porter admired Grant's "administrative capacity which he displayed from the very start."[28] Then Porter elaborated in detail on Grant's working methods as the plan for breaking the siege of Chattanooga was gradually implemented:

> My attention was soon attracted to the manner in which he went to work at his correspondence.... His work was performed swiftly and uninterruptedly.... He sat with his head bent low over the table, and when he had occasion to step to another table or desk to get a paper he wanted, he would glide rapidly across the room without straightening himself, and return to his seat with his body still bent over at about the same angle at which he had been sitting when he left his chair. Upon this occasion he tossed the sheets of paper across the table as he finished them, leaving them in the wildest disorder. When he had completed the dispatch, he gathered up the scattered sheets, read them over rapidly, and arranged them in their proper order.[29]

Porter judged Grant's writing skills to be formidable, remarking, "His thoughts flowed as freely from his mind as the ink from his pen; he was never at a loss for an expression, and seldom interlined a word or made a material correction."[30] Porter's observations on Grant were not alone in this respect and provide a glimpse into one reason for his consistently successful management of personnel during the war.

In truth, the plan for opening the cracker line at Chattanooga had originated with General Smith and others, but as Colonel Arthur Conger remarked:

In Grant's case the question of copyright on ideas and military plans troubled him not at all during the war itself ... when the decision was forthcoming, it came out, more and more as the war progressed, with a torrent of energy, and was speedily clothed by Grant himself in concise and forceful orders.[31]

In essence, Grant was a successful facilitator and improviser, rather than a planner of grandiose schemes, and the "key" to his success—if such a term can be applied—was attributable just as much to his communication and administrative skills, as to his courage, poise, and military experience. Captain Porter, like everyone else, also observed that Grant's physical appearance and bearing were less than what eastern officers had been taught to expect; on the other hand, as Arthur Conger further asserted:

There is always hope for a country in which public opinion has come to recognize that while a real general is often seen in a well-tailored uniform and sitting on a horse, neither the horse nor the uniform matters very much, provided that certain qualities and characteristics of the general are in order.[32]

Eastern-bred Federal officers and soldiers such as Porter had by now been through enough defeats at the hands of Robert E. Lee and company to know that appearance and bearing were not enough to ensure success in a commanding general, and were perhaps not even relevant at all. Conger again:

By the fall of 1863, however, the heavy casualties and numerous disappointments and reverses had brought home the lesson to the people that neither glittering uniforms nor prancing steeds were vital factors, and it was realized that a Grant on crutches—or even in a litter—was more certain to produce the desired victory if placed in command than any other generals, however physically fit the others.[33]

Beginning on October 23, 1863, Porter and the other eastern Federal soldiers sent to Chattanooga were about to get a seminar in the successful western-style warfare of Ulysses S. Grant and his Midwestern armies. For the first time during the war, eastern and western Federal armies would effectively cooperate.

The day after Grant arrived at his command post (October 24), he took a tour of the lines and discovered the pickets of each army within hailing (and shooting) distance of each other. Gazing at the Confederate sentries, Grant marveled, "They did not fire upon us nor seem to be disturbed by our presence."[34] Then again, this was similar to Vicksburg, and as in most civil wars, opposing armies tended to fraternize when not killing each other. Also on October 24, Grant ordered implementation of the elaborate plan to open up a supply line out of Chattanooga, commencing in two days after all the details had been worked out. This delay was necessary given the complexity of the scheme, which involved General Hooker's army marching towards Chattanooga from Bridgeport as another task force under General Smith simultaneously moved towards Hooker out of Chattanooga. On October 26, these movements began.[35] The first critical step was for the Federals under Smith to seize the river crossing at Brown's Ferry. This was accomplished by stealth with a daring, late-night operation in which Confederate pickets were over-powered by Smith's troops, silently floating downstream in makeshift boats. The Federals quickly consolidated their position with reinforcements and by October 27, Smith and Hooker had linked up, thus opening the "cracker line." Grant noted with pride, "In five days from my arrival in Chattanooga the way was open to Bridgeport and with the aid of steamers and Hooker's teams, in a week the troops were receiving full rations. It is hard for any one not an eye-witness to realize the relief this brought." Grant pointedly added, "I do not know what the effect was on the other side, but assume it must have been correspondingly depressing."[36] Depressing it was, as well as setting off the final chain of events leading to Bragg's most foolish decision yet of the campaign.

Perceptive students of military operations may wonder why the Confederates did not guard Brown's Ferry with everything they had, and then counterattack with everything they had after it had been lost. The answer seems to be that few (if any) of them appreciated the geographic importance of the point, especially given the region's devilishly confusing topography. Grant and his engineers, however, understood it all too well. Brown's Ferry was under the view of Lookout Mountain, a sector occupied by General Longstreet—a skilled soldier in everyone's estimation, but geography was evidently not his best subject. Not wishing to embarrass his friend Longstreet, Grant merely noted, "The enemy was surprised by the movements which secured to us a line of supplies."[37] When Bragg ordered Longstreet to retake Brown's Ferry, he first delayed, then attempted to do so indirectly and half-heartedly, still believing the place to be of secondary importance. On October 28, Longsteet opted to counterattack Hooker's rear guard at Wauhatchie (rather than Brown's Ferry itself).[38] This was another night action and the Confederates were repulsed by both timely Union reinforcements and an accidental stampede of 200 mules. When Federal teamsters became frightened during the firefight and ran away, the mules decided to do the same, but—as fate would have it—in the opposite direction, towards the Confederates. Thinking that non-existent Federal cavalry was coming, the Southerners ran for cover, and that was the end of Longstreet's counterattack. One Union soldier, to commemorate the event, composed a mock–Tennyson poem titled "Charge of the Mule Brigade."[39]

With the opening and securing of the cracker line, guns and butter now poured into the Federal lines at Chattanooga. Moreover, within a week since Grant's arrival, the corresponding morale of each army had been reversed. A Union veteran later wrote:

> You have no conception of the change in the army when Grant came. He opened up the cracker line and got a steamer through. We began to see things move. We

felt that everything came from a plan. He came into the army quietly, no splendor, no airs, no staff. He used to go about alone. He began the campaign the moment he reached the field.[40]

This turnabout had been achieved mainly by Grant and his staff's making geography work for them rather than against them, along with effective communication and delegation of tasks. It was mind over matter. As Shelby Foote eloquently surmised, "[T]here was no better example, in the whole course of the war, of what the combination of careful planning, ingenuity, and great daring could accomplish under intelligent leadership."[41] Now, in reality, it was the Confederates who were besieged, although their own leaders would have been the last ones to admit it.

The same day that the Confederate counterattack at Wauhatchie was scattered by the Union mule brigade, omnipresent journalist Sylvanus Cadwallader rode his own mule into Chattanooga. Cadwallader had picked up Grant's trail in Memphis on October 16, and had been furiously trying to catch up with him ever since. By the time Cadwallader reached Federal camp in Chattanooga on October 28, he was greeted by chief-of-staff Rawlins and Colonel Duff (Grant's respective guardian and whiskey enabler). Cadwallader was told by Rawlins that he had been expected and was invited to stay in their tent.[42] Not long after arriving in Chattanooga, Cadwallader busted a photographer for selling phony portraits of Grant, who by that time had become everyone's man of the hour.[43]

As the Chattanooga campaign shifted into its final phase, Grant found himself involved in some of the most unusual and surreal incidents of the war. Inspecting the new lines near Brown's Ferry, Grant was first acknowledged by the Federal sentries with, "Turn out the guard for the commanding general." Promptly ordering this not to be done, Grant then heard the nearby Confederate pickets call out in a like manner, "Turn out the guard for the commanding general ... General Grant." After being saluted by the enemy, Grant wandered near a popular watering spot by the river and encountered a soldier who "wore blue of a little different shade from our uniform." This turned out to be a member of Longstreet's Virginia corps, who wore light blue uniforms rather than cadet grey or butternut. Instead of having panic attacks, Grant and Longstreet's Confederate both exchanged pleasantries and small talk before going their respective ways.[44] It appears as though Grant's Federal troops were not the only ones who respected him at this point, and the respect seems to have been mutual.

The real rebels in blue suits, however, were Grant's own western Federal troops.[45] Many had come a long way from their isolated farms of "Egyptian" Illinois, Indiana, and beyond. They did not set out to free slaves—quite the opposite, in fact—nor were they crusaders; rather, they believed in Union and youthful adventure, barely in that order. Now, they had effectively become the enforcers of Emancipation. Although defeated at Chickamauga, they were now united under the general who had brought them repeated victory, and the momentum of the campaign had shifted. After two years of campaigning, Grant's armies were poised to deliver yet another great blow to the Southern Confederacy, once again in its own heartland. This time, though, it would be delivered in tandem with eastern Federal troops brought in especially for the occasion, perhaps to learn how the job should be done. General Hooker's eastern troops (mostly from New York and Pennsylvania) were for the first time getting a close-up look at their less-polished but fabled western allies. Eastern Confederate diarist Mary Chesnut pejoratively referred to western battles as "bloody street brawls,"[46] and yet it had been just such street brawls that were deciding the outcome of the war. Grant's final and decisive engagement of this type in the West would soon take place outside of Chattanooga along Missionary Ridge.

CHAPTER 32

November 1863:
Missionary Ridge

... my later experience has taught me two lessons: first, that things are seen plainer after events have occurred; second, that the most confident critics are generally those who know the least about the matter criticized.

—Grant[1]

On November 2, Grant wrote to Julia, "I see the papers again teem with all sorts of rumors of the reasons for recent changes. This time however I do not see myself abused. I do not know whether this is a good omen or not."[2] It was a good omen. For the first time during the war, Grant was conducting a major campaign without his critics and enemies hounding him. Rivals like McClernand and Rosecrans were gone. Now it was a case of whether Grant could pull an iron out of the fire. Perhaps the biggest disadvantage for him in Chattanooga, unlike previous campaigns in which he personally participated, was that there was no gunboat support along the Tennessee River (access had been first blocked, then restricted), nor was there any cavalry to speak of (there was nothing to feed the horses with). The upcoming battle would be won or lost by the infantry acting on its own. On the positive side, Grant would eventually assemble at Chattanooga (with the exception of General McPherson, who remained in Vicksburg) the finest talent in the western Federal officer corps, including individuals such as Sherman, Sheridan, and Thomas. The Confederates also had many good officers (even after the departure of Forrest), but these were at the mercy of a petty-minded general-in-chief (Bragg), more intent on imposing his will on subordinates than beating the Yankees. In many ways, Chattanooga represented a reunion of many western personalities on both sides of the conflict who had fought with and against each other at Shiloh (downstream on the Tennessee River) some 18 months earlier.

The Chattanooga theater of operations by this time extended approximately a hundred miles northeast to Knoxville, where a Federal garrison under General Ambrose Burnside maintained a tenuous hold on that mostly Union-

239

ist part of Tennessee. Burnside, like many otherwise unsuccessful Union generals during the war,[3] showed signs of competency when asked to fight on the defensive, which is what he was now preparing to do at Knoxville. Burnside, like Joseph Hooker in Chattanooga, was also another eastern general falling under the sphere of Grant's western command. President Lincoln's priority of protecting pro–Unionist eastern Tennessee was longstanding; therefore, the preservation of Federal authority in places like Knoxville and Chattanooga now justified the deployment of reinforcements from the Army of the Potomac. Consequently, and for the first time during the entire war, eastern Federal officers were taking orders from their western counterparts. In contrast to the dysfunctional relations between General James Longstreet's Virginians and Bragg's Army of Tennessee (even in victory at Chickamauga), the corresponding East-West combination on the Federal side seems to have come off without a hitch. Primary credit for this should go to Grant, if anyone. Grant himself noted with pride that the combined armies worked together seamlessly, or as he put it, "There was no jealousy—hardly rivalry."[4]

On November 4, Bragg committed another blunder in a series of mistakes, any one of which made the worst of Grant's errors appear miniscule. With the endorsement of Jefferson Davis, Bragg sent Longstreet and his corps to besiege Knoxville, ostensibly to create a fire in Grant's rear, but in reality to defuse the irretrievably damaged relationship between Longstreet and Bragg. Earlier, Bragg had also sent away cavalry under General Joseph Wheeler to raid behind Federal lines, but only succeeded in achieving minor psychological gains (before Grant's arrival), which the Confederates already had in their possession after Chickamauga. Then Wheeler found himself cut off and unable to return to Chattanooga. Now it was Longstreet's turn to go. As eloquently summed up by historian Thomas Connelly, "[T]he danger and the impracticable nature of sending Longstreet had given way to personal motives. Bragg simply wanted to be rid of the man."[5] So desirous was Bragg to exile Longstreet that he got rid of him despite knowing that Grant's cracker line had been opened and that Sherman was on the way with reinforcements. After the cracker line opened, Bragg, according to most military second-guessers, should have made another vigorous and urgent attack to close the breach. Instead, he committed a goof that made Rosecran's mistake at Chickamauga look like a routine miscalculation. In one fell swoop he both depleted his army and deprived it of one its best combat leaders. Twenty years after the fact, Grant was still incredulous both of Bragg's stupidity and his own good fortune: "I have never been able to see the wisdom of this move."[6]

Thomas Connelly once again went to the core of the problem by noting that Bragg did not respond well to Davis' praise and affirmation of his command in mid–October.[7] Instead of being conciliatory and patching up his seemingly endless differences with subordinates, Bragg lashed out and attempted to purge all dissent. Grant in his worst moment would never have done such a thing. In addition to Longstreet, Confederate generals driven away for having been too outspoken now included Forrest, Buckner, Polk, and D.H. Hill. All were either good officers or at the very least commanded the loyalty and respect of their troops. Confederates who remained at Chattanooga under the respective commands of Cleburne, Hardee, Cheatham, Breckinridge and others, were now thoroughly demoralized and (even worse) appallingly supplied. As at Shiloh (in which Bragg had played such a conspicuously counterproductive role), the Confederate high command had ceased to function, this time on the very eve of battle.

When Grant heard of Longstreet's detachment, he was beside himself with excitement to take advantage of this unexpected handout. Fortunately, General Thomas talked him out of a making a premature attack. For starters, the Federal artillery (which was without horses) could not be brought into action yet; more importantly, Sherman would be there soon with reinforcements.[8] Grant was also frustrated because, with Knoxville threatened, he was being regularly urged by Lincoln to send help for Burnside, which he was loath to do until Bragg had been defeated. Reason prevailed, however, and the attack was postponed. The delay was also fortuitous because Bragg was far from through making foolhardy decisions. Finally, on November 13, Sherman's army reached Bridgeport, and, on November 15, marched into Chattanooga. From all accounts, the reunion between Grant, Sherman, and Thomas was a high-spirited, casual affair, even though Grant and Thomas rarely (if ever) would see eye to eye on micro-strategy. One eastern observer present at the meeting, General Oliver Howard from the Army of the Potomac, later stated that he had never witnessed a military strategy conference so relaxed.[9] Certainly, one cannot even begin to imagine Braxton Bragg having such a conference with his alienated subordinates.

After Sherman arrived it would still be over a week before the Federals could resume the offensive. During this anxious interlude for Grant, it appears that once again he fell off the wagon. On November 16, chief-of-staff John Rawlins wrote a letter to his fiancée in which he alluded to Grant getting drunk the night before, and also referred to Grant's indiscretion at New Orleans back in August.[10] Such an occurrence is believable given that Julia was not there, and that a golden military opportunity was presenting itself yet could not be rapidly pursued, despite Grant's reunion with Sherman. Moreover, Grant apparently used this involuntary lull in the action to have his first portrait painted (see Chapters 33–34).[11] That same day (November 16), however, Longstreet's forces laid siege to Burnside's garrison at Knoxville, and Washington then began again applying pressure on Grant to lend defensive help to Burnside. Having an immediate, pressing task at hand always seemed to be the best cure for Grant's episodes of overindulgence. As things turned out at Knoxville, Burnside's defense was skillful and Longstreet's siege lackluster, thereby giving Grant time to put into motion his plans at Chattanooga.

Grant and fellow officers near the summit of Lookout Mountain, Tennessee, shortly after the battle of Chattanooga in November 1863. Grant is at left with a cigar (courtesy Library of Congress Prints and Photo Division).

As the beefed-up Federal army at Chattanooga prepared for its breakout move, Bragg made his precarious situation even more vulnerable on November 22 by sending away forces previously commanded by General Simon Bolivar Buckner to aid Longstreet at Knoxville. With the departure of both Longstreet and Buckner, plus the recent arrival of Sherman, the Federals now enjoyed nearly a 2–1 advantage in numbers at Chattanooga,[12] with Bragg deluded into thinking that his army would be protected by their high ground and supposedly superior moral values. More devastating for the Southerners was that their opponents were now well-fed, armed to the teeth, and seething for revenge. Leading them were men like Grant, Sherman, and Sheridan— generals not shy in employing aggressive offensive tactics. While Bragg had been busy starving, depleting, and demoralizing Confederate forces, Grant did just the opposite for his. In retrospect, the rapidity with which the tables were turned at Chattanooga—in less than a month—leaves one awed by the superiority of Grant's leadership.

To the immediate southeast of Chattanooga are the imposing heights of Missionary Ridge, which provide the gateway from southeastern Tennessee to northwest Georgia. Bookending Missionary Ridge are, to the northeast, Tunnel Hill and, to the southwest, Lookout Mountain—the latter being the highest point in the region. Dividing Lookout Mountain from Missionary Ridge is Chattanooga Creek, a rather substantial tributary of the Tennessee River. For the last two months, the Confederates had occupied these formidable heights, first in an attempt to starve out Federal forces huddled in Chattanooga, then after October 27 (when Grant's cracker line opened)—God knows why. Perhaps Bragg still thought the Federals would retreat towards Knoxville, or, if they attacked, that he could win. Perhaps Bragg thought he was still fighting someone like Rosecrans. Beginning on November 23, however, Bragg's motives and intentions would become irrelevant.

In addition to the caustic remarks of Tennessee infantryman Sam Watkins (see Chapter 31), the problems of food and clothing supply for the Confederate army at Chattanooga have been well documented.[13] This handicap was even later acknowledged by some of the victorious Federals after the battle.[14] Basic problems such as these, combined with seemingly endless disputes along the Confederate chain of command, effectively extinguished any mood of Southern victory after Chickamauga, leading to widespread negative attitudes in the ranks. It was a recipe for the disaster about to happen.[15] By total contrast, the morale of the combined Federal forces in Chattanooga had been completely restored, and by November 23 Grant's troops—particularly those under General Thomas who had been defeated at Chickamauga—were eagerly looking for the first opportunity to redeem themselves and their lost pride.

The first phase of this Federal reclamation project began on November 23 when Thomas's troops ejected Confederate outposts around Orchard Knob, losing about 200 men in the process.[16] This extended the Union lines front and center, closer to the ridge, and allowed Grant an even more advantageous observation post to monitor the fighting over the next two days. The following day (November 24), eastern Federal troops under General Hooker captured Lookout Mountain with a direct assault in plain view of both armies and planted the Stars and Stripes on the summit. Hooker's loss was so small (less than a hundred) that Grant and his staff laughed in disbelief and made fun of Sylvanus Cadwallader when he first reported the numbers to them. Other journalists later tried to romanticize Hooker's success at Lookout Mountain as the "Battle Above the Clouds,"[17] but the real epic event would take place along Missionary Ridge the following day. By November 25 (Thanksgiving Day), Federal forces were massed both directly in front of and on either side of the ridge.

Grant's "Plan A" for the main assault against Missionary Ridge on November 25 called for Thomas's Army of the Cumberland to threaten the Confederate center (which was perceived to be the strongest position), while Hooker and Sherman attacked the flanks. "Plan B" was to exploit any unforeseen opportunities. It was expected that Sherman's veterans would achieve the first breakthrough on the Confederate right at Tunnel Hill; instead they were stopped cold in their tracks by an elite division under the command of General Patrick Cleburne. Although Sherman's maneuver should have been anticipated by Bragg, the truth is that Cleburne's crack infantry were being sent away by Bragg to join Longstreet in Knoxville, and just happened to be in the neighborhood when Sherman attacked. Observing Sherman's severe repulse through his field glasses from the Union command post at Orchard Knob, Grant remarked nonchalantly to Cadwallader, "Driving our boys quite lively, aren't they?"[18] On the Confederate left, things were going no better for the Federals. Hooker found himself stymied by retreating Confederates who destroyed the only bridge over Chattanooga Creek. This proved to be a much greater obstacle for Hooker than the token opposition he had faced on Lookout Mountain the previous day, and most of the afternoon was spent building another bridge.

In the midst of these setbacks, the Federals commenced what Grant had originally intended to be little more than a demonstration at the center of Missionary Ridge. After a short delay in which Grant queried Thomas and his staff as to why they were hesitating to charge the most daunting defensive position any of them had ever seen, the movement began to lurch forward.[19] Upon driving the Confederate defenders back and reaching their supposed objective at the base of the ridge, Federal officers leading the charge then made a spontaneous and unanimous decision. Noticing the weakness of the Confederate defense, and rather than waiting to be shot at from above, the Federals kept charging up the ridge. Within minutes, panic descended on the Confederates and their position disintegrated. Watching the whole thing transpire, Grant had to resist initial panic as well, because this was not according to his plan and there were no reserves if anything went amiss. Having a few minutes earlier asked Thomas why his men were not advancing, Grant now asked Thomas why they *were*, and was once again informed that Thomas did not know why.[20]

Spearheading the Federals' impromptu, uphill rush was General Philip Sheridan, perhaps the most combative and talented of all Union officers.[21] An angry Sheridan allegedly began things when a Confederate gunner responded to his respectful flask toast at the base of the ridge by taking a shot at him.[22] Following in Sheridan's impetuous wake were a bevy of illustrious Union combat leaders that included Wisconsin Captain Arthur MacArthur (father of World War II General Douglas MacArthur) and Ohio Colonel Emerson Opdyke—the same man who would later wreak such havoc on the Confederacy at the battle of Franklin. As the Southern defense of Missionary Ridge totally collapsed, an awestruck Cadwallader witnessed (and later recorded) the entire spectacle while sitting with Colonel James Wilson on an exposed earthwork at Orchard Knob. Cadwallader described the charge as "an experience never to be encountered twice in one life time."[23]

For the first time during the war, a large Confederate army had broken under fire and run for their lives. Their feelings were perhaps best described by the hyperbole of Sam Watkins, who began the day on picket duty near Lookout Mountain and then became separated from his company, which probably saved his life as the throngs of Federal troops rushed by him:

> I was willing to be taken prisoner, but no one seemed disposed to do it. I was afraid to look at them, and I was afraid to hide, for fear some one's attention would be attracted toward me. I wished I could make myself invisible. I think I was invisible. I felt that way anyhow ... a column of Yankees advancing to the attack swept right over where I was standing. I was trying to stand aside to get out of their way, but the more I tried to get out of their way, the more in their way I got. I was carried forward, I knew not whither....[24]

Having barely survived this ordeal, Watkins found his way back to the rear guard of the Confederate retreat, where he encountered general-in-chief Braxton Bragg, of whom he had more, not-so-kind kind things to say: "Bragg was trying to rally them. I heard him say, Here is your commander, and the soldiers hallooed back, here is your mule." (Note: "Here is your mule" had become a western Confederate byword after the soldiers had commandeered a peddler's mule and refused to give it back.) Watkins then added the priceless observation that Bragg was "cursing like a sailor ... and running like a scared dog," finally declaring his own judgment from a ground-level view:

> ... if he [Bragg] had cultivated the love and respect of his troops by feeding and clothing them better than they were, the result would have been different. More depends on a good general than the lives of many privates. The private loses his life, the general his country.[25]

At the end of the day, over 5,000 Federals had been killed or wounded as opposed to less than 3,000 Confederates, but an additional 4,000 Confederates were captured or missing, and those who were not casualties were rushing back to northern Georgia and beyond.[26]

The hidden weakness of the Confederate position at Missionary Ridge was itself the result of numerous factors coalescing into a perfect storm for its hapless defenders. These have been analyzed by other students of the campaign in far more detail than would be within the scope of this study. In brief, however, causes for the collapse included faulty troop alignment and artillery placement (though this was not readily apparent at the time), as well as insufficient numbers manning key positions. These problems were further aggravated by Bragg's sending away many of his best troops to Knoxville—even the ones under Cleburne who defeated Sherman at Tunnel Hill were there more by accident than design. In addition, the Southerners were critically handicapped by horrendous supply problems, which included a basic lack of food, clothing, and ammunition. Above all, the Confederates defending Missionary Ridge were demoralized by a command structure rife with dissension, beginning at the top with a general-in-chief who was neither loved nor respected, nor up to the task. Historian James Lee McDonough was firm in his conclusion: "The Confederate disaster on Missionary Ridge was clearly preventable."[27] The average private who lost the battle was underfed, underclothed, outnumbered, and devoid of meaningful leadership. That they fought as well as they did and inflicted as many casualties on the Federals as they did is a marvel.

Among the comrades of Private Sam Watkins in the Army of Tennessee who fled Missionary Ridge were my ancestors. Some of these included my great-grandfather, Private Frederick A. Cox (age 18), and my great-granduncles, Private John T. Cox (age 17) and Private William Richardson Cox (age 14), all members of the 37th Georgia Infantry. Young William, because of his age, was a teamster. After my great-great-grandfather, Private Thomas J. Cox, had been disabled at Sharpsburg, and after Confederate defeats at Vicksburg and Gettysburg, the three sons of Thomas J. Cox responded to the growing crisis by signing up and were immediately thrown into the battles of Chickamauga and Chattanooga, where they got a heavy dose of Braxton Bragg, Jefferson Davis, and Ulysses S. Grant. Frederick and John Cox went on to participate in John Bell Hood's 1864 campaign against Franklin and Nashville, surviving the war with serious wounds—in fact, my great-grandfather (like his father, my great-great-grandfather) ended up with a disabled leg. Fourteen-year-old William, however, was not so fortunate; he died of wounds and/or illness at Dalton, Georgia, in early 1864. My grandfather, William Edward Cox (son of Frederick), may have been named in memory of his young deceased uncle, and I was in turn named in honor of my grandfather.[28] Though I never knew any of these individuals beyond my grandfather, it could be said that the indirect influence of events from those times are still being felt today, however unaware of it I—and other relations—may be.

Looking beyond these lamentable consequences, Grant's stunning success at Missionary Ridge is worthy of some additional reflection. In one sense, his serendipitous good fortune is reminiscent of Buster Keaton's silent movie classic *The General.* Like Keaton's "Johnny Gray" character, no one seemed to want Grant at the beginning of the war. Now, after two years of battles and unlikely victories, even Confederate pickets were saluting him. On the other hand, to view Grant merely as being more lucky and having more resources to work with than his opponents does a complete disservice both to the man and to the powers of Providence. Grant's style, on such conspicuous display at Chattanooga, was to try everything and see what worked. The Federal assault on Missionary Ridge may not have developed as Grant planned,[29] but it was chaotic only in the narrowest sense of the word. Grant prevailed through superior preparation, utilization of resources, and flexible contingency planning. That the entire operation had elements of unintentional comedy should not reflect badly on Grant's achievement, either—in the broken Confederate ranks, even Sam Watkins sounded amused, at least in retrospect. Grant himself rightfully noted, "The victory at Chattanooga was won against great odds, considering the advantage the enemy had of position, and was accomplished more easily than was expected by reason of Bragg's making several grave mistakes...."[30] Grant also had an honorable mention for the role of Jefferson Davis in the final outcome: "Mr. Davis had an exalted opinion of his own military genius.... On several occasions during the war he came to the relief of the Union army by means of his *superior military genius.*"[31] Grant concluded his analysis with, "It would have been a victory for us to have got our army away from Chattanooga safely. It was a manifold greater victory to drive away the besieging army; a still greater one to defeat that army in his chosen ground and nearly annihilate it."[32]

Some critics have tried to characterize Grant's victory at Missionary Ridge as being solely the inevitable result of Confederate ineptitude, superior resources, and above all, luck. Others have attempted to proclaim it as the work of towering genius. The truth, however, lies somewhere in between, and was perhaps best expressed by military historian J.F.C. Fuller:

> At the battle of Chattanooga Grant's distribution is in form classical, for it closely resembles that established in the Macedonian army by Philip in the fourth century B.C., and made use of by his son Alexander the Great throughout his astonishing career ... it was a three-fold organization ... the central phalanx was the trunk ... attached to it the arms which, hinged on the trunk and protected by it, could punch right or left ... in my opinion, it was the most perfect ever devised for war, and with certain modifications remains so.... It was because Grant's distribution was flexible that he was able to modify his plan and yet maintain his idea; had it been rigid Sherman's failure would have ended the battle.... It is in this distribution that we see his Grant's generalship far more clearly than in the final results of this battle."[33]

Fuller's "three-fold organization" roughly corresponded to the three armies Grant commanded simultaneously at Chattanooga, a far cry from a mere 27 months earlier when he was having trouble obtaining the command of a single regiment. His successful coordination of several Federal armies from East and West, working together towards a common objective, would also prove to be a forerunner of Grant's future campaigns in the East during 1864–1865.

For the next two days, Grant's victorious and elated army pursued the broken Confederate forces fleeing into northern Georgia. By November 27, Grant had arrived in person at Ringgold, Georgia. Here, General Hooker, whose contribution at Missionary Ridge had been minimal, launched a reckless attack against the Confederate rear guard commanded by General Cleburne. As he had done with Sherman at Tunnel Hill, Cleburne gave Hooker a complete thrashing and the relentless Federal advance finally came to a halt.

Grant then returned to Chattanooga only to discover that a Federal relief force ordered to Knoxville under General Gordon Granger had yet to start out, apparently because it was perceived to be a perilous and thankless job. Aggravated that things only seemed to move when he was physically present, Grant ordered Sherman to take over the relief force, which then speedily departed.[34] That same day (November 29), after hearing of the Confederate disaster at Missionary Ridge and correctly deducing that Federal reinforcements were on the way, Longstreet launched a desperate, all-out assault against Knoxville, which was completely repulsed. As a result of these multiple Confederate failures, and now that the damage had already been done (from a Southern viewpoint), Braxton Bragg was finally relieved of his command on November 30 and temporarily replaced by General William Hardee.

Northern public reaction to the results at Chattanooga and Missionary Ridge were probably best summed up by Grant's son Jesse upon first hearing there had been a battle. According to Julia, young Jesse merely asked, "Who whipped?," and upon being told "Grant," called out joyfully, "Hurrah! Hurrah! Bully for Grant."[35] His father-general, now that the press was finally leaving him alone, offered the remarkable comment, "If the same license had been allowed the people and press in the South that was allowed in the North, Chattanooga would probably have been the last battle fought for the preservation of the Union."[36] Though probably an exaggeration, it was not far from the truth. Historian Nathaniel Cheairs Hughes wrote, "The battles around Chattanooga came close to destroying the morale of the Army of Tennessee."[37] Thomas Connelly added, "The army was shamed by the retreat and angry at both Bragg and the President."[38] Looking at the big picture, James Lee McDonough opined, "When the campaigns of the Civil War are analyzed, the struggle for Chattanooga stands out as a decisive engagement."[39] Connelly, McDonough, and Hughes are all Southern historians writing from a Southern point of view. I agree; and yet the battle of Chattanooga is often demoted to second-class status among Civil War buffs and historians. As with Fort Donelson, there is little in the campaign for Southern apologists to be proud of, with the exception of Patrick Cleburne's magnificent performance.

Perhaps the most credible observation on the battles of Chattanooga and Missionary Ridge came during the Confederate retreat as one dejected Southern officer remarked to another, "Sir, this is the death knell of the Confederacy."[40] That such a remark was allegedly made in November 1863, with a year and a half of fighting left and Grant having yet to meet Robert E. Lee in the field, is notable. Though many severe battles were yet to be fought, something in the national struggle had changed—both territorially and psychologically. The next step in this unlikely saga would be for Major-General Ulysses S. Grant to receive greater authority than ever before, and to take this new authority in person to the eastern theater of operations. Sam Watkins' proverbial "side show of the big show" had now become the big show itself.

CHAPTER 33

December 1863: "The Question Astonishes Me"

Something for us is pouring now more than Niagara pouring,
Torrents of men, (sources and rills of the Northwest are you
Indeed inexhaustible?)

—Walt Whitman[1]

His all-out assault in late November having been repulsed with heavy loss, and learning that Sherman was marching to the relief of Knoxville,[2] Confederate General James Longstreet raised the siege and retreated east into the mountains. Sherman marched into Knoxville on December 4, marking the end of large-scale fighting in the West for the momentous year of 1863. The Federal liberation of Unionist Knoxville served as an appropriate coda for Grant's unbelievable Chattanooga campaign, which began only six weeks earlier when Grant rode into the beleaguered city on October 23. Longstreet would spend the winter in Greeneville, Tennessee, and remain a continual threat. For all practical purposes, however, President Lincoln's long-cherished (and long-frustrated) dream of shielding eastern Tennessee from the Confederacy had been finally realized, thanks to Grant, his officers, and his troops. Not until the insane invasion of John Bell Hood during late 1864 would the peace of that part of the country be again seriously disturbed, and soon after that, permanently established.

On the Confederate side, 1863 was the year that the bottom fell out of the tub. The twin disasters at Vicksburg and Gettysburg, one brought about by Grant directly and the other by him indirectly, then led to a brief glimmer of hope at Chickamauga, only to be quickly extinguished again by Grant at Chattanooga. The Confederate officer who referred to Missionary Ridge as the death knoll of the Confederacy was absolutely right. Although the war would last another 17 months and those with the most at stake would fight to the bitter end, things had changed at Missionary Ridge. It was at Missionary

Ridge that the original Confederate vision or dream—one of sweeping, transcontinental domination—came to an end. If Vicksburg had been the turning point, then Chattanooga was the affirmation, the point of no return. From then on, even if the Confederacy were to win its independence, it would be on a smaller scale, more or less confined to the southeastern states. This was now true no matter how many Federal armies invading Virginia were trounced by Robert E. Lee. Any cursory glance at a map showing Confederate territory for the years 1861, 1862, and 1863, told a dramatic, twofold story.[3] The first aspect was that the Confederacy had gradually lost most of its western holdings since 1861; the second was that Grant had personally supervised most of the Federal repossession of that territory. Even back east in haughty Richmond, reality was beginning to sink in, although few could yet admit it out loud. Mary Chesnut wrote on December 7, "Gloom and unspoken despondency hang like a pall everywhere."[4]

Grant would have agreed. On December 5, he wrote to his friend J. Russell Jones, a former Galena neighbor and now a U.S. Marshal in Chicago, "An Army never was whipped so badly as Bragg was."[5] Jones would play an unorthodox but significant role in the next phase of Grant's career. While Grant had been cooped up in Chattanooga during mid–November, waiting for his opportunity to break out (and drinking heavily on at least one occasion), Jones had commissioned the artist John Antrobus to sketch Grant's likeness in the field, to be later used for a formal, painted portrait. This was a first for Grant. His photo portrait had been (and would continue to be) taken many times. Now, the artists were creating painted canvases, and this was a definite step up from the fabricated newspaper accounts of Grant's physical appearance during the Fort Donelson campaign. An image of Grant was now being molded, or least the attempt was being made. This was perhaps appropriate for a man who had during the course of some 19 months gone being a complete unknown to the most popular living American hero. Something larger was at work as well. The American Civil War had brought to the forefront of public attention the western states, and men like Lincoln, Grant, Sherman, and Sheridan, as well as the seemingly invincible western armies that did their bidding. Westerners now wanted to celebrate their new prominence in political and military affairs, while easterners (such as the poet Walt Whitman) were, at the very least, highly curious about it.

Grant knew he had done well and would be rewarded, but nevertheless seemed genuinely surprised at what followed, perhaps because for over two years he had been so continuously pummeled by the media. On December 8, things began with yet another thank-you note from President Lincoln:

MAJ.-GENERAL U.S. GRANT:

Understanding that your lodgment at Knoxville and Chattanooga is now secure, I wish to tender to you, and all under your command, my more than thanks, my profoundest gratitude for the skill, courage, and perseverance with which you and they, over so great difficulties, have effected that important object. God bless you all.

A. LINCOLN,
President U.S.[6]

Lincoln then added his name to a joint resolution of Congress on December 17, thanking Grant for his victories at Chattanooga and Vicksburg, and striking a commemorative gold medal for the occasion. Concurrently, the citizens of Galena and Jo Daviess County, Illinois, subscribed to the first in a long series of baubles that would be presented to Grant. This was a diamond-hilted sword with a gold scabbard, ornamentally inscribed with the names of Grant's battle victories and dubbed the "Chattanooga sword."[7] Julia Grant, with a good eye for such things, pronounced the sword "magnificent."[8] The odd little man with a checkered past and drinking problem who slinked into Galena circa late 1860 had, by late 1863, come a long way, to be sure.

Such attentions may appear somewhat less overwrought in hindsight since, as Bruce Catton accurately observed, "Chattanooga and Vicksburg added up to something bigger than any Northern general had yet accomplished...."[9] For that matter, Vicksburg alone—which had also resulted in Gettysburg—was more than anyone had yet accomplished. Now combined with Chattanooga, these two campaigns were irrefutable proof of Grant's extremely high value to the Republic. On the other hand, what immediately followed was truly unprecedented, at least in terms of the rapidity with which it occurred. On December 9, an editorial in the New York Herald read as follows: "It is proposed in Congress to revive the office of Lieutenant-General. It is stated that the rank is to be revived that it may be conferred on General Grant, in the hope no doubt that such a high military position will switch him off the Presidential track...."[10] Thus in two sentences, a leading opinion barometer (and maker) suggested both that Grant would be elevated to a military rank last held by George Washington, and in addition, that he was now a leading presidential contender. Moreover, both assertions were absolutely true.

While Grant was always a keener student of politics than he is usually given credit for, it is unknown whether he anticipated any of this. His outward reaction certainly disguised it, and we want to believe that, though the thought may have crossed his mind, it was quickly dismissed, especially given all that he had been through in life. By December 12, Grant must have heard something was afoot because he wrote to his benefactor Congressman Washburne, the gist of which was, "I have been highly honored by the government and do not ask or feel that I deserve anything more in the shape of honors or promotion."[11] This was, of course (whether Grant knew it or not), exactly the right thing to say in order to ensure more honors and promotion. On December 14, Washburne introduced a bill reviving the rank of Lieutenant-

General, with Republican James Doolittle of Wisconsin as co-sponsor in the Senate.[12] The bill would be destined to pass two months later (see Chapter 35) against token opposition, although persuading Lincoln that it was good idea would be the first and foremost hurdle (see Chapter 34). Lincoln had been desperate for a winner like Grant since the war began; now that he had one, his own job appeared to be threatened.

Talk in the *New York Herald* of Grant as the next President was not idle. On December 7, the same day that Mary Chesnut lamented the Southern public mood, one Barnabas Burns, Chairman of the Ohio Democratic Central Committee, wrote a direct letter to Grant sounding him out as a possible Presidential candidate for the next election in 1864. On December 17, Grant responded: "The question astonishes me. I do not know of anything I have ever done or said which would indicate that I could be a candidate for any office whatever within the gift of the people."[13] Continuing in this vein, Grant forcefully assured Burns that he was completely uninterested in politics, at least until the war was over:

> Nothing likely to happen would pain me so much as to see my name used in connection with a political office. I am not a candidate for any office nor for favors from any party. Let us succeed in crushing the rebellion, in the shortest possible time, and I will be content with whatever credit by then be given to me, feeling assured that a just public will award all that is due.[14]

Grant concluded his letter by directing that their correspondence be kept private and confidential.[15] Reading what is not said in this letter, nowhere does Grant say that he will never enter politics, only not while the war is in progress. It is also tempting to surmise that Grant's reference to a reward from a "just public" meant someone other than members of the Democratic Party. Although having strong Democratic leanings thus far his entire adult life, Grant by this time may have realized who his real friends had been. He may have also begun considering politics as a postwar livelihood, especially given that the prewar private sector had been such a bust for him.

At this point, it is useful to briefly survey who had been Grant's friends and enemies during the last two-and-a-half years. His greatest friends had been men like Washburne, Yates, and Lincoln—all Republican office holders. It was they who put him in a position to succeed and they alone who sustained him against withering criticism. The biggest exceptions were Democrats like John Rawlins and Sylvanus Cadwallader, who were also indispensable friends, but on a more personal and less political level. Rawlins never could raise or sustain Grant the way that Republican politicians had. Far more Democrats (nearly all of them in fact) had been rival generals like John McClernand or William Rosecrans who sought to embarrass if not destroy Grant, or worse, Copperhead journalists and officeholders who arguably had more power to accomplish what McClernand and Rosecrans never could. By December of 1863, though having no immediate political aspirations, Grant may have been having an epiphany as to which party would best serve his future interests.

It is difficult for modern readers to appreciate that the re-election of Abraham Lincoln in 1864 was a very, very controversial proposition. The bloodiest war in American history was being fought, its prosecution from a Federal standpoint had been rife with error, and public opinion, even in the North, was deeply divided. Though the end of the war was now in sight, no one knew exactly how long it was going to take and the final result was still far from being a foregone conclusion. The last two-term President had been the Southern, slave-owning, Native American-killing Andrew Jackson in 1832.[16] Abraham Lincoln had yet to be assassinated, mythologized and canonized.[17] One could even credibly argue that in December 1863, Grant had made far more progress in becoming a public icon than Lincoln. This would of course quickly change, but on December 29, Sherman wrote to Grant (accurately), "You occupy a position of more power than ... the President.... Your reputation as a general is now far above that of any man living...."[18]

Having rebuffed the first overture to make him literally commander-in-chief, Grant now returned to the business of being merely western general-in-chief. On December 18, he arrived in Nashville from Chattanooga and by December 20 had established his new headquarters there.[19] Then he invited Julia to join him. In Grant's priority of military strategy, the presence and support of his wife and family were foremost, just as they had been several times before. In her memoirs, Julia recalled arriving in Nashville by train and being met at the station by her husband, who later told her, "I moved my headquarters to Nashville for the sole purpose that I might have you near me." Julia also recalled riding into Nashville with Mr. and Mrs. General William "Baldy" Smith, who barely spoke with each other during the trip. Smith had been a successful point person for Grant at Chattanooga but later became an erratic and jealous rival. With undisguised satisfaction, Julia recounted how Smith seemed both surprised and a little annoyed that the nation's leading hero (Grant) would take time out to meet his wife at the train station with an army ambulance specially commandeered for the occasion. Unfortunately, the Grants' reunion in Nashville was short-lived, since Confederate General James Longstreet began to make threatening (and ultimately empty) gestures from the mountains of eastern Tennessee. Nevertheless, Grant was called away to Knoxville and had to leave Nashville on Christmas morning.[20]

Earlier on December 7, the same day that he had been solicited as a presidential candidate and that Mary Chesnut recorded gloom within the Confederacy, Grant wrote to Halleck, giving recommendations in wake of his staggering success. Foremost among these recommendations was a renewal of his proposal for a campaign against Mobile, Alabama, first suggested after Vicksburg and now more forcefully advocated after Chattanooga.[21] Grant's first instinct after routing Bragg had been to chase him all the way back through northern Georgia to Atlanta, but this preference was offset by Lincoln's prioritization of eastern Tennessee, as well as horrendous seasonal weather in the region. Then Grant revisited the Mobile project, which would involve striking east from New Orleans, thereby bypassing the harsh climate of the Cumberland Mountains. Once again, however, Grant's proposal went nowhere because the President would not be satisfied until Longstreet's forces were driven completely out of Tennessee and back to Virginia. Though Grant's proposed Mobile campaign had been stillborn for the second time in less than five months, he was nevertheless being listened to in a way that he never had been previously. Moreover, his strategic thinking was taking on new dimensions. From Grant's point of view, the best way to take Richmond, Virginia, was to chip away at everything around it. As Bruce Catton summarized the new Federal strategy, "It was time, in short, to get away from the old idea of the war in the West as something separate and to make it part of an overall design."[22] This was, after all, what had inadvertently transpired with Gettysburg via Vicksburg.

In effect, the brutal winter season of 1863-1864 in eastern Tennessee immobilized both Union and Confederate forces alike. Neither would be able to take meaningful action until the spring thaw. On December 16, Jefferson Davis temporarily faced up to reality and grudgingly appointed General Joseph Johnston to take command over the recently beaten Army of Tennessee. Johnston formally assumed command on December 22 and instantly whipped the demoralized Confederates back into shape. They were soon prepared to give northern Georgia a memorable defense during the spring of 1864 that would be far more costly from a Federal standpoint than is generally acknowledged even today. Though unable to do anything against Longstreet from Knoxville (or vice versa), Grant did take note of the comparative loyalty to the Federal government demonstrated by the citizens of that region,[23] who no doubt felt more appreciation for his services than other Southern towns that he had previously garrisoned. By way of contrast, in the immediate aftermath of Chattanooga, Grant had corresponded with the governor of Kentucky regarding far-off Paducah, which Grant's troops had taken by stealth back in September 1861 (see Chapter Six). Despite conciliatory proclamations and successful, extraordinary measures taken to protect private property and personal rights, Grant's only thanks at Paducah had been intractable civilian resentment, directed on at least one occasion against his wife. Now, in an effort to fast-track the rebuilding of military railroads around eastern Tennessee, portions of existing rails around Paducah were moved south, and consequently, loud protests were heard from that quarter. Unmoved, Grant wrote the governor, "My experience satisfies me that the citizens of Paducah, almost to a man, are disloyal and entitled to no favors from the government." Then, with a mock gesture of compromise, Grant promised to confiscate only that portion of the

Paducah railroad that had been installed by the Federal government, which was about 10 miles' worth.[24]

Grant ended the epic year of 1863 holed up within the freezing confines of Knoxville, Tennessee, separated from Julia and unable to do anything militarily at that particular moment. If he touched the bottle during that time he can be forgiven for it. More likely, he thought about the future—the war and beyond. Indeed, the remaining chapters of this book will have little to do with great battles or Grant's Virginia campaign of 1864–1865. These things are beyond the scope of this study. What does capture our intense interest is the fitting manner in which the first three months of 1864 would cap off Grant's miraculously swift journey from disgraced ex-captain to Lieutenant-General. As for the 33 months that preceded these, we are at a loss for precedent. Prior to May 16, 1863, as the smoke blew away at Champion Hill—a mere seven months before Missionary Ridge—Grant was risking everything and could have easily become just another Civil War footnote, an initially successful general who then suffered irretrievable defeat, or possibly cashiered before then for reasons that had nothing to do with the battlefield. On the subject of Grant's progression in the art of military command, Colonel Arthur Conger observed:

> Whether one is disposed to believe that Grant's education as a higher commander was deliberately planned by some guiding intelligence or that it was purely accidental, it cannot be gainsaid that had some able schoolmaster in the military art ... arranged the course of training for an apt pupil, he could not have done so in any more simple, orderly, and progressive manner than that which the natural course of events provided for Grant during the Civil War.[25]

Grant's river warfare campaigns in the West from Belmont through Chattanooga had demonstrated an unrivaled combination of luck and skill. As a consequence of this success, he was now faced with both military and political challenges on a scale perhaps never before encountered by any individual.

CHAPTER 34

January 1864:
Celebrity in St. Louis

... how little men control their own destiny.

—Grant[1]

Grant began the new year of 1864 in Knoxville, Tennessee, during what proved to be one of the colder winters for that region in recent memory.[2] Two days later on January 3, Grant pushed east towards the mountains in order to monitor the activities of Confederate forces under General James Longstreet, then camped at Strawberry Plains, Tennessee. Longstreet's veterans had never known failure south of the Mason-Dixon before they were detached from Robert E. Lee and sent west to fight a doomed campaign against Ulysses S. Grant and company. Their retreat from Knoxville at the end of 1863 was a precursor of what would happen to the rest of the Army of Northern Virginia later in 1864 and 1865 when Grant was sent east. Conversely, Grant's assigned management (for the first time) of elements borrowed from the eastern Federal armies at Chattanooga and Knoxville foreshadowed his eventual success later in the war with these same troops against Lee in the Virginia theater of operations.

Among Longstreet's corps that winter season were two great-great-granduncles of the author, Privates James M. Rape and Milton A. Rape of the 53rd Georgia Infantry. Neither had likely been previously exposed to this kind of harsh weather, let alone the likes of Grant, Sherman, and Sheridan. Twenty-six-year-old Milton A. Rape succumbed to illness and/or wounds on January 13, 1864. His then 19-year-old brother, James M. Rape, would survive the war after being wounded during Philip Sheridan's blistering counterattack at Cedar Creek, Virginia, later that same year. Their father (the author's great-great-great-grandfather), Private Allen Rape, had also enlisted in the 53rd Georgia Infantry, but had been confined to a Richmond hospital since 1863 and died there on February 1, 1864, not long after possibly learning that his eldest son Milton had passed away a few weeks before. His daughter, Martha Hannah

This formidable-looking bunch is the Rape clan of Henry County, Georgia, including the author's great-great-grandmother Martha Hannah Rape (upper right). Her brother James M. Rape is seated because he was a disabled Confederate veteran. Their father, Allen Rape and brother Milton A. Rape (inset), did not survive the war, the latter dying in eastern Tennessee during the aftermath of Grant's Chattanooga campaign.

Rape, after the war married another Confederate veteran from Lee's army, Burl Washington Nail, and these two were the author's great-great-grandparents. The Rapes of Henry County, Georgia, were of course only one of thousands of such families from the time whose lives were permanently scarred by the events narrated herein.

While Union and Confederate forces shivered in the winter cold of eastern Tennessee and warily eyed each other, Grant and Sherman began to formulate a strategy for the next significant Federal action in the West, although it would be one in which Grant did not personally participate. Being prevented by the weather from doing anything tangible in Tennessee or Georgia, Grant directed Sherman (and upon the latter's urging) to return to Vicksburg, Mississippi, via Memphis and concentrate his forces for a contemplated move from that point. Sherman's chosen target would be the town of Meridian, Mississippi, near the Alabama border.[3] By mid–January, Grant was informing General Halleck in Washington of this plan as Sherman simultaneously made his preparations from Vicksburg.[4] Grant hoped that Longstreet could be indirectly dislodged from eastern Tennessee by having Sherman cut a Federal swath through east-central Mississippi. Confederate cavalry under Nathan Bedford Forrest, though highly adept at harassing Yankee stragglers and ambushing mediocre Union commanders, were no match in numbers or firepower for Sherman's consolidated army. This was especially true whenever Sherman's forces were on a rapid march and deliberately wasting everything in their path.

A world away from Strawberry Plains, Tennessee, the attempted process of turning U.S. Grant into a public icon was moving to its next level at the Chicago studios of the English-born American artist John Antrobus. Employed by Grant's friend J. Russell Jones to paint the very first portrait of the war's most successful general, Antrobus had been busy putting the finishing touches on the full-length work, based upon his sketches made of Grant during the battle for Chattanooga—Missionary Ridge is visible in the background behind Grant, who is resting his hand on a spiked Confederate artillery piece (see cover art). Antrobus was partners with the politically connected Chicago sculptor Leonard Volk, brother-in-law of deceased Illinois Democratic Senator Stephen Douglas. Volk's own artistic subjects included Senator Douglas, President Lincoln, and many other notable figures. On January 14, Jones wrote from Chicago to Grant's sponsor, Congressman Elihu Washburne, mentioning that the portrait had been completed. The timing of this work was concurrent with the popular movement in Congress to make Grant Lieutenant-General. In the same letter to Washburne, Jones also mentioned Grant's potential for the presidency four years down the road.[5]

The author makes no claims as to his artistic taste or judgment, but the Grant portrait by John Antrobus has always held a certain amount of fascination. There is a noticeable tension between the myth and the reality. Grant's frivolous dress uniform (which he disdained to wear, like his idol, Zachary Taylor) is a dead giveaway—so is the erect, statuesque posture. The facial features, a bit harried and out-of-balance (to borrow Shelby Foote's paraphrase of Horace Porter's description), are more on target, as are the sideways glance and reliance on field glasses. Are we looking at Bonaparte or Buster Keaton? The artist seems to have not quite made up his mind; neither had the general public at this point in time, no doubt. For certain, however, is that the real Grant of Chattanooga is better represented by a famous photograph taken on Lookout Mountain. Here we see a slouching and hunched-over Grant, clenching a stogie in his mouth while standing off to the side and barely distinguishable from the members of his staff.

For the remainder of January, the Antrobus portrait of Grant was put on public display in Chicago and received half a dozen favorable notices in the *Chicago Tribune* alone. On January 20, no less a critic than Grant's long-time chief-of-staff John Rawlins came to Chicago, viewed the portrait for himself, and then wrote of the experience to Washburne with a mixture of admiration and concern. Rawlins' concern was over the possible inflationary effect on Grant's ego.[6] The alarmed Rawlins, a small-town lawyer who had spent the last two-and-a-half years trying to shield Grant from public scrutiny, may have realized for the first time (while in Chicago) that his once-humble employer had now become public property. Later, the Antrobus portrait of Grant was forwarded to Washington for similar public display and comment. Today, a three-quarters-length version of the portrait hangs in the lobby of the Harold Washington Library Center in Chicago, while the original, full-length version is privately owned. The now-public version of the painting was donated by Jones to the library upon the owner's death at the turn of the 19th century.[7]

Another indicator of Grant's newly acquired clout was his ability to effectively clash over military matters with the Secretary of War, Edwin Stanton. Stanton, the reader may recall, may have been foremost among Grant's fair-weather friends, having conspired for Grant's removal as recently as the previous spring during the Vicksburg campaign (by re-commissioning William Kountz). Now it was time for Grant to successfully defy Stanton's well-known highhandedness, and there is no indication that President Lincoln disapproved of this defiance. Before leaving Nashville for Strawberry Plains, Grant— for logical reasons—had demanded that a reluctant telegraph operator hand over military ciphers to a designated staffer accompanying Grant on his trip. This move was in direct defiance of a standing order by Stanton, who insisted on maintaining strict and limited access to these ciphers. Grant, however, by now had made a successful career out of breaking and bending rules as common sense dictated. Explaining to the hesitant operator that punishment for disobedience would come a lot sooner from Grant (who was standing right there) than it would from Stanton, who was a long way away in Washington, Grant obtained the ciphers.[8]

Upon returning to Nashville on January 12,[9] Grant learned that the same operator had been reprimanded and relieved for his acquiescence. It seems that Grant came to the hapless man's rescue by informing Stanton (through an officer whom Grant disparagingly referred to as Stanton's "assistant secretary") that if the operator was punished then Grant himself would have to be punished as well. This "little spat," as Grant termed it, reflected both his new authority within the Federal government, and his personal dislike of Edwin Stanton.[10] While acknowledging Stanton's great abilities, Grant had a much lower opinion of Stanton's character, and was particularly irked by any favorable comparison of Stanton with President Lincoln. In complete contrast to Lincoln, Grant wrote that Stanton "never questioned his own authority to command, unless resisted. He cared nothing for the feelings of others. In fact it seemed to be pleasanter to him to disappoint than to gratify...." Then Grant delivered his final dig: "The Secretary was very timid.... The enemy would not have been in danger if Mr. Stanton had been in the field."[11] These putdowns were probably true, but also may have reflected Grant's unwritten awareness that Stanton was his friend only when Grant was successful, and not always even then. By way of comparison, Lincoln not only supported Grant when he was down, but also continued in the name of friendship to try to help the ostracized John McClernand long after McClernand had self-destructed and done little to merit a second chance. It is therefore not surprising that Grant was later offended by any attempted favorable comparisons in character between the fallen President and the oftentimes petty Secretary of War.

Like poor John Rawlins, it may have dawned for the first time on Stanton during January of 1864 that he was now grappling with a public icon. Whereas this produced a feeling of concern in Rawlins, it probably made the would-be presidential candidate Stanton furious, and there was little he could do about it. On the other hand, the wide (though temporary) gap between the myth and reality of Ulysses S. Grant still often continued to produce comical results. Returning to Nashville via Knoxville and remote eastern Tennessee, Grant related in his memoirs how the townsfolk, though supportive, were easily misled. Traveling with a small entourage that included his elderly, gray-haired medical director, Grant upon his arrival at any particular village would pass entirely unnoticed as people assumed that the famous general was literally the senior officer in the group. This enabled Grant to both eavesdrop and make a quick exit into the nearest building. With respect to what he heard said by the locals, Grant noted, "Those remarks were apt to be more complimentary to the cause than to the appearance of the supposed general...."[12]

After straightening out with Stanton which of them was in charge at Nashville, Grant once again found himself wrestling more with the false preconceptions of Northern supporters than with hostile movements of the Confederate army. Meeting Grant in Nashville for the first time was the young

Colonel James Rusling, who, expecting another Bonaparte or at least a John Brown, instead found himself under the direct authority of a rumpled and shabbily-dressed little man. Rusling later wrote that Grant's appearance to him was "a decided disappointment," but rationalizing this letdown added that Grant was "evidently intent on everything but show."[13] Perceptively, Rusling took particular notice of Grant's prodigious facility in the telegraph office, as well as his dislike for long letters and wordy reports.[14] Grant's written communication skills always set him apart. Then came the first hard decision that Grant had to make in the presence of Rusling. Acting like the junior officer that he was, Rusling asked Grant if he was sure about assumptions that affected his decision. According to Rusling, Grant told Rusling that he was most certainly not certain, but that "...in war anything is better than indecision. *We must decide.* If I am wrong we shall soon find it out and can do the other thing. But *not to decide* wastes both time and money and may ruin everything."[15] What is striking about this alleged remark is not that Grant assumed the mantle of "The Decider," but rather openly admitted that one must be flexible and willing to try other things if the proverbial "Plan A" did not go according to plan.

A few days later, on January 20—the same day that Rawlins wrote to Washburne from Chicago—Grant sat down to write a carefully worded response to Isaac Morris, son of Ohio Democratic Senator Thomas Morris. Senator Morris had been a friend of Grant's father Jesse and one who had played a role in getting Grant admitted to West Point some 20 years earlier.[16] The younger Morris had written to Grant, like Barnabas Burns in December, to sound him out regarding a future presidential bid. Grant continued to play hard-to-get, but in a sincere manner no doubt reflecting his acute awareness that the war still needed to be won before the value of any political office fully assessed, replied: "Allow me to say however that I am not a politician, never was and hope never to be, and could not write a political letter." Then he comes to the main point:

> In your letter you say that I have it in my power to be the next President! This is the last thing in the world I desire. I would regard such consummation as being highly unfortunate for myself if not for the country. Through Providence I have attained to more than I ever hoped, and with the position I now hold in the Regular Army, if allowed to retain it will be more than satisfied. I certainly shall never shape a sentiment, or the expression of a thought with the view of being a candidate for office. I scarcely know the inducement that could be held out to me to accept office, and unhesitatingly say that I infinitely prefer my present position to that of any civil office within the gift of the people.[17]

Grant's use of the phrase "Through Providence" suggests that by this time Grant himself realized he was being propelled forward by unseen forces, and that additional exertions on his part were unnecessary, even had he cared to. On January 25, Jesse Grant also wrote to Morris and admitted that his now-famous son seemed to be temporarily content as a Major-General in the regular army.[18]

Lincoln noticed the commotion as well. In 10 months he would be up for reelection against a Democrat, probably during wartime (which proved to be the case), and nomination as his own party's candidate was no sure thing. Grant was now the obvious frontrunner among his potential opponents, and one who could most likely beat him. To repeat, the Abraham Lincoln of 1863–1864 was not the deified and sanitized martyr that he would later become in 1865—in fact, Grant came far closer than Lincoln to holding such a claim on Northern public affection during January of 1864. Now, with the congressional bill reviving the rank of Lieutenant-General about to go to the floor in February, Lincoln had to decide whether to throw in his support. The alternative was to join a minority who either believed that no one should be raised to such power or continued to dislike Grant for unspoken personal reasons. At this point, a worried Lincoln, who had yet to even meet Grant, turned to Congressman Elihu Washburne—the same man who, along with Lincoln, had brought Grant thus far along. According to the story, Washburne—now more panicked over Grant's celebrity than he had ever been over Grant's shortcomings—made the remarkable admission to Lincoln that he really did not know Grant that well either and that they should both turn to outside help for advice.[19]

The man that Lincoln and Washburne turned to for advice, at least according to the man himself, was J. Russell Jones, the same who had commissioned the Antrobus portrait of Grant. Jones had allegedly written to Grant about the presidential rumors (just as he had written to Washburne about these), and Grant allegedly wrote back to Jones that he was throwing all such mail into the garbage. Then Jones says he was summoned to Washington by Lincoln and Washburne, and just happened to pick up his mail at the train station, which included the alleged letter from Grant.[20] Taking this to Washington, Jones showed the letter to a tickled-pink Lincoln, who immediately decided to support Grant as Lieutenant-General.[21] The only problem with this attractive story is that the aforementioned letters between Jones, Grant, and Lincoln have never been produced. Unlike the occasional journalistic exaggerations of Sylvanus Cadwallader, the recollection of these particular events by J. Russell Jones has a distinct air of romance; on the other hand, there is also likely to be more than a grain of truth found within.

This recent run of spectacular good fortune for Ulysses S. Grant had not made him forget the opposite feeling, which had been the prewar norm for him and even during the war sometimes seemed to prevail. He had lost his favorite brother Simpson not long after becoming a Brigadier General in 1861, and in Grant's life personal happiness was invariably followed by personal tragedy. It was therefore probably with a sense of dread and impending misfortune that Grant learned from a frantic Julia in late January that their son

Fred lay ill with typhoid fever and camp dysentery in St. Louis.[22] This was the same deadly combination that had killed Sherman's young son only a few weeks earlier. On January 24, Grant obtained leave to rush to the bedside of his eldest boy, "hardly expecting to find him alive on my arrival."[23] By the time Grant arrived in St. Louis a few days later, Fred had miraculously rebounded and the family was once again reunited. In this state of emotional extremity, Julia related to her husband that she herself had recently sought medical advice for the purpose of correcting her crossed eyes, but was told by the doctor that she was too old to be a good surgical candidate. Her motive for doing this, she explained to Grant, was that, "Why, you are getting to be such a great man, and I am such a plain little wife." Grant, according to Julia, chivalrously responded with, "Did I not see you and fall in love with you with these same eyes? I like them just as they are...." He then threatened to not like her as much if she changed them.[24]

No sooner had Grant realized that his son was going to live than he found himself to be the man of the hour in St. Louis. This was the same town that he had left only three years before without a cent to his name, having been reduced to selling firewood on the street in return for bread money. Now, while attending the theater, Grant was given a spontaneous standing ovation and compelled to sit down front near the stage where everyone could see him. On January 29, Grant was the guest of honor at a banquet hosted by the Lindell Hotel, one more magnificent in scale than the dinners he had attended in Memphis the previous summer. Once again declining to speak in public, Grant merely bowed, shook hands, and tried not to look frightened. After the banquet, Grant investigated an uproar outside of the hotel by going to his room balcony, only to discover that his presence had been the cause of the crowd down in the street. A silent gesture by Grant acknowledging their adoration seemed to calm them down a bit.[25]

Other than wanting to correct her own physical imperfections, Julia's feelings during these events are not elaborated in her memoirs. She, like her husband, was probably above all things happy that their son had not died. Beyond this, we can surmise that she felt the Grants were finally where they belonged— in the limelight—although Grant himself would likely have disagreed. Julia does at this point in their story rather curiously record (with a small hint of resentment) that her long-time "nurse" (read: slave) had run away to get married in Louisville.[26] Although the slaves had been officially emancipated in the rebellious states, these did not include the state of Missouri. Julia, thanks to her husband and the unseen powers of fate, had finally found the place in the sun that she always considered her birthright since antebellum times. Now that she had found this lofty status, however, some of the specific antebellum trappings would have to be shed, and one of these included human property. Such adjustments would also be absolutely necessary in order to maintain a public image of her husband that was now rapidly emanating all across the country.

CHAPTER 35

February 1864:
Georgia Preparations

Every one has his superstitions. One of mine is that in positions of great responsibility every one should do his duty to the best of his ability where assigned by competent authority, without application or the use of influence to change his position.

—Grant[1]

While Julia Grant was unabashedly proud that her husband had now become the most prominent, if not most popular, man in the North, Grant's long-time chief-of-staff John Rawlins was feeling worried and negative. As accurately surmised by Bruce Catton, "Rawlins was frightened by Grant's approaching elevation to supreme command," adding that "Grant had come up from far down and he was reaching the high place, where there were no concealing shadows and the steady light was pitiless." Rawlins no doubt correctly sensed, among other things, that the highly distorted and false image of his boss as a George Washington-like savior of the nation would prove to be unsustainable, as indeed it did in the long term. Thus during the month of February, as Grant was being officially promoted to a place that no then-living man had been before, he also found himself the object of Rawlins' "querulous nagging" (Catton again). First he was unhappy that Grant was basking in glory at St. Louis when he should have been working at headquarters in Nashville. Then after Grant finally arrived back in Nashville on February 4—where he would spend most of the month—Rawlins was buried in paperwork (a "thankless undertaking," as he put it). Later in the month, Grant took a side trip to Louisville with Rawlins as a chaperon. Grant's Calvinist Galena townsman promptly took exception to just about everything that Grant considered to be fun. This included going to the theater, which Rawlins disapproved of on principle, and Grant's conspicuous use of opera glasses, which he viewed as unseemly.[2] But the big embarrassment came when Grant was offered a glass of wine by some ladies—Rawlins apparently was strongly indignant even after Grant had politely refused. In defense of Grant's long-suffering chief-of-staff, it should be added that his health from lingering consumption began to deteriorate that winter (he had five years left to live), just as Grant's star began to rise higher than ever.[3]

One thing that Rawlins did approve of was that Grant began attending Methodist church services in Nashville, just as he had back in Galena during the spring of 1861. Whether this was because Julia joined him later in the month, or because Grant was concerned about his new responsibilities, or because he was just trying to keep up his new image, or all of the above, it was better than being seen in public with opera glasses. Although the home of Grant's parents in Covington, Kentucky, was not much farther away from Nashville than Louisville, Julia still preferred to live at camp headquarters with her husband whenever possible. This was due to her long-standing, reluctant interaction with her father-in-law, part of which stemmed from her Southern antebellum upbringing and ownership of slaves.[4] This conflict, which surely contributed to Grant's own difficult relationship with his father, surfaced at irregular intervals, such as in November 1862 during the first Vicksburg campaign, when Grant berated Jesse for his condescending attitude towards Julia (see Chapter 20).

The anxiety among Grant's family and friends was not premature. On February 1, the same day that President Lincoln ordered half a million additional men be drafted for the continued war effort, the House of Representatives voted 117–19 in favor of the bill restoring the rank of Lieutenant-General. This lopsided vote had been mainly due to Lincoln's enthusiastic support.[5] On February 10, Grant wrote to Julia, "It looks now as if the Lieut. Generalcy bill was going to become law." The immediate impact of this, Grant pointedly added, would be a significant pay raise.[6] Given his prewar (and later postwar) failures in the business world, Grant's emphasis on this aspect of the event should not be minimized. On February 16, Grant wrote a cordial letter of response to his boyhood friend, Commodore David Ammen, reiterating his views on the potential overlap between politics and his pending promotion:

> Your letter was duly received and advice fully appreciated, particularly as it is the same I would give any friend: i.e. to avoid all political entanglements. I have always thought the most slavish life any man could lead was that of a politician. Besides I do not believe any man can be successful as a soldier whilst he has an anchor ahead for other advancement. I know of no circumstances likely to avail which could induce me to accept of any political office whatever. My only desire will be, as it has always been, to whip out the rebellion in the shortest way possible and to retain as high a position in the Army as the Administration then in power may think suitable for me.[7]

That Grant would turn around four years later and wholeheartedly embrace this "most slavish life" is a topic beyond the immediate scope of this study. The main point of this particular letter, as in other sincere expressions made by Grant during this same period, was first things first; namely, win the war.

Four days after Grant's letter to Commodore Ammen (on February 20), Grant wrote another one of his many angry letters to his father. One can almost feel the table pounding as Grant berated Jesse in writing: "I am not a candidate for any office. All I want is to be left alone to fight this war out, fight all rebel opposition, and restore a happy Union, in the shortest possible time." Then came the real beef against Jesse's behavior: "You know, or ought to know, that the public prints are not the proper mediums through which to let a personal feeling pass. I know that I feel that nothing personal myself could ever induce me to accept a political office."[8] Obviously, Jesse had been talking to the press again, and word had somehow reached Grant, perhaps even through Jesse himself. To leave no doubt as to whether he had changed his mind later after cooling down, Grant followed this letter up with another missive to Jesse some 10 days later in which he firmly reiterated his earlier sentiments.[9]

On February 26, the Senate passed the Lieutenant-General bill by a decisive vote of 13–6.[10] Congressman Elihu Washburne immediately notified Grant by telegram.[11] Three days later, on February 29, 1864, President Lincoln signed the bill into law. The day before (February 28), Grant responded to yet another letter of inquiry, this time written from someone whom he apparently respected more than his own father—General Francis P. Blair, who had served under Grant at Vicksburg and would later become a U.S. senator for the state of Missouri.[12] One thing that made Blair special, or at least probably set him apart in Grant's view, was that Blair was one of the most successful political generals (that is, a non–West Point graduate) of the war. Blair was also the polar opposite of a political general such as John McClernand, who had given Grant so much grief from Belmont through Vicksburg. Accordingly, Blair belonged to a small group of men (which included John Logan and Richard Oglesby) whom Grant respected both as politicians and as soldiers. Regarding his political future, Grant wrote to Blair:

> It is on a subject upon which I do not like to write, talk, or think. Everybody who knows me knows I have no political aspirations either now or for the future. I hope to remain a soldier as long as I live, to serve faithfully any and every Administration that may be in power and which may be striving to maintain the integrity of the *whole Union*, as long as I do live.[13]

For Grant, the "whole Union" meant North and South alike, a pointed reference for Blair, who was an Abolitionist even before the war began, and one that Blair seems to have later taken to heart by softening his attitude towards former Confederates. Grant added that he would accept the promotion merely as a means for "crushing out the rebellion in the shortest possible time," and that he wanted to stay in the field—not Washington, D.C. Grant signed off with both a warning and encouragement: "I hate to see my name associated with politics either as an aspirant for office or as a partisan. Write to me again. Sincerely, your friend, U.S. Grant."[14]

Beyond receiving better pay, Grant's specific, personal reaction to being named Lieutenant-General was unusual, if not one-of-a-kind. Some 20 years later in his memoirs, Grant wrote, "The passage of that bill, and my promotion, blasted my last hope of ever becoming a citizen of the further West."[15] In hindsight, he recognized that being named general-in-chief translated into spending most of his time around Washington, D.C., both during and after the war. Julia, in her memoirs, confirmed Grant's longing to go west (particularly to the Pacific coast) and how being called east effectively and permanently thwarted that dream.[16] Grant's desire to settle on the frontier, probably somewhere in northern California, Oregon, or Washington, likely stemmed from his early days as a young officer stationed in that region. He later recalled in wonder that some of the scenes he witnessed around San Francisco exceeded in strangeness and improbability anything that he had ever read in fictitious novels—of which he had read many.[17]

As the Lieutenant-General bill successfully worked its way through Congress in Washington, a much different kind of debate was taking place within the Georgia state legislature at Milledgeville. The irretrievable Confederate disasters of 1863 led Jefferson Davis in early February to do on a large scale what President Lincoln had been doing selectively since the outset of the war; namely, suspend the writ of habeas corpus (the right to appear before a judge soon after detention). Like President Lincoln, Davis was trying to enforce a new draft, as well as suppress disloyal expressions, of which there were many by this time. Georgia as a state had never been a big fan of Jefferson Davis, and Confederate Vice President Alexander Stephens of Georgia had been selected partly to offset this unpopularity. Now Stephens was joined by Georgia governor Joseph Brown and former Georgia Senator Robert Toombs (who fought under Lee at Sharpsburg) in a joint and massive protest against the Confederate administration at Richmond. This faction, described by historian James McPherson as "pro-war but anti-administration," was also rightfully concerned about their state's being sighted next in the Federal crosshairs of Grant and Sherman during the spring of 1864.[18]

In addition to publicly declaring that current policies were leading them all to destruction, these men and their numerous followers branded Jefferson Davis a hypocrite for his suspension of civil liberties. Brown, in particular, became defiant by shielding Georgians from conscription through massive administrative appointments and, more surprisingly, by proposing some kind of peace negotiations that would salvage whatever the Confederacy had left. This was before Sherman even began his spring offensive. Now gone were the pre–Chattanooga fantasies of transcontinental domination—Brown and other Georgians just wanted to keep the Yankees out. Stephens supported Brown but then a backlash set in, with other Georgia politicians and journalists reassert-ing their commitment to the war, even if doomed to failure.[19] The stage was now set for the tragedy that soon became Sherman's Georgia campaign of 1864.

By February 12, Grant—always open to the advice of his subordinates—had been persuaded not to directly attack Confederate forces under James Longstreet in the mountains of eastern Tennessee. Bad weather had immobi-lized everyone, Sherman was launching his own diversion in Mississippi, and Longstreet was best left where he was, as opposed to forcing him into battle or back to Virginia where he could reinforce Lee.[20] Suspending a move against Longstreet, Grant instead ordered General George Thomas, like Sherman, to make a massive demonstration between Chattanooga and Dalton in north-ern Georgia. Unfortunately, Thomas was no Sherman when it came to tear-ing up the countryside, and had to be ordered by Grant to move out three times over the course of 10 days before he would budge from Chattanooga.[21] By February 26, the Federals had advanced south to the appropriately named citadel of Buzzard Roost, Georgia, where they found General Joseph John-ston's reinvigorated and well-positioned Confederate Army of Tennessee dar-ing them to come on. Sherman in this situation would have tried to maneuver but Thomas simply turned around and headed back to Chattanooga. As a native Southerner (from Virginia), Thomas never had Sherman's or Grant's inclination to terrorize civilian populations when on the march, and was by temperament a defensive fighter—and a highly effective one at that.

Meanwhile, with no fanfare and little concern over lack of communica-tions (a mere go-ahead from Grant was enough), Sherman's Federal army cut a deliberate swath of destruction through east-central Mississippi. Having departed from Vicksburg on February 3, Sherman's forces first advanced to the state capital of Jackson, thus giving an earth-scorching encore to their per-formance from last July. Then, instead of heading back to Vicksburg, Sher-man plunged straight east towards Meridian and the Alabama state line, confiscating or wrecking everything of value in his path. Opposing him in the most meager sense was Jefferson Davis crony and Confederate General Leoni-das Polk. Polk seems to have learned nothing about modern warfare since first provoking Grant into Kentucky some two-and-a-half years earlier, and after getting over his surprise, retreated to Alabama as Sherman entered Meridian on February 14. The only thing resembling Southern resistance in this sector came when, careless of his own safety, Sherman was nearly captured by parti-sans.[22] Far more typical among the local population, however, were some 1,000 whites who (along with even greater numbers of emancipated slaves) marched back with Sherman to Vicksburg, hoping to find a better life and some sem-blance of government protection.[23] Less than two years earlier, these same Mississippi farmers had been uselessly throwing away their lives at Shiloh under bad Confederate leadership, while doing their very best to drive Sher-man and his troops out of the region entirely.

The calculated mayhem that was perpetuated by Sherman and his army during the Meridian campaign represented a practice run for what would transpire on a much larger scale in Georgia later that same year. These activities may have been wanton and in many cases even criminal, but they also served a premeditated purpose—to break the will of the South to fight. Military historian Arthur Conger noted that, from the standpoint of the Federals, simply beating Robert E. Lee and Joseph Johnston were no longer enough:

> There was needed something deeper than the mere driving back of the Confederate armies. To convince the Confederate population that peace was desirable, it was necessary to change their mental attitude in two respects. Their conviction that they could never again feel themselves at one with the United States had to be overcome; and their faith in the possibility—even the barest possibility—of the ultimate success of their cause had to be dissipated.[24]

Chattanooga may have ended Confederate imperialist hopes, but the idea of a Confederacy—reduced in size to the southeastern states—was still going strong in February of 1864. The concept of total war, or war against civilians, pioneered by Grant and Sherman during the Vicksburg campaign, would be the primary weapon used to defeat, or at least suppress, this civilian Confederate mindset, while Confederate armies themselves would be compelled into formal surrender.

Some Confederates were a long way from being compelled. While Sherman was busy having his way at Meridian, a large Federal cavalry force under General William Sooy Smith, attempting to link up with Sherman from the north, met with resounding defeat at the hands of Nathan Bedford Forrest. After a slow start caused by the late arrival of detachments, plus perhaps his own innate sense of dread, Smith set out for Meridian from Memphis in mid–February but did not get very far. Barely halfway to his objective, Smith was intercepted by Forrest's troopers in north-central Mississippi, then sent scampering back to Memphis in a panic with a series of embarrassing (from the Federal viewpoint) rear-guard actions on February 21–22. Grant and Sherman, later learning of these events, were both disgusted by the poor Federal performance. Smith proved not to be another Benjamin Grierson, the cavalry hero of Vicksburg. Once again, however, Grant was reluctantly impressed with the unschooled but highly successful tactics of Forrest. Grant particularly admired the way Forrest knew how to keep an enemy, once beaten, on the run:

> The fact is, troops who have fought a few battles and won, and followed up their victories, improve upon what they were before to an extent that can hardly be counted by percentage. The difference in result is often decisive victory instead of inglorious defeat. This same difference, too, is often due to the way troops are officered....[25]

Though not a West Pointer or even a politically correct person, Forrest instinctively understood exactly how to do what Grant had been urging his Federal colleagues to do for the last two years—keep on pushing after a win. Now, as Lieutenant-General, his main challenge would be to get his many underlings to show half the aggressiveness and cunning that had been repeatedly demonstrated by Forrest.

CHAPTER 36

March 1864:
Lieutenant-General Grant

*"Man proposes and God disposes." There are but few important events in
the affairs of men brought about by their own choice.*

—Grant[1]

On March 1 the nomination of Ulysses S. Grant as Lieutenant-General
was sent to the Senate and confirmed on the following day. On March 3,
Grant was ordered to Washington to receive his commission, and he departed
from Nashville on March 4.[2] That same day (March 4) he wrote a letter of
heartfelt thanks—not to Congressman Washburne, not to John Rawlins, not
even to his wife Julia—but rather to William Tecumseh Sherman for the latter's indispensable role in Grant's unprecedented rise to power over the last
three years. While also giving some credit to Union General James McPherson, who would die a few months later during the battle for Atlanta, Grant
wrote to Sherman in so many words that he could not have done it without
him.[3] Given Sherman's superhuman performance at Shiloh, which in retrospect was the make-or-break point in Grant's career, as well as Sherman's personal and professional support at Corinth, Vicksburg, and Chattanooga, there
is no reason to disagree with Grant's assessment. Sherman, for his part, wrote
to Grant urging him to maintain his "simple, honest, and unpretending" qualities, to keep his strategic focus on the West, and, above all, to stay away from
Washington, D.C.—in hindsight, all sound advice.[4]

News of Grant's elevation had also reached the Confederacy. The official
reaction in Richmond, to whatever extent preserved for history, is best represented by the journal of government insider Mary Chesnut. This attitude
towards Grant can be described in a single word: disdain. Moreover, this disdain was based on a false image of Grant that still pervades today. Whereas
Northern image-makers attempted to transform Grant into a Bonaparte or
George Washington, admirers of Jefferson Davis tried to portray him as a thug
or petty despot, depending on their mood. Chesnut repeatedly compares

Grant to the famous Russian field marshal, Alexander Suvorov—whose name she cannot even spell or pronounce correctly ("Suwarrow").[5] Suvorov had risen from obscure origins to become one of the greatest (as well as most popular) military leaders of the 19th century. Rather tellingly, Chesnut liked neither Suvorov nor Grant, and what many people would take as a compliment, Chesnut issued as a slur: "So they have made their brutal (*Suwarrow*) Grant lieutenant general."[6] As prelude to this event, she gives us valuable excerpts of Confederate table talk from early 1864 in which it was noted that Grant had been forced out of the old army for "habitual drunkenness," but that "since Vicksburg they have not a word to say against Grant's habits."[7] Both of these observations were true, but offered as evidence of Grant's unworthiness—his combat record over the last three years seems to have escaped them.

What was their explanation for Grant's success? Lack of humanity and superior resources, with luck thrown in for good measure, it would seem. More table talk: "He is their man, a bullheaded Suwarrow. He don't care a snap if they fall like the leaves fall. He fights to win, that chap. He is not distracted by a thousand side issues. He does not see them. He is narrow and sure, sees only in a straight line." What Sherman saw as Grant's "simple faith in success" became qualities that were "narrow," "straight," and "sure" in the eyes of Richmond. The closest thing to a compliment came as, "He has the disagreeable habit of not retreating before irresistible veterans.... You need not be afraid of a little dirt on the hands which wield a field marshal's baton, either." In other words, Grant is not very smart and has no gentility, but those can be virtues on the battlefield—this was Richmond's idea of fair and balanced analysis. The most ridiculous assertion, however, was that Grant resembled "Louis Napoleon—from a bath in the gutters, he goes straight up."[8] That Grant was seriously compared to a

Undated photograph (probably early 1864) of Grant in the uniform of a major-general, representing a significant change in image and demeanor from late 1861 (courtesy Library of Congress Prints and Photo Division).

man that he went on record in his memoirs as despising and disrespecting—Louis Napoleon—is the absolute height of absurdity.[9] Nevertheless, these comments provide good insight into the twisted and demented mindset of Confederate political leadership that had been losing the war over the last three years with its stunningly bad decision-making.

The delusional views regarding Grant that dominated Richmond politics were of course not shared by all Confederates, as shown through the pages of this study. Perhaps the most notable exception was Robert E. Lee, who, whatever his faults may have been, was not known for making catty comments about his opponents, with the exception of perhaps John Pope, whom he accurately called a "miscreant" before dealing him a crushing defeat at Second Manassas.[10] Mary Chesnut's social circle, while improperly deifying Lee, was also fond of maintaining that if Lee had Grant's resources or Grant's designated powers, it would be a different war.[11] The same would be true, they maintained, if Albert Sidney Johnston had not been killed at Shiloh, or if Stonewall Jackson had not died at Chancellorsville, and so forth. The remarkable thing about these rationalizations is that had Jefferson Davis or any of his favorites for one moment recognized Grant's special talents anytime before 1864, it indeed might have been a different war. By this time, however, it was too late and remnants of the Confederacy were fighting for their very survival.

On March 8, Grant arrived with his son Fred in Washington. Arrangements for a welcoming party fell through and the Grants—father and son—made their way to the Willard Hotel with no fanfare or recognition. The immortal tale of Grant's reception at the Willard has been related by others far better than this one ever could, but my favorite is perhaps Shelby Foote, who dwelled on eyewitness accounts of Grant's physical unimpressiveness. These describe "A short, round-shouldered man in a very tarnished major-general's uniform" with "no gait, no station, no manner" and "rather a scrubby look ... as if he was out of office and on half-pay, with nothing to do but hang around the entry of Willard's, cigar in mouth." Grant, it was observed, definitely had "rather the look of a man who did, or once did, take a little too much to drink."[12] Some things for Grant, especially external appearances, had not changed much since three years ago in Galena. His insignia rank counted for nothing in the eyes of a hotel clerk only slightly less disdainful than Mary Chesnut, since Major-Generals in Washington were a dime a dozen. Upon seeing Grant's registry signature ("U.S. Grant and son, Galena, Illinois"), however, the same clerk switched Grant's meager room to the best one in the house, and word quickly spread who had arrived. Then after dinner at the hotel during which Grant was given a spontaneous standing ovation by the patrons, he received his invitation to an ongoing White House reception.[13]

At the White House, Grant met President Lincoln face-to-face for the first time. Towering over Grant, Lincoln exclaimed, "Why here is General

Grant! Well, this is a great pleasure I assure you!"[14] Then Lincoln proceeded to hustle Grant around the room, as the latter pressed flesh and, according to one eyewitness, "blushed like a schoolgirl."[15] Lincoln followed in his wake grinning, if not laughing. Then the diminutive Lieutenant-General was forced to stand on a couch so that the unruly crowd could stare at him better. Journalist Noah Brooks later remarked that "it was the only real mob I ever saw in the White House.... For once at least the President of the United States was not the chief figure in the picture. The little, scared-looking man who stood on a crimson-colored sofa was the idol of the town."[16] The combat leader who had kept his cool at Fort Donelson, Shiloh, and Champion Hill had now entered a new theater of operations—Washington politics—and appeared unnerved.[17] After this unscripted farce, Grant was ushered into a back room to be briefed by Lincoln for the following day's ceremony in which Grant would receive his new commission.

According to Presidential aide John Nicolay, Lincoln gave Grant a copy of his short speech for the ceremony, as well as a copy of a suggested response for Grant. Lincoln obviously did not realize he was now dealing with a man who had unbounded confidence in his own abilities at written expression. Lincoln wanted Grant in his acceptance to defuse potential jealousy among rival eastern generals and to praise the Federal Army of the Potomac.[18] Grant opted to do neither. During the March 9 proceedings, which included Lincoln and his entire cabinet, as well as Grant, his son Fred, and John Rawlins, Lincoln began with:

> General Grant, the nation's appreciation of what you have done, and its reliance upon you for what remains to do, in the existing great struggle, are now presented with this commission, constituting you Lieutenant General in the Army of the United States. With this high honor devolves upon you also a corresponding responsibility. As the country herein trusts you, so, under God, it will sustain you. I scarcely need to add that with what I here speak for the nation goes my own hearty personal concurrence.[19]

Grant then responded with:

> Mr. President, I accept this commission with gratitude for the high honor conferred. With the aid of the noble armies that have fought on so many fields for our common country, it will be my earnest endeavor not to disappoint your expectations. I feel the full weight of responsibility now devolving on me and know that if they are met it will be due to those armies and above all to the favor of that Providence which leads both Nations and men.[20]

Grant may have been telling everyone at this point that he was no politician, but he was not going to let any politician—even Lincoln—tell him how to give an acceptance speech for a military command, especially if it went against his instincts. Later Grant recalled Lincoln telling him that he only wanted someone who would take responsibility, and advised Grant not to bother him with details. In effect, Lincoln told Grant that he did not know how he did what he did, but that he just wanted him to keep doing it. Grant also candidly recalled that he had not been a "Lincoln man" at the outset of the war.[21]

Grant later told Julia that his experience in the Washington limelight was "very embarrassing" and that he wished himself back in camp.[22] For those not put off by his appearance, though, Grant's unaffected humility in a land of prima donnas was something new and it played well. Jean Edward Smith wrote that "Grant's modesty captured the nation's imagination," while a more skeptical contemporary labeled him "a man who could remain silent in several languages."[23] One perceptive British journalist in Washington at the time recorded:

> I never met a man with so much simplicity, shyness, and decision.... He is a soldier to the core, a genuine commoner, commander of a democratic army from a democratic people. From what I learn of him, he is no more afraid to take responsibility of a million men than of a single company.[24]

Indeed Grant had been barely able to obtain command of a single company not so very long ago. Perhaps the most discerning comment on Grant's character came from his Federal colleague General John Schofield, who made a distinction between modesty and self-esteem, and felt Grant particularly had the latter. Because of this, according to Schofield, Grant was one of the few commanders he knew who could make a mistake but then quickly recognize and acknowledge it with a smile.[25]

After inspecting the defenses around Washington, Grant went to Virginia and was introduced to his new command. There, to everyone's surprise, he hit it off with General George Meade, victor of Gettysburg, and decided to retain Meade's immediate command over the Army of the Potomac.[26] Meade's staff, though, were snippety rather than grateful, some having the audacity to tell Grant to his face, "You have not fought Bobby Lee yet."[27] It was also at this point that Grant decided to eventually stay in the East where he could supervise the overall war effort. After informing Lincoln, "Really, Mr. President, I have had enough of this show business,"[28] Grant departed back to the West to visit family and confer with old colleagues.

After visiting his father in Covington, Kentucky,[29] Grant arrived back in Nashville on March 17 to assume formal command. Nashville proved to be a political circus environment as well, beginning with military governor (and future president) Andrew Johnson, whose nonstop, exhibitionist blustering offended Grant's entire staff.[30] Before getting down to business (and in order to unwind), Grant, along with Sherman and other colleagues, had a night out on the town, highlighted by a theater performance of William Shakespeare's *Hamlet*. During the show, Sherman, it seems, made some loud remarks, and as Hamlet began his soliloquy holding the skull of poor Yorick in Act V, one of Grant's curious Midwesterners in the audience hollered out, "Say, pard, what is it—Yank, or Reb?" This brought the house down with uproarious laughter, giving Grant and his entourage an opportunity to make a quick exit. Then at a nearby oyster bar, Grant's company was informed by their host— who may or may not have recognized them—that they could not be served due to the imposed Yankee military curfew. Rather than suspend their own martial law, the architects of Federal military strategy decided to call it a night.[31]

The idea of the theater-loving Grant attending *Hamlet* in Nashville was not so unlikely as it may seem. In fact, Grant probably had a better appreciation of the performing arts than Mary Chesnut's bluebloods in Richmond and Charleston. As early as 1846, when the young Lieutenant Grant was stationed in Corpus Christi, Texas, he was an enthusiastic participant in the sophisticated Army Theatre organized by that king of military thespians, John Magruder, later a prominent Confederate general.[32] Grant, according to biographer Lloyd Lewis, auditioned for the female role of Desdemona in Shakespeare's *Othello*, after it was determined that Grant's friend, the hulking James Longstreet (also later a Confederate general) could not physically carry it off. Grant, though he looked the part with his small, delicate frame and convincing feminine manner, could not deliver with conviction the lines that he had memorized so well. Magruder eventually opted to bring in a professional actress from New Orleans, but Grant (along with Longstreet) went on to act in light comedy roles for other productions.[33] It is also worth recalling that Grant was probably later saved from sharing Lincoln's fate at Ford's Theatre (Grant wanted to go and was invited to attend) by his wife Julia's distaste for the company of Mary Todd Lincoln.[34]

On March 18, Grant was formally presented his "Chattanooga sword" in Nashville by the mayor of Galena and the citizens of Jo Daviess County, Illinois. According to a March 29 article in the *Galena Weekly Gazette*, the ornamental gold and diamond-studded heirloom cost a (then) whopping $1,000 to manufacture.[35] Grant thanked everyone by noting that the sword was "evidence of their devotion to their country, and their appreciation of the progress towards a final triumph, marked by an unbroken series of successes in every battle named upon it, from Belmont to Chattanooga...."[36] Sherman, who was also present at the ceremony, recalled Grant awkwardly fumbling around in his pockets to find this short speech and remarked, "I could not help laughing at the scene so characteristic of the man who then stood prominent before the country, and to whom all had turned as the only one qualified to guide the nation in a war that had become painfully critical."[37] The art of anticlimax continued to be Grant's forte.

How much of this comedy was intentional it is difficult to say. Immediately after the sword presentation ceremony, however, Grant and Sherman left for Cincinnati to escape the public eye. There, with their maps in the privacy of a hotel room, they devised the grand strategy for winning the war, both simple in concept and vague in its allowance for flexibility. Sherman was given charge of the campaign in the West, while Grant would return to the East and supervise operations there.[38] Grant in his memoirs remembered instructing an eager Sherman that, in Georgia, "Johnston's army was the first objective, and that important railroad centre, Atlanta, the second."[39] As Sherman later recalled the same meeting with Grant, "He was to go for Lee and I was to go for Joe Johnston. That was the plan."[40] Grant would also take Philip Sheridan east with him to assume overall command of the Federal cavalry and spearhead the offensive in Virginia.[41] It would prove to be a shrewd and crucial choice. Finally, Grant and Sherman decided to try to reactivate a number of Federal commanders whom they felt had been too quickly relieved from duty because of past failures. This represented an attempt to apply pressure against the Confederates in all sectors simultaneously. Though good in theory, Grant never seemed to grasp that his colleagues were not as selfless as himself, and personal egos continued to get in the way. George McClellan, for one, would challenge Lincoln for the presidency in November. Others, such as Don Carlos Buell, who had fought side by side with Grant and Sherman at Shiloh, refused to serve under anyone who once served under him. Years later, an exasperated Grant asserted in his memoirs, "The worst excuse a soldier can make for declining service is that he once ranked the commander he is ordered to report to."[42] It was just as well; few Federal commanders other than Grant, Sherman, and Sheridan would prove successful at making offensive headway and tended to merely occupy the Confederates while being defeated by them in the process.[43]

By March 23, Grant had returned to Washington and was joined there by Julia and his son Fred.[44] Before departing by train for the Virginian front that same day, he was escorted by Secretary of War Edwin Stanton to the famous photographic studios of Mathew Brady, where the new Lieutenant-General would have his latest image recorded for posterity. As Brady recalled, late in the afternoon Grant sat for his portrait like hundreds of other VIPs, when Brady sent an assistant to the roof in order to uncover the overhead skylights and brighten the room. In doing so, the assistant tripped and caused the fragile skylight to collapse, with glass and steel crashing to the floor below. Before anyone could react, Grant sat amidst the rubble, which somehow had fallen all around him but not on top of him. Brady marveled, "It was a miracle that some of the pieces didn't strike him.... And if one had, it would have been the end of Grant; for that glass was two inches thick." It was another of the many times in three years that Ulysses S. Grant had dodged death. As for Grant's reaction to the mishap, Brady recorded that there was "a barely perceptible quiver of the nostril." Grant brushed himself off slightly, and then acted as if nothing had happened. It was, Brady said, "the most remarkable display of nerve I ever witnessed." Stanton was not as nonchalant, and he gave one of his notorious, hyperventilated warnings to the shaken photographer:

"Not a word about this, Brady, not a word! You must never breathe a word of what happened here today.... It would be impossible to convince the people that this was not an attempt at assassination!"[45]

After surviving his photo-op, Grant headed straight south, six miles beyond Brandy Station (where Meade was headquartered) to Culpepper Court House, where he and his staff set up shop. A few days later, after another quick commute to Washington, Grant would end the month of March 1864 back at Culpepper, where he personally represented the lead advance of the world's largest and most powerful army.[46] It is not overstatement to say that the eyes of the world were upon him, nor is it exaggeration to claim that Ulysses S. Grant then commanded more pure, raw power than the President himself, or even the most absolute and remote dictator. Three years earlier to the day he had been listlessly clerking at the family store in Galena, thankful to be making ends meet. Now, waiting for him approximately 10 miles to the south along the banks of the Rapidan River, were Robert E. Lee and the Army of Northern Virginia.

Aftermath: 1864–1885

All things are said to be wisely directed, and for the best interest concerned.
This reflection does not, however, abate in the slightest our sense of bereave-
ment....

—Grant[1]

The South should have won. This is not to say that the Confederacy was
morally in the right—legally and constitutionally, in the strict sense, perhaps
it was, but not as these principles applied to the heinous institution of human
slavery. The modern (and currently eroding) notion of Federal Union was a
construct of the war that many of the Founding Fathers would have abhorred.
Moreover, the argument that the Confederacy was doomed to failure from
the start because of inferior manpower and resources has never been very persuasive. Countless military struggles throughout history—not the least of
which was the American Revolution itself—have demonstrated otherwise. At
the beginning of the conflict, the Confederacy had better soldiery and better
officers to lead them. Most of the war would be fought on Southern soil,
where the overwhelming majority of the civilian population fanatically supported independence. Northern political and military leadership was deeply
divided on a wide spectrum of issues. Yet in spite of all this and more, Federal Union was preserved after the bloodiest war in American history. The
person who most embodied this unlikely accomplishment was Ulysses S.
Grant. For all of President Lincoln's great leadership and rhetorical skills, it
was Grant who did the fighting, the winning, and much of the politicking
later during Reconstruction.

Many commentators, especially those sympathetic to the South (such as
this one), often try, four generations after the fact, to re-fight the Civil War
in their writings; consequently, there tends to be a shortage of bona fide critical
analysis. The latter requires distance or detachment, and the author has only
a tenuous claim to either quality, given the heavy participation in events by
his ancestors. On the other hand, it was not he who did the fighting. Furthermore, the North and the Midwest are his native land. Most importantly, I am

279

struck by how the two people most responsible for the North's victory—Grant and Lincoln—were Midwesterners with strong personal ties to the South. This writer may not be a soldier or a politician, but he does know what it feels like to have conflicted opinions. While his opinions may or may not be biased, we like to at least think that these are rooted in a very real, American oral tradition.

The fiery cauldron that was the war in Virginia during 1864–1865 finally ended at Appomattox, approximately one year after Grant arrived in that theater of operations. It represented some of the hardest fighting the world had ever seen and, as more than one military historian has noted, was in many ways a precursor of the horrors of trench warfare associated with World War I. Grant's long, relentless struggle with Robert E. Lee, from the Wilderness to Petersburg, was of a much different character than his western campaigns for a number of reasons. Not the least of these was that Grant was up against, perhaps for the first time, a truly worthy opponent. One commonality between Grant in Virginia and Grant in the West, however, was that his incredible luck continued to hold. For example, not long after he arrived in Virginia, he was nearly captured by the legendary Confederate cavalry leader, Colonel John S. Mosby. After the war, the two became friends and Grant agreed that had Mosby captured him in 1864, Mosby might have been elected President instead of Grant.[2] Whether one studies Grant's western campaigns or those against Robert E. Lee, there can be no discounting the role of luck in Grant's success, as Grant himself was always the first one to acknowledge.

Arguably, Grant's public reputation as a warrior-hero never got any higher than in March of 1864, after he was promoted to Lieutenant-General. From the moment in May that Lee's veterans stopped the Federal Army of the Potomac in its tracks at the battle of the Wilderness, many remembered what had been said about Grant before Vicksburg—that he was not, shall we say, infallible. Nevertheless (and true to his character), Grant did not retreat after this thumping; instead he kept flanking, advancing and ordering his men to fight until the brutal war of attrition had been won. At times, he even managed to outwit Lee, such as the Federal move against Petersburg after their useless and bloody repulse at Cold Harbor. His true savvy, though, manifested itself by using men like Sherman and Sheridan as key lieutenants—men who truly knew how to exploit enemy mistakes as opportunities presented themselves. After Lee's surrender at Appomattox, Grant, it is true, had accomplished what no one else had before him. A very high cost, though, had been paid; consequently, Grant has never enjoyed widespread acclaim as a military genius, despite his breathtaking accomplishments in the West during the first three years of the war and a few, perceptive acknowledgments of this achievement. The term "genius" has been more often applied to Lee, whether deservedly or not.

Curiously, one of the first things that Grant did after being named general-in-chief in 1864 was to have a backdated and revised report made of his first controversial battle fought at Belmont, Missouri, in November 1861.[3] Rather than concern ourselves with the details of the original report that Grant wanted to clarify or finesse, the timing of this revision by itself is noteworthy. By the spring of 1864, an iconographic image of Grant was taking shape in the public mind, as exemplified by the over-idealized Antrobus portrait of Grant. Even if Grant truly had no political aspirations, as he insistently maintained during that time, he was nonetheless surely concerned with his public image as a soldier. Despite his famous lack of concern for appearances, Grant was beginning his first tentative steps towards cultivating what he believed to be an appropriate image, and this process would continue on and off for the duration of his life. Part of the reason, after all, that Grant was such a successful military leader was that his opinions and methods typically evolved for the better as time went on. To repeat, the word "inflexible" was not part of his vocabulary, even though many Grant apologists often try to recreate him in their own image as someone with an "iron will"—a man who supposedly never changed his mind about anybody or anything.

While Grant grappled with Lee in the East, his "Egyptians" and other Midwestern volunteers under Sherman plowed through Georgia and the Carolinas, just as they had previously done through Tennessee and Mississippi under Grant. By the spring of 1865, Grant (along with many others in the know) was in fact genuinely concerned about Sherman's army getting to Richmond before he did.[4] Even after Lee surrendered at Appomattox and Joseph Johnston at Greensboro, it was the western Federal troops who stole the show at the massive Grand Review for the combined armies in Washington. People then tended to know (more than they do now) who exactly won the war. The western armies won major victories before their eastern counterparts had even gained a foothold in Virginia. Fort Donelson was the first important Union victory, and the first crisis was survived at Shiloh. Vicksburg not only produced its own turning-point victory but led to another one at Gettysburg as well. Chattanooga represented the true end of the original Confederacy. Then, under Sherman, the western Federals eliminated what was left of resistance in Georgia—which led to Lincoln's reelection—and menaced the Carolinas while Grant gave Lee everything he could handle around Richmond. In summation, one cannot downplay the contribution of Grant's western Federal armies without completely distorting the history of the war.

After Appomattox and Lincoln's assassination came three years during which Grant exerted more real authority than did President Andrew Johnson. For example, if Johnson had his way, Robert E. Lee would have been put on trial for his life—but he was not, thanks mainly to Grant.[5] Then came Grant's own presidency, during which he turned away from the Democrats (the party of his mother and in-laws) and embraced the Republicans, who had been so instrumental in his initial rise to fame and power. Grant's tenure in the Oval Office is widely viewed as a failure, although more recent, astute historians such as Jean Edward Smith have made a convincing case that it perhaps was not as big a failure as previously thought.[6] After Grant's shameless bid for a third term in 1876 was rejected by his own constituents, he and Julia devoted their time to travel and conspicuous consumption. All this came to an abrupt halt when Grant simultaneously learned that he had been swindled out of his savings and had terminal throat cancer. Rather than die the pathetic death that most of us would have under similar circumstances, however, Grant rallied—with the help of Mark Twain—to write his classic memoirs while on his deathbed, often under the influence of morphine. The deserved though posthumous success of this timeless work provided for his family long after Grant's death in 1885.

The author's own grandfather, William Edward Cox, was born in 1885—the same year that Grant died—in fact, their lives overlapped about two months. Having known this grandfather very well during childhood (he passed away in 1962), I am struck by how our lives can be affected by events that have taken place over a hundred years before. All of those who had the privilege of knowing him agree that "Granddaddy" Cox (as he was called), though never wealthy in the financial sense, was one of the finest human beings they ever knew—strong, compassionate, and morally upright. His memory is an unqualified pleasure; and yet, there was never any talk about his childhood, even to his own children. There were no fond memories of his own father or grandfather, both of whom were physically disabled by the war. There was no talk of the grinding poverty he must have experienced as a sharecropper's son growing up in Wilkes County, Georgia, during the late 1800s. There was no talk of his own mother's parents, William and Mary Dozier of Columbia County, Georgia, who seemed to have vanished without a trace during the war years. What shaped my grandfather's mysterious character? Was he a good man because of what had happened to his family, or in spite of it, or both?

As for the man who affected my own family (and the nation) so decisively, Grant himself may be the greatest enigma among American heroes. Journalist Sylvanus Cadwallader relayed to posterity a story from one James Earnest, a businessman from Mineral Point, Wisconsin. Earnest had known Grant during the Galena days, recalling one time when he condescended to notice that his lowly wagon driver knew how to make intelligent conversation. Earnest later reflected: "That man Grant is President of the United States.... I will never doubt the truth of scriptural miracles hereafter."[7] Cadwallader himself made the profound observation that it was Grant's very flaws—his business ineptitude, his alcoholism, his political inconsistencies, etc.—that seemed to make him an even greater man than he would otherwise be: "His blemishes of character were incident to our common humanity; and instead of seriously damaging him in the estimation of right-minded men, will tend to emphasize his

The little boy in the middle is the author's grandfather, William Edward Cox, born in Wilkes County, Georgia, the same year that Grant died (1885). To the lower right is his mother, Rebecca Jane Dozier Cox, a teenager during the war and whose family was ruined by it. Not pictured are William's father and grandfather, both of whom were disabled Confederate veterans.

virtues, which were many and strongly pronounced."[8] Cadwallader's assessment of Grant from the perspective of an American sensationalist news reporter is not unlike that of say, the largely favorable (but certainly not uncritical) view of the Roman Emperor Augustus Caesar handed down to us by that ancient tabloid journalist turned historian, Suetonius. It is certainly true that, because of Grant's glaring, inescapable faults, we have a better appreciation of his greatness than that of many other American notables, whose marble images are routinely presented to us by the custodians of our heritage.

Hypothesizing "What if the South had won?" can be like asking who's buried in Grant's tomb, a question taken seriously by a few people but not the rest of us. A more relevant question is why did the Confederacy lose? Two reasons are suggested by this study—bad leadership (especially political) and Ulysses S. Grant. This book was more than half-written before I realized what it was really all about; namely the ancient philosophical debate over the respective roles of Free Will and Predestination in human affairs. Was Grant just lucky or was there more to it than that? For now, let us conclude by saying that the many special and unique qualities of Ulysses S. Grant proved to be God's own instrument in directing the course and outcome of the American Civil War.

Notes

Introduction

1. From Whitman's poem titled "Virginia—The West." Walt Whitman, *Complete Poetry and Collected Prose* (New York: The Library of America, 1982), p. 429.

2. In Shakespeare's *Twelfth Night*, this line is intended to be ironic, but in Grant's case the application is certainly literal.

3. John Y. Simon (quoting Whitman), "The Paradox of Ulysses S. Grant," *Register of the Kentucky Historical Society* 81, no. 4 (1983), p. 368.

4. J.F.C. Fuller, *The Generalship of Ulysses S. Grant* (1929; reprint, New York: Da Capo Press, Inc., 1991), p. xiii.

5. Ulysses S. Grant, *Personal Memoirs of U.S. Grant* (Lincoln, NE: University of Nebraska Press, 1996), p. 27.

6. Grant, *Memoirs*, p. 25. Grant was reputedly tone-deaf.

7. Grant, *Memoirs*, p. 37.

8. Grant, *Memoirs*, p. 66.

9. Grant, *Memoirs*, p. 49. Grant admitted that he would rather observe wildlife than hunt. He was also disgusted by the sight of blood.

10. Grant, *Memoirs*, p. 40.

11. Grant, *Memoirs*, p. 39.

12. Grant, *Memoirs*, p. 69.

13. Grant, *Memoirs*, p. 24.

14. Grant, *Memoirs*, pp. 64–65.

15. Gore Vidal, "President and Mrs. U.S. Grant," in *United States: Essays 1952–1992* (New York: Random House, 1993), p. 721. Grant, like many other intelligent persons, also longed to travel from an early age. See Grant, *Memoirs*, p. 25.

16. Grant, *Memoirs*, pp. 129–130, 135.

17. Grant, *Memoirs*, pp. 17–18.

18. Grant, *Memoirs*, p. 20.

19. Grant, *Memoirs*, p. 27. In a similar manner, Grant caustically recalled that he and many others began smoking (the eventual cause of his death) because it had been so stigmatized by their teachers. See Grant, *Memoirs*, p. 41.

20. Lloyd Lewis, *Captain Sam Grant* (Boston: Little, Brown, 1950), p. 93.

21. Grant, *Memoirs*, p. 19.

22. Grant, *Memoirs*, p. 488.

23. Grant, *Memoirs*, p. 36.

24. Grant, *Memoirs*, p. 85.

25. Jean Edward Smith, *Grant* (New York: Simon & Schuster, 2001), p. 166.

26. For example, Grant later wrote "their marching could not be excelled." See Grant, *Memoirs*, p. 655.

27. Grant, *Memoirs*, p. 32.

28. Julia was from Missouri, technically not a state in rebellion, and therefore temporarily exempt from the Emancipation Proclamation.

29. John S. Mosby, *The Memoirs of John S. Mosby*, ed. Charles Wells Russell (Bloomington, Indiana University Press, 1959), p. 399.

30. Mosby, p. 383.

31. These four brothers from Henry County, Georgia (all Army privates), were Burl Washington Nail, Thomas J. Nail, Robert J. Nail, and Rubin W.J. Nail.

32. Grant, *Memoirs*, p. 666.

Chapter 1

1. Smith, p. 628. By this time, Grant's throat cancer prevented him from speaking in conversation.

2. The second Galena home appears mainly to have been used by Grant as a springboard for his later presidential campaigns, both successful and failed.

3. Julia Dent Grant, *The Personal Memoirs of Julia Dent Grant (Mrs. Ulysses S. Grant)*, ed. John Y. Simon (Carbondale, IL: Ulysses S. Grant Association, 1975), pp. 84, 86.

4. Lewis, p. 373. Today, the same storefront has an address of 122 Main Street.

5. Lewis, p. 373.

6. Of his brother Simpson, Grant wrote, "A more honorable man never transacted business." See Grant, *Memoirs*, p. 129.

7. Lewis, p. 373.
8. James M. McPherson, *Battle Cry of Freedom: The Civil War Era* (New York: Ballantine, 1988), p. 296.
9. Shelby Foote, *The Civil War: A Narrative*, vol. 1, *Fort Sumter to Perryville* (New York, Random House, 1958-1974), pp. 196-197.
10. Foote, vol. 1, p. 148. This is taken from Horace Porter's description of Grant at Chattanooga. See Smith, p. 269.
11. McPherson, p. 296.
12. Vidal, pp. 709, 718, 722.
13. Brooks D. Simpson, *Ulysses S. Grant: Triumph Over Personal Adversity, 1822-1865* (New York: Houghton Mifflin, 2000), p. 74.
14. Smith, p. 96 (citing Lewis, p. 377).
15. Grant, *Memoirs*, p. 128.
16. Lewis, pp. 389-390.
17. Lewis, p. 376.
18. Grant, *Memoirs*, p. 26.
19. Lewis, p. 391.
20. Grant, *Memoirs*, pp. 128-129.
21. Simpson, p. 75.
22. Lewis, pp. 415-416.
23. Julia Grant, p. 87.
24. Smith, p. 99.
25. See *www.galenahistorymuseum.org/ninegenerals.htm*.
26. John Y. Simon, "From Galena to Appomattox: Grant and Washburne," *Journal of the Illinois State Historical Society* 58 (Summer 1965): p. 189.
27. Lewis, p. 377.
28. Smith, p. 97.
29. Lewis, p. 396 (quoting Albert Deane Richardson). This theme is repeated by Grant in a letter to his father dated April 21, 1861. See Ulysses S. Grant, *The Papers of Ulysses S. Grant*, vol. 2, ed. John Y. Simon (Carbondale, IL, Southern Illinois University Press, 1967-1995), pp. 6-7.
30. Lewis, pp. 399-400.
31. Lewis, p. 401.
32. Timoleon, Plutarch's successful Hellenic liberator of Sicily, was mysteriously nominated for his presumed suicidal mission after spending some 20 years in seclusion and disgrace.
33. Grant, *Memoirs*, p. 138.
34. Grant, *Memoirs*, p. 138.
35. Smith, p. 100 (citing Lewis, p. 403).
36. Lewis, p. 409.
37. Smith, p. 101.
38. Lewis, p. 411.
39. Lewis, p. 411. Pope and Grant had been at West Point together and also served together under General Taylor during the Mexican War. See Grant, *Memoirs*, p. 143.
40. Grant implies that the conversation occurred right before he returned to Galena and wrote his letter to General Lorenzo Thomas at the end of May 1861, but this appears to be mistaken. Grant remarks that Pope was a mustering officer at the time, a position from which Pope had resigned by the first week of May. See Lewis (p. 419) and Grant, *Memoirs* (pp. 142-143).
41. Pope's Civil War career would effectively end in 1862 with the crushing defeat of his army at the battle of Second Manassas.
42. Lewis, p. 416.
43. Smith, p. 103.
44. Lewis, p. 417.
45. Grant, *Papers*, vol. 2, p. 16.
46. Grant, *Memoirs*, p. 140.
47. Grant, *Papers*, vol. 2, pp. 12-13. This appears to be the first mention of Grant's services in the official war record.
48. Lewis, p. 418.

Chapter 2

1. Grant, *Memoirs*, pp. 549, 653. Confederate General Joseph Johnston stated his belief that the last military force in history comparable to the western Federal armies of the American Civil War were the Roman legions of Julius Caesar.
2. Pope received his promotion shortly afterwards while Prentice would later serve with distinction under Grant at Shiloh.
3. Lewis, p. 419. See also Smith, p. 105.
4. McPherson, p. 296.
5. Grant, *Papers*, vol. 2, p. 21. This sentiment appears contrary to the one that Grant expressed to fellow townsmen the previous month (see Chapter One); however, they seemed to think there would be no fighting at all.
6. Grant, *Papers*, vol. 2, p. 24.
7. Grant, *Papers*, vol. 2, p. 22.
8. Grant, *Papers*, vol. 2, p. 26.
9. Grant, *Memoirs*, pp. 140-142.
10. Lewis, p. 422.
11. Grant, *Memoirs*, p. 142. Journalist Sylvanus Cadwallader noted that Grant alluded to this unhappy stint in St. Louis many years later. Grant recalled that no one gave him anything when he needed it, but when he could afford things after the war, gifts were lavished upon him. See Sylvanus Cadwallader, *Three Years with Grant*, ed. Benjamin P. Thomas (Lincoln, NE: University of Nebraska Press, 1996), p. 351.
12. Smith, p. 92.
13. Smith, pp. 90-95.
14. Smith, p. 94.
15. Grant, *Papers*, vol. 2, p. 22.
16. Lewis, p. 423.
17. Grant, *Papers*, vol. 2, p. 32n.
18. Lewis, p. 423.
19. Smith, p. 107.
20. Grant, *Papers*, Vol. II, p. 25.

21. Grant, *Memoirs*, p. 145.
22. Lewis, p. 427.
23. See Mark Twain, "The Private History of a Campaign That Failed," in *Tales, Speeches, Essays, and Sketches* (New York: Penguin, 1994).
24. Grant, *Papers*, vol. 2, p. 30n.
25. Lewis, pp. 423, 427.
26. Lewis, p. 423.
27. Julia Grant, p. 75. Gore Vidal opined that the phrase "low-spirited" was "a nice euphemism for full of spirits." See Vidal, p. 715.
28. Smith, p. 105.
29. Grant, *Papers*, vol. 2, p. 33.
30. Grant, *Papers*, vol. 2, p. 33.
31. Grant, *Papers*, vol. 2, pp. 33–35n.
32. For example, detached from Grant's command, the 21st Illinois was nearly annihilated under General William Rosecrans at Chickamauga in September 1863. Its commander, regimental Colonel John Alexander of Paris, Illinois, was killed in that same engagement. See Bruce Catton, *Grant Moves South* (Boston: Little, Brown, 1960), p. 4.
33. Lewis, p. 424.
34. Smith, p. 105.
35. Thomas, Adjunct General, was the recent replacement for Joseph Johnston, who had defected to the Confederacy. See Lewis, p. 424.
36. Grant, *Memoirs*, p. 143.
37. Grant, *Memoirs*, p. 144.
38. Grant, *Papers*, vol. 2, p. 37.
39. Smith, pp. 105–106. See also Lewis, p. 425.
40. Grant, *Memoirs*, p. 405. Grant's idealistic attitude unwittingly applied to those who eventually proved his most powerful benefactors.

Chapter 3

1. Grant, *Memoirs*, p. 405. Essayist Gore Vidal, somewhat unconvinced, characterized this attitude as a "Cromwellian assertion." See Vidal, p. 717.
2. Julia Grant, p. 89. See also Grant, *Memoirs*, p. 143.
3. Lewis, p. 413.
4. Lewis, p. 425. Politically, McClellan was a Democrat as well.
5. Grant, *Papers*, vol. 2, pp. 37–39.
6. Grant, *Papers*, vol. 2, pp. 40–42.
7. McPherson, pp. 364–365.
8. McPherson, p. 359.
9. Grant, *Papers*, p. 41n.
10. Smith, p. 107.
11. Lewis, p. 426.
12. Grant, *Memoirs*, p. 35.
13. Plutarch, vol. 2, p. 201.
14. Smith, p. 107.
15. Lewis, p. 426.

16. Grant, *Papers*, vol. 2, pp. 43n–44.
17. Lewis, p. 427.
18. Grant, *Papers*, vol. 2, p. 42.
19. Grant, *Papers*, vol. 2, p. 45n.
20. Smith, p. 107. See also Simpson, p. 83.
21. Julia Grant, pp. 90–91.
22. Smith, p. 108.
23. Lewis, p. 427.
24. Lewis, p. 428.
25. Grant, *Papers*, vol. 2, p. 51n.
26. Grant, *Papers*, vol. 2, pp. 44n–45n, 50–51n. See also Lewis, p. 428.
27. Grant, *Papers*, vol. 2, pp. 45–46.
28. Lewis, p. 428. I assume that Grant's approximate words were "I guess I'll take command."
29. Smith, pp. 108–111. See also Grant, *Papers*, vol. 2, pp. 45–46.
30. Grant, *Papers*, vol. 2, p. 47n.
31. Grant, *Memoirs*, p. 145.
32. Grant, *Papers*, vol. 2, p. 50.
33. Grant, *Papers*, vol. 2, pp. 47n, 49, 52.
34. Grant, *Memoirs*, p. 146.
35. Grant, *Memoirs*, pp. 145–147.
36. Lincoln was one of the few cognizant of this. He is quoted as saying "keep Egypt right side up," that is, keep Southern Illinois on the Federal side. See Victor Hicken, *Illinois in the Civil War*, 2nd ed. (1966; reprint, Chicago: University of Illinois Press, 1991), p. 13.

Chapter 4

1. Twain, p. 182.
2. Smith, p. 111.
3. Julia Grant, p. 92.
4. Grant, *Papers*, vol. 2, pp. 60, 66.
5. Grant, *Papers*, vol. 2, pp. 59–60.
6. Grant, *Papers*, vol. 2, p. 59n.
7. Smith, p. 111.
8. Smith, p. 112.
9. Grant, *Papers*, vol. 2, p. 64n.
10. Grant, *Memoirs*, p. 148.
11. Twain's family would later settle in nearby Hannibal, Missouri.
12. Hannibal was located in Marion County, Missouri; Florida in Monroe County.
13. Grant, *Papers*, vol. 2, pp. 66–67, 69–70.
14. Grant, *Memoirs*, p. 149.
15. Grant, *Memoirs*, p. 58.
16. Grant, *Memoirs*, p. 45.
17. Grant, *Memoirs*, p. 149.
18. Twain, p. 183.
19. Twain, pp. 182–183.
20. Grant, *Papers*, vol. 2, p. 72n.
21. Grant, *Papers*, vol. 2, p. 73.
22. Grant, *Memoirs*, p. 149.
23. Grant, Papers, vol. 2, p. 69n.
24. Grant, *Memoirs*, p. 150.

25. Some asserted that Twain was Grant's main influence, if not the real author.
26. Grant, *Memoirs*, p. 151.
27. Grant, *Papers*, vol. 2, p. 77n.
28. Grant, *Papers*, vol. 2, p. 67.
29. William Tecumseh Sherman, whom Grant saw during his St. Louis days, agreed with this assertion. See Smith, p. 92.

Chapter 5

1. Grant, *Memoirs*, p. 28.
2. Grant, *Papers*, vol. 2, p. 82n. See also Smith, p. 644. Grant said it was a St. Louis newspaper. See Grant, *Memoirs*, p. 151.
3. Grant, *Papers*, vol. 2, p. 82n. See also Smith, p. 113.
4. Simon, "From Galena to Appomattox," p. 172.
5. Foote, vol. 1, p. 148. Foote also relates the amusing story that when Grant's surprised father heard the news, he nervously wrote to his son, warning him, "Be careful, Ulys ... you're a general now; it's a good job, don't lose it." See p. 197.
6. Washburne was among the many civilian observers who fled from the battlefield after the Federal defeat.
7. Simon, "From Galena to Appomattox," pp. 169, 171–182.
8. In correspondence Pope variously referred to Grant as "thoroughly a gentleman & an officer of intelligence and discretion" and "a Soldier by education & experience & a discreet prudent man who is eminently needed now...." See Grant, *Papers*, vol. 2, pp. 86n, 124n.
9. Grant, *Papers*, vol. 2, pp. 80–81.
10. Grant, *Papers*, vol. 2, p. 83.
11. Grant, *Papers*, vol. 2, p. 86n.
12. Grant, *Papers*, vol. 2, pp. 96–97n.
13. Grant, *Papers*, vol. 2, p. 97n.
14. Grant, *Memoirs*, p. 152.
15. Grant, *Papers*, vol. 2, pp. 85, 87. See also Smith, p. 115.
16. Grant, *Memoirs*, pp. 152–153.
17. Grant, *Papers*, vol. 2, pp. 89–90.
18. Grant, *Papers*, vol. 2, p. 87n. See also Grant, *Memoirs*, p. 153.
19. Grant, *Papers*, vol. 2, pp. 94–95, 105, 107, 120, 122. See also Grant, *Memoirs*, p. 153.
20. Grant, *Papers*, vol. 2, p. 105.
21. McPherson, pp. 299–303.
22. McPherson, pp. 351–352.
23. Two days earlier, Grant had written to Julia, "tomorrow I move South," but in point of fact, he was about to be ordered North so as to deal with the brewing crisis in Jefferson City, Missouri. See Grant, *Papers* (vol. 2, pp. 115, 123n) and Catton, *Grant Moves South* (p. 22).

24. Grant, *Memoirs*, p. 153.
25. These missteps, in addition to defeat at Wilson's Creek and the temporary loss of a huge portion of Missouri to the Confederates, included making draconian proclamations. Then both Frémont and his wife simultaneously succeeded in alienating President Lincoln by refusing to follow his advice. See McPherson, pp. 352–353.
26. Grant, *Papers*, vol. 2, p. 124n. See also Smith, p. 116.
27. Grant, *Memoirs*, pp. 153–155.
28. Grant, *Papers*, vol. 2, p. 131.
29. Grant, *Papers*, vol. 2, pp. 149n–151n. See also Grant, *Memoirs*, p. 155.
30. Smith, p. 117.
31. Grant, *Papers*, vol. 2, pp. 151n–152n.
32. Grant, *Papers*, vol. 2, p. 158.
33. Smith, p. 117.
34. This decision was apparently in doubt right up to the moment Grant sat waiting to be interviewed by Frémont in St. Louis. It seems as though Grant's reputation for drinking was an issue. See Catton, *Grant Moves South*, pp. 37–38.

Chapter 6

1. Grant, *Memoirs*, p. 156.
2. Grant, *Memoirs*, pp. 156–157. In retrospect, Grant was also grateful to Prentice for his heroic performance at Shiloh.
3. Grant, *Papers*, vol. 2, p. 170n.
4. Grant, *Memoirs*, p. 157.
5. Grant, *Papers*, vol. 2, p. 177.
6. This was Colonel Leonard Ross.
7. Grant, *Papers*, vol. 2, p. 172n.
8. Grant, *Papers*, vol. 2, p. 188.
9. Grant, *Memoirs*, p. 157. Oglesby would go on to become one of Grant's most reliable and highly decorated point men, and after the war was elected Governor of Illinois.
10. Polk may have also received nudges from his colleague Gideon Pillow and Jefferson Davis, but not the Confederate high command or legislature, who appear to have been just as surprised by the move as everyone else. See Bruce Catton, *Grant Moves South*, pp. 42–43, 56.
11. Smith, p. 118. Thomas Connelly wrote, "Polk had made what was probably one of the greatest mistakes of the war...." See Thomas Lawrence Connelly, *Army of the Heartland: The Army of Tennessee, 1861–1862* (Baton Rouge: Louisiana State University Press, 1967), p. 52.
12. Grant, *Papers*, vol. 2, p. 189.
13. Smith, pp. 118–119.
14. Paducah was also the adopted hometown of Tilghman.
15. Grant, *Memoirs*, p. 159.

16. Grant, *Memoirs*, p. 158. Julia, in her own memoirs, related an unpleasant encounter soon afterwards with a woman in Paducah, who threw a tantrum when she heard Julia drop the phrase "mania for secession." See Julia Grant, p. 95. In fact, the women of Paducah appear to have been more spirited than the men, taunting Federal troops with cries of "Hurrah for Jeff Davis!" See Catton, *Grant Moves South*, p. 49.

17. Smith, pp. 119–120.

18. Confederate General Jeff Thompson, sense of humor intact, made a mockery of Frémont's proclamation by declaring, in so many words, that he could act more excessively than Frémont on any matter. See Catton, *Grant Moves South*, p. 43.

19. Grant, *Papers*, vol. 2, pp. 194–195.

20. Smith, p. 120.

21. Grant, *Memoirs*, p. 159. In effect, Grant was reprimanded for issuing a better proclamation than his superior.

22. Grant, *Memoirs*, p. 158.

23. Grant, *Papers*, vol. 2, pp. 210–211.

24. Julia Dent, p. 115n.

25. See Smith, pp. 120–121. See also McPherson (p. 392) and Catton, *Grant Moves South* (p. 82).

26. Catton, *Grant Moves South*, p. 66. The exact date was September 10. See Colonel Arthur L. Conger, *The Rise of U.S. Grant* (1931; reprint, New York: Da Capo Press, 1996), p. 79.

27. Smith, p. 120. C.F. Smith, despite his impeccable credentials, had somehow at the outbreak of the war been tagged by politicians as a soldier of dubious loyalty to the Union, and was only ranked a Colonel until August 1861, when in the wake of Bull Run, and thanks to McClellan, he finally got the promotion that he deserved. See Catton, *Grant Moves South*, pp. 50–51.

28. Grant, *Memoirs*, p. 158.

29. Smith, pp. 120–121.

30. Grant, *Papers*, vol. 2, p. 239.

31. Grant, *Papers*, vol. 2, p. 247.

32. Julia Dent, p. 115n.

33. Smith, p. 122. Lexington was later retaken by the Federals on October 16; nevertheless, Frémont's reputation in Missouri continued to plummet as a result.

34. Grant, *Papers*, vol. 2, p. 289.

35. Grant, *Papers*, vol. 2, p. 299.

36. Grant, *Papers*, vol. 2, p. 313.

37. Grant, *Papers*, vol. 2, pp. 299, 328.

38. Grant, *Papers*, vol. 2, pp. 166, 179, 250, 253, 300. This was Colonel William H.L. Wallace of Ottawa, Illinois, later promoted to Brigadier General and who fell at Shiloh.

39. Today, Belmont Landing in southeastern Missouri is curiously flanked north and south by portions of land belonging to the state of Kentucky, which (contrary to popular perception) occupies pieces of the Mississippi west bank in this region.

Chapter 7

1. Grant, *Memoirs*, p. 160.

2. McPherson, pp. 353–354. See also Smith, pp. 122–123.

3. Grant mentions Belmont eight times in his dispatches during October, or twice per week on average, reflecting a remarkable preoccupation with a place that most people had never heard of. See Grant, *Papers*, vol. 3, pp. 4, 11, 14, 16, 18, 58, 66.

4. Grant, *Papers*, vol. 3, pp. xxi, xxii, 18.

5. Grant, *Papers*, vol. 3, p. 64.

6. Grant, *Papers*, vol. 2, p. 300.

7. Grant, *Papers*, vol. 3, p. 10.

8. Grant, *Papers*, vol. 3, p. 11.

9. Grant, *Papers*, vol. 3, p. 58.

10. Grant, *Papers*, vol. 3, pp. 42, 54.

11. Catton, *Grant Moves South*, p. 57. William Hardee had followed the same path earlier. See Conger, p. 76.

12. Conger, p. 76.

13. Grant, *Papers*, vol. 3, pp. 39–40.

14. Conger, p. 79.

15. Conger, p. 79.

16. This was Captain Chauncey McKeever.

17. Grant wrote, "My own impression however is that they are fortifying strongly and preparing to resist a formidable attack and have but little idea of risking anything upon a forward movement." See Grant, *Papers*, vol. 3, p. 24.

18. Conger, p. 74.

19. Conger, p. 78.

20. Grant, *Papers*, vol. 3, p. 42.

21. Sherman was angrily accused by some of his men that he had ordered them out of a barn during a rainstorm because he wanted to use it as a horse stable. See Charles Bracelen Flood, *Grant and Sherman: The Friendship that Won the Civil War* (New York: Farrar, Straus and Giroux, 2005), p. 56.

22. Flood, pp. 58–59, 66, 68.

23. Grant, *Papers*, vol. 3, p. 212.

24. Grant, *Papers*, vol. 3, pp. 43–44.

25. Grant, *Papers*, vol. 3, p. xxii.

26. Grant, *Papers*, vol. 3, p. 80n. The exact number of Federal casualties at Fredericktown was never disclosed.

27. Grant, *Papers*, vol. 3, pp. 73, 79–80.

28. Grant, *Papers*, vol. 3, p. xxii.

29. Grant, *Papers*, vol. 3, pp. 54–57, 63.

30. Smith, pp. 123n–124.

31. On October 31, 1861, Grant was called in to testify before a House committee investi-

gating contractor corruption in Frémont's department. See Grant, *Papers*, vol. 3, pp. xxii, 90–98.
    32. For example, on October 9, Grant or-
dered Colonel W.H.L. Wallace to monitor the
sale of beer around Bird's Point, Mo. See
Grant, *Papers*, vol. 3, pp. 32–33.
    33. Grant's later photos have no weaponry.
See Grant, *Papers*, vol. 2, overleaf notes.
    34. Grant, *Papers*, vol. 3, pp. 63, 76–77.
    35. Grant, *Papers*, vol. 2, overleaf notes.

Chapter 8

    1. Grant, *Memoirs*, p. 536. Grant refers to
General Lewis Cass but then a few pages later
(p. 540), perhaps unconsciously—this was years
after the Little Big Horn—mentions George
Armstrong Custer (whom he disliked) in another context.
    2. Smith, p. 122.
    3. Grant, *Memoirs*, pp. 160–161. The wily
Thompson managed to vanish yet again once
he quickly became aware of this plan.
    4. Smith, p. 124–125.
    5. Grant, *Papers*, vol. 3, pp. 105–106, 124.
Grant was in agreement with the sentiments of
Oglesby, reporting to St. Louis later in the
month, "There is not a sufficiency of Union
sentiment left in this portion of the state to
save Sodom." See p. 212.
    6. Grant was specifically ordered by Fré-
mont not to attack on either side of the river,
only to menace and go after Jeff Thompson.
See Smith, pp. 124–125.
    7. Smith, pp. 125–126.
    8. Foote, vol. 1, pp. 150–151.
    9. Grant, *Memoirs*, p. 161.
    10. John Y. Simon, "Grant at Belmont," *Mil-
itary Affairs: Journal of the American Military Institute* 45 (December 1981): p. 164.
    11. Future author of the novel *Ben-Hur* and
no relation to Colonel William Wallace.
    12. Smith, pp. 126–127.
    13. Conger, pp. 83–84. Commodore Foote
later accepted Grant's explanation for this.
    14. The recent combination of Pillow's
insufferable behavior and A.S. Johnston's
daunting reputation seems to have temporarily
unnerved Polk, who sought a return to the min-
istry. See Parks, p. 189.
    15. Smith, p. 128.
    16. Grant, *Memoirs*, p. 163.
    17. Smith, p. 128–130.
    18. See McPherson, Chapter 10, "Amateurs
Go to War."
    19. Grant, *Memoirs*, p. 166.
    20. Grant, *Papers*, vol. 3, pp. 138, 142.
    21. Foote, vol. 1, p. 199.
    22. Catton, *Grant Moves South*, p. 78.

    23. Grant, *Memoirs*, p. 162.
    24. Grant, *Memoirs*, pp. 164–165, 167–168.
    25. Grant, *Memoirs*, p. 165. Military histo-
rian J.F.C. Fuller was especially praiseworthy of
Grant's conduct in this regard: "At Belmont ...
in spite of the danger he was the last to leave
the field, as a trusty captain is the last to leave
a sinking ship." See Fuller, p. 189.
    26. Grant, *Memoirs*, p. 165.
    27. Julia Grant, p. 93.
    28. Simon, *Grant at Belmont*, p. 161.
    29. Simon, *Grant at Belmont*, p. 165.
    30. Mary Chesnut, *Mary Chesnut's Civil War*,
ed. C. Vann Woodward (New Haven: Yale University Press, 1981), p. 233 (and note).
    31. Smith, p. 131.
    32. Foote, vol. 1, p. 152.
    33. Smith, p. 131.
    34. Grant, *Memoirs*, p. 166.
    35. Conger, pp. 99–100.
    36. Conger, p. 95.
    37. Smith, p. 131.
    38. William Tecumseh Sherman later wrote
to Grant, "At Belmont you manifested your
traits...." See Smith, p. 288.
    39. Grant, *Memoirs*, p. 166.
    40. Grant, *Papers*, vol. 3, pp. 130–131.
    41. Grant, *Papers*, vol. 3, p. 133.
    42. Grant, *Papers*, vol. 3, p. 133n.
    43. Grant, *Papers*, vol. 3, p. 134.
    44. Grant, *Papers*, vol. 3, p. 138.
    45. Grant, *Memoirs*, p. 166.
    46. Catton, *Grant Moves South*, p. 84.
    47. Grant, *Papers*, vol. 3, p. 131.
    48. Grant, *Memoirs*, p. 167.
    49. Polk's biographer son later changed this
to "I was favorably impressed with him; he is
undoubtedly a man of much force." See Joseph
H. Parks, *General Leonidas Polk C.S.A.: The Fighting Bishop* (Kingsport, TN: Kingsport Press/
Louisiana State University Press, 1962), pp.
194–195.
    50. This cannon had been appropriately
nicknamed "Lady Polk." See Nathaniel Cheairs
Hughes, Jr., and Roy P. Stonesifer, Jr., *The Life
and Wars of Gideon J. Pillow* (Chapel Hill, NC:
University of North Carolina Press, 1993), p. 205.
    51. Grant, *Memoirs*, p. 168.
    52. Foote, vol. 1, p. 182.
    53. Julia Grant, pp. 93–94.
    54. Julia Grant, p. 94.
    55. A large Federal cannon at Cairo had
been nicknamed "Lady Grant" in honor of
Julia. That one did not explode. See Catton,
Grant Moves South, p. 109.
    56. Grant, *Memoirs*, p. 159
    57. According to Grant, this officer was one
Major Barrett, whom Grant had known before
the war in St. Louis, although Grant also reported that Jeff Thompson had led the raid in

person. Grant added that Barrett had been involved in negotiations for prisoner exchanges (presumably after the battle of Belmont), and had at that time overheard plans for Grant's aborted trip to Cape Girardeau. See Grant, *Memoirs* (p. 159) and Grant, *Papers*, vol. 3 (p. 186).

58. Grant, *Papers*, vol. 3, pp. 186–187n, 210.

Chapter 9

1. One historian of the battle, Nathaniel C. Hughes, wittily wrote that Pillow had been sent to Grant by "the tooth fairy." See Nathaniel Cheairs Hughes, Jr., *The Battle of Belmont: Grant Strikes South* (Chapel Hill: University of North Carolina Press, 1991), p. 20.

2. According to Thomas Connelly, "The debacle" of Fort Donelson "began with the command failures of Polk in late autumn and early winter of 1861–62." Polk "became completely absorbed in preparing the town [of Columbus] against attack." See Connelly, *Army of the Heartland*, pp. 103–105.

3. Connelly, *Army of the Heartland*, pp. 103–106, 109–111. Johnston was concerned, however, that Grant might attempt to flank Columbus to the east, and urged Polk to detach troops under Pillow for Clarksville, Tennessee, which both Polk and Pillow opposed. See Parks, p. 198.

4. Smith, p. 134.

5. Smith, p. 134.

6. Connelly, *Army of the Heartland*, p. 104.

7. Conger, p. 98.

8. Grant, *Papers*, vol. 3, p. 245.

9. Grant, *Papers*, vol. 3, pp. 260–261n.

10. Grant, *Papers*, vol. 3, pp. 280–284.

11. Connelly, *Army of the Heartland*, p. 105.

12. Grant, *Papers*, vol. 3, p xxv.

13. Fuller, pp. 77–83. See also Smith, pp. 134–135.

14. Grant, *Papers*, vol. 3, pp. 295–296, 316–318n.

15. Smith, p. 138.

16. Grant wrote, "No one regrets the occurrance more than I do." See Grant, *Papers*, vol. 3, pp. 322–323n.

17. Grant, *Papers*, vol. 3, pp. 334–335.

18. Hicken, *Illinois in the Civil War*, p. 10.

19. Grant, *Papers*, vol. 3, pp. 266n–268n.

20. The chaplain, Father Louis A. Lambert, was also allowed to stay.

21. Grant, *Papers*, vol. 3, pp. 301–304n, 314–315n, 338–339, 340–341n, 365–366n.

22. Grant, *Papers*, vol. 3, pp. 320–322n.

23. Julia Grant, p. 96.

24. Grant, *Memoirs*, p. 168.

25. Grant, *Papers*, vol. 3, pp. 289–290, 299, 324–328n, 351–352n.

26. Catton, *Grant Moves South*, p. 95.

27. Grant, *Papers*, vol. 3, p. 257.

28. Grant *Papers*, vol. 4, pp. 116n–118n. It is implied that this evidence included the eyewitness testimony of Bross himself.

29. Grant, *Papers*, vol. 3, pp. xxiv–xxv, 227, 262–269, 271.

30. Conger, p. 122.

31. Grant, *Papers*, vol. 3, p. 353.

32. Conger, p. 129.

Chapter 10

1. Grant, *Memoirs*, p. 660.

2. Conger, pp. 134–136. See also Catton, *Grant Moves South*, pp. 117–118.

3. Fuller, pp. 79–80.

4. Fuller, p. 81.

5. Regarding Halleck, Grant later wrote, perhaps intending a pun, that "... it was much easier for him to refuse a favor than to grant one." See Grant, *Memoirs*, p. 341.

6. Conger, p. 136.

7. Fuller, p. 82.

8. Conger, pp. 138–139.

9. Grant, *Papers*, vol. 4, pp. 3–4n.

10. Conger, p. 151.

11. Smith, pp. 137–138. According to Grant, he had contemplated the move against Fort Henry even before the reconnaissance by Smith. See Grant, *Memoirs*, p. 169.

12. From these circumstances, one may surmise that McClellan possibly sent Kountz out West to be the proverbial fox in charge of chicken coop.

13. Grant, *Papers*, vol. 4, pp. 53–54. In addition to the complaints recited in this letter, Grant was no doubt exasperated by Kountz's allegations of drunkenness against him. Grant was also probably irritated that another subordinate, Captain Rueben B. Hatch, had recently been arrested and charged with corruption of the type that Kountz and the *Chicago Tribune* had been loudly railing against. Hatch was later exonerated and had been probably accused more as a result of having a spat with other junior officers. See pp. 79–84n. Grant may have decided that it was high time for other, worse offenders, such as Kountz, to be detained.

14. Julia Grant, pp. 95–96. See also Catton, *Grant Moves South*, p. 120.

15. Grant, *Papers*, vol. 4, p. 22.

16. Grant, *Papers*, vol. 4, p. 114n.

17. Grant, *Papers*, vol. 4, pp. 110–113n.

18. Grant, *Papers*, vol. 4, pp. 107, 110n. This whole scenario calls to mind Julius Caesar's quick exit from Rome for the Gallic Wars in order to escape his many political accusers.

19. Grant, *Papers*, vol. 4, pp. 118n–119n. Lincoln, for his part, may have been offended by

the bit about "secesh wives," having himself married into a slave-holding family.

20. Catton, *Grant Moves South*, p. 122.

21. Grant, *Memoirs*, p. 170. See also Grant, *Papers*, vol. 4, p. 94.

22. Foote, vol. 1, p. 184.

23. Connelly, *Army of the Heartland*, pp. 76–77.

24. Connelly, *Army of the Heartland*, pp. 78–85.

25. Conger, pp. 147–151.

26. The decision of Thomas contrasted with that of his fellow Virginian, Robert E. Lee, whom many expected to accept a Federal commission.

27. Fuller, p. 81.

28. Zollicoffer was the first Confederate general killed in the West during the war. See Connelly, *Army of the Heartland*, p. 99.

29. Smith, p. 137.

30. Smith, p. 138.

31. Grant, *Memoirs*, p. 170. Many reputable commentators have suggested that Grant was rebuffed, not for having a bad plan, but for trying to tell a superior things already known. While I believe there may have been an element of this involved, subsequent events in Tennessee and Mississippi demonstrated that Halleck was not one to move quickly in the field, if at all.

32. Catton, *Grant Moves South*, p. 124.

33. Catton, *Grant Moves South*, p. 127.

34. Smith, p. 139.

35. Foote ended his dispatch with, "Have we your authority to move...?" Grant, *Papers*, vol. 4, p. 99n. See also Smith (p. 138) and Fuller (p. 82).

36. Grant, *Papers*, vol. 4, pp. 103–104.

37. Catton, *Grant Moves South*, pp. 129–130.

38. Conger p. 141.

39. Smith, p. 140. See also Catton, *Grant Moves South*, p. 131.

40. Smith, p. 140.

41. Catton, *Grant Moves South*, p. 134.

42. Grant, *Papers*, vol. 4, pp. 123n–126n.

43. Conger, p. 154.

Chapter 11

1. Grant, *Memoirs*, p. 360.

2. Grant, *Papers*, vol. 4, pp. 130–131n, 139–140n.

3. Smith, p. 142.

4. Catton, *Grant Moves South*, p. 138.

5. Connelly, *Army of the Heartland*, p. 109.

6. During the engagement, several of these guns malfunctioned and/or exploded. See Foote, vol. 1, p. 187.

7. Connelly, *Army of the Heartland*, p. 107.

See also Smith (pp. 143–144) and Foote, vol. 1 (p. 188).

8. Grant, *Memoirs*, p. 171.

9. Flood, p. 78. See also Smith, p. 142. Sherman was still recovering from his panic attacks of the previous year and was, in effect, being given a second chance by Halleck.

10. Grant, *Papers*, vol. 4, p. 149.

11. In making a mistake that probably did not affect the final outcome of the battle, Tilghman, once he realized that the Federal host was upon him, ordered the west bank of the river evacuated and then appealed for reinforcements The west bank consisted of yet another incomplete fortification, dubbed Fort Heiman. The decision allowed Grant and Foote's gunboats to focus all of their attention on the east bank and Fort Henry. See Smith, pp. 145–146.

12. Smith, p. 147.

13. Grant, *Papers*, vol. 4, p. 160n.

14. Smith, p. 147. See also Flood, p. 81.

15. Grant, *Papers*, vol. 4, p. 157.

16. Grant, *Papers*, vol. 4, p. 163.

17. See Smith (p. 149) and Foote, vol. 1 (p. 192).

18. Pillow, even more vacillating than Johnston, first wanted to attack Grant like Beauregard, but then decided there were not enough troops to do this and then did not want to participate in an offensive campaign under the command of Floyd. See Connelly, *Army of the Heartland*, pp. 113, 115–116.

19. Jean Edward Smith called the decision to defend Fort Donelson (rather than attack from it) "an error of catastrophic proportions." See Smith, p. 149.

20. Connelly, *Army of the Heartland*, p. 112. Grant himself agreed with this particular assessment: "Johnston made a fatal mistake in intrusting so important a command to Floyd.... Pillow's presence as second was also a mistake," adding, "I knew that Floyd was in command, but he was no soldier, and I judged that he would yield to Pillow's pretensions." See Grant, *Memoirs*, pp. 192, 173. Floyd arrived in Tennessee after having recently helped to lose West Virginia for the Confederacy.

21. Mosby, p. 103.

22. Grant, *Memoirs*, p. 175.

23. Smith, p. 148.

24. In the words of Shelby Foote, "A highway of invasion had been cleared." See Foote, vol. 1, p.191. Grant, in a slam against his wife's home state, wrote to her on February 10, "The Union sentiment up there [Florence, AL] is much stronger than we have found it through Missouri." See also Grant, *Papers*, vol. 4, p. 188.

25. Grant, *Papers*, vol. 4, p. 180.

26. Grant, *Papers*, vol. 4, p. 188.

27. Grant, *Papers*, vol. 4, pp. 189n–191n.

28. Smith (quoting Shelby Foote), p. 209.
29. Connelly, *Army of the Heartland*, pp. 111, 146.
30. Fuller, pp. 85–86.
31. Connelly, *Army of the Heartland*, p. 112.
32. Catton, *Grant Moves South*, p. 159.
33. Connelly, *Army of the Heartland*, p. 120.
34. Conger, p. 172.
35. Grant, *Memoirs*, p. 180. While Grant was busy winning the battle and his men bled, his superiors (Halleck, Buell, and McClellan) bickered amongst themselves. See the excellent discussion by Conger, pp. 178–192. One conspicuous exception was Sherman, who, inspired by Grant's campaign, on February 15 offered to send reinforcements and waive his then-senior status. See also Flood, pp. 87–88.
36. Smith, p. 159.
37. Smith, pp. 157–158.
38. Grant told Colonel J.D. Webster, "[T]he one who attacks first now will be victorious and the enemy will have to be in a hurry if he gets ahead of me." See Grant, *Memoirs*, p. 181.
39. Smith, p. 159.
40. Catton, *Grant Moves South*, p. 170.
41. Connelly, *Army of the Heartland*, p.114. Also escaping, along with the cavalry under his command, was the indomitable Nathan Bedford Forrest, who learned his first of several hard lessons about being under the command of fools during moments of crisis. See McPherson, pp. 398, 401–402.
42. Smith, p. 155.
43. There is no doubt in this commentator's mind that Fort Donelson would have been a completely different battle, perhaps with a different result, had Buckner and Forrest been in command of the Confederates. Grant himself agreed in the case of Buckner. See Grant, *Memoirs*, pp. 184–185.
44. Grant, *Papers*, vol. 4, p. 218. C.F. Smith is credited with using the phrase first and Grant incorporating it into what his former commandant called "smoother words." See Smith, p. 162.
45. Smith, p. 166.
46. Smith, pp. 24–25. It has often been remarked that Grant's failure to correct West Point's misspelling of his name was due to a sort of shyness or timidity; rather it must have reflected a sense of relief. See also Foote, vol. 1, p. 196.
47. Smith, p. 160.
48. See Smith (pp. 160, 165) and Catton, *Grant Moves South* (p. 173). Federal dead, wounded, and missing at Fort Donelson, approaching 3,000, outnumber Confederate casualties (approximately 2,000), but at the time of surrender the starving Confederates were surrounded and outgunned with no hope of outside relief.

49. See Benjamin Franklin Cooling, *Forts Henry and Donelson: The Key to the Confederate Heartland* (Knoxville, University of Tennessee Press, 1987), pp. 219–222, and Frances H. Casstevens, "*Out of the Mouth of Hell*": *Civil War Prisons and Escapes* (Jefferson, NC: McFarland, 2005), pp. 27–28).
50. Incidentally, the many families of African-American veterans present that Memorial Day at Oakwoods Cemetery were extremely cordial towards the author.
51. Mary Chesnut recorded the defeat in her diary the very same day as the surrender (February 16), even though the Southern press initially reported a stalemate. See Chesnut, p. 290.
52. Grant, *Memoirs*, p. 187.
53. Julia Grant, p. 97.
54. See Catton, *Grant Moves South* (p. 179) and McPherson (p. 402).
55. Foote, vol. 1, p. 214.
56. Smith, p. 165.
57. Fuller (quoting Stone), p. 93.
58. Flood, p. 89. See also Smith, p. 164.
59. Smith (quoting Sherman), p. 288.
60. Cooling (quoting Catton), p. xiii.
61. Connelly, *Army of the Heartland*, p. 145.
62. McPherson, p. 403.
63. Grant, *Memoirs*, p. 188. J.F.C. Fuller firmly pronounced the reasons for this delay to be jealousy, stupidity, and lack of unified command. See Fuller, p. 96. Jean Edward Smith added, "[E]vidence suggests [Halleck] was more concerned with advancing his career than advancing against the Confederate army." See also Smith, p. 168.
64. Grant, *Papers*, vol. 4, p. 258n. See also Flood (quoting Commodore Foote), p. 93.
65. Grant, *Papers*, vol. 4, p. 271.
66. Smith, p. 169.
67. It is possible that Buell thought he was getting rid of the irascible Nelson by sending him to Grant.
68. Grant, *Papers*, vol. 4, p. 284.
69. Grant, *Papers*, vol. 4, pp. 299n–300n.
70. Grant, *Papers*, vol. 4, pp. 293–294n, 298n. See also Smith, pp. 171–172.
71. Grant, *Memoirs*, p. 190.
72. Smith, pp. 152–153.

Chapter 12

1. I am aware of at least one physical monument cataloguing Grant's victories that does not even mention Fort Donelson; I assume (giving the benefit of the doubt) that the designers of the monument viewed Donelson as a footnote to the Shiloh campaign.
2. Benjamin Franklin Cooling, perhaps the most thorough student of the campaign, asked

provocatively, "Did the stigma of shame and surrender so taint the mythic shield of southern valor that ex–Confederates blotted out such images of defeat from their Lost Cause?" See Cooling, p. xiii.

3. See Smith, p. 166, and Foote, vol. 1, p. 214.

4. Smith, p. 166. This would also no doubt contribute to his death from throat cancer in 1885.

5. Grant, *Papers*, vol. 4, pp. 195n–197n.

6. Grant, *Papers*, vol. 4, pp. 318, 320n–321n.

7. Flood, p. 95.

8. Flood, p. 95. Journalist Sylvanus Cadwallader added, "That Halleck had been insincere and treacherous to Grant was firmly believed by every member of the latter's staff...." See Cadwallader, p. 345.

9. Grant, *Papers*, vol. 4, p. 320n.

10. Grant, *Memoirs*, p. 194.

11. Grant, *Papers*, vol. 4, pp. 116.

12. Grant, *Papers*, vol. 4, pp. 229–230. Again to Julia on March 29, Grant wrote, "Such men as Kountz busy themselves very much." See p. 444.

13. Grant, *Papers*, vol. 4, p. 344n.

14. On April 2 (four days before Shiloh), Kountz responded to the paper in writing that he was ready to provide witnesses. See Grant, *Papers*, vol. 4, pp. 113n–114n.

15. Grant, *Papers*, vol. 4, p. 331.

16. Smith, p. 176.

17. Grant, *Papers*, vol. 4, pp. 354n–355n.

18. Catton, *Grant Moves South*, p. 207.

19. Grant, *Papers*, vol. 4, p. 349.

20. The rough equivalent to today's "Liberal media."

21. Grant, *Papers*, vol. 4, pp. 413, 418.

22. Connelly, *Army of the Heartland*, pp. 136–137. Connelly also wrote with disdain of how the Nashville social elite had boisterously supported Secession but within a year submitted to Yankee authority in particularly groveling fashion. See pp. 73, 137. This is in keeping with Grant's assertion that the loudest Secessionists tended not to be the ones who fought.

23. Connelly, *Army of the Heartland*, p. 21.

24. On March 5, Beauregard styled this force "The Army of the Mississippi," an appropriate moniker since the fate of the Mississippi Valley would be decided by their actions.

25. In the words of Shelby Foote, Beauregard "was planning a Cannae." Cannae was the proverbial ancient battle in which the Carthaginian general Hannibal, though heavily outnumbered, routed and scattered the combined Roman legions that had been sent against him. Foote, vol. 1, p. 319.

26. These were Tennessee, Alabama, and Mississippi.

27. Blanton and Cook, p. 10.

28. Smith, p. 184. Grant's forces at Pittsburg Landing by April 6 consisted of an equal or somewhat lesser number, but many of these were non-combatants.

29. Johnston had earlier suggested that Jefferson Davis take command. See McDonough, *Shiloh*, p. 60.

30. Harry T. Williams, *P.G.T. Beauregard: Napoleon in Gray* (Baton Rouge: Louisiana State University Press, 1954), p. 272.

31. Alfred Roman, *Military Operations of General Beauregard in the War Between the States 1861 to 1865* (New York, Harper & Brothers, 1884), vol. 1, p. 266.

32. Flood, p. 98. See also Wiley Sword, *Shiloh: Bloody April* (New York: William Morrow, 1974), p. 91.

33. Smith had seriously injured his leg in a freak accident while attempting to jump into a boat. See Smith, pp. 177, 179.

34. Flood, p. 98.

35. Grant, *Papers*, vol. 4, p. 379n.

36. Grant's phrase writing to Julia on March 18. See Grant, *Papers*, vol. 4, p. 389.

37. Grant, *Papers*, vol. 4, pp. 378, 387, 393, 447–448.

38. Grant, *Papers*, vol. 4, p. 400.

39. Grant, *Papers*, vol. 4, p. 411.

40. Grant, *Papers*, vol. 4, pp. 428–431n.

41. Grant, *Papers*, vol. 4, pp. 437–438n.

42. All eight of these maternal surnames were represented at Shiloh in the Federal army as well, although my relations among these soldiers tended to be more distant. Was it literally brother against brother?

Chapter 13

1. Grant, *Memoirs*, p. 216.

2. Grant, *Memoirs*, p. 210. Survivors of subsequent engagements in the West such as Perryville, Stone's River, Chickamauga, and Franklin have occasionally disagreed, but no one has ever denied that Shiloh was the first of its kind.

3. Smith, p. 204.

4. McDonough (quoting Sherman), p. 219.

5. Grant, *Papers*, vol. 5, p. 21.

6. Grant, *Memoirs*, p. 219.

7. McDonough, *Shiloh*, p. vi.

8. Catton, *Grant Moves South*, p. 255.

9. Fuller, p. 103.

10. Smith, pp. 182–183.

11. McPherson, p. 407.

12. Smith, p. 184. A good comparison is the worst term that Robert E. Lee ever used for the enemy—"those people"—demonstrating a more healthy respect for what he was up against.

13. Noting that he had modeled the plan after his hero Napoleon's strategy at Waterloo, many commentators have rightfully joked that Beauregard seems to have forgotten what happened to Napoleon at Waterloo.

14. Conger, p. 269.

15. The exact figures have always been disputed. Some of these casualties included women fighting disguised as men. See Deanne Blanton and Lauren M. Cook, *They Fought Like Demons: Women Soldiers in the Civil War* (Baton Rouge: Louisiana State University Press, 2002), pp. 10–11.

16. Foote, vol. 1, p. 351.

17. Grant, in a letter to Congressman Washburne on November 22, 1861, had praised Wallace, a lawyer from Ottawa, Illinois, and recommended his promotion to Brigadier General. Grant, *Papers*, vol. 3, p. 205.

18. Grant, *Papers*, vol. 5, p. 23.

19. Catton, *Grant Moves South*, p. 243.

20. Sam R. Watkins, Co. *Aytch: A Confederate Memoir of the Civil War* (New York, Macmillan, 1962), p. 27.

21. As it was dubbed by a Confederate soldier who survived one of many charges made against it.

22. Flood (quoting Sherman), p. 119.

23. Catton, *Grant Moves South*, p. 223.

24. Both Grant and Sherman were in physical pain during the battle, Grant from his leg injury and Sherman from being shot through the hand.

25. Grant, *Memoirs*, pp. 197–198.

26. Union General Lew Wallace later wrote that if Grant at Shiloh "had studied to be undramatic, he could not have succeeded better." Catton, *Grant Moves South*, p. 244.

27. Smith, p. 201. With respect to calmness under fire, plainness in dress and manner, and clear expression of orders, Grant himself expressed admiration for his role model Zachary Taylor, adding, "These qualities are more rarely found than genius or physical courage." See Grant, *Memoirs*, p. 63.

28. Grant remembered it as a musket ball. Grant, *Memoirs*, p. 209.

29. Smith, p. 195.

30. Foote, vol. 1, pp. 339–340. See also Flood, p. 111.

31. Grant, *Papers*, vol. 5, p. 7. Around this time, Julia Grant had a premonition that Richmond had fallen. It would fall literally in three years to a Federal army led by her husband. See Julia Grant, p. 99.

32. Control of the river also prevented Shiloh from being a Fort Donelson-in-reverse situation for the Federals.

33. McDonough, *Shiloh*, p. 171.

34. McDonough, p. 180. For the rest of the war, the strongest testimony that soldiers could give to the fury of a particular battle was "I was worse scared than I was at Shiloh." See Catton, *Grant Moves South*, p. 243.

35. Smith, p. 185.

36. Grant wrote, "It was a case of Southern dash against Northern pluck and endurance." Grant, *Memoirs*, p. 201.

37. The ardor of the Confederate volunteers in this engagement was exemplified in many ways, one of which was that many of them ignored huge quantities of Federal greenbacks left in the Union camps. The main focus of looting was food and supplies, a practice eventually adopted by both sides in the war.

38. Conger, p. 253.

39. McDonough, *Shiloh*, p. 221. Rough estimates vary, but after deducting stragglers and non-combatants, the Confederates may have had (before the arrival of Union reinforcements) as much as a 30% numerical superiority on Day One. Grant initially believed the Federals were facing twice their number.

40. Fuller, pp. 108, 100.

41. Grant, *Memoirs*, p. 213.

42. For a highly persuasive but searingly critical analysis of A.S. Johnston's generalship, see the discussion by Connelly in *Army of the Heartland*, Chapter Three, "An Uncertain Hand," pp. 59–77.

43. Grant, *Memoirs*, p. 215.

44. Bruce Catton observed, "The intimacy that would bind these two men together all the rest of the war was born this day at Shiloh." Catton, *Grant Moves South*, p. 229. Sherman also deserves credit for choosing the ground (see Chapter 12), the superb defensive nature of which likely saved the day for the Federals.

45. Grant, *Memoirs*, pp. 199–200.

46. Wallace died from his wounds a few days later. At his bedside was his wife, who came for a surprise visit but ended up looking for and finding him on the field incapacitated. A very similar incident occurred involving the mortally wounded Union Colonel Herman Canfield, discovered by his visiting wife among the dying at the end of Day One. See Julia Grant, pp. 99–100.

47. It appears at this point in the battle, the entire Confederate force foolishly focused their exclusive attention on reducing the Hornet's Nest.

48. Hurlbut was a South Carolina transplant to Belvidere, Illinois.

49. Lew Wallace was the future author of *Ben-Hur* and no relation to W.H.L. Wallace.

50. Bruce Catton correctly surmised, "Buell was not the man to crowd anybody." Catton, *Grant Moves South*, p. 245.

51. Jean Edward Smith used the German

word *Schadenfreud* to describe Buell's attitude
towards Grant at Shiloh. Smith, p. 195. Such an
attitude is not surprising after Grant had recently embarrassed Buell in Nashville (see
Chapter 12). Grant himself was alert to such
behavior: "Boys enjoy the misery of their com-
panions ... and in later life I have found that all
adults are not free from the peculiarity." See
Grant, *Memoirs*, p. 23. More seriously, there
were doubts as to whether Buell intended to reinforce Grant or cooperate in the Day Two
counterattack. Both of these doubts, however,
were dispelled.

52. McDonough, *Shiloh*, p. 205.
53. Grant, *Memoirs*, p. 212.
54. Grant, *Memoirs*, p. 132.
55. Grant, *Memoirs*, p. 218.
56. Grant, *Memoirs*, p. 211.
57. Mary Chesnut caustically wrote, "Cock
Robin is as dead as he ever will be now." Chesnut, p. 336.
58. Connelly, *Army of the Heartland*, pp. 175.
59. McDonough, *Shiloh*, p. vii.
60. James C. Bresnahan, ed. (quoting
Symonds), *Revisioning the Civil War: Historians on
Counter-Factual Scenarios*, (Jefferson, NC: Mc-
Farland, 2005), p. 54.
61. The Federal army began its elephantine
advance against Corinth, Mississippi, on April
29, with Halleck in command. On April 30,
Grant was given the symbolic and meaningless
position of second-in-command.
62. Grant, *Papers*, vol. 5, p. 72.
63. This opinion is offered with all due respect those African-Americans whose ancestors
were slaves; it was at Shiloh that the evil finally
caught up with everyone.
64. McPherson, p. 414.
65. Catton, *Grant Moves South*, p. 255.
66. Fuller, p. 116.
67. McDonough, *Shiloh*, p. 221.
68. McDonough, *Shiloh*, p. 225.
69. Michel de Montaigne, "On the Uncer-
tainty of Our Judgment," in *The Complete Essays*,
trans. and ed. by M.A. Screech (New York: Penguin Putnam, 1991), p. 319.

Chapter 14

1. Shiloh unleashed demons. Many simi-
lar-scaled battles followed over the next three
years, but few provoked the same kind of reaction. For example, nine months later, the battle of Stone's River in Murfreesboro, Tennessee,
would see similar casualty numbers and a
higher casualty rate, yet since it was one in a series of such after Shiloh, the public outcry was
not nearly as vocal.
2. Catton, *Grant Moves South*, p. 254.

3. Larry J. Daniel, *Shiloh: The Battle That
Changed the Civil War* (New York: Touchstone,
1998), p. 306.
4. Fuller, p. 118.
5. Both Julia Grant and Jesse Grant wrote
letters of thanks to Washburne for this speech.
See Grant, *Papers*, vol. 5 (p. 120n) and Catton,
Grant Moves South (pp. 260–261, 515, n28).
6. Smith, p. 205.
7. Flood, p. 122. See also Catton, *Grant
Moves South* (p. 257) and Grant, *Papers*, vol. 5 (p.
116).
8. Catton, *Grant Moves South*, p. 257.
9. Grant, *Papers*, vol. 5, pp. 110, 116.
10. Grant, *Papers*, vol. 5, p. 72.
11. Catton, *Grant Moves South*, p. 514, note
24.
12. Grant, *Papers*, vol. 5, p. 132.
13. Catton, *Grant Moves South*, p. 261.
14. Catton, *Grant Moves South*, pp. 259,
262–263, 515n26.
15. Catton, *Grant Moves South*, pp. 261,
525n29.
16. Daniel, p. 306.
17. On May 24, some time after his relief by
Halleck, Grant wrote to Julia, "My duties are
now much lighter...." Grant, *Papers*, vol. 5, p.
130.
18. Grant, *Papers*, vol. 5, pp. 87–88, 94n–
95n, 121–123n, 125–126n, 128–129n.
19. This Stanton was no relation to the Secretary of War.
20. Flood, p. 121.
21. Catton, *Grant Moves South*, p. 258.
22. Grant, *Memoirs*, p. 224. In the eyes of
Halleck, according to Professor Smith, Grant
was merely "an insurance policy" while Grant
himself was "temperamentally incapable of
being second in command." See Smith, pp.
208–209.
23. Smith, p. 210.
24. Fuller, p. 117.
25. Smith, p. 209.
26. Grant, *Memoirs*, p. 224.
27. Smith, p. 209.
28. At the time Halleck thought the numbers were about equal, but there was no firm
basis for this estimate.
29. Grant, *Memoirs*, p. 225. More precisely,
Grant suggested that a recently arrived army
under General John Pope block the Confederates' escape hatch. Pope's army had arrived on
the scene after Shiloh and after enjoying a
small-scale victory at Island Number 10 on the
Mississippi River. Consequently, at this point
in time, Pope had momentarily eclipsed Grant
in the public favor.
30. Smith, p. 213.
31. Catton, *Grant Moves South*, p. 276.
32. Catton, *Grant Moves South*, p. 273.

33. Recently, Beauregard had experienced the indignity of having one of his messages to Richmond intercepted, decoded, and printed in the Northern newspapers, for which he was criticized by Robert E. Lee. Catton, *Grant Moves South*, p. 269.

34. Grant, *Papers*, vol. 5, p. 124.

35. Grant, *Memoirs*, p. 226.

36. Grant, *Memoirs*, p. 226.

37. Catton wrote that "the men came to feel they had done a great thing" and the army "was beginning to be very proud of itself." Catton, *Grant Moves South*, p. 261.

38. Grant, *Memoirs*, p. 50.

Chapter 15

1. Smith, p. 211.

2. Grant, *Memoirs*, p. 227.

3. Grant, *Papers*, vol. 5, p. 138.

4. Grant had sent his latest request to Halleck on May 11, which was initially refused. The request was sent in writing though their tents were some 200 yards apart, a reflection of Grant's isolation and Halleck's insistence on strict protocol. See Smith, p. 209.

5. Smith, p. 212. See also Grant, *Memoirs*, p. 228.

6. Grant, *Papers*, vol. 5, p. 141n. Saratoga was the first important U.S. victory during the American Revolution, leading to French intervention.

7. Grant, *Papers*, vol. 5, p. 140.

8. Grant, *Memoirs*, p. 227.

9. Smith, p. 213.

10. Grant, *Memoirs*, p. 229.

11. This information came from a drover of Federal cattle that Jackson later intercepted and then released. In a similar incident, Grant was nearly captured by Confederate Colonel John B. Mosby shortly after becoming Lieutenant-General in 1864. See Grant, *Memoirs*, pp. 419–420.

12. Grant, *Memoirs*, pp. 230–231.

13. Grant, *Papers*, vol. 5, pp. 149–150.

14. Grant, *Memoirs*, p. 231.

15. Grant, *Papers*, vol. 5, pp. 168–169. See also Smith, p. 214.

16. Grant, *Papers*, vol. 5, pp. 153n–154n.

17. Grant, *Papers*, vol. 5, pp. 141n–142n.

18. Grant, *Memoirs*, p. 232.

19. Grant, *Papers*, vol. 5, p. 143.

20. To be more precise, the Proclamation held that slaves from any states still in rebellion against the Federal government by January 1, 1863, would be freed.

21. Catton, *Grant Moves South*, pp. 292–293.

22. Catton, *Grant Moves South*, p. 293.

23. Catton, *Grant Moves South*, p. 295.

24. Catton, *Grant Moves South*, p. 294.

25. Another example of the family's misfortune was that E.A. Dozier's eldest son (my great-great-grandfather's nephew), Tillman H. Dozier, joined the Confederate army (as a chaplain) in 1861 at age 21, only to succumb to disease three months later, a fate shared by thousands of others. On this point (and others), *Gone With the Wind* was accurate.

26. Julia Grant, pp. 101, 116n27.

27. Conger, p. 274.

Chapter 16

1. Grant, *Memoirs*, p. 236.

2. Grant, *Papers*, vol. 5, pp. 181n–182n.

3. Grant, *Papers*, vol. 5, p. 190.

4. Grant, *Papers*, vol. 5, pp. 192n–193n.

5. Grant, *Papers*, vol. 5, pp. 193n–194n.

6. Catton, *Grant Moves South*, p. 299.

7. Julia Grant, p. 101.

8. Fuller, p. 123.

9. Grant described Halleck as "very uncommunicative." Grant, *Memoirs*, p. 233.

10. Catton, *Grant Moves South*, pp. 287–288.

11. Grant, *Papers*, vol. 5, p. 207n. Columbus had been evacuated by the Confederates shortly after Grant's victory at Fort Donelson in February.

12. Flood, pp. 136–137.

13. Julia Grant, pp. 102–103.

14. Grant, *Papers*, vol. 5, pp. 218n–220. See also Catton, *Grant Moves South*, p. 298.

15. Julia Grant, pp. 102–103.

16. Grant, *Memoirs*, p. 234.

17. Smith, p. 216.

18. Grant wrote, "I was put entirely on the defensive in a territory where the population was hostile to the Union." Grant, *Memoirs*, p. 233.

19. Within six months, Sheridan would go on to establish his own impressive combat record at the battles of Perryville (under Buell) and Stone's River (under Rosecrans). By the end of July, Rosecrans was pressing for Sheridan's promotion to Brigadier General.

20. Grant, *Papers*, vol. 5, p. 221.

21. Price commanded troops remaining in Tupelo, and Van Dorn the Confederate forces in Vicksburg.

22. Smith, p. 217.

23. Grant, *Memoirs*, p. 237.

24. Grant, *Papers*, vol. 5, pp. 239n–241n. McClernand's endorsement in this one instance is particularly noteworthy, for it would be one of the few remaining times during the war that Grant had full support from his troublesome subordinate.

25. Grant, *Papers*, vol. 5, p. 238.

26. Grant, *Papers*, vol. 5, pp. 255–256.

27. Conger, pp. 278–279.

Chapter 17

1. Grant, Memoirs, p. 659.
2. Grant, Memoirs, p. 235.
3. Grant, Papers, vol. 5, p. 264.
4. Grant, Papers, vol. 5, p. 264.
5. Grant, Papers, vol. 3, p. 227.
6. McPherson, p. 510.
7. McPherson, p. 510.
8. Grant, Papers, vol. 5, p. 311.
9. Grant, Papers, vol. 5, p. 274.
10. Grant, Papers, vol. 5, p. 275n. See also Cadwallader, p. 4.
11. Catton, Grant Moves South, pp. 301–303.
12. Cadwallader, p. 4.
13. Cadwallader, p. 4.
14. Grant, for his part, had earlier encouraged Sherman "to write freely and fully on all matters of public interest." Grant, Papers, vol. 5, p. 275n.
15. Grant wrote, "In the South no opposition was allowed to the government...." Grant, Memoirs, p. 637 (see also p. 263).
16. Catton, Grant Moves South, p. 302.
17. Grant, Papers, vol. 5, p. 310.
18. Julia Grant, p. 103.
19. Grant, Papers, vol. 5, p. 299–302n.
20. Grant, Papers, vol. 5, p. 330.
21. Grant, Papers, vol. 5, p. 305.
22. Grant, Papers, vol. 5, p. 258.
23. Julia Grant, p. 104.
24. Grant, Memoirs, p. 236.
25. Grant, Memoirs, p. 234.
26. Flood, p. 139.
27. "First" Manassas was the Battle of Bull Run, fought on roughly the same ground in July 1861.

Chapter 18

1. Grant, Memoirs, p. 240.
2. Grant, Memoirs, pp. 238–239.
3. Smith, p. 217.
4. Grant, Memoirs, p. 240–241.
5. Smith, p. 218.
6. Grant, Memoirs, p. 240.
7. Grant, Papers, vol. 6, p. 43.
8. Grant, Memoirs, p. 240.
9. Grant, Papers, vol. 6, p. 44.
10. Thomas J. Cox was apparently wounded at South Mountain before the main battle. This probably saved his life, since he was a member of the same Gordon's Brigade that would soon be overrun by the Federals at the infamous "Bloody Lane" along Antietam Creek.
11. Grant's reputation was still suffering everywhere, thanks to an unsympathetic Northern press. Confederate sympathy around Cincinnati was strong to begin with.

12. Grant, Papers, vol. 6, p. 61–62.
13. Grant, Papers, vol. 6, p. 63.
14. Grant, Memoirs, p. 244.
15. Grant, Memoirs, p. 243.
16. Catton, Grant Moves South, p. 312.
17. Catton, Grant Moves South, p. 310.
18. This was a characterization given by Rosecrans. Foote, vol. 1, p. 718.
19. Grant, Papers, vol. 6, pp. 70–71.
20. Grant, Memoirs, p. 245.
21. By contrast, a Confederate, rather than Union, commander was killed at Iuka, General Lewis Little. Grant, Papers, vol. 6, pp. 72, 74n.
22. Conger, p. 279.

Chapter 19

1. Grant, Memoirs, p. 133.
2. Grant, Papers, vol. 6, p. 99.
3. Among many Confederate blunders, it was thought that they would enjoy a large numeric advantage when in fact this advantage was only slight. This was partly due to the rapid-response consolidation of Federal troops in the area by Grant and Rosecrans.
4. Grant, Papers, vol. 6, p. 107.
5. Grant, Papers, vol. 6, pp. 126–127n.
6. Grant, Memoirs, pp. 246–247.
7. Grant, Papers, vol. 6, p. 123.
8. Grant, Memoirs, pp. 247–248.
9. This would in fact happen to Rosecrans a year later at Chickamauga.
10. Grant, Papers, vol. 6, pp. 133–136n.
11. "Not a single soldier in the entire army ever loved or respected him." See Watkins, pp. 33–34.
12. Grant, Memoirs, p. 388.
13. Fuller, pp. 122–123.
14. Grant, Memoirs, p. 248.
15. It has been suggested that the Confederate army in Kentucky was as preoccupied with plundering the locals as the Federals would later become during the Vicksburg campaign in Mississippi.
16. Bragg, it appears, often tried to emulate Robert E. Lee by dividing his forces in the presence of a larger enemy, though without Lee's cunning instincts or knowledge of his opponent. This type of move invariably led to disaster for Bragg, culminating at Missionary Ridge the following year in November.
17. McPherson, pp. 517–518.
18. Connelly, Army of the Heartland, p. 238.
19. In a pep talk to his troops, Bragg referred to Lincoln as an "Abolition tyrant." See McPherson, p. 517.
20. Foote, vol. 1, p. 725.
21. Catton, Grant Moves South, p. 318.
22. Grant, Papers, vol. 6, p. 165.

23. Grant, *Papers*, vol. 6, pp. 166n–167n.
24. Catton, *Grant Moves South*, pp. 319–320.
See also Julia Grant, pp. 104–105.
25. Cadwallader, p. xxi.
26. Cadwallader, pp. 6–7.
27. Smith, p. 201.
28. Cadwallader, pp. 113–115.
29. Cadwallader, p. 133.
30. Grant, *Papers*, vol. 6, p. 200. See also
Conger (pp. 280–281) and Cadwallader (p. 16).
31. Fuller, p. 123.
32. Fuller, p. 122.

Chapter 20

1. Grant, *Memoirs*, p. 35.
2. The Confederates also held Port Hudson, Louisiana, to the south, the position of which mainly depended on Vicksburg for support.
3. Terrence J. Winschel, *Triumph and Defeat: The Vicksburg Campaign*, 2 vols. (New York: Savas Beatie, 1999, 2006), pp. 1–2.
4. Samuel Carter, *The Final Fortress: The Campaign for Vicksburg 1862–1863* (New York: St. Martin's, 1980), p. 11.
5. Winschel, p. 90.
6. Grant himself recalled that at this point he still considered the East to be the main theater of the war. Grant, *Memoirs*, p. 271.
7. Fuller, p. 125.
8. Mary Chesnut, with typical regional bias, felt that Pemberton was "unlucky" because he was a "born Yankee." After the fall of Vicksburg, she would describe him as a "stupid log of a halfhearted Yankee." The author in fact believes that Davis was less than brilliant himself. See Chesnut, pp. 332, 469.
9. Catton, *Grant Moves South*, p. 460.
10. Grant, *Papers*, vol. 6, 341–342n. Grant had known Pemberton in Mexico. See Grant, *Memoirs*, p. 329.
11. Bragg, after his recent failure in Kentucky, was retained by Davis to command the Army of Tennessee, despite his growing unpopularity among both staff and troops after the Perryville campaign. Historian James McPherson referred to the new group of western Confederate generals as a "kettle of catfish." McPherson, p. 576.
12. Thomas Lawrence Connelly, *Autumn of Glory: The Army of Tennessee, 1862–1865* (Baton Rouge: Louisiana State University Press, 1971), pp. 34–35. See also Carter, p. 89.
13. Catton, *Grant Moves South*, p. 328.
14. Foote, vol. 1, p. 764.
15. Cadwallader, p. 16.
16. Cadwallader, pp. 17–19.
17. Cadwallader, pp. 20–22.

18. Grant, *Papers*, vol. 6, pp. 266–267n, 273–276n.
19. In this same letter, Grant also warned Washburne against one Leonard Swett, who was one of Lincoln's closest confidants and with whom Grant butted heads back in Cairo over the activities of dishonest contractors. See Grant, *Papers*, vol. 6, pp. 273–276n. Four years later, Swett would support Grant's candidacy for president.
20. Grant, *Papers*, vol. 6, p. 283.
21. Grant, *Papers*, vol. 6, p. 283n.
22. Cadwallader, pp. 22–23. See also Grant, *Papers*, vol. 6, p. 333n.
23. Smith, p. 221.
24. This compensation would be in the form of food and supplies rather than money. See Grant, *Memoirs*, pp. 251–252.
25. "Oh, you are the man who has all these darkies on his shoulders," was one snide comment. See Kenneth P. Williams, *Grant Rises in the West: From Iuka to Vicksburg, 1862–1863* (1956; reprint, Lincoln, NE: University of Nebraska Press, 1997), pp. 163–165.
26. Grant, *Memoirs*, pp. 251–252. See also Grant, *Papers*, vol. 6, p. 316n.
27. McClernand had apparently told an incredulous Admiral David Porter that he could take Vicksburg in a week while simultaneously celebrating his honeymoon with his second wife. See Carter, pp. 86–87.
28. Smith, p. 222.
29. Halleck was not an attorney but was a master of army administrative bureaucracy. Shelby Foote quipped that "Halleck was something of a lawyer too...." See Foote, vol. 2, p 61.
30. Upon the urging of Halleck, McClernand's commission had language inserted that made his supposedly independent expedition subject to the discretion of Halleck. In effect, Lincoln reserved the right to bait and switch.
31. Smith, p. 222. See also Flood, p. 147.
32. Carter, p. 86.
33. Grant for his part, writing to his cousin Silas Hudson on November 15, praised Sherman, McPherson, Crocker, Hamilton and others, but not McClernand. See Grant, *Papers*, vol. 6, pp. 319–320.
34. Fuller, p. 127.
35. Grant, *Papers*, vol. 6, p. 288.
36. Catton, *Grant Moves South*, p. 329.
37. Foote, vol. 2, p. 61.
38. Grant, *Papers*, vol. 6, p. 310.
39. Grant, *Papers*, vol. 6, p. 312n. This retrograde route was chosen for speed, safety, and (no doubt) to avoid McClernand, should he appear.
40. Julia Grant, p. 105.
41. Grant, *Papers*, vol. 6, pp. 344–345.
42. Smith, p. 221. See also Fuller, p. 128.

Chapter 21

1. Grant, p. 127.
2. Federal cavalry reached Oxford on December 1 and Grant arrived in person on December 4.
3. Julia Grant, p. 117, n36.
4. Julia Grant, pp. 105–109.
5. Grant, *Papers*, vol. 7, p. 50.
6. See the excellent discussion on this topic by Jean Edward Smith, pp. 226–227.
7. Grant, *Papers*, vol. 7, pp. 393–394.
8. Grant, *Papers*, vol. 7, pp. 43–44.
9. Catton, *Grant Moves South*, pp. 352–353. See also Flood (pp. 144–145) and Grant, *Papers* (vol. 7, p. 53n).
10. Catton, *Grant Moves South*, p. 362.
11. Grant, *Papers*, vol. 7, p. 56.
12. Grant, *Papers*, vol. 7, p. 24.
13. Smith, p. 226.
14. Cadwallader, pp. 33–34, 40.
15. Julia Grant, p. 107.
16. Grant, *Memoirs*, p. 666.
17. McPherson, p. 574.
18. Colonel Murphy had earlier come under censure by General Rosecrans for his conduct at the Battle of Iuka, and his career was saved at that point only because Grant was trying to defend all of his troops from the criticism of Rosecrans. Murphy's dereliction of duty at Holly Springs was underscored by the heroics of Colonel William Morgan at nearby Davis Mills, who though with a much smaller command (but with preparation and skill) still managed to force Van Dorn to go around him. See Cadwallader, p. 37.
19. Grant, *Memoirs*, p. 257. See also Grant, *Papers* (vol. 7, p. 104) and Cadwallader (pp. 34–38).
20. Smith, p. 223.
21. Grant, *Memoirs*, p. 400.
22. Cadwallader, p. 39.
23. Julia Grant, pp. 107, 117, n36. Julia later returned the favor by helping to secure from Grant a parole for Confederate P.O.W. Jack Govan. See also pp. 110–111.
24. Julia Grant, pp. 107–109.
25. Grant, *Memoirs*, pp. 258–259.
26. Grant, *Memoirs*, p. 258.
27. Grant, *Memoirs*, p. 108.
28. Catton, *Grant Moves South*, p. 322.
29. Grant, *Memoirs*, p. 636. For emphasis, Grant repeats the assertion on p. 637. The obvious paradox here is that the Confederacy, while supposedly advocating more freedom than the North, became in reality a police state supported by slave labor.
30. Grant later learned that Pemberton's sprint back to Vicksburg, in contrast to Grant's bountiful and leisurely withdrawal, more resembled a panicked and disorderly retreat. See Grant, *Memoirs*, p. 258.
31. Connelly, *Autumn of Glory*, p. 40.
32. Connelly, *Autumn of Glory*, p. 38.
33. Connelly, *Autumn of Glory*, p. 37. See also Carter, p. 97.
34. Foote, vol. 2, pp. 10–16.
35. Smith, pp. 224–225.
36. Grant, *Memoirs*, p. 255. Grant would take personal command in January at the beginning of the second Vicksburg campaign.
37. Present at McClernand's nuptials with the young Minerva Dunlap was Governor Richard Yates of Illinois, who had helped to jump-start Grant's career the previous year. See Carter, pp. 92–93, 104.
38. Catton, *Grant Moves South*, p. 340.

Chapter 22

1. McPherson, pp. 580–583.
2. Flood, p. 145.
3. Grant, *Papers*, vol. 7, pp. 53n–56n.
4. Julia Grant, p. 107.
5. Williams, *Iuka to Vicksburg*, p. 292
6. Grant, *Papers*, vol. 7, p. 209. See also Grant, *Memoirs*, p. 260.
7. Catton, *Grant Moves South*, p. 346.
8. Smith, p. 227.
9. Grant, *Papers*, vol. 7, p. 220.
10. Grant, *Memoirs*, p. 260. See also Catton, *Grant Moves South*, p. 346.
11. Grant, *Memoirs*, p. 261.
12. Williams, *Iuka to Vicksburg*, p. 301.
13. Foote, vol. 2, pp. 188–189.
14. Grant, *Papers*, vol. 7, pp. 234–235.
15. Flood, pp. 141–142.
16. Foote, vol. 2, p. 187.
17. Williams, *Iuka to Vicksburg*, p. 311.
18. Cadwallader, p. 54.
19. Grant, *Papers*, vol. 7, pp. 264–265n.
20. Grant, *Papers*, vol. 7, p 270.
21. Carter, p. 109.
22. Grant, *Memoirs*, p. 262.

Chapter 23

1. Grant, *Papers*, vol. 7, pp. 265n–268n. See also Catton, *Grant Moves South*, pp. 375–376.
2. Grant, *Papers*, vol. 7, p. 274.
3. Williams, *Iuka to Vicksburg*, pp. 307–308.
4. The side movement suggested by McClernand would have been against Pine Bluff, Arkansas. See Williams, *Iuka to Vicksburg*, p. 324.
5. Fuller, p. 135.
6. Fuller, p. 134.
7. Grant, *Memoirs*, pp. 262–263.

8. Grant, *Memoirs*, p. 264.
9. Fuller, p. 134.
10. Fuller, p. 135.
11. Smith, p. 229.
12. Grant, *Papers*, vol. 7, p. 281.
13. Williams, *Iuka to Vicksburg*, p. 321.
14. Grant, *Papers*, vol. 7, p. 311.
15. Fuller, p. 134.
16. Grant, *Memoirs*, p. 274.
17. Grant, *Memoirs*, pp. 274–275.
18. Foote, vol. 2, pp. 200–201. See also Catton, *Grant Moves South* (pp. 416–417) and Williams, *Iuka to Vicksburg* (pp. 314–315).
19. Grant, *Memoirs*, pp. 103, 629.
20. Cadwallader, pp. 56–57.
21. Grant, *Papers*, vol. 7, p. 316.
22. Grant, *Papers*, vol. 7, pp. 324–325.
23. Sherman referred to Knox as "a spy and an infamous dog." Catton, *Grant Moves South*, p. 397. See also Flood, pp. 150–151 and Williams, *Iuka to Vicksburg*, pp. 317–318.
24. Williams, *Iuka to Vicksburg*, p. 318.

Chapter 24

1. Smith, p. 229.
2. Cadwallader, p. 51.
3. Smith, p. 230. See also Grant, *Memoirs*, pp. 268–269.
4. Cadwallader, p. 53.
5. Cadwallader, p. 53.
6. Porter was not a particular favorite among the Confederates, either, especially after his practical joke on them in February. Soon after, General Pemberton wrote Grant a harsh letter criticizing the perceived uncivilized conduct of Porter in various matters. Grant felt a need to respond in writing on March 2, defending the admiral and noting that the recent behavior of Confederate partisans had been less than exemplary. See Grant, *Papers*, vol. 7, pp. 370–372n.
7. Smith, p. 230.
8. Carter, p. 133.
9. Carter, p. 134.
10. Smith, p. 230.
11. McPherson, p. 590.
12. McPherson, p. 588.
13. Grant, *Papers*, vol. 7, p. 275n.
14. In his memoirs, Grant seems to lament the earlier altercation with Prentice, particularly the latter's decision to temporarily resign from the service. It is heavily implied that had it not been for Prentice's rash decision, he would have outranked McClernand throughout the war and Grant would have had a much abler corps commander at his side during the Vicksburg campaign. See Grant, *Memoirs*, pp. 156–157.
15. Grant, *Papers*, vol. 7, p. 275n.
16. Williams, *Iuka to Vicksburg*, p. 340.
17. Cadwallader, p. 60.
18. Julia Grant, pp. 111–112.
19. Grant, *Papers*, vol. 7, pp. 396–397.
20. Grant, *Papers*, vol. 7, pp. 490–491.
21. Grant, *Papers*, vol. 7, pp. 479–480.
22. Grant, *Memoirs*, pp. 262–265.
23. Smith, p. 27.
24. Smith, p. 234.
25. Conger, p. 288.

Chapter 25

1. Cadwallader, p. 114n.
2. Foote, vol. 2, p. 217. See also Smith, p. 231.
3. Smith, p. 231.
4. Smith, p. 231. Julia Grant also repeated this story, although Lincoln reportedly later disclaimed it. See Julia Grant, pp. 114, 118n45.
5. Grant, *Memoirs*, p. 272.
6. Grant, *Papers*, vol. 8, pp. 3–4.
7. Smith, p. 235.
8. Smith, pp. 235–236.
9. Fuller, pp. 137–138.
10. Grant, *Papers*, vol. 8, pp. 8–9.
11. Catton, p. 389.
12. Williams, *Iuka to Vicksburg*, pp. 335–336. See also Flood, pp. 154–155.
13. Cadwallader, p. 60.
14. Catton, *Grant Moves South*, p. 388.
15. Williams, *Iuka to Vicksburg*, p. 335.
16. Flood, p. 155.
17. Cadwallader, pp. 70–72.
18. Cadwallader, pp. 61–62.
19. Grant, *Papers*, vol. 8, pp. 30–31.
20. Cadwallader, p. 46.
21. Grant, *Papers*, vol. 8, pp. 38–39.
22. Grant, *Papers*, vol. 8, pp. 29–30.
23. Julia Grant, p. 111.
24. Flood, p. 158.
25. Julia Grant, p. 112. See also Flood, pp. 156–157.
26. Julia Grant, p. 113. Eleven days later, Grant wrote to Julia that Fred would accompany him on the campaign. See Grant, *Papers*, vol. 8, p. 130. This extraordinary decision is rarely discussed among biographers. Was Fred Grant his father's insurance policy against drunkenness?
27. Williams, *Iuka to Vicksburg*, pp. 337–338.
28. In fairness to Pemberton, he was not the only one fooled. Even Robert E. Lee in Richmond did not anticipate what Grant would soon attempt. See Smith, pp. 236–237.
29. Smith, p. 239.
30. Catton, *Grant Moves South*, p. 422.
31. Foote, vol. 2, p. 341.

32. Smith, p. 239.
33. Smith, p. 237.
34. Grant, *Papers*, vol. 8, pp. 100–101.
35. Grant, *Papers*, vol. 8, pp. 109–110.
36. Grant, *Papers*, vol. 8, p. 130.
37. Catton, *Grant Moves South*, p. 423. See also Foote, vol. 2, p. 332.
38. Flood, p. 152.
39. Smith, p. 239.
40. Fuller, p. 239.
41. McPherson, p. 628.
42. Grant, *Papers*, vol. 8, pp. 126–127.
43. Grant, *Memoirs*, p. 282.
44. Fuller, p. 139.
45. Foote, vol. 2, p. 342.
46. Smith, p. 238.
47. Flood, p. 158.
48. Catton, *Grant Moves South*, p. 420.
49. Foote, vol. 2, p. 342. See also Smith, p. 238.
50. Grant, *Memoirs*, p. 284.
51. Foote, vol. 2, p. 331.

Chapter 26

1. Smith (quoting Hovey), p. 250.
2. McPherson, p. 645.
3. In round numbers, the Federals brought approximately 23,000 troops to Port Gibson against 6,000 Confederates. See McPherson, p. 629.
4. Smith, p. 240.
5. Grant, *Papers*, vol. 8, p. 139.
6. Smith, p. 240.
7. McPherson, p. 629.
8. See Fuller (p. 147) and Foote (vol. 2, p. 347)
9. Smith, p. 241.
10. Foote, vol. 2, p. 353.
11. Smith, p. 243.
12. Grant, *Memoirs*, pp. 290–291.
13. Sherman gleefully wrote to General Francis Blair that the victimized reporters "were so deeply laden with weighty matter that they must have sunk." Catton, *Grant Moves South*, p. 430.
14. Grant, *Memoirs*, p. 291.
15. Grant, *Papers*, vol. 8, pp. 170–171.
16. Grant, *Papers*, vol. 8, p. 155.
17. Grant, *Papers*, vol. 8, p. 189.
18. See Foote (vol. 2, p. 350) and Williams (*Iuka to Vicksburg*, p. 359).
19. Cadwallader, p. 66.
20. Grant, *Memoirs*, pp. 287–288.
21. Grant, *Papers*, vol. 8, p. 169. See also Smith, p. 240.
22. Grant, *Papers*, vol. 8, pp. 192–193.
23. Grant, *Papers*, vol. 8, p. 195
24. Fuller, p. 142.
25. Fuller, pp. 143–144.
26. Fuller, p. 146.
27. Smith, p. 243.
28. Fuller, p. 142.
29. Smith, pp. 245–246.
30. Timothy B. Smith, *Champion Hill: Decisive Battle for Vicksburg* (New York: Savas Beatie LLC, 2004), p. 88.
31. Cadwallader, pp. 70–71.
32. McPherson, pp. 629–630.
33. Timothy B. Smith, p. 102.
34. Catton, *Grant Moves South*, p. 441.
35. A bemused Grant also describes how the factory owner later came to him in the White House asking for reparations. Grant, *Memoirs*, p. 298.
36. Grant, p. 298.
37. Catton, *Grant Moves South*, p. 442.
38. Fuller, p. 149.
39. Grant, *Memoirs*, pp. 299–300. See also Smith, p. 248.
40. Grant, *Memoirs*, p. 302.
41. Grant, *Papers*, vol. 5, p. 152n.
42. Catton, *Grant Moves South*, p. 443. Eyewitness accounts of the concentrated musketry suggest a resemblance to machine-gun fire.
43. Grant, *Memoirs*, p. 302.
44. According to commentators such as J.F.C. Fuller, "[H]ad McClernand ordered a charge, he would have cleared his front in a few minutes." See Fuller, p. 151.
45. Grant, *Memoirs*, pp. 304–305.
46. Smith, pp. 249–250.
47. Grant, *Memoirs*, p. 294.
48. Foote, vol. 2, p. 374.
49. Smith, p. 250.
50. Fuller, p. 153. Grant's bad fortune, such as the insubordination of McClernand, was invariably offset by good fortune, such as Pemberton's stupid decision to retreat into Vicksburg—McClernand's mortifying incompetence offset by Pemberton's incredible lack of judgment. Grant himself always felt that Pemberton should have linked up with Johnston at this point. See Grant, *Memoirs*, p. 306.
51. Williams, *Iuka to Vicksburg*, p. 385.
52. McPherson, p. 630.
53. Smith, p. 250.
54. Grant, *Papers*, vol. 8, pp. 220–230.
55. Cadwallader, pp. 80–82.
56. Cadwallader, p. 80.
57. Cadwallader, p. 83.
58. Grant, *Memoirs*, pp. 307–308. Early in Grant's Civil War career, Lawler had been court-martialed for basically being a pain in the neck, but was reinstated by Halleck (see Chapter Nine).
59. Cadwallader, p. 83.
60. Smith, p. 251.
61. McPherson, p. 631.

62. Conger, p. 291.
63. Fuller, p. 188.
64. Smith, p. 252.
65. Smith, p. 252.
66. Grant, Memoirs, p. 313.
67. Grant, Memoirs, p. 310.
68. Foote, vol. 2, p. 385.
69. Grant, Memoirs, pp. 310–311.
70. Cadwallader, p. 92.
71. Catton, Grant Moves South, pp. 453.
72. Catton, Grant Moves South, pp. 456–457.
73. Cadwallader, pp. 91–92.
74. Grant, Memoirs, pp. 503–504.
75. Grant, Papers, vol. 8, p. 261.
76. Grant, Memoirs, p. 312.
77. Cadwallader, pp. 94–95.

Chapter 27

1. McPherson, pp. 648–649.
2. Foote was referring to the Confederacy, but the same could be said for the Federal Union as a whole. See Foote, vol. 2, p. 431.
3. Blanton and Cook, pp. 16–17. For the amazing story of Hodgers and other female soldiers during the war (both Union and Confederate), see the remarkable study by Blanton and Cook, They Fought Like Demons.
4. Foote, vol. 2, p. 417.
5. Smith also acknowledges the key roles played by Grant's wife Julia and chief-of-staff John Rawlins in checking Grant's drinking habits. See Smith, pp. 231–232.
6. Flood, p. 137.
7. Lyle W. Dorsett, "The Problem of Ulysses S. Grant's Drinking During the Civil War," Hayes Historical Journal 4 (1983): pp. 37–38.
8. Dorsett, pp. 39–40.
9. Dorsett, p. 42.
10. Dorsett, pp. 46–47.
11. Foote, vol. 2, p. 417. Julia Grant criticized this letter's being made public. See Julia Grant, p. 114.
12. Cadwallader, pp. 102–105.
13. Cadwallader, pp. 105–107.
14. Smith, p. 303.
15. Cadwallader, pp. 107–108.
16. Cadwallader, pp. 108–109.
17. Cadwallader, pp. 110–112.
18. Cadwallader, pp. 113, 120.
19. Cadwallader, pp. 118–119.
20. Cadwallader, p. 114.
21. Cadwallader, p. 105n. Nevertheless, Dana elsewhere recalls that Grant was once "stupidly drunk" on board Admiral Porter's flagship Blackhawk, but the next day "came out fresh as a rose." See Smith (quoting Dana), p. 231.
22. Grant, Papers, vol. 8, pp. 324–325n. See also Dorsett, p. 44.
23. Grant, Papers, vol. 8, pp. 332, 376–377.
24. Grant, Papers, vol. 8, pp. 375–376.
25. Blair, another political general (like McClernand), was nevertheless praised by Grant. See Grant, Memoirs, p. 338.
26. Foote, vol. 2, p. 421. See also Flood, pp. 175–176.
27. Foote, vol. 2, p. 421.
28. Grant, Memoirs, pp. 321–322.
29. Foote, vol. 2, p. 422.
30. Flood, p. 176.
31. Foote, vol. 2, pp. 422–423.
32. Conger, p. 287.
33. Grant, Memoirs, pp. 261–262.
34. Grant, Memoirs, p. 585.
35. Grant, Memoirs, p. 306.
36. Grant, Memoirs, p. 435.
37. Smith, pp. 253–254. See also Johnston, p. 202n.
38. Foote, vol. 2, p. 426.
39. Smith, p. 254.
40. Grant had in fact intercepted another dispatch from Johnston on June 21 stating his intent to make a move. See Grant, Memoirs, p. 325.
41. Grant, Memoirs, p. 324.
42. Foote, vol. 2, pp. 173–174.
43. Flood, p. 178.
44. Flood, pp. 178–180.
45. Grant, Papers, vol. 8, pp. 444–445.
46. Flood, p. 180.
47. Grant, Memoirs, p. 318.

Chapter 28

1. Grant, Memoirs, p. 38.
2. Grant, Memoirs, p. 326.
3. Grant, Memoirs, pp. 326–327.
4. Cadwallader, p. 125.
5. Grant, Memoirs, p. 327.
6. Grant, Memoirs, p. 328.
7. Smith, p. 255.
8. Grant, Memoirs, pp. 329–331.
9. Grant, Memoirs, pp. 332–33.
10. Smith, p. 256.
11. McPherson, pp. 636–637.
12. Julia Grant, p. 120.
13. Smith, p. 303.
14. Grant, Memoirs, p. 45.
15. McPherson, p. 638.
16. Smith, p. 257.
17. Geoffrey C. Ward, with Ric Burns and Ken Burns, The Civil War: An Illustrated History (New York: Alfred A. Knopf, 1990), p. 242.
18. Catton, Grant Moves South, pp. 482–483.
19. Bresnahan (quoting Bearss), p. 150.
20. Williams, Iuka to Vicksburg, p. 319.

21. Conger (quoting Greene), p. 158.
22. McPherson, p. 637.
23. Grant, *Memoirs*, p. 334.
24. Grant, *Memoirs*, p. 339.
25. McPherson, p. 637.
26. Julia Grant, p. 119.
27. Chesnut, pp. 459–460.
28. Grant, *Memoirs*, p. 335.
29. Catton, *Grant Moves South*, p. 482.
30. Cadwallader, p. 125.
31. Foote, vol. 2, p. 623.
32. Julia Grant, p. 120. The Lum Mansion had also been Pemberton's headquarters during the siege. See Cadwallader, p. 123.
33. Grant, *Papers*, vol. 9, p. 70.
34. Grant, *Memoirs*, p. 340.
35. Grant, *Memoirs*, p. 662.
36. Smith, pp. 260–261.

Chapter 29

1. Catton, *Grant Moves South*, pp. 7–9.
2. Grant, *Papers*, vol. 9, p. 147.
3. Grant, *Papers*, vol. 9, pp. 223n–224n.
4. Grant, *Papers*, vol. 9, pp. 172–174.
5. Grant, *Papers*, vol. 9, pp. 172–174.
6. Grant, *Papers*, vol. 9, pp. 195–197.
7. Grant, *Papers*, vol. 9, pp. 217–218.
8. Grant, *Papers*, vol. 9, pp. 217–218.
9. Catton, *Grant Moves South*, pp. 3–6.
10. Julia Grant, p. 113.
11. Julia Grant, p. 113.
12. Grant, *Memoirs*, p. 131.
13. Grant, *Papers*, vol. 9, p. 200.
14. Smith, pp. 261–262. See also Catton, *Grant Takes Command*, p. 20.
15. Foote, vol. 2, p. 677.
16. Connelly, *Autumn of Glory*, p. 165.
17. Grant, *Memoirs*, p. 103.
18. Catton, *Grant Takes Command*, p. 14.
19. Bruce Catton, *Grant Takes Command* (Boston: Little, Brown, 1968), p. 13. Grant later complained, "I had tried for more than two years to have an expedition sent against Mobile when its possession would have been of great advantage. It finally cost lives to take it when its possession was of no importance, and when, if left alone, it would within a few days have fallen into our hands without any bloodshed whatever." See Grant, *Memoirs*, p. 647.
20. Cadwallader, pp. 126–127.
21. Cadwallader, pp. 127–128.
22. Cadwallader, p. 128.
23. Grant, *Papers*, vol. 9, p. 109.
24. Cadwallader, p. 127.
25. Catton, *Grant Takes Command*, p. 21.

Chapter 30

1. Grant, *Memoirs*, p. 464.
2. Smith, p. 262.
3. Grant, *Memoirs*, pp. 342–343.
4. Cadwallader, p. 118n.
5. Grant, *Memoirs*, p. 343.
6. Flood, p. 194.
7. Grant, *Papers*, vol. 9, pp. 221–222.
8. Julia Grant, pp. 120–121.
9. Julia Grant, pp. 121–122, 143n.
10. Fuller, p. 161. Fuller states that over 16,000 Federals were lost and nearly 21,000 Confederates.
11. Smith, pp. 262–263. See also McPherson, p. 672.

Chapter 31

1. Whitman, p. 418. Whitman's poem is titled "Eighteen Sixty One" but it represented an accurate vision of what would occur at Chattanooga in 1863.
2. Fuller, p. 166.
3. McPherson, p. 675.
4. Relative figures at Chattanooga vary according to the source, due in large part to both armies having a limited number of effective troops, as opposed to roll numbers. Most sources agree that the Confederates enjoyed an initial advantage after Chickamauga. According to Jean Edward Smith, the Federals numbered approximately 40,000 while the Confederates under Braxton Bragg had roughly 70,000 troops. See Smith, p. 270. These numbers would change dramatically over the next two months.
5. Fuller, p. 166. See also James Lee McDonough, *Chattanooga: A Death Grip on the Confederacy* (Knoxville: University of Tennessee Press, 1984), pp. 44–45.
6. Grant, *Memoirs*, p. 352.
7. Grant, *Memoirs*, p. 347.
8. Grant, *Memoirs*, pp. 343–344.
9. Julia Grant recalled that their ferry across the Ohio River to Louisville was a very hush-hush affair, due to fear of espionage in this highly pro–Confederate region. See Julia Grant, p. 123.
10. Grant, *Memoirs*, pp. 348–349.
11. Grant, *Papers*, vol. 9, p. 302.
12. Grant, *Memoirs*, p. 353.
13. See, for example, Mary Chesnut's opinion (p. 634).
14. Foote, vol. 2, pp. 816–819. This conference had been urged upon Davis by (among others) General Robert E. Lee and Colonel James Chesnut, husband of Confederate diarist Mary Chesnut. Colonel Chesnut had earlier in

the month gone west and was startled by the widespread anger expressed against Bragg. See Connelly, *Autumn of Glory*, p. 241.

15. Connelly, *Autumn of Glory*, pp. 240–241. See also Foote, vol. 2, pp. 813–814.

16. McDonough, *Chattanooga*, p. 96. For a concise though excellent discussion of the feud between Confederate leaders at Chattanooga, see McDonough, *Chattanooga*, Chapter Two, "War Between the Generals."

17. Foote, vol. 2, pp. 816–819. Any choice would have been better than the one Davis made.

18. Defenders of Davis have argued that he had no one but Bragg to turn to since others declined when offered the job; however, if Davis had been nearly as insistent with these offers as he was in other things, someone may well have changed his mind. There were certainly enough candidates.

19. Watkins, p. 98.

20. The most notable occurrence during this leg was Grant's stop in Nashville, where he was compelled to listen to a long-winded speech by military governor Andrew Johnson. In the words of a highly annoyed Grant, Johnson's speech "was by no means his maiden effort." See Grant, *Memoirs*, p. 353.

21. Smith, p. 265.

22. Grant, *Memoirs*, p. 354.

23. Grant, *Papers*, vol. 9, p. 317.

24. Smith, p. 266. See also Catton, *Grant Takes Command*, p. 38.

25. Catton, *Grant Takes Command*, p. 42. A more specialized student of the campaign, James Lee McDonough, concurred with this assessment: "To understand the plan one must grasp the geography of the region." See McDonough, *Chattanooga*, p. 55.

26. Grant, *Papers*, vol. 9, pp. 334–335.

27. Flood, p. 204.

28. Smith, p. 267.

29. Smith, p. 267.

30. Smith, p. 267.

31. Conger, p. 298.

32. Conger, p. 294.

33. Conger, p. 295.

34. Grant, *Memoirs*, p. 355.

35. Grant, *Memoirs*, p. 358.

36. Grant, *Memoirs*, pp. 359–360.

37. Grant, *Memoirs*, p. 361. By this time, Grant's leg was also starting to feel much better. Writing to Julia on October 27, he remarked that physical exertion, "instead of making my injury worse has almost entirely cured me." See Grant, *Papers*, vol. 9, pp. 334–335.

38. Grant, *Memoirs*, p. 361.

39. Foote, vol. 2, pp. 810–811.

40. Catton, *Grant Takes Command*, p. 56.

41. Foote, vol. 2, p. 808.

42. Cadwallader, pp. 134–137.

43. Cadwallader, pp. 138–139.

44. Grant, *Memoirs*, p. 362.

45. The author first read this expression given by an eastern Federal officer who viewed Grant's western troops with a combination of awe and contempt. Unfortunately, he cannot remember the exact source.

46. Chesnut, p. 634.

Chapter 32

1. Grant, *Memoirs*, p. 100.

2. Grant, *Papers*, vol. 9, p. 352.

3. Burnside had earlier been completely defeated by Lee at Fredericksburg (after a lackluster showing at Sharpsburg/Antietam), and would later confirm his reputation for inept offensive warfare with the Crater debacle in front of Petersburg, Virginia.

4. Grant, *Memoirs*, p. 387.

5. Connelly, *Autumn of Glory*, p. 263.

6. Grant, *Memoirs*, p. 393.

7. Connelly, *Autumn of Glory*, p. 247.

8. Smith, pp. 272–273. See also McDonough, *Chattanooga*, p. 104.

9. Smith, p. 272.

10. Cadwallader, p. 118n. Grant's biographer Bruce Catton denies that Grant was drunk that night, pointing out that Rawlins also wrote a letter to Grant which was never sent. Rawlins, though, did speak personally to Grant about the incident. See Catton, pp. 65–66.

11. See letter to J. Russell Jones in Grant, *Papers*, vol. 9, pp. 406–407.

12. Grant estimated there were by then approximately 60,000 Federals and 35,000 Confederates. See Grant, *Memoirs*, p. 392.

13. McDonough, *Chattanooga*, pp. 63–64. See also Connelly, *Autumn of Glory*, p. 274.

14. Foote, vol. 2, pp. 858–859.

15. Connelly, *Autumn of Glory*, p. 274.

16. Catton, *Grant Takes Command*, p. 72.

17. Cadwallader, p. 146.

18. Cadwallader, p. 152.

19. Grant, *Memoirs*, p. 383.

20. Smith, p. 280.

21. According to Cadwallader, Grant thought Sheridan was the most talented of the bunch. See Cadwallader, pp. 305–306.

22. Ward, pp. 260–261.

23. Cadwallader, pp. 150, 152.

24. Watkins, p. 102.

25. Watkins, pp. 102–103.

26. Smith, p. 281.

27. McDonough, *Chattanooga*, p. 205.

28. The same applies to one of this book's dedicatees, William Eugene Cox, who is my uncle. My first name may have also come from my great-great-grandfather, William E. Dozier.

29. For the best discussion see McDonough, *Chattanooga*, pp. 161–168.

30. Grant, *Memoirs*, p. 387.

31. Grant, *Memoirs*, p. 388. Confederate General P.G.T. Beauregard had an even more harsh opinion of Jefferson Davis: "The curse of God must have been on our people when we chose him." See Foote, vol. 2, p. 896.

32. Grant, *Memoirs*, p. 394.

33. Fuller, pp. 197–198.

34. Grant, *Memoirs*, pp. 390–391.

35. Julia Grant, p. 124.

36. Grant, *Memoirs*, p. 394.

37. Hughes Nathaniel Cheairs, Jr., *General William J. Hardee: Old Reliable* (Baton Rouge: Louisiana State University Press, 1965), p. 176.

38. Connelly, *Autumn of Glory*, p. 277.

39. McDonough, *Chattanooga*, p. 230.

40. Foote, vol. 2, p. 859.

Chapter 33

1. From Whitman's poem titled "Rise O Days from Your Fathomless Deeps" (pp. 427–428).

2. Longstreet apparently got his information from one of Grant's covert messengers. Grant, it seems, wanted Longstreet to retreat as opposed to fighting Sherman. See Grant, *Memoirs*, p. 392.

3. For a good illustration of this map, see Foote, vol. 2, p. 952. Grant himself seems to have had such a map in his possession. See also Conger, p. 308.

4. Chesnut, p. 501.

5. Grant, *Papers*, vol. 9, p. 496.

6. Grant, *Memoirs*, pp. 394–395.

7. Grant, *Memoirs*, pp. 395–396.

8. Julia Grant, p. 128.

9. Catton, *Grant Takes Command*, p. 105.

10. Catton, *Grant Takes Command*, p. 103.

11. Catton, *Grant Takes Command*, p. 103.

12. Smith, p. 284.

13. Grant, *Papers*, vol. 9, pp. 541–542n.

14. Grant, *Papers*, vol. 9, p. 541.

15. Grant, *Papers*, vol. 9, p. 541.

16. Smith, p. 285.

17. Nowadays, the joke in the North is that Old Abe was a good guy but he should have just let the South go.

18. Flood, p. 225.

19. Grant, *Memoirs*, p. 395.

20. Julia Grant, pp. 124–125.

21. Grant, *Papers*, vol. 9, p. 500.

22. Catton, *Grant Takes Command*, p. 95.

23. Grant, *Memoirs*, p. 397.

24. Catton, *Grant Takes Command*, pp. 96–97.

25. Conger, p. 284.

Chapter 34

1. Grant, *Memoirs*, p. 65.

2. Memoirs of both Grant and his wife Julia recount this winter. See Grant (*Memoirs*, p. 396) and Julia Grant (p. 125).

3. Grant, *Memoirs*, pp. 399–400.

4. Fuller, p. 180.

5. Grant, *Papers*, vol. 9, p. 542n.

6. Grant, *Papers*, vol. 9, p. 543n.

7. Grant, *Papers*, vol. 9, p. 409n.

8. Grant, *Memoirs*, pp. 397–398.

9. Grant says it was January 13. See Grant, *Memoirs*, p. 397.

10. Grant, *Memoirs*, pp. 398–399.

11. Grant, *Memoirs*, p. 656.

12. Grant, *Memoirs*, p. 397.

13. Catton, *Grant Takes Command*, p. 105.

14. Catton, *Grant Takes Command*, p. 105.

15. Catton, *Grant Takes Command*, p. 105.

16. Grant, *Memoirs*, pp. 24–25.

17. Grant, *Papers*, vol. 10, pp. 52–53.

18. Grant, *Papers*, vol. 10, p. 53n

19. Smith, p. 286.

20. It is possible that the trip to Washington by Jones was rather made in connection with arranging for the move of the Antrobus portrait of Grant to that location for public display.

21. Professor John Y. Simon, with a healthy dose of skepticism, thought these events may have occurred soon after January 14, when Jones wrote to Washburne. See Grant, *Papers*, vol. 9, p. 243n. See also Smith (p. 286) and Catton, *Grant Takes Command* (pp. 111–112).

22. Julia Grant, pp. 125–126.

23. Grant, *Memoirs*, p. 401.

24. Julia Grant, pp. 126–127.

25. Catton, *Grant Takes Command*, p. 114.

26. Julia Grant, p. 126.

Chapter 35

1. Grant, *Memoirs*, p. 271.

2. Rawlins may have believed that real men hold field glasses, like the ones Grant was painted holding by John Antrobus.

3. Catton, *Grant Takes Command*, pp. 115–117.

4. Catton, *Grant Takes Command*, p. 113.

5. Smith, p. 286.

6. Grant, *Papers*, vol. 10, pp. 100–101.

7. Grant, *Papers*, vol. 10, pp. 132–133.

8. Grant, *Papers*, vol. 10, pp. 148–149.

9. Grant, *Papers*, vol. 10, p. 183.

10. Smith, p. 286.

11. Grant, *Papers*, vol. 10, p. 188n.

12. Politically, during the war, Blair was a Free-Soil Republican, but after the war became a Democrat, breaking with the Reconstruction policies of the Johnson administration.

13. Grant, *Papers*, vol. 10, pp. 166–167.

14. Grant, *Papers*, vol. 10, p. 167. Blair, then a Republican, seems to have received a much more cordial reply than earlier, similar overtures from Democrats (see Chapter 34), or even from Grant's father Jesse. Whereas Grant would become a Republican after the war, Blair would switch to Democrat.

15. Grant, *Memoirs*, p. 125.

16. Julia Grant, p. 127.

17. Grant, *Memoirs*, p. 120.

18. McPherson, pp. 692–693.

19. McPherson, pp. 693–694. In its hostile attitude towards Jefferson Davis and the Richmond-directed Confederate war effort, Georgia was outdone only by North Carolina, particularly the western, Unionist part of the state, which by this time seemed to favor Reconstruction. See also pp. 694–698.

20. Grant, *Memoirs*, p. 402.

21. Grant, *Memoirs*, pp. 402–403.

22. Grant, *Memoirs*, pp. 400–401.

23. Flood, p. 229.

24. Conger, pp. 307–308.

25. Grant, *Memoirs*, p. 400.

Chapter 36

1. Grant, *Memoirs*, p. 7.

2. Grant, *Memoirs*, pp. 403.

3. Grant, *Papers*, vol. 10, pp. 186–187.

4. Sherman favorably compared Grant's "simple faith in success" to the Christian religious faith. See Catton, *Grant Takes Command*, pp. 133–134.

5. Chesnut, pp. 520, 585, 609, 616, 640.

6. Chesnut, p. 585.

7. Chesnut, pp. 520–521.

8. Chesnut, pp. 520–521.

9. Unlike Napoleon Bonaparte, whose ability Grant at least respected, (Louis) Napoleon III, in Grant's estimation, had neither ability nor character. Grant, *Memoirs*, p. 662.

10. McPherson, p. 501.

11. At the end of this particular tirade, the manuscript is mutilated, probably with good reason. See Chesnut, pp. 520–521.

12. Foote, vol. 3, p. 1.

13. Catton, *Grant Takes Command*, pp. 124–125. See also Smith, p. 289.

14. Catton, *Grant Takes Command*, p. 125.

15. Smith p. 290.

16. Catton, *Grant Takes Command*, p. 126.

17. Julia, for her part, beamed with pride at these incidents in her memoirs. See Julia Grant, pp. 127–128.

18. Catton, *Grant Takes Command*, p. 126. See also Smith, p. 290.

19. Grant, *Memoirs*, p. 403.

20. Grant, *Memoirs*, p. 403.

21. Grant, *Memoirs*, pp. 407–408. Julia recalled being impressed by meeting Lincoln as well, but also taken aback at the way in which Washington socialites stared at her, sometimes close-up with spectacles. See Julia Grant, p. 129.

22. Julia Grant, p. 128.

23. Smith, p. 294.

24. Smith, p. 291.

25. Catton, *Grant Takes Command*, p. 135. This also jives well with Sherman's comment regarding Grant's "simple faith in success."

26. Grant, *Memoirs*, pp. 403–404.

27. Catton, *Grant Takes Command*, p. 131.

28. Catton, *Grant Takes Command*, p. 132.

29. At Covington-Cincinnati, as in Washington, DC, Grant's official welcoming committee failed to connect with or recognize him at the station. Grant ended up strolling up to his father's house with a carpetbag. See Catton, *Grant Takes Command*, p. 137.

30. Catton, *Grant Takes Command*, p. 137.

31. Catton, *Grant Takes Command*, pp. 137–138.

32. Confederate forces under Magruder, Civil War buffs may recall, completely fooled Union General George McClellan with their theatrical posturing during the Peninsula campaign of 1862.

33. Lewis, p. 129.

34. See Cadwallader, p. 283.

35. Years later, a bankrupt Grant would give the sword to William Vanderbilt to help pay off his debts, and Vanderbilt immediately donated it to the Smithsonian. Julia glosses over the whole sordid affair in her memoirs. See Julia Grant, p. 128.

36. Grant, *Papers*, vol. 10, p. 214.

37. Smith, pp. 295–296.

38. Smith, pp. 294–295.

39. Grant, *Memoirs*, pp. 405–406.

40. Smith, p. 296.

41. Smith, p. 299.

42. Grant, *Memoirs*, p. 407.

43. For example, the highly successful Union General George Thomas won almost all of his victories while fighting on the defensive.

44. Catton, *Grant Takes Command*, p. 140.

45. Foote, vol. 3, pp. 8–9. Grant was less intimated by Stanton than most. When challenged by Stanton for depleting Washington of troops for the Virginia campaign, Grant responded with, "I think I rank you in this matter, Mr. Secretary." See Smith, *Takes Command*, p. 297.

46. Smith, p. 301.

Aftermath

1. Grant, *Memoirs*, p. 648. Grant speaks here of Lincoln's assassination, but it could apply to the American Civil War as a whole.
2. Mosby, p. 392.
3. Smith, pp. 130, 647n204.
4. Grant, *Memoirs*, pp. 612–613.
5. Smith, p. 18n.
6. Reconstruction, many now agree, was in some ways a more difficult task for the Federal Union than winning the war that came before it.
7. Cadwallader, pp. 349–350.
8. Cadwallader, p. 353.

Bibliography

Ballard, Michael B. *U.S. Grant: The Making of a General, 1861-1863*. Lanham, MD: Rowman & Littlefield, 2005.
_____. *Vicksburg: The Campaign that Opened the Mississippi*. Chapel Hill: University of North Carolina Press, 2004.

Bearss, Edwin Cole. *The Vicksburg Campaign*. Dayton, OH: Morningside, 1991.

Blanton, Deanne, and Lauren M. Cook. *They Fought Like Demons: Women Soldiers in the Civil War*. Baton Rouge: Louisiana State University Press, 2002.

Bresnahan, James C., ed. *Revisioning the Civil War: Historians on Counter-Factual Scenarios*. Jefferson, NC: McFarland, 2005.

Cadwallader, Sylvanus. *Three Years with Grant*. Edited by Benjamin P. Thomas. Lincoln: University of Nebraska Press, 1996.

Carter, Samuel. *The Final Fortress: The Campaign for Vicksburg 1862-1863*. New York: St. Martin's, 1980.

Casstevens, Frances H. *"Out of the Mouth of Hell": Civil War Prisons and Escapes*. Jefferson, NC: McFarland, 2005.

Catton, Bruce. *Grant Moves South*. Boston: Little, Brown, 1960.
_____. *Grant Takes Command*. Boston: Little, Brown, 1968.

Chesnut, Mary. *Mary Chesnut's Civil War*. Edited by C. Vann Woodward. New Haven: Yale University Press, 1981.

Conger, Colonel Arthur L. *The Rise of U.S. Grant*. 1931. Reprint, New York: Da Capo Press, 1996.

Connelly, Thomas Lawrence. *Army of the Heartland: The Army of Tennessee, 1861-1862*. Baton Rouge: Louisiana State University Press, 1967.
_____. *Autumn of Glory: The Army of Tennessee, 1862-1865*. Baton Rouge: Louisiana State University Press, 1971.

Cooling, Benjamin Franklin. *Forts Henry and Donelson: The Key to the Confederate Heartland*. Knoxville: University of Tennessee Press, 1987.

Daniel, Larry J. *Shiloh: The Battle That Changed the Civil War*. New York: Touchstone, 1998.

Dorsett, Lyle W. "The Problem of Ulysses S. Grant's Drinking During the Civil War." *Hayes Historical Journal* 4 (1983): pp. 37-49.

Flood, Charles Bracelen. *Grant and Sherman: The Friendship that Won the Civil War*. New York: Farrar, Straus and Giroux, 2005.

Foote, Shelby. *The Civil War: A Narrative*. Vol. 1, *Fort Sumter to Perryville*; Vol. 2, *Fredericksburg to Meridian*; Vol. 3, *Red River to Appomattox*. New York: Random House, 1958-1974.

Freeman, Douglas Southal. *R.E. Lee: A Biography*. 4 vols. New York: Scribner's, 1935.

Fuller, J.F.C. *The Generalship of Ulysses S. Grant*. 1929. Reprint, New York: Da Capo Press, 1991.

Grant, Julia Dent. *The Personal Memoirs of Julia Dent Grant (Mrs. Ulysses S. Grant)*. Edited by John Y. Simon. Carbondale, IL: Ulysses S. Grant Association, 1975.

Grant, Ulysses S. *The Papers of Ulysses S. Grant*. 20 vols. Edited by John Y. Simon. Carbondale: Southern Illinois University Press, 1967-1995.
_____. *Personal Memoirs of U.S. Grant*. Lincoln: University of Nebraska Press, 1996.

Hicken, Victor. *Illinois in the Civil War*. 2nd ed. 1966. Reprint, Chicago: University of Illinois Press, 1991.

Hughes, Nathaniel Cheairs, Jr. *The Battle of Belmont: Grant Strikes South*. Chapel Hill: University of North Carolina Press, 1991.
_____. *General William J. Hardee: Old Reliable*. Baton Rouge: Louisiana State University Press, 1965.

Hughes, Nathaniel Cheairs, Jr., and Roy P. Stonesifer, Jr., *The Life and Wars of Gideon J. Pillow*. Chapel Hill: University of North Carolina Press, 1993.

Johnston, Joseph E. *Narrative of Military Operations Directed during the Late War between the States*. New York: D. Appleton, 1874.

Lewis, Lloyd. *Captain Sam Grant.* Boston: Little, Brown, 1950.

McDonough, James Lee. *Chattanooga: A Death Grip on the Confederacy.* Knoxville: University of Tennessee Press, 1984.

_____. *Shiloh: In Hell Before Night.* Knoxville: University of Tennessee Press, 1977.

McFeely, William S. *Grant: A Biography.* New York: W.W. Norton, 1981.

McPherson, James M. *Battle Cry of Freedom: The Civil War Era.* New York: Ballantine, 1988.

Montaigne, Michel de. *The Complete Essays.* Translated and edited by M.A. Screech. New York: Penguin Putnam, 1991.

Mosby, John S. *The Memoirs of John S. Mosby.* Edited by Charles Wells Russell. Bloomington: Indiana University Press, 1959.

Parks, Joseph H. *General Leonidas Polk C.S.A.: The Fighting Bishop.* Kingsport, TN: Kingsport Press, Inc./Louisiana State University Press, 1962.

Plutarch. *The Lives of Noble Grecians and Romans.* Vols. I–II. Dryden translation. Edited by Arthur Hugh Clough. New York: The Modern Library, 1992.

Roman, Alfred. *Military Operations of General Beauregard in the War Between the States 1861 to 1865.* New York: Harper & Brothers, 1884.

Simon, John Y. "From Galena to Appomattox: Grant and Washburne." *Journal of the Illinois State Historical Society* 58 (Summer 1965).

_____. "Grant at Belmont." *Military Affairs: Journal of the American Military Institute* 45 (December 1981).

_____. "The Paradox of Ulysses S. Grant." *Register of the Kentucky Historical Society* 81, no. 4 (1983).

Simpson, Brooks D. *Ulysses S. Grant: Triumph Over Personal Adversity, 1822–1865.* New York: Houghton Mifflin, 2000.

Smith, Jean Edward. *Grant.* New York: Simon & Schuster, 2001.

Smith, Timothy B. *Champion Hill: Decisive Battle for Vicksburg.* New York: Savas Beatie LLC, 2004.

Sword, Wiley, *Shiloh: Bloody April.* New York: William Morrow, 1974.

Twain, Mark. *Tales, Speeches, Essays, and Sketches.* New York: Penguin, 1994.

Vidal, Gore. "President and Mrs. U.S. Grant." In *United States: Essays 1952–1992.* New York: Random House, 1993.

Ward, Geoffrey C. with Ric Burns and Ken Burns. *The Civil War: An Illustrated History.* New York: Alfred A. Knopf, 1990.

Watkins, Sam R. *Co. Aytch: A Confederate Memoir of the Civil War.* New York: Macmillan, 1962.

Whitman, Walt. *Complete Poetry and Collected Prose.* New York: The Library of America, 1982.

Williams, Harry T. *P.G.T. Beauregard: Napoleon in Gray.* Baton Rouge: Louisiana State University Press, 1954.

Williams, Kenneth P. *Grant Rises in the West: The First Year, 1861–1862.* 1952. Reprint, Lincoln: University of Nebraska Press, 1997.

_____. *Grant Rises in the West: From Iuka to Vicksburg, 1862–1863.* 1956. Reprint, Lincoln: University of Nebraska Press, 1997.

_____. *Lincoln Finds A General.* Vol. 5. New York: Macmillan, 1959.

Winschel, Terrence J. *Triumph and Defeat: The Vicksburg Campaign.* Vols. 1–2. New York: Savas Beatie, 1999, 2006.

Index